T0244369

Prophets without Honor

Prophets without Honor

The 2000 Camp David Summit and the End of the Two-State Solution

SHLOMO BEN-AMI

OXFORD
UNIVERSITY PRESS

OXFORD
UNIVERSITY PRESS

Oxford University Press is a department of the University of Oxford. It furthers
the University's objective of excellence in research, scholarship, and education
by publishing worldwide. Oxford is a registered trade mark of Oxford University
Press in the UK and certain other countries.

Published in the United States of America by Oxford University Press
198 Madison Avenue, New York, NY 10016, United States of America.

CIP data is on file at the Library of Congress
ISBN 978–0–19–006047–3

DOI: 10.1093/oso/9780190060473.001.0001

1 3 5 7 9 8 6 4 2

Printed by LSC Communications, United States of America

To Itai, Mika, Liv, Zoe, and Daphne

Let the failures we bequeath you refine your gift of restraint and moderation

The Place Where We Are Right
From the place where we are right
Flowers will never grow
In the spring.
The place where we are right
Is hard and trampled
Like a yard.
But doubts and loves
Dig up the world
Like a mole, a plow.
And a whisper will be heard in the place
Where the ruined
House once stood.

Yehuda Amichai,
https://princeton57.org/dynamic.asp?id=Amichai, with permission
of the poet's widow, Hannah Amichai

Tragedies are resolved in one of two ways, the Shakespearean way or the Anton Chekhov way. In a tragedy by Shakespeare the stage at the end is littered with dead bodies. In a tragedy by Chekhov, everyone is unhappy, bitter, disillusioned and melancholy, but they are alive. I prefer a Chekhovian not a Shakespearean conclusion.

Amos Oz in an interview with Roger Cohen,
*https://www.nytimes.com/2013/01/29/opinion/global/roger-cohen-sitt
ing-down-with-amos-oz.html.*

"If there were a party of those who aren't sure they're right, I'd belong to it," Albert Camus quoted by Tony Judt, *https://www.nybooks.com/
articles/1994/10/06/the-lost-world-of-albert-camus/*

Men make their own history, but they do not make it just as they please; they do not make it under circumstances chosen by themselves, but under given circumstances directly encountered and inherited from the past.

Karl Marx, *The Eighteenth Brumaire of Louis Bonaparte*

CONTENTS

ACKNOWLEDGMENTS

The idea for this book originated from a conversation with Jonathan Freeland of the *The Guardian*. Jonathan came to see the diaries I had written throughout the Israeli-Palestinian peace negotiations in the last two years of Bill Clinton's presidency. His plan was to write a play about the Camp David summit and the drama of the mis-encounter between the leaders at the summit. As the brilliant journalist and essayist that he is, Jonathan probably got absorbed by more important, and I hope more fulfilling, tasks. I finally ended up writing a critical account of the entire process from 1999 to these days, the first part of which is mostly based on my diaries. I wish to thank Jonathan for inadvertently drawing me back to a bygone era where the task of struggling for peace was still a necessary, and noble, endeavor. Peace diplomacy seems to have lost its appeal everywhere.

Inevitably, one accumulates debts of gratitude throughout the writing and publication of a book. I am first and foremost deeply indebted to Andrew Stuart, an agent and a friend. His vast experience in the editorial world and his advice on ways to improve the manuscript were truly invaluable. I am obliged also to David MacBride, the social sciences editor of Oxford University Press, New York, for his meticulous examination of the manuscript. His assistant editor, Holly Mitchell, was always kindly responsive and so was Emily Benitez. Thanks are due also to Cheryl Merritt for the editing process. Colonel (res.) Dr. Shaul Arieli, who worked with me in government, is today probably the most knowledgeable scholar of the intricacies of the Israeli-Palestinian situation. I wish to thank him for making available to me all the maps in this book. I also hope for his indulgence for leaving him as one of the last believers in the two-state idea. I gave up; he still resists heroically. I am also obliged to Lieut. Colonel (res.) Dr. Ephraim Lavie, with whom I worked closely during the entire negotiating process, for his invaluable help in locating bibliographical material.

Hussein Agha has unwittingly been a mentor on Palestinian affairs. Whatever may be good in my analyses draws to a large degree from his brilliance and teachings. Gilead Sher was an obliging partner throughout our close work to-gether. His knowledge of the intricacies of the Israel-Palestine situation, and his experience in both military and political affairs as well as in the legal aspects of the conflict made him the man to work with.

The many backchannel peace seminars organized by the Toledo International Center for Peace in Spain were an instructive experience that further helped me shape my views on the Israeli-Palestinian conundrum. I am also indebted to the University of Columbia's School of International and Public Affairs (SIPA) for offering me the George S. McGovern Visiting Professorship for fall 2016, and to UCLA's Nazarian Center for Israel studies for the Visiting Professorship in the Winter of 2018–2019. The work on the seminar and lectures I gave at these institutions turned out to be an essential part in the preparation of this book.

My academic upbringing, and life experience on the whole, taught me the validity of the Jewish aphorism "wisdom from all my teachers." But, the shortcomings of my work, this book included, are entirely my responsibility.

Shlomo Ben-Ami

LIST OF MAPS

The copyright for all the maps is Dr. Shaul Arieli's, who kindly gave his consent for their use in this book.

Source: All the maps except the Alon Plan and Olmert's Realignment Plan, are from Shaul Arieli, *The Truman Institute Atlas of the Jewish-Arab Conflict* (Mount Scopus: Hebrew University of Jerusalem, 2020). The Allon and Olmert's Realignment Plans are from Shaul Arieli, *A Border between Us: Toward a Solution to the Israeli-Palestinian Conflict* (Tel Aviv: Yedioth Ahronoth, 2021).

A NOTE ON VOCABULARY

Conflicts and peace processes tend to have their own particular vocabulary. *Religion* was central to the Northern Ireland conflict and to the India-Pakistan dispute, but was entirely absent from the Colombian armed conflict, or from the drama of South Africa's apartheid, the civil wars in Central America, and the Morocco-Southern Sahara conflict. *Power-sharing* was key to the solution of the Northern Ireland situation, but is entirely irrelevant in the case of Palestine and Colombia. In none of these conflicts, except in the cases of Morocco and India-Pakistan has *territory, annexation,* and the *delineation of borders* played any role whatsoever. The vocabulary of the Israeli-Palestinian drama, and the attempts to solve it are overwhelmingly pervaded with the yearning of *return* (of Palestinian refugees), with claims over *holy shrines,* with Israel's affirmation of its right to keep her *settlements* in occupied lands and her needs for *security.* The ultimate purpose of the peace process is the creation of a *Palestinian state,* the definition of its *borders,* and the amount of *territory* it would allow Israel to *annex,* in exchange for Israeli *swapped territory,* for the purpose of accommodating its *settlement blocs.*

The Interim Agreement that was signed between Yitzhak Rabin and Palestinian Liberation Organization (PLO) chairman Yasser Arafat on September 28, 1995, required that Israel offer the Palestinians, ahead of the negotiations on the final settlement, parts of the West Bank and redeploy accordingly its military forces. These *withdrawals-redeployments* were to be defined in term of *percentages* of the total surface of the West Bank. *Percentages* were also to be traded in the final peace agreement, for it was understood that a solution to the problem of settlements would require it.

In the first stage of the Interim Agreement, the Israeli Defense Forces (IDF) withdrew from the populated areas of the West Bank, that is, six cities—Jenin, Nablus, Tulkarem, Kalkilya, Ramallah, and Bethlehem—and 450 towns and villages. With the end of this redeployment, hardly any Israeli military presence remained in Palestinian population centers. The agreement also provided that additional redeployments would take place at six-month intervals so that, by the completion of the redeployment phases, Palestinian jurisdiction will cover West Bank territory except for the areas where jurisdiction is to be determined under the final status negotiations. In his Wye River Agreement with Arafat in October 1998, Benjamin Netanyahu, who had earlier redeployed from the city of Hebron, pledged handing over to the Palestinians 13 percent of the West Bank, but his right-wing government could not stomach such a "sellout" of biblical lands, and it turned down the agreement. It was left to us, the Barak government, to deliver on the Wye River redeployment if we wanted to proceed toward a final peace settlement in strict observance of the Interim Agreement framework. But, Barak's idea was to skip the whole redeployment process by moving directly to negotiations on the final settlement.

Barak's leap into the endgame was a transparent attempt to eschew the pattern of interim agreements where Israel relinquished territory at such a prohibitive political price that it could bring about the collapse of the government, as indeed was the case with Netanyahu's, and the end of the peace process. Knowing that we would need every drop of public and political support for the difficult concessions required by the endgame, Barak thought it politically advisable to integrate all redeployments into the final settlement. But Arafat needed signals of Barak's seriousness as a peacemaker, and on September 4, 1999, an agreement was signed at Sharm el-Sheikh dividing Netanyahu's unaccomplished redeployment into three phases, September 5, November 15, and January 20, 2000. This would have left Israel in control of 59 percent of the West Bank ahead of the negotiations for a final peace. It was also agreed that Israel would release a total of 350 Palestinian prisoners.

Barak complied with the first stage on September 5, and also released the first group of prisoners. Also the safe passage connecting Gaza with the West Bank, which I negotiated with Palestinian Minister of Civil Affairs, Jamil Tarifi, was signed in Jerusalem on October 5 to Arafat's satisfaction. He even hailed it for creating a "geographic and demographic unity between Gaza and the West Bank"; Tarifi saw it as an important "trust building move between the two peoples and the two leaders."[1] Droves of Palestinians making use of the safe passage and the start of the construction of a seaport in Gaza went in the same promising direction.

But, Arafat's expectations would soon clash with Barak's constraints. Pressured by his focus on the peace talks he had started with Syria and ever present domestic concerns, Barak went back on his pledge of a further release of prisoners and also skipped altogether the third phase of the promised redeployment that was scheduled for January 20. To stave off the inevitable crisis of confidence, he gave in to Arafat's demand for compensation in the form of a transfer to the Palestinians of three Arab villages on the outskirt of Jerusalem—Abu Dis, Azariyya, and el-Ram—as part of the remaining 6.1 percent redeployment. On March 20, however, Barak executed the final withdrawal, but avoided including in it the promised villages. He also released only fifteen prisoners instead of the more than a hundred that were requested.

Clearly inadequate, Barak's gestures were part of a maintenance task to allow him to focus on his Syria negotiations. There is no other way to define also the peace talks with the Palestinians he entrusted to Ambassador Oded Eiran, a brilliant diplomat who served as Israel's ambassador in Jordan, to conduct. These were held on March 21 and April 7 in Bolling Air Force Base near Washington, DC, and on May 4, in the Israeli southern resort of Eilat. The Palestinian negotiator Saeb Erakat rightly defined the meetings as being more brainstorming sessions than real negotiations. In practical terms, Eran offered a Palestinian state on 66 percent of the West Bank, with 20 percent to be annexed by Israel and another 14 percent to be kept for an indefinite period of time for security purposes. It was a humiliating nonstarter no Palestinian could have taken seriously. If Barak's ambition for an era of peace with the Palestinians was to have any realistic prospects, we needed to do better.

Introduction

No Zionist panegyric can convincingly blur the responsibility of the Jews' return to their ancestral homeland for the Palestinian tragedy of disinheritance and exile. Yet the enduring clash between Zion and Palestine is not a tale of absolute righteousness. Partisan accounts are bound to pervert the complex truth of a story that started when a decimated people, resolute as only a nation desperately gasping for life can be, clashed with a fragmented indigenous Arab community. It later evolved into a tragedy of discrepant historical rhythms where peace overtures aimed at splitting the land were defeated in order to be missed when history had already swept them into oblivion. Ill-conceived perceptions of the other, all-or-nothing theological fanaticism, and a lack of bold, enlightened leadership combined to turn the conflict into a cruel lesson about the inherent amorality of history.

Not in vain has the enthralling drama of the clash between Zion and Palestine been one of the most emotionally engaging causes for the Western mind. It is an absorbing odyssey of two nations to the same landscapes, a story of mutually exclusive claims on sacred lands and religious shrines that are central in the lives of millions around the world. Israel-Palestine is a story far bigger than the current conflict; it is also the story of an extraordinary symbiosis between Jewish heritage and Western civilization that ended in a cataclysmic tragedy. The plight of the Palestinians, the victims of Israel's resurgence, rightly touches another neuralgic center in the Western mind.

Consequently, Israel's suppression of Palestine resonates in a way that no other conflict does. From London to Rome, from Antwerp to Berlin, and from Istanbul to Casablanca, Israel is frequently denounced as a "Terror State." Seventy-five years after the annihilation of European Jewry in the Holocaust, and shocked by the burning of synagogues in France and Germany, Jews throughout Europe see again the shadow of *Kristallnacht* looming over their communities, with angry pro-Palestinian demonstrators inviting them back "To the Gas."

Israel apologists are these days facing pro-Palestine activism on Western campuses, the kind of which is unparalleled since the Vietnam War. The apparent demise of the two-state solution has also made legitimate among Americans the idea of a one-state solution where Palestinians should have equal rights in all and every aspect. A Brookings Institution poll in August 2021 found that 84 percent of Democrats and 60 percent of Republicans favor a single democratic state with Arabs and Jews as equal.[1]

Israel's critics would scornfully repudiate her claim that the Palestinian national movement has four times in its history rejected offers of statehood, in 1937, 1947, 2000, and 2008. To this day, it is still normal in the anti-Zionist left to dismiss peace offers such as the Clinton peace parameters and the Ehud Olmert Annapolis peace deal—both proposing a Palestinian state over practically 100 percent of the occupied territories—as nothing but a crippled Palestinian state in "isolated Bantustans." Gullibility is a weakness that even supposedly educated authors can sometime share with the anonymous masses. Robert Fisk, who found room in his 1,336 page book to pervert the truth of what was offered at the Camp David summit—he insists on only 64 percent of the occupied West Bank for a Palestinian state (it actually was 92 percent)—could not find room for even mentioning the Clinton parameters that offered 97 percent, as if they never existed.[2] I sadly believe that those offers will go down in history as the last chance we had for a negotiated solution to the plight of the Palestinians.

Spread practically among all the relevant stakeholders, the inglorious task of preventing the creation of a Palestinian state was not an exclusive Israeli responsibility. In their rejection of the 1947 UN Resolution 181 partitioning Palestine into a Jewish and an Arab state, the Palestinians opted for high stakes with inadequate resources. The war they started on the very morrow of the UN vote ended with what would become engraved in their memory as the *Nakba*, the disaster of dispossession and exile. By intervening in the 1948 war, the Arab states did not seek to secure for the Palestinians their promised state. Rather, they sought to kill the partition plan and acquire new territory for themselves. Palestinian blunders and an unholy alliance of Arab states, American mediators, and Zionists have been jointly responsible for making Palestinian statehood a historical impossibility.[3]

But the war whose consequences still reverberate to this day is the 1967 Six Day War. Israel's lightening victory brought her military grandeur and moral decay. The nationalist-religious intoxication that followed the conquest of Jerusalem and the biblical lands of Judea and Samaria, the Palestinian West Bank, reached dangerous heights to the degree that this "mother of all victories" was now being interpreted as a messianic, providential event. The 1967 *annus mirabilis* threw the Jewish state into the realm of the fantasy of Greater Eretz Israel. The new zeitgeist gave popular legitimacy to the irresistible Bacchanalia of nationalist ardor. "We have returned to our holiest shrines in order not to part from them ever again," affirmed then Defense Minister Moshe Dayan.[4]

For a while, it looked as if reality could convincingly intrude into ideological purity. It was an Egyptian president, Anwar Sadat, who, in his peace negotiations with Israel at Camp David in September 1978, forced a hawkish Israeli prime minister, Menachem Begin, to endorse such concepts as "a recognition of the legitimate rights of the Palestinian people and their just requirements," and "the resolution of the Palestinian problem in all its aspects." The text was indeed promising, but not so much the political will to make it true. For all practical purposes, Anwar Sadat signed a separate peace with Israel while paying verbal tribute to the Palestinian cause. "Sadat does not give a shit about the West Bank," confided Jimmy Carter to his Middle East adviser, William Quandt.[5] The most that Begin was willing to offer the Palestinians was a bizarre autonomy plan that drew its inspiration from the Habsburg polyglot empire, and from his mentor, Ze'ev Jabotinsky, who had advocated the principle of individual rights for the Arabs, but no collective entitlement to a territory.

Yet, Sadat did revolutionize the entire geostrategic structure of the Middle East by indicating to Arab leaders that only by extricating themselves from the Soviet Union's grip and embracing instead the US-led peace diplomacy could they get back their territories. This was also true of the Palestinian Liberation Organization (PLO). From the early 1970s, it started a process of change that would eventually lead its legendary leader, Chairman Yasser Arafat, to embrace in the November 1988 Algiers Declaration the two-state solution. But Israel's infatuation with the conquered Palestinian lands was such that it preferred to discard any diplomatic approach; it was more politically convenient to fight the PLO as a terrorist organization. This was fine so long as Cold War bipolarity condemned the conflict to oscillate between paralysis and war. But with the collapse of the Soviet Union, the opportunities started to overshadow the risks. This was ceremoniously reflected in the October 1991 Madrid Peace Conference under the co-chairmanship of US President George H. Bush and Russia's Mikhail Gorbachev. For the first time in the history of the century-old Israeli-Arab conflict, the parties and the major international stakeholders launched a concerted effort for a comprehensive solution to the conflict.

It took, however, a change of government in Israel from Yitzhak Shamir's Likud to a transformed Laborite, Yitzhak Rabin, to reach in 1993 the historic Oslo Accord between Israel and the PLO. Oslo was an interim agreement that allowed the creation of a Palestinian autonomy in Gaza and parts of the West Bank, and established a roadmap for negotiations of the core issues of the conflict— Jerusalem, Palestinian refugees, Israeli settlements, and Palestinian statehood.

Alas, Oslo was designed to function under sterile laboratory conditions, for it assumed that trust could be built between the occupied and the land-hungry

occupier. Oslo lacked monitoring mechanisms of compliance and agreed
sanctions for breaking pledges. Its architects assumed as a given the goodwill of
the parties and their commitment to march together, hand in hand, to the final
settlement on the most divisive issues imaginable. Rabin also expected Arafat to
be the subcontractor of Israel's security by putting an end to the First Intifada in
the occupied territories that had been going on unabated since 1987. But Arafat
was incapable of delivering. He rightly gathered that clamping down on the
Islamist radicals from Hamas and Islamic Jihad would portray him in the eyes
of his people as a "collaborator" of the Israelis. Israel could do little to help him,
for Yitzhak Rabin was trapped in his unsustainable double-edged approach of
fighting terrorism as if there was no peace process and pursuing the peace process as if there was no terrorism.

A fatal vicious cycle was created whereby the Palestinians were hit by collective punishment, economic decline, and the expansion of settlements, whose
population increased under Rabin's government by 48 percent in the West Bank
and 62 percent in the Gaza Strip. Rather than as a modern state bound by international law, Israel behaved in the territories as possessed by an irresistible
agrarian hunger.

When Rabin was assassinated by a Jewish fanatic as a traitor who sold out
Eretz Israel, he was already severely crippled politically by a series of devastating
suicide terrorist attacks. Benjamin Netanyahu's premiership (1996–99) gave
the *coup de grâce* to an already moribund peace process. Ehud Barak, a highly
decorated former IDF chief of general staff and now head of the Labor Party,
defeated Netanyahu in May 1999 to become Israel's new prime minister. A hybrid of right-wing sentiments and left-wing political persuasions, Barak cultivated his self-image as Rabin's successor, a general turned statesman. He lost no
time in spelling out his intention of reaching a peace settlement with Syria and
the Palestinians as well as pulling out from Southern Lebanon in line with UN
Security Council Resolution 425.

* * *

Historic breakthroughs do not occur in a vacuum. They demand a rare syn-
ergy between ripe social and strategic conditions and a leadership capable of
leveraging the new circumstances and rallying the nation behind its vision. By
the end of the millennium, Barak still believed that the window of opportunity
of Rabin's times, although narrower, was yet open, and he was determined to
pursue Rabin's peace legacy before a brutal wave of Islamic fundamentalism
could topple the region's pro-Western regimes, and before fundamentalist Hamas
could gain control of Palestinian society and dispel any chance of an agreement.
Arafat, with all his weaknesses, was the last obstacle in Hamas's snowballing
path. We were acting against the drifting sands of time. For Iran too was rising to

the level of a regional superpower, spreading its patronage over a swelling fundamentalist wave. As we were briefed immediately upon assuming power, Iran was making progress in her nuclear program. The rising Shiite empire had a strategic interest in blocking the chances of an Israeli-Arab rapprochement.

These were also the last eighteen months of Bill Clinton's presidency, and it made much sense to have him and his peace team—supposedly the group of foreign officials most proficient in the intricacies of the Israel-Palestine situation—accompany us in this fateful voyage to a final and definitive peace agreement, one that would address all the issues that Oslo had defined as necessary for an end of conflict. Clinton's emotional attachment to Israel, and his admiration for the late Yitzhak Rabin, whose assassination he took as the intimate loss of a father figure, consumed him with a sense of mission to accomplish the peace legacy of his fallen hero well into the very last days of his presidency. Eager to end his presidency in the kind of dramatic crescendo that a Palestinian peace would give him, he was even willing to divert his last drops of presidential power from the burning North Korean nuclear showdown to the Palestinian problem, which now became the central foreign policy endeavor of the prodigiously tenacious president. It was also evident to us that Arafat, just like Anwar Sadat in the late 1970s, saw his newfound working relations with Washington as a strategic asset. His friends in the old Soviet Union and Eastern Europe had all evaporated, and Vladimir Putin, who had just come to power in Russia, was still a long way from being the destabilizing, revisionist tsar that he is today.

It all now converged in a showdown between the right's view of the biblical lands of Judea and Samaria as articles of faith and a Rabin-style pragmatic approach to peacemaking. Alas, our peace enterprise was to be marked by a fatal misencounter between the outer limits of our capacity for compromise as Jews and Israelis and the Palestinians' expectations. History is made of such imperfect opportunities, which, if missed, end up throwing its desolate subjects into even deeper abysses.

* * *

This book should be read as an obituary to the two-state solution. The story of the Camp David process and that of all the attempts at peacemaking that followed it, which are all reviewed and scrutinized in this book, needs to be seen as a defining failure of the entire peace paradigm based on the two-state concept. This rote religion that continues to dominate the international discourse on Palestine is dead and buried, and it is about time that all stakeholders shift their attention to other possible scenarios, some ominous and other less so, which are also examined in this book. Whatever "solution" happens in the future, it is not going to be the classic two-state solution with an orderly settlement of the refugee problem and arithmetically calculated land swaps; it would be a situation born out of chaos amid broad regional changes, the exact nature of which one cannot predict.

Not all was bad news in this torturous story, however. The funereal historiography and poignant memoirs that have emerged in the wake of the Camp David process, where for the first time ever Israelis and Palestinians engaged in the Sisyphean task of dealing with all of the core issues of the conflict, should not overshadow its achievements, if only for the sake of the historical record. This is the story of a tortuous drama which, as in almost all peace enterprises elsewhere, is always paved with crises and violence. Clinton's decision to convene the summit was not an irresponsible act of desperation of a lame-duck president. Palestinians and Israelis gave his team pre-summit ideas from which they believed a conceivable endgame could emerge. The president, moreover, as we could ascertain in meetings in Congress with his Republican nemeses, such as Senator John McCain, Senate Majority Leader Trent Lott, and a score of others in the House, enjoyed wide bipartisan support for his peace enterprise.

The summit itself made enormous progress in breaking taboos no one before had ever dared touching, and it ended with an outline that became the foundation upon which the Clinton peace parameters were produced six months later. These parameters became eventually the litmus test of every serious peace proposal since then, all of which are scrutinized in Part III of this book. Against the unpromising background of the Oslo legacy of the expansion of settlements and terrorism, we succeeded in coming closer than ever to breaking the genetic code of the Israeli-Palestinian dispute. The two-state solution that was bequeathed by the Netanyahu government in a comatose state, was given in these negotiations a living form, and a precise set of peace parameters.

But, the two-state solution proved eventually to be undeliverable. It eluded us not only because of the shortcomings of leaders and negotiators, but because of the inherent intractability of the conflict. "Ending the occupation," which friends and detractors keep clamoring for, remains, of course, a sublime objective. But this account of our voyage into the boundaries of the quest for peace as well as the description of the peace process as it evolved in future years until the current impasse offers a taste of how innocent can such a noble objective be.

The Camp David story is not short of witnesses—Palestinians, Americans, and Israelis—who chronicled the process in informative and enlightening ways. The former prime minister Ehud Barak was the last to offer his account. His book is, however, essentially the story of his life and his exploits as a military man. The chapter that deals with the Camp David process is incomplete and disappointingly apologetic. The entire Taba experience is not even mentioned in his book. Nor is the Taba story a first hand account in the American memoirs, for it happened after the participants had left office. Clinton's and Barak's accounts are written from the heights of their leadership positions; they certainly are not self-critical analyses.

History should not be what we choose to remember; hence Henry David Thoreau's advice that "it takes two to speak the truth" is such an essential tool in historical research. My many flaws as a politician probably stemmed from my obsession with not abandoning my vocation as a student of history or, dare I say, as an intellectual as well? As such, I did my best to follow Albert Camus's adage on the role of the intellectual not being "to excuse the violence of one side and condemn that of the other."[6] This book pretends, therefore, to offer the most nonpartisan, comprehensive, and balanced account by an insider representing one of the parties. I have read all previous accounts and compared my notes with theirs, at times correcting my own original perceptions, in order to offer the most accurate story possible. Evidently, these were all instant accounts, written immediately after the collapse of the process; mine is written with the advantage of historical perspective. This is not the work of a peace negotiations practitioner, which I am not, but that of a historian with a compulsive tendency to collect notes and evidence, and to draw from them policy implications. Nor is this an apologia of Israel's behavior throughout the negotiations; it is an attempt to weave together love and loyalty to Israel with truth-telling. This is also the account of a minister who formed part of the decision-making process, and also traveled the region and the world to engage the international stakeholders. This international dimension, which remains vital if the flaws of the US monopoly on "the process" are to be superseded, gets due attention in this book.

Camp David should also be understood through the drama of the interplay between its actors. Barak's character flaws, Clinton's ineffective leadership of the summit, and his team's utterly unrealistic views as to the margin of maneuver the Palestinians had for making concessions contributed to the outcome. Barak was desperately slow in understanding the depth of the concessions that needed to be made. We tried to make peace while destroying the Palestinians' trust by expanding settlements, and by not respecting goodwill pledges. Also, the incompatibility in character between the two leaders was truly abysmal. Barak was a man of brilliance, broad strategic understanding, and the necessary courage to take difficult decisions such as the dramatic withdrawal from Lebanon in May 2000. In our team's internal deliberations, he was open-minded, responsive, ironic at times, and always wittily humorous. In wrapping up such meetings, he tended, however, to display an almost preternatural capacity for opaque and ambiguous instructions that left one with the liberty of interpreting them. A uniquely gifted and thrusting military man with the calling of a statesman, Barak had an unorthodox mind and a vast knowledge. But his character flaws were a major handicap when he needed to reach out to others. He was inept at managing the sensibilities of either friends or rivals, and he lacked the intuitive tactile sense that makes a great politician. He was blessed with an elephantine skin that shielded him against criticism, and a mental fortitude that made him impervious to pressure, which was perhaps what also made him at times an overbearing negotiator. He expected people to act according to the scenario he had written for them and, when they refused, he tended to lose his composure, and dig in his heels. He obstinately assumed that what he considered a "reasonable agreement" must also appear thus in the eyes of whomever he was talking to, in this case the historic leader of a disinherited nation who had been forged by long years of struggle and steadfastness. Arafat's "stubbornness" in acting against his own interests, as Barak saw them, was intellectually incomprehensible to him. A conceited and bumptious Cartesian, he was too abrasive to be able of levelling with a Palestinian counterpart who was wholly consumed in theological hallucinations and national mythologies.

Throughout the negotiating process, Barak, and at times others in our team, myself included, wrongheadedly behaved like Noam Chomsky's "new mandarins."[7] "The best and the brightest" of the American administrations analyzed projections regarding the behavior of the Vietcong in the Vietnam War in a rational, perhaps even scientific way. They certainly made use of the best tools that the elite American universities could offer in areas such as systems analysis, decision-making, game theory—you name it. There was one thing they did not take into account: the unbounded human will of the enemy, as well as the basic fact that the ethos of his struggle did not answer to the same "rational" patterns upon which the Americans had built their working assumptions. What "logic," to return to the Palestinian arena, was there in the Al-Aqsa intifada, which was to drive this battered, defeated people to the depths of Destruction that could only be compared to the days of the *Nakba*? This, indeed, was not "logical," but it represented the fundamental ethos of a national struggle with a strongly Islamic and nationalistic flavor. Our rage at the enemy for not taking the steps that we expected him to take was of no use whatsoever.

Referring to the Vietnam war, the historian and journalist James C. Thomson wrote in April 1968 of the "effectiveness trap" dilemma of officials willing to serve under a leader whose positions they did not share, in the assumption that at some point down the road they would be able to be effective in improving them.[8] I admit that was my attitude when Barak tried to convince me how reasonable his idea of a Palestinian state in 66 percent of the land was. Expecting that Barak could make the leap to more realistic standpoints made all of us around him hostages to fortune, though. His initial negotiating positions were, indeed, of monumental absurdity, and his febrile conviction of their validity was truly perplexing. No less surprising was his assumption that with such delusionary positions a final agreement could still be reached in the breakneck speed of a tight timetable that he imposed on all sides. These negotiations, he confided to the head of the peace process administration, Colonel (res.) Shaul Arieli, were not about the creation of two states but about "a just partition of the West Bank between the parties."[9] He also rejected the idea that UN Resolution 242 should have any bearing whatsoever on the Palestinian question. And when Arieli prepared a plan for a Palestinian state on 87 percent of the West Bank, Barak asked him to shelve it. The myth surrounding Yitzhak Rabin's peace legacy should not, however, obscure the fact that Barak's positions were practically identical to those of his slain mentor. On October 4, 1995, one month before his assassination, Rabin spelled out before the Knesset his peace plan. He wanted "less than a state" for the Palestinians, a Jerusalem that is linked to Maale Adumim, an Israeli "extensive" military presence on the Jordan River, and sizable blocs of settlements east of the green line.[10]

In Palestinian iconography, Arafat was a metahistorical figure, a *pater patriae* almost devoid of human features. In his own insatiable appetite for adulation he saw himself as the reincarnation of Saladin, the redeemer of Jerusalem from the infidel Crusaders in the twelfth century. It was through Arafat that the Palestinian keffiyeh became the icon of an internationally acclaimed national cause. To be sure, he was also a cunning and deceitful politician, always capable of rising like a phoenix from the ashes of innumerable setbacks and defeats. He deserved much of his people's adoration, though, for it was he who extricated the Palestinian national movement from the cynical grip of Arab leaders, gave it a sense of purpose, and turned it into the most widely resonant national cause in recent times. Alas, he also was responsible for missing the optimal peace deal once it was offered. With Arafat, everything was complex and indecipherably ambiguous. He was incorrigibly evasive, his penchant for doublespeak disguised and distorted his intentions, and his showmanship made his interlocutor's capacity to distinguish between reality and performance a truly disconcerting task. The way Lloyd George described his talks with the Irish nationalist Eamon de Valera—a hopeless exercise in picking up mercury with a fork—is perfectly applicable to talks with Arafat as well. Arafat also could never resist the temptation of trading with Palestinian blood, which, admittedly, did not make him unique among nationalist leaders throughout history. Leaders of national movements have always used and abused the blood of their people to advance the national cause. The Zionists did it brilliantly on the way to statehood with the Holocaust of European Jewry.[11] But, they were also determined state-builders, which Arafat was not. He was a freedom fighter who fought to redress an injustice, not to build a future.

An Israeli leader has yet to emerge to genuinely commiserate on, let alone admit, Israel's share of responsibility for the Palestinian tragedy of dispossession and exile. Israel owes its existence to the Jews' extraordinary memory of history; it now relies on the Palestinians forgetting theirs. This compulsive ignorance of the givens of human nature greatly contributed to making the Israeli-Palestinian dispute such a desperately protracted conflict. Israel's moral abdication and her complete insouciance, a failure of imagination to conceive the suffering of the other, so typical otherwise of bitter national conflicts that tend always to metamorphose into a story of competitive victimhood, are common to both the right and the left. We, who incessantly fight for the retrieval of Jewish property confiscated by the Nazis and other executioners of the Jewish people, created, through the 1950 Absentees' Property Law, a legal instrument to take possession of the movable and immovable property belonging to Palestinian refugees across the state. At Camp David and after, we adamantly rejected the Palestinians' demand that compensation for the refugees be drawn from such properties. The people of the book applied its teachings to the letter: they "rushed greedily upon the spoil, and took sheep and oxen and calves, and slew them on the ground."[12]

Alas, history is a textbook of moral paradoxes, and it is absurd political correctness, or postcolonial patronization, to assume that the weaker side can never have a responsibility for the tragedies that have befallen them. The Jews are a living testimony of the maxim that being the underdog is not to be blameless. That an independent Jewish state existed for only short periods of Jewish millenarian history was the result of the blunder of ignoring political realities and suicidally challenging the world powers that governed the international system of the time.

Self-determination is never handed on a silver platter. Oppressed nations throughout history reached it not only because they had the right or held the moral high ground, but because they were capable of meeting the historical moment with a sagacious balance of force and diplomacy. The Kurds probably deserve the dignity of statehood as much as the Palestinians, but trapped as they are in impossible geostrategic conditions, they fail time and again in their struggle for independence. It was a brilliant Palestinian scholar, Yezid Sayigh, who warned Arafat during the Second Intifada that the Kurdish fate awaited the Palestinians if he continued to miss the encounter with history. From the perspective of what today looks like the end of the two-state solution and, indeed, of any realistic promise of Palestinian redemption, how can the Palestinians defend the case that they did not fail in the crucial test of seizing historical moments and their inevitably imperfect offers? How can they not rue the day that they turned out the Clinton parameters and later Ehud Olmert's 2008 peace offer, now that Palestine has been cast away from both the regional and global agenda?

Nabil Amr, a minister in Arafat's cabinet, valiantly made precisely such an accusation in an open letter to Arafat, two years into the Al-Aqsa Intifada, that is, when it was becoming tragically clear that Arafat's failure to give a final yes to Clinton's peace proposals had doomed the Palestinian cause:

> *Didn't we dance when we heard of the failure of the Camp David talks? Didn't we destroy pictures of President Bill Clinton who had the temerity to propose a Palestinian state with small border modifications? We are not being honest. Today, after two years of bloodshed we are asking for exactly what we rejected then, and now it is beyond our reach . . . How often have we agreed to compromises, only to change our mind and reject them, and later still find ourselves agreeing to them once again? We were never willing to learn from either our acceptance or our rejection. How often were we asked to do something that we could have done, and did nothing? Afterwards, when the solution was already unattainable we roamed the world in the hope of getting what had already been offered to us and rejected. And we discovered that in the span of time between our "rejection" and subsequent "acceptance" the world had changed, and we were faced with additional conditions which again we felt we could not accept. We failed to rise to the challenge of history.*[13]

Amr eventually paid for his daring with the amputation of his leg after being shot at by Arafat's men.

On January 8, 2001, a few days after Arafat had turned down Clinton's peace plan, Fouad Ajami, the eminent Lebanese-born Shiite scholar and one of the world's foremost orientalists, published his explanation of Arafat's conduct in *US News and World Report*. Arafat's behavior, he wrote, reflected an inherent failure within the Palestinian national movement, its innate refusal to surrender to the logic of things, to understand and differentiate between the possible and the impossible. He said the Palestinians believed that a mysterious higher power would always come to their rescue, as if the laws of history did not apply to them.

What, indeed, is an Israeli negotiator to think when, while Ariel Sharon was *ante portas*, and the Israeli negotiating team in Taba was accepting going beyond the Clinton parameters, which the president had presented as a take-it-or-leave-it offer, he is told by the chief Palestinian negotiator that "the boss is not interested in an agreement"?[14] What sense did it make for Palestinian negotiator Mohammed Dahlan to define then the Taba talks as "bullshit" (*Harta Barta* in Arabic is also a popular expression among Israelis), an expression captured in a headline by *Yedioth Ahronoth*, the newspaper with the highest circulation in the country, a few days before Sharon's landslide victory? Dahlan later apologized for his mischief. What is one to think when, immediately upon the formation of Sharon's hard-line government, Arafat asks him to resume negotiations from the point they were left at by an Israeli team consisting of the most emblematic peace dreamers in Israeli politics ever? Sharon, as expected, buried what remained of the peace process and reconquered with massive force the entire area under the control of the Palestinian authority. And what is one to think when, in a desperate attempt to break the deadlock, a bold proposal of mine to concede full sovereignty for the Palestinians on the Temple Mount, something Arafat valued even more than the refugees' right of return, if only they would acknowledge the existence of the remains of a holy Jewish shrine in the depth of the Mount, was rejected on the ground that there had never existed such a holy Jewish site? The same Palestinian negotiator through whom I made the proposal, Yasser Abed-Rabbo, later endorsed this very same idea into the 2003 Geneva Understandings. It was not an Israeli negotiator subscribing to the "traditional Israeli position," but the Saudi ambassador, Bandar bin Sultan, who defined in an interview with *The New Yorker*[15] Arafat's rejection of the Clinton peace parameters as a "crime against the Palestinian people and the Arab nation."

* * *

That the Israeli right has dominated Israeli politics ever since Camp David is the direct result of the discredit of the peace camp's trounced core message. It is this consequential defeat, more than Netanyahu's extraordinary canvassing proficiencies, which explains his fifteen-year rule at the head of far-right coalitions of annexationists and peace refuseniks. Only one more Israeli government, Ehud Olmert's, would still embark on a genuine attempt to reach a Palestinian peace. He also failed. We were only a link in a chain. Peace offers came and went. From Oslo to these very days, all attempts at peacemaking have failed resoundingly. There never was a textbook solution to this conflict. It was always going to be a voyage of trial and error.

Parts I and II of the book, essentially based on my diaries, always contrasted with other published accounts, are the story of the different phases of the negotiations throughout the last eighteen months of Bill Clinton's presidency. Part I—"Anatomy of a Seminal Misencounter"—covers the political voyage that started in secret talks in Israel and Sweden and moved then to the Camp David summit. Part II—"A Savage War for Peace"—starts with an analytical account of the Al-Aqsa Intifada. It then addresses the diplomatic struggle under fire for the elaboration of the Clinton peace parameters six months later, and the last-ditch attempt, amid the most savage war between Israelis and Palestinians since 1948, to salvage the peace in Taba. The blow-by-blow account of the Camp David process offered in Parts I and II of the book should also be read as the anatomy of a true-to-life essay in Israeli-Palestinian peace negotiations, with all its hopes and disappointments, its real and fake dramas, the clash of myth and reality underlying it, and the always unbridgeable gap between what is *necessary* and what it is *possible* to do under the compelling pressure of political constraints. It should also be read as a demonstration of how the failure to reconcile the diametrically opposed national narratives and core interests of the parties has made the two-state solution a historical impossibility. Israelis and Palestinians are capable of narrowing down the ocean that separates them into a river, but one with such troubled waters that they are simply incapable of crossing it. Too rich in history and too desperately poor in geography, Israel-Palestine proved incapable of accommodating such divergent monumental narratives and national aspirations. The last chapter (Chapter 26) in Part II, *Post-Mortem,* offers an interpretation of the reasons for and consequences of the outcome of the Camp David process.

Part III—"2001–20: A Story of Promise and Deceit"—is about the undeliverability of the two-state solution. It comprises six chapters offering different perspectives of the structural and political conditions that made the conflict such a resilient dispute. Its first two chapters (Chapters 27 and 28) are an interpretive account of the different phases of negotiations that took place during the presidencies of George W. Bush and Barak Obama (2001–14). Empires have never gone quietly, and Israel cannot be an exception, particularly as hers is both an empire, admittedly miniscule, and an ancestral homeland. One wonders why the bad press the Camp David experiment received has not been extended to the negotiations orchestrated by US Presidents George W. Bush and Barack Obama. Precisely because of the promising regional and international context, and despite the benefit of Camp David's lessons, the mismanagement and eventual failure of these peace enterprises is particularly revealing. They were a Rashomon of clumsiness and incompetence by the American side, Israeli erratic behavior, typical Palestinian indifference the moment they were not offered exactly their dream agreement, a bazaar over concessions and incentives for the Palestinians, and always a last moment walkaway by the Palestinians without even responding to a last, improved peace offer. Chapter 29 analyzes the Track Two, 2003 Geneva Understandings as a parable of the paradoxes and eventual undeliverability of the two-state idea. Chapter 30 addresses the fragmentation and innate lack of a state-building ethos in the Palestinian national movement. Chapter 31 is about how the international community failed to rise to the challenge when it was most needed by the peacemakers. Chapter 32 describes how the occupation's traits of permanence—Israel's insatiable quest for *Lebensraum,* economic dominance, and territorial security, and her chronically dysfunctional polity coupled, paradoxically, with her growing international clout—became major impediments to a solution.

Part IV—"Denouements"—brings under scrutiny the alternative options to an orderly move to a two-state solution. Chapter 33 conveys the overriding sense of futility of the ominous alternatives that politicians and pundits toy with, such as the binational state, a unilateral pullout from much of the West Bank and, finally, Donald Trump's "Deal of the Century." Gaza's evolving tragedy these days is a direct consequence of Ariel Sharon's unilateral disengagement from that troubled strip. Chapter 34 is a discussion of the Jordanian-Palestinian option, a solution with a long pedigree that is revisited here from different perspectives.

This author believes that with the Oslo bilateral way of peacemaking in irremediable disarray, the 1991 Madrid Peace Conference's way of peace through a Jordanian-Palestinian association needs to be revisited.

Part V—"Defying the Logic of Conflict Resolution"—consists of one chapter that examines the Palestinian conflict in a broad comparative perspective. The clash between Zion and Palestine transcends facile analogies, but examining it in a broader context is essential if the singularities of the Israeli-Palestinian situation are to be fully assumed by would-be peacemakers and potential mediators. I also hope that policymakers, pundits of the Middle East story, students of conflict resolution, and the many fervent activists for either Zion's or Palestine's cause will draw lessons from this revisiting of the Israeli-Palestinian conundrum about what was right and wrong in our peace enterprise. Questions raised in this book, and discussed from a comparative perspective in this chapter, stand at the center of any peace enterprise everywhere. This is the case, for example, with the difference between interstate negotiations and asymmetrical peace talks between a democratic state and a national movement; the utility of secret peace talks; the link between peacemaking and domestic constraints; the dilemma of negotiations under fire and the consequent deficit of legitimacy for peace talks that they tend to create in a democracy; the question of why war can be conducive to peace in some cases and not in others; the question of whether the importance of trust in peace negotiation has been overblown; the role of the mediator and the consequences of his faltering methods; the tension between tangible and nontangible categories—that is, the stuff of politics and of theology—in peace negotiations; the built-in tension between peace and justice; the link between ripeness (social, political, and even regional and global) and the prospects of peace that worked in some conflict theaters but fell short of producing peace in others; the influence that the way the parties frame the conflict can have—the Palestinians' framed it in colonial terms—on the prospects for its resolution; and so on.

History seldom has single inflection points, where one act or omission proves decisive. Rabin's assassination has been accorded a disproportionate bearing on the prospects of peace. Our failure to clinch a final settlement was a defining failure, for the two-state solution has proved to be a structural impossibility. I took from the Camp David experience a sense of the irrevocability of our dispute, a perception that would subsequently be borne out by the serial failures of each and every future peace enterprise discussed in this book. This was why, immediately after the Taba conference, I pinned my hopes, vainly it turned out, on an international solution that would save the parties from themselves and succor the two-state idea.[16] The preponderant world powers have simply lost interest.

The book ends with an Epilogue of conclusions and reflections on the consequences of Israel's supposed defeat of the Palestinian national movement for both her moral profile and her international standing. The dichotomy between Israel's improved standing in international affairs and her poor image in world opinion, mostly right in its critique but frequently ill-informed, will persist so long as Palestine is subjugated. If, predictably, all the avenues to a peaceful solution of Palestine's tragedy remain blocked, history will have the last word, either through a major war over explosive contentions, such as Jerusalem or Iran, or following any other regional geostrategic earthquake. Ours is the case of a protracted condition waiting for Clio, for the impersonal forces of history, to produce a geostrategic earthquake from which a solution of sorts might emerge. Indeed, any step leading to peace in the Middle East has always come about only after such tectonic shifts. "Events, dear boy, events," was how the late British prime minister, Harold MacMillan, defined the unpredictability of politics. Similarly, our failures leave the future of Palestine at the mercy of such indefinite "events."

History is not reversible, but it is not predetermined either. It is true that in peace enterprises, domestic politics and traditions largely determine success and failure. But, there is always a balance between determinism and free will, choice and responsibility. Alas, the classic two-state solution we fought for throughout our political and intellectual life is not on the menu of choices anymore; it has probably never been. This book illuminates turning points at Camp David and after that could have, some believe, led to different results, but the fact that they did not is not accidental; it is built into the structural fault of the two-state idea. Wronged nationalisms, ours and the Palestinians' included, tend to raise the cult of grievances, and the expectation of their redress, to the level of the absolute. One can only hope that if any new opportunities emerge again, the parties will address them through an informed comprehension of reality and in context, and, above all, by avoiding self-deception.

PART I

ANATOMY OF A SEMINAL MISENCOUNTER

First Steps, Harsh Truths

Peace on two fronts—Syria and Palestine—can be no less painful than war on two fronts. The more dovish members of Barak's cabinet, such as Yossi Beilin and myself, supported a Palestine-first strategy. And so did Ami Ayalon, the head of Israel's Internal Security Service (Shin Bet), and General Shaul Mofaz, the Chief of Staff. They both thought the public would not support relinquishing the vitally strategic Syrian Golan Heights, and they feared a violent explosion in the Occupied Territories should the Palestinians be relegated. I could understand the position of Ami Ayalon, a political dove who knew the high price of a Palestinian peace. But it was not clear what price General Mofaz, an indomitable hawk, was willing to pay. But Barak was obsessed with Syria. Like Rabin before him, he believed that an agreement with Syria would not only neutralize a serious strategic threat on our northern border, but would ultimately lead to a "cheaper" settlement with the Palestinians, who would then be deprived of the ability to inflame the region if their national aspirations remained unfulfilled.

Palestine was, nonetheless, present in our internal deliberations and in papers that some of us exchanged with the prime minister. In one such paper I sent him dated October 13, 1999, I referred to a basic contradiction in his peace policy: his attempt to end the conflict without facing up to the crucial question of Jerusalem. I stressed that it was in Israel's interest "to gain pan-Arab, Islamic, and international recognition of Jerusalem as her capital." Moreover, it would be impossible to develop trade-offs between the various core issues at stake without discussing Jerusalem. At Barak's house in Kochav Yair, we frequently brainstormed together with Gilead Sher, the head of the prime minister's Bureau, and General (res.) Danny Yatom, his security adviser. It was an established Israeli axiom that the 1967 line between Israel and the West Bank needed to be redrawn. My own view was that this could only be achieved through a strategic trade-off between that border and the Jordan Valley, which should become the international border of the future Palestinian state to the east. Barak agreed that "strategically," the western part of the West Bank was more important to Israel's vital interests than the eastern part, but he was not that eager to concede sovereignty to the Palestinians there. I proposed that we see the issues at stake as being divided in two clusters: *tangible* assets such as land, settlements, and security; and *narrative categories,* Jerusalem and refugees. My assessment was that from Arafat's perspective, the right of return was not negotiable against borders and territory, as Barak assumed, but might be in return for concessions on Jerusalem. That much we later heard from Hassan Asfour, a minister in Arafat's government and a member of the Palestinian negotiating team. "Arafat," he said, "would consider sacrificing the refugees in return for Jerusalem."

Barak's instructions ahead of my first meeting with the Palestinian negotiator Abu Ala on March 28, 2000, reflected a profound contradiction between his unquestionable desire to reach an agreement and his opening positions. Nor was the frenetic timetable he wanted to impose on both sides—two and a half months culminating in a leaders' summit at Camp David in early June—a signal that he really gauged the complexity of the enterprise. The tools he gave me to work with, though interesting opening positions for a man who had never been enamored of the left's "peace industry," would turn out to be clearly not tempting enough to induce the Palestinians to hurry to the summit, let alone to agree to an end of conflict.

His instructions were as follows:

- To seek an end of conflict.
- No return of refugees to Israel, other than small numbers on a humanitarian basis.
- Blocs of Israeli settlements to remain in Palestinian lands without being hemmed in. He entirely ruled out, however, swaps of territory.
- Jerusalem would "for the time being have to be postponed." He alluded, however, to the idea, popular among Israeli pundits, of expanding the city in order to divide it later into an Israeli Jerusalem and a Palestinian Al-Quds in one or two villages on the city's eastern outskirts. He also added the extravagant idea of a "flyover" under Israeli sovereignty across the Kidron River connecting Al-Quds to the Temple Mount, Haram al-Sharif for the Palestinians, where they could maintain the status quo. He also ruled out any kind of Palestinian sovereignty in the Old City.
- The demilitarized Palestinian state would have "qualified sovereignty" but its territory would be a single contiguous area. Its frontiers would be controlled by Israel, but there would be a Palestinian "gateway" to the outside world.
- Israel was to have sovereignty in the Jordan Valley for an extended period of time, and would now withdraw from only "a part" of the settlements in the Valley.

In the meetings with Abu Ala that were held intermittently in hotels in Jerusalem and Tel Aviv, I was joined by Former Chief of Staff Major General (Res.) Amnon Lipkin Shahak, now our minister of tourism, and later also by Gilead Sher. On the Palestinian side Abu Ala was sometimes joined by Mahmoud Abbas (Abu Mazen), one of the PLO's founding fathers and, in effect, Arafat's undeclared second-in-command. Gentle, soft-spoken, and reserved, he was an intellectual of sorts—he had written a revisionist dissertation questioning the magnitude of the Holocaust—whose status lay paradoxically in his lack of public or political support on the Palestinian street. His image as a politician who had not taken part in the armed struggle engendered, however, a degree of objection, and he would frequently become the scapegoat of the public's frustration with Arafat. To his credit, Abbas had been consistent in his call for switching from the armed struggle to a diplomatic strategy. However, during and after the Camp David negotiations, he was, regrettably, unable to rise to the occasion. It was as if he was present in body but not in mind, often apathetic and indifferent rather than playing the role of a leader advancing initiatives and identifying areas of compromise and decision. He would show signs of leadership only during the Second Intifada, when he had the courage to stand up to the armed militias and call for an end to the military way.

The discussions with Abu Ala were a rewarding personal experience. His proverbial rectitude, impeccable logic, and patriotic dedication made him the best envoy of peace that his suppressed nation could ever hope to have. He was pleasant, clever, experienced, and sophisticated in his own cumbersome way, a *bon vivant*, a lover of good food and cigars, with a keen sense of humor and a rare talent for telling jokes. A master in the art of tactical concessions, "Here is a concession," he would say with the cunning of a chess player, sacrificing a pawn in the hope of capturing the queen. He is endowed with a rare combination of strategic vision and the ability to handle details, and was willing, when necessary, to go to the very brink and risk a complete breakdown in the negotiations. One could not have, however, too many illusions as to his underlying rejection of the Israeli national narrative. Not unlike Arafat, Abu Ala believed, as he wrote in a programmatic article commemorating the fiftieth anniversary of the *Nakba*, that Jews never actually lived in Palestine, and Zionism was based on the manipulation of invented mythologies. He even compared the loss of Palestine to that of Islam's loss of Al-Andalus. I have always been indulgent with these kinds of myths; aren't we all in varying degrees trapped in the lies of our past? I found in Abu Ala a partner who appreciated what he defined as my earnest attitude, and in his cunning way believed to have detected what he viewed as my persistent attempts to push Barak's instructions to the most flexible extremes possible.[1] Barak's instructions were, indeed, a straitjacket that one needed to untie carefully. That we would eventually conclude this tortuous process in January 2001 with peace parameters that remain to this very day the most realistic foundation ever laid down for an Israeli-Palestinian peace had to do not only with our drive to explore ideas that went beyond official instructions, but also with Barak's own embrace of positions he never thought he would.

Abu Ala stated his objectives at the very outset: a Palestinian state within the 1967 borders and Jerusalem as its capital, and, once Israel had accepted the right of return, an "acceptable" way for its implementation would be agreed upon. Yet, like burned children avoiding the fire, all the Palestinian negotiators, Abu Ala included, avoided quantifying the number of returnees involved in his "acceptable" solution. It was practically impossible to ever know what they really meant by the term. On the broader meaning of an Israeli-Palestinian peace, Abu Ala was preaching to the converted. Peace, he said, was about restoring Palestinian honor, and it could not be the continuation of the occupation and humiliation by other means. True, the Palestinians were a nation without an economy and an army but, he said, it was they who held the key to war and peace in the Middle East. But, he asked,

> What happened after your peace with Egypt? Nothing. Not a single Arab country established relations with you, and your international standing remained unchanged. But the Oslo Agreement with us entirely altered your international standing, and for the first time Arab states began establishing economic and political ties with you.

Only by linking up with the Palestinians, Abu Ala insisted, would the Israelis be able to reach into the heart of the Arab and Muslim world. Israel, he tried to persuade me, must abandon its piecemeal approach to the peace talks—a percentage here and a percentage there, "arrangements" of one kind and another. "It's as if you are all the time preparing for the next war instead of laying the foundations for peace."

I also introduced my interlocutor to Israel's perspective. Israel was not yet ready to peg her security to the pledges of her Arab neighbors. That level of trust might develop in the future, but there would have to be a critical period of transition while our Palestinian peace took hold and the behavior of regimes in the area changed. The poor geography that we shared was such that our security demands were not aimed at the Palestinians but rather at wider strategic concerns, at our ability to respond to threats that could always arise in an unstable region in which a Palestinian peace would not end our security problems.

Yet, while he was decisive on the principles Abu Ala claimed to be flexible on their implementation. He could not endorse the Zionist ethos of the farthest kindergarten in the remotest settlement on Palestinian occupied land also defining Israel's political and security border. Yet he was ready for all the settlements to remain in place under Palestinian sovereignty with the Jewish residents being offered Palestinian citizenship. And, though "unlawful," the settlements, he said, could be accommodated through "minor" border changes. As for security, he wished to develop "an innovative approach," a mix of "joint patrols, American presence, and early warning systems" rather than annexation or an Israeli presence on the ground. When applied to the question of refugees, the Palestinian mix of steadfastness on the principle and a soft approach in its implementation was far less digestible. We did converge on the idea of an international commission—in which Israel and the Palestinian state would participate but which would be led by the United States, Canada, Europe, Japan, and those Arab states which hosted the refugees—that would manage the mobilization of resources, and the compensation and rehabilitation of the refugees, either in their host countries or in the Palestinian state, or in third countries. We even managed to dilute the obstacle represented by the Palestinians' insistence on UN Resolution 194 of December 11, 1948, defining the principles for the return of refugees or compensation for those who opted not to return. We agreed that when a mechanism for solving the refugee problem had been approved, it would be viewed as an "implementation of resolution 194." What we could not agree to, however, was Abu Ala's insistence on the right of return and its implementation *à la carte*—the free choice for every refugee to stay in his host country, move to a third country, or return to Israel. The Palestinian longing for peace offers of yesteryear that were either ignored or bluntly repudiated has been a recurrent pattern in this conflict. Resolution 194 was a non-binding General Assembly Resolution that was rejected at the time by the entire Arab world, the Palestinians included. They had also rejected an Israeli proposal made a few months later at the UN-sponsored Lausanne Peace Conference to admit 100,000 refugees. Nor did the Palestinians accept in 1967 the UN Security Council Resolution 242 that was now the fundamental premise upon which our entire peace process was based.

These initial discussions ended up exposing five fundamental Palestinian truths. Oslo represented the major historic compromise in which they had ceded 78 percent of mandatory Palestine; in the 22 percent left they were prepared for small reciprocal adjustments, but were unwilling to accept a substantive redrawing of the map. Second, while they said they wanted a practical solution to the refugee problem, they always insisted that Israel recognize first the principle of the Palestinian right of return. Third, they insisted absolutely that Jerusalem be divided into two capitals. Four, unlike our critics in Israel who thought that we should have gone for an interim agreement instead of getting bogged down in negotiations over an impossible final settlement, the Palestinians were sick and tired of interim situations. "It would be better to postpone the deadline for a final settlement, so long as there are no partial agreements," Abu Ala averred time and again. "The Palestinians are interested in a full package," I was also told by Dennis Ross, the head of the American Peace Team overseeing our talks, "They have come to hate these interim arrangements." Five, the Palestinians made it unequivocally clear that the era of "constructive ambiguity" that characterized the old Interim Agreements had come to an end. In simple terms, they argued: "What is yours is yours, and what is ours is ours; one color for you another color for us. Don't cover the land in a multi-colored mosaic."

|| 2 ||

"A Secluded Nordic Castle"

The Palestinian philosophy whereby they entered negotiations on the basis that they had already made their compromises by waiving their right to 77 percent of historical Palestine, and that all that was left for them to do was to dot the i's and cross the t's, had never been the working assumption of the Israeli side. Unlike the case of Syria and Egypt, where the result of the negotiations was practically a given, we all agreed, the Palestinian process was more open-ended. This massive gulf between the working assumptions of the parties was bridgeable if only we were all ready to go substantively beyond our preconceived suppositions. "The Swedish track" was supposed to test our capacity to do so. Ehud Barak, who used to ridicule the Oslo Accords idea of "secret talks in remote Scandinavian castles," finally agreed to precisely such a Scandinavian venue, not exactly a castle, but rather the country residence of the Swedish prime minister Göran Persson in Harpsund, about two hours south of Stockholm.

Before setting off for Sweden, we went to an impossible mission, calming Arafat's stormy temperament. Our meeting took place in Abu Mazen's spacious house in Ramallah in the evening hours of May 8, 2000. I joined Prime Minister Barak, Danny Yatom, and Yossi Ginnossar, a former deputy head of Shin Bet who, bizarrely, became an Arafat confidant as well as a business partner, in what was to be an almost surreal encounter. Barak vainly explained to Arafat the political difficulties he faced handing over the promised Jerusalem villages. Arafat showed his anger by nervously shuffling his feet and saying almost nothing. He was also dissatisfied with the outcome thus far of my talks with Abu Ala. "Very good atmosphere but no results," he complained. "I should get 100 percent of the land, you should dismantle all the settlements, and there would then be peace," he said. He also complained of Barak's inflexible attitude: "Rabin used to listen to me; you are never willing to change your positions."[1]

Not making the army's senior command privy to the government's peace policy was a major flaw of the Oslo Accord. On May 9, before leaving for Sweden, we came, then, to the Ministry of Defense to share our assessment with the generals. The Head of Military Intelligence, General Amos Malka, predicted that Arafat would be ready to settle on the basis of Israel annexing 5–6 percent of the territory. Military Intelligence assumed that the territorial issue was the paramount Palestinian concern, and a core narrative such as the refugees was just a bargaining card.[2] This certainly was not the case with Arafat. At Camp David he was willing to give away 10 percent of his land in exchange for an acceptable offer in Jerusalem. The Head of Military Planning, General Shlomo Yanai, spoke at the meeting of the need to secure our interests without offending Palestinian honor. He thought that the IDF would have to maintain some military presence in given areas along the Jordan Valley for a limited period of time and in as "low a key" as possible. I suggested the term "phased Israeli withdrawal" to encapsulate General Yanai's concept. In this way we would clearly signal to the Palestinians that at a stage to be agreed, these security territories would be transferred to their sovereignty. Even though the Palestinians were never too happy with the idea—"You conquered the West Bank in six days and you can also withdraw from it in six days," Abu Ala would tell me in moments of anger—they would try to bargain in order to reduce the "phased withdrawal" to eighteen months. Summing up the discussion, Barak instructed that we get an annexation by Israel of between 13 percent and 15 percent (of the West Bank), a Palestinian state on 77 percent of the territory, with 8–10 percent designated as security zones in which the withdrawal would be phased. Though clearly still a nonstarter for the Palestinians, Barak's instructions, on the eve of our Swedish exercise, amounted to a demilitarized state on 87 percent of the area of the West Bank as well as the whole of Gaza emptied of all its settlements.

There is nothing that a Swedish leader wants more than to serve the cause of peace in Palestine. Prime Minister Göran Persson, a soft-spoken Social Democrat, austere in his manners and a committed Protestant philo-Semite, the highly efficient head of his bureau Pär Nuder, and Foreign Minister Anna Lindh, a more typical left-wing Nordic peacenik, spared no effort by way of goodwill and discreet help to facilitate the talks. The Swedish monarch's personal aircraft was on standby to take us to Stockholm. We arrived in Harpsund, the prime minister's summer residence in the early hours of the morning of May 11. In the dark pre-dawn chill we could still only imagine the unique beauty of the place. The cottages at our disposal were modest and unostentatious, as befits the austere Protestant Swedish lifestyle. There were no curtains at all, so at sunrise one woke to a scene of breathtaking beauty. A lake was surrounded as far as the eye could see by tall lush grass and a variety of other plant life, with picturesque houses dotting the entire colorful landscape. It was our hope that here, light years away from the tribal Israeli-Palestinian feud, we could, for the first time in our century-old conflict, delve into a thorough discussion of its intractable core issues.

Abu Ala was joined by Hassan Asfour. Despite his relative youth, Hassan Muhammad Asfour (Abu Ali) had a long political history behind him. After being active in the 1970s in a string of communist organizations in Russia, Syria, and Iraq, he joined the PLO in Lebanon and went with them to Tunis. There, he was a militant member in unions of Palestinian students and journalists. He advised the negotiating team that paved the way for the Oslo Accords and, in the wake of what was seen as a "surrender" on the issue of Palestinian prisoners during the negotiations of the 1998 Wye River Memorandum, Asfour led the harsh critique of Abu Mazen's performance. The two have been archenemies ever since.

But Abu Mazen's hasty opposition to the Stockholm track, of which he himself was, ironically, one of the initiators, had deeper roots than his personal rivalries. He wanted the Swedish channel to be run along the lines of the Oslo model, that is, first Track Two among academics to define the gaps and if possible bridge them, and only later bring in the officials. Academics had the liberty to engage with imagination and the privilege of denial, which the officials obviously lacked. It was Barak who, in his utter detestation of Oslo, insisted on the Swedish model. This episode was to have dire consequences for the prospects of our entire peace enterprise, for from that moment Abu Mazen lost trust in the process and practically disengaged from it. Arafat was no negotiator, and he now lost the man whom he always needed to help him navigate through the intricacies of a process about whose details Arafat was neither well informed, nor interested.

Yet Abu Ala's opening remarks at Harpsund boded well. He was prepared to formulate, immediately and in writing, ideas on such issues as borders, refugees, Jerusalem, and security. And there was a clear hint by him of a Palestinian readiness to compromise when he said, "We must prepare public opinion *on both sides* for difficult decisions." It was not particularly helpful, though, that in my own opening statement, in line with Barak's explicit instructions, I had to make it clear that although it was apparent that there would not be a comprehensive agreement without the issue of Jerusalem being resolved, it was best "for now" to leave it to a later stage.

The Palestinians had come to view our security demands as nothing more than a smokescreen for the continuation of the occupation by other means. If we were to progress, it was important that we present the issues in as nonconfrontational a manner as possible. I spoke of borders that were "militarily defensible without them being politically unreasonable." Abu Ala's response was far from being confrontational. Initially, he had insisted that border changes to accommodate the settlements would have to be topographical rather than substantive geographical changes. Now, as the talks progressed, he began to adopt a more generous approach. He also did not reject out of hand our demand that the

Israeli Air Force could fly within Palestinian airspace. While rejecting the maps we presented, the Palestinians showed, nevertheless, an increasing willingness to recognize Israel's need to adjust the western border of the future Palestinian state so as to accommodate approximately 80 percent of the settlers in a number of settlement blocs under our sovereignty.

"What percentages do you *really* need?" Abu Ala asked me in a private conversation. When in a deviation from Barak's instructions I responded, "Eight percent seems to me an appropriate final figure," he neither fell off his chair nor accepted the suggestion. Despite the fact that the Palestinians always maintained that "the whole area of the settlements does not exceed 2 percent" (of the territory), Hassan Asfour admitted that "the area of the settlements was really 4 percent" and in an off-the-record conversation he even went as far as to say, "If it is, say, 8 percent or 9 percent, we can discuss it and reach a compromise." In a frank exchange between the two delegations, Asfour even acknowledged that Etzion Bloc as well Jewish neighborhoods in East Jerusalem such as Gilo, and Ariel would be under Israeli sovereignty.

The discussion on the refugees was also practical and purposeful, and we were able to further elaborate the mechanisms we had agreed upon in our Tel Aviv meetings. Yet the Palestinians did not at any stage give up on the principle of the right of return, and insisted that a "significant number" of refugees should be admitted into Israel. Our position was that only a few thousand over a period of time and for the humanitarian purpose of family reunification could be allowed. Another bone of contention was the Palestinians' demand that compensation be drawn from "the properties of the absentees." This was a question of principle—that there should be an Israeli recognition that it was built on the back of the abandoned property of the refugees—to which we responded that a cap should be established to Israel's financial participation in the compensation scheme.

Regrettably, the promising Swedish track ended up being wrecked by malevolent leaks to Agence France Press, allegedly through Abu Mazen, who felt sidelined by Arafat. The leak was a hard blow for Abu Ala and undermined his ability to give of his best. Once the whistle had been blown, he felt pressure from the Palestinian street, where rumor had it that he was "selling off the Palestinian people's national assets." He acknowledged in his memoirs that the leak "changed the nature of our meeting . . . We felt we had to tread more carefully."[3]

By the time the second round opened in Harspund on May 20, the previous air of practicality and purposefulness within the entire Palestinian team had evaporated. As accounts of disturbances in the territories became more disturbing, Abu Ala began to cool and even to go back on previous understandings. Now just one question preoccupied him: How was he to ensure that he had upheld Palestinian orthodoxy so that no one at home could dare accuse him of "a treacherous sellout"?

Following two days (May 19–20) of violent Palestinian disturbances—"Days of Wrath" commemorating the *Nakba* Day—Barak announced the recall of the team from Sweden. The riots, inspired by what was then seen as a hasty, precipitate Israeli withdrawal from Lebanon and a victory for Hezbollah's resistance, highlighted a quintessential Arafatian strategy, or that of his militia chief and head of Tanzim, Marwan Barghouti. "Lebanon today, Palestine tomorrow!" shouted Palestinian demonstrators in Gaza. While there was still time, President Clinton sent an urgent message to Arafat in an attempt to cut short the waves of violence. Arafat's response was characteristically evasive: "I will try but am not sure that I will succeed." But Arafat did not really regret the death of the secret talks—he referred to our back channel as "the bad channel"—and lost no sleep over Barak's political difficulties. The *ra'is* was clearly no longer interested in the Swedish channel. Significantly, even though Barak had a few days earlier sent a message to Arafat through Yossi Ginossar that he would have the transfer of the Jerusalem villages approved by the Knesset, to which a peaceful *Nakba* Day could be a welcome contribution, Arafat did not lift a finger to prevent the riots. Arafat was always utterly indifferent to Israel's domestic politics, even though he should have known how vitally central they were to her capacity to deliver on the peace process.

The interruption of the Stockholm talks was a major setback, for they produced truly substantial progress on each and every chapter of a potential peace agreement. We, the Israelis, endorsed the "100 percent minus" territorial formula for a Palestinian state, a far cry from Barak's initial positions. Also, the principle of annexing between 4 percent and 8 percent of the West Bank to accommodate 80 percent of the settlers was not turned down provided Israeli territories of the same size and quality were handed over to the Palestinian state. They also acknowledged that Jewish neighborhoods in the wider Jerusalem area could be part of Israel. The concept whereby the use of Israeli assets such as port facilities and safe passage between Gaza and the West Bank would be calculated as "territory" within a land swap arrangement was also raised. Nor did Abu Ala rule out the concept of "phased Israeli withdrawal" from security areas, although he had in mind areas of Israeli deployment that were far smaller than Israel would have wanted.

A brilliant drafter and resourceful negotiator, Gilead Sher led the progress made with Abu Ala's team in Harpsund in the preparation of the Framework Agreement of the Permanent Status (FAPS). The document acknowledged principles such as UN Security Council Resolutions 242 and 338, border demarcation to be based on demographic changes, the recognition of the Palestinians' right of self-determination (which the Oslo accords had ignored) within a territory that is contiguous with Gaza and the West Bank forming one territorial unit, and the stipulation that neither side should join military alliances against the other. Differences on issue such as refugees or the timing of the release of Palestinian prisoners were also defined and registered.

In my report to Barak back home I defined the problem of these negotiations as one of methodology. The Palestinians wanted to nail down principles, such as the 1967 border and the right of return, and then deal with the details. Ours was a diametrically opposite approach of progressing with the practical arrangements and then applying the principles accordingly. This methodological difference was to remain a factor well into the discussions at Camp David.

A few months later, Abu Ala would speak with nostalgia about our Swedish talks. He explained the failure of the Camp David summit as stemming from the "major American mistake" of neglecting what "we had already achieved at the Stockholm talks," where, he wrote, they were "surprised by the progress made on some issues, particularly territory and frontiers."[4] There was always a caveat, however. To what degree did Arafat truly stand behind his negotiators? It was Arafat's way to use multiple channels and create competition among his men. Abu Ala was never sure he had Arafat's backing; he also knew that back home others prayed for his failure.

Not that on our side was all perfect. At no stage were we allowed to present a comprehensive proposal which the other side could see as a reasonable outline of an endgame worth fighting for. We did not offer a territorial package they could accept, nor a timetable for handing over the security "gray areas" which they, anyway, hated. I believed throughout, as I repeatedly said to Abu Ala and others, that the ultimate justification for their concessions on terror and refugees was their gaining, on behalf of the entire Muslim world, positions in Jerusalem that Islam had not had for more than 1,500 years. Yet, on Jerusalem, I only offered generalities. Be that as it may, the pragmatic, businesslike atmosphere at Harspund was destroyed by sour grapes, for good.

3

Back to Square One

The collapse of the Swedish track boded ill for the future of the process. Its aftermath became an uphill struggle to stem the loss of its achievements by engaging both Palestinian negotiators and Arab leaders in the region. That Barak dug his heels in and refused to offer his negotiator more leeway was not particularly helpful in assuaging the Palestinians' rising resentment. Removing from the equation the thorniest of issues, Jerusalem, was a Barak pipedream. He feared that "clear-cut decisions on Jerusalem would not pass the test of a national referendum." But this blatantly contradicted his own assertion made in an internal deliberation after our Swedish experiment. "We Israelis," he said then, "need to achieve a settlement that includes all the problems and issues and all the pain in one go. We are not equipped to cope with phased agreements." This looked like talking the talk without daring to walk the walk.

Muhammad Rashid was a Kurd who rose during the siege of Beirut in 1982 to become Arafat's smooth-talking—in perfect English—confidant, particularly on financial and economic matters. He presumably controlled the Chairman's secret funds. Always pragmatic and moderate, he was close to the Israeli business community with which he shared the quest for peace as the key to good business. He would occasionally send up trial balloons such as the one he tried on me upon our return from Sweden. It was possible, he said, to reach a territorial arrangement based on "somewhere in the range of 80–100 percent or 85–98 percent," provided Arafat got what he wanted in Jerusalem. Jerusalem, he said, was "a killing point." He proved to be right. On Jerusalem, that is.

And what did Arab leaders think? These negotiations were not conducted in a regional or international vacuum. When considering difficult decisions, Arafat would always pit us against the Arab world, the Palestinians' strategic hinterland. He would also frequently use the "Arab world" as an excuse for his inability to make grand, game-changing decisions. It made, then, sense for us to engage Arab leaders.

On May 23, 2000, I arrived in Cairo to report to President Hosni Mubarak on the state of the negotiations. We met in his dazzlingly luxurious Cairo palace, which, he stressed, was not his actual residence. The robust and athletic *ra'īs* looked younger than his actual age. His grandson, he told me, hated Arafat, for whenever he wanted to see his grandfather, one of the interminable Arafat visits to Cairo took place. He asked me about his Israeli acquaintances, and when I told him that Shimon Peres might become Israel's next president, he noted sarcastically, "We'll probably have now another Casablanca Economic Summit [on regional economic cooperation]." The Egyptians were never enthusiastic about Peres's concept of a "New Middle East." They always regarded it, and continue to do so today, as an expression of Israeli neocolonialism, a way for the Jewish state to dominate the region by virtue of its technological superiority. Mubarak was surprisingly sanguine about our need for modifications to the 1967 borders and did not seem shocked when I showed him our proposed map suggesting that 87 percent of the territory would go to the Palestinians, and 13 percent be annexed by Israel to accommodate the settlement blocs. He insisted, though, that the blocs remain adjacent to the Green Line. "Don't ask for isolated areas in the heart of the Palestinian territory," he urged. Mubarak's comment fully concurred with the late Yitzhak Rabin's opposition to what he used to denounce as "political settlements" deep inside Palestinian territory.

Nothing made the Jordanians more indignant than being left out of the loop when it came to Palestine. King Abdullah II asked that I pay him a visit; he even dispatched a special helicopter to take me to Amman. The helicopter sent was the cleanest, shiniest military craft I had ever seen, and I wondered whether this was due to tradition inherited from the days of British rule or a symbol of Jordanian royalty. It was probably both. The meeting took place at the king's private residence on the outskirts of Amman. He was joined by both Foreign Minister Abdul Ilah al- Khatib and his closest adviser, Abdullah Tarawneh. The king received me wearing battle fatigues and explained that he had come directly from a military drill. This was my second meeting with the likable and friendly young monarch. I briefed him on the package of proposals that had so far been discussed. He took particular interest in the two thorniest issues, both vitally central to Jordan's concerns, Jerusalem and the refugees. Jordan is home to the largest community of Palestinian refugees, and unlike elsewhere in the region, they all hold Jordanian citizenship. The Jordan Valley was an obvious strategic interest for the kingdom, and I assured the king that "our interest was not based on politics but on security."

Jordan's Palestinian story was a tale of contradictions. Torn between its Bedouin destiny and its predominantly Palestinian population, and pressured by the Arab League, King Hussein had relinquished in 1988 his claim to the West Bank. He tried, however, to curb the rise of a sovereign Palestinian state across the Jordan River, which he saw as a threat to the future integrity and identity of the kingdom. The Oslo Accords, which paved the way for the realization of Palestinian national ambitions, were the reason Hussein hurriedly signed a peace treaty with Yitzhak Rabin. If he could not prevent the birth of a Palestinian state, with its inherent risks to Jordan's future, he would at least be able to help shape its features and exert some control over it. Significantly, King Abdullah was not entirely free of his late father's reservations about Palestinian statehood. He clearly preferred that Israel first pursue a peace deal with Syria before tackling the Palestinian problem with its uncertain consequences for Jordan. He told me that he had been receiving "positive signals from Syria." "All the issues between us and Israel are solvable," he had been told by President Hafez al-Assad in the course of his recent visit to Damascus. Subtly, the king disguised his own views on Palestine under the cover of his report of the Syrian positions, which were, he said, highly skeptical about the prospects for a negotiated Israeli-Palestinian peace. Abdullah insisted that "the Syrian track promised quicker results," and expressed the hope that immediately after the Ba'ath Congress on June 17 the Americans would again revive the Israeli-Syrian talks. The message, admittedly implicit, I got was fully consistent with Jordan's traditional apprehension at the rise of a fully independent, revolutionary, and probably irredentist Palestinian state across the river.

The day after my return from Amman, we discussed with Barak alternative solutions to the core issues. Both Gilead Sher and the prime minister did not concur with my view against the 13 percent annexation fantasy. Still apprehensive with regard to raising the Jerusalem issue, Barak only agreed to "discreet discussions among ourselves." Which we held. The conventional formula in Israeli peace games was to expand Jerusalem's municipal borders in order to allow a Palestinian capital in some of the city's external villages, such as Abu Dis, the seat of the Palestinian parliament from which the golden Dome of the Rock in the Old City could be seen. I believed that eventually we would have to transfer to full Palestinian sovereignty the outer parts of Arab east Jerusalem, while the inner Palestinian neighborhoods (Wadi al-Joz, Silwan, Sheikh Jarrah, and Salah a-Din) should be granted an autonomy status, a "sovereignty-minus" arrangement. I also suggested a "super-municipality" that would coordinate planning and zoning for the two capitals. Barak was not shocked, but was still afraid of the political dynamite involved in the Jerusalem issue. "Talk to the Palestinians in a general way," he said, "but postpone the solution for five years."

Unsurprisingly, Barak was not enthusiastic at all about US Secretary of State Madeleine Albright's planned visit to the region. He foresaw that a close scrutiny of the two sides' positions would reveal that the time was not yet ripe for a peace summit. In Barak's defense, one could say that seeking a summit was also the consequence of the difficult political and security environment. Each day produced more leaks from the peace talks, swelled the number of local and international actors seeking to play a role, and increased the political cost of confidence-building gestures to the Palestinians. Furthermore, the Palestinians were beginning to exhibit clear signs of impatience. On Tuesday, May 30, Yossi Ginossar passed on to me messages from the Palestinian "young guard," Mohammed Dahlan and Muhammad Rashid, warning that the situation was explosive. Arafat, they said "was no longer capable of controlling the impatient public mood."

Unlike Rashid, who gained Arafat's trust precisely because he was an outsider, Mohammed Dahlan was a local rising star and a leader on his own merit. Born in Gaza, where he would become in the early 1960s the head of the Shabaiba, Fatah's youth movement, he was arrested by the Israelis for his activities as Fatah's man in the local students' association. His two years in prison (1983–84) allowed him to learn fairly good Hebrew and, more importantly, acquire a keen understanding of the Israeli mentality and weaknesses. Likable and quick to respond to a good joke, he was highly proficient in making Israeli friends. In 1987, he was expelled to Egypt, from where he later moved to the PLO head-quarters in Tunis. His five years in Arafat's entourage turned him into one of the Chairman's closest advisers on security matters, and when he was allowed to return to Gaza in the wake of the Oslo Accords, he became the head of the Palestinian security apparatus in the Strip. We used to call him "the beautiful" for his good appearance since he was always well dressed with his hair neatly combed. He was quick to laugh and no less so to explode in rage when he felt humiliated or misunderstood by his Israeli interlocutors. His English was poor, and he would always prefer Arabic or Hebrew. "*Tarjem*" ("Translate"), he would ask you when you made a proposal in English.

Israel's failure to keep its promise to transfer the Jerusalem villages led to an ever-increasing distrust between Barak and Arafat. Arafat was right to assume that a handover of the villages would help him demonstrate to his people that not only had he not been sidelined by the progress of the Syrian track, but that he was, in fact, at the heart of the peace process. The villages affair was also a breach of trust with President Clinton, who had assured Arafat that they would be transferred only after getting Barak's green light. But building trust was not Barak's métier. The insult was so stinging that Arafat raised the public profile of the dispute and warned that he would reject any territory which he was due to get under the terms of the Sharm El-Sheikh Interim Agreement if the handover did not include the villages.

Israel's Byzantine domestic politics never made this kind of Gordian knot easy to untie. Shas, the Sephardi religious party in our disparate coalition, made its support for the transfer of the villages conditional on a solution being found to the financial problems plaguing their autonomous school system. Shas's spiritual mentor, the octogenarian Rabbi Ovadia Yosef, with whom I pleaded to approve the transfer of the villages, mentioned to me some other obscure rabbi who claimed that the whole thing was "a security threat." Rabbis in Israel are multipurpose creatures, indeed, politicians, spiritual leaders, and, for their flock, even field marshals all rolled into one. Shas was not alone; the National Religious Party also threatened to quit the coalition if the villages were transferred. And as if this were not enough, the Attorney General made a puzzling decision which made the whole matter subject to a Knesset resolution.

Both Barak and Arafat were now trapped by their own constraints. Barak was dreaming of an endgame summit with a cumbersome coalition that was not even capable of delivering three marginal villages. The affair severely shook the Palestinians' faith in him as a "strong" leader. If he could not push through the transfer of Abu Dis, they wondered, how could they rely on him to carry out the difficult concessions involved in a permanent settlement? Arafat's anger was manifested in a typical bout of sulking, lashing out, and losing patience in order to apply pressure. An endgame summit was what he most dreaded, and Barak's miserable failure to meet his pledge gave him the otherwise understandable pretext.

Barak wrongly believed that one way to handle the crisis of confidence with the Palestinians was by waging a worldwide PR campaign. We would use it, he said, to make clear to the rest of the world that Israel had fulfilled all of its commitments, and the Palestinians were responsible for a long list of transgressions. I felt differently, and shared this with him. Such a campaign would create a feeling that the talks had already failed and that all we were now doing was apportioning blame. The goal was still to reach a settlement, not to explain a failure which might or might not occur. Besides, I said, that "no one in the West would be surprised that a people under occupation failed to honor agreements with its occupier: 'Accusations made by a dominant society about how a people it was oppressing was breaking rules to attain its rights did not have much credence.'"[1] I would later reiterate these assertions at a Cabinet meeting in the middle of the Intifada.

Barak was not alone in his contradictions; I also had my own. While fully understanding the logic of an oppressed nation's struggle for emancipation, I could not resist being alienated by the Palestinians' failure to assume the limits imposed by the historical conjuncture.

What we needed to do now was put the floundering negotiations back on track. From what Mohammed Dahlan told me over the telephone and from intelligence reports we had received, it became clear that, for tactical reasons, the Palestinians were acting tough in an attempt to apply pressure on Israel. US Ambassador Martin Indyk called to tell me that President Clinton's pressure had done the trick: Arafat had been "appeased," as Indyk put it. But was it really so? That evening, I got another call from Indyk, this time after he had met with

Arafat. "I don't have a good feeling," he told me. "Arafat is still playing the role of the victim." Arafat understandably rebelled against Barak's obsessively coercive timetable. But it is also true that, to him, negotiations needed to be part of a revolutionary process mired in crisis and bloodshed. For the national liberation warrior that he was, nations were born in war, not around the negotiating table. The late Yitzhak Rabin's description of the process—"We'll negotiate as if there were no terror, and fight terror as if there were no negotiations"—was to Arafat like a soothing balm.

4

Longing for Hezbollah

Shifting to a strategy of fighting while negotiating was to be, indeed, the lesson that Arafat would draw from the pullout of Israeli forces from Lebanon on May 24. What was planned to convey the government's earnest commitment to peace only enhanced the Palestinians' resentment at our foot-dragging. "Everyone tells us that the example of Hezbollah in Lebanon is the only way," warned Abu Ala in a negotiating session on June 1 after describing the criticism throughout the Arab world of the concessions the Palestinian had supposedly made in Sweden. Our pullout from Lebanon became a defining event; it hung like the sword of Damocles over our heads and infused the Palestinian negotiations with the specter of a Lebanon-like scenario. Mutual recriminations and almost zero progress marked the coming days.

Raising with the Palestinians Israel's security requirements was now met with scornful rejection. The deployment of an American military force in the Jordan Valley, not an Israeli presence, was the best the Palestinians could offer. That was a far cry from the Sweden talks, where Abu Ala had agreed that security arrangements could be made "even on the roof of my house." Now he claimed that the central component of security was peace. "Why," he asked, "are you prepared to accept UN peacekeepers in Lebanon, on the Golan, and in Sinai but not with us?" "Strategic depth and the poverty of the geographic conditions," we responded. More importantly, General Yanai added, virtually waiving Israel's claim to sovereignty in the Jordan Valley: "The Jordan Valley doesn't have to be under Israeli sovereignty. We only need a dividing line with Jordan, the crossing of which would be a *casus belli*." What the Palestinians could never accept was that Israel's peace with Arab states had all been about full withdrawal while they were being asked to negotiate the extent of Israel's annexation of Palestinian land. "You are offending our honor," said Asfour.

Abu Ala could be a charming poseur who enjoyed showing off his tactical skills, but the sentiment of humiliation underlying his negotiating positions was genuine. He would repeatedly invoke the destructive effect which the withdrawal from Lebanon had had on the atmosphere. "Hezbollah humiliated

Arafat," he said, "Sheikh Nasrallah is laughing at him." Arafat, Abu Ala reminded me, had recently been forced to close down a TV station in Ramallah that had been ridiculing his claim that Israel's withdrawal from Lebanon had been the result of Israel's implementation of Security Council Resolution 425 and not the consequence of Hezbollah's guerilla activity.

During a night long vigil, Abu Ala reiterated his objection to another partial settlement. It was all or nothing. Nor was he ready to postpone the question of Jerusalem, or just that of the holy places. He also advised that we forget about a Palestinian capital in Abu Dis; Jerusalem has to be partitioned along the 1967 lines. At a recent joint trip he had made with Abu Mazen to Saudi Arabia, Crown Prince Abdullah had told him that if they reached a settlement with Israel, he would have the whole of the Muslim world join it, but under no pretext would he approve of a deal that included concessions on Al-Quds. Abu Ala also retreated from the practical atmosphere of the Stockholm talks on refugees; he now claimed that the concept of "family reunification" was unacceptable. First, the principle of the right of return would have to be agreed and then we would talk of the details, such as, perhaps, five to ten thousand refugees to be admitted every year until "the matter dies a natural death." On our way out into the chill of Tel Aviv at dawn, Abu Ala made it clear that without Abu Mazen's support, he would not be able to face Arafat with the kind of positions he had defended in Sweden. In the same vein, he advised me that the so-called Beilin-Abu Mazen agreement, a 1995 informal peace deal that included ideas such as a Palestinian capital in Abu Dis, had never been endorsed by Abu Mazen.

It was all desperately disconcerting. There was nothing linear or sequential in these peace talks. One could be abruptly thrown from a promising move to an adverse one and back without any obvious cause. And so, the following day, Friday, June 2, in the same Tel Aviv hotel, Abu Ala suddenly accepted a formula of mine he had always resisted of negotiating on the basis of hypothetical working assumptions. It would have allowed Israel not to endorse a priori the principle of the 1967 borders, for example, but make its acceptance conditional on an agreement on security and blocs of settlements. Alas, that was a moment of grace that would not be repeated; he would never approve that methodology again. But his partner, Hassan Asfour, then came with stunning ideas for a breakthrough. He sensibly questioned as untenable our claim to accommodate 170,000 settlers in 13 percent of their land, a territory equivalent in size to an area in which 1.2 million Palestinians lived. But he valiantly defined the outline of what could be an acceptable endgame, where Israel annexed the Etzion Bloc of settlements, and even the Ariel Bloc, even though it was deep inside Palestinian territory, provided they were defined in a more restricted way. On Jerusalem, he was truly revolutionary. He proposed a change in the municipal boundaries of the city so that Arab neighborhoods like Beit Hanina and Shuafat, and an eastern strip adjacent to Abu Dis (Tzur Bacher, Issawyah) could be joined to make Al-Quds the Palestinian capital. Within the Israeli capital, he said, there would be a Palestinian district that would receive its municipal services from the municipality of Al-Quds. When I demanded that Jewish neighborhoods in East Jerusalem be part of Jewish Jerusalem, he replied that this would be possible provided the sovereign Palestinian capital included, in addition to the city's periphery, Palestinian inner-city neighborhoods too. He did not think it was right that remote neighborhoods that were, in effect, themselves separate townships should be part of Jewish Jerusalem, while Arab neighborhoods that were clearly part of Jerusalem—like Wadi al-Joz, Sheikh Jarrah, and Silwan—were not part of the Palestinian capital of Al-Quds. We had here a broad outline of a Jerusalem solution to which one would have still to add the question of the Old City and the holy places. A whole summit and a bloody Intifada would still have to take place before we were allowed to produce a fuller proposal on Jerusalem.

At this stage, such views as those expressed by Hassan Asfour were anathema to Barak, who deprecated the idea of even discussing Jerusalem. Later on, when it came to accepting the Clinton parameters, his position was to change. Timing, General Barak should have known, is vital in peacemaking, not only in warfare. Nor was Barak yet willing to endorse the realistic intelligence analysis that was presented to me by General Amos Malka, head of Military Intelligence, and General Amos Gilead, his head of research, in my house in Kfar Saba. Arafat, they said, was a historic leader, not a run of the mill politician; he operated under "deep pressures of history." He understood Oslo as a prelude to a return to the borders of 1967, and he therefore resisted Israel's insistence on border modifications to accommodate settlements blocs. He was innately unable to disavow such iconic values as Jerusalem, refugees, and the Temple Mount without betraying his historic mission. On refugees, General Malka believed that Arafat could live with an Israeli acknowledgment of responsibility for the creation of the problem and the practical return of between twenty and thirty thousand refugees. Military Intelligence maintained that a package that could be described as representing for Arafat the point of no return was not yet offered. Arafat, they reported, had expressed to Clinton a readiness to change the western border line by 2 percent, provided he got back land in Israel on a similar scale. In other words, the Palestinians wanted 98 percent of the West Bank and for now we had only agreed to 87 percent. As for Jerusalem, a recognition by Israel that Resolution 242 applied would satisfy Arafat prior to the summit. Since the intelligence failures leading to the 1973 Yom Kippur War, Israel's intelligence had been taught not to lock itself into one single interpretation, but to present divergent assessments on issues of war and peace. A previous intelligence analysis forecasting that Arafat was nearing the point of no return and feared losing the package deal that was now taking shape proved to be utterly wrong. Neither Camp David, nor the Clinton parameters, not even Taba, were points of no return so far as Arafat was concerned. At each of these junctures, the Palestinian leader had no qualms about taking the risk that his actions might result in him losing the entire deal, which should perhaps explain why, strikingly, Nabil Abu Rudeineh, Arafat's personal secretary, was said to have suggested an imposed American settlement. The Palestinians, he said, were simply unable to compromise on the key issues and would prefer to accept a solution enforced by the Americans.

But the Americans were not in the business of imposing anything. Ahead of Madeleine Albright's visit—she arrived in Jerusalem on June 4—Barak reacted apprehensively to my suggestion to hold a pre-summit meeting at the ministerial level before venturing into an uncertain leaders' summit. Every meeting prior to the summit eroded our positions and reduced our room for maneuver at the summit itself, he said. But the Americans eventually bought into the pre-summit idea. They justifiably feared a hasty, premature summit, and wanted Arafat to be there in the right mood. They also expected us to promise him ahead of the summit a third-phase redeployment, to release funds due to the Palestinians and free a significant number of prisoners.

The Secretary of State's visit was not a dazzling success. She got nothing from Barak. The Americans could have pressured him, but did not, to offer them a "deposit" in any of the areas in which, at the moment of truth, a conditional Israeli promise might have paved the way for a breakthrough. Their lenient approach to the Israeli side naturally fed Arafat's feelings of victimization and of being dragged to Camp David like the proverbial sacrificial lamb. Eventually, Barak's willingness to agree to a pre-summit meeting was of less importance than whether he was ready to give us, his negotiators, enough leeway to make progress there. And he was not. In his meeting with the Secretary of State, Arafat made harsh comments about Barak. "The third-phase redeployment," scheduled for June 23, "is a test of Barak's trustworthiness and credibility," he told Albright. He had, however, totally unfounded fantasies about that redeployment. He would consistently lie about what he told everybody was Rabin's pledge that the third redeployment would leave him in control of 91 percent of the West Bank. This should partly explain his lukewarm attitude to the need for a summit. Why go for an uncertain summit when he was already entitled to most of the West Bank even before it?

That day ended, nonetheless, on a promising note. Barak had in him the will for compromise, but he always got entangled in considerations of tactics and timing that eventually defeated his good intentions. When we later met with him and the heads of the army and security services at the Ministry of Defense, he consistently avoided a categorical statement that there was to be no concession on Israeli sovereignty in the Jordan Valley. This prompted Chief of Staff Mofaz to say that Barak's instructions showed "a lack of clarity in respect of the Jordan valley." But, in the National Security Council there were no doubts. Already on December 22, a Council document entitled *Initial Positions for Negotiation*[1] had envisaged the possibility of "Palestinian sovereignty in the Valley."

5

Forcing the Leaders' Hands

Barak grudgingly acceded to a pre-summit meeting but with the unequivocal condition that we not fritter away any of our assets ahead of the summit. We should eschew any on-the-record talks on Jerusalem. Jerusalem was for Arafat what the Lake of Galilee had been for Hafez alAssad, a sacrosanct principle. Trapped in an impossible coalition and still under attack from a combative opposition, Barak assured President Clinton that the summit would be his moment of truth. He was "willing at the summit to go further than any previous Israeli leader had ever done." He warned, though, that this needed to be "a negotiating summit," unlike the encounter with Assad where the endgame was given. What he did not expect was that we, his team, would deviate from his paralyzing instructions and make this into a substantive pre-summit meeting.

Even though the Egyptians played a double game in their meetings with Secretary Albright, the voices coming from Cairo encouraged us to be more creative on our way to Andrews. President Mubarak and Foreign Minister Amr Moussa, according to Aaron Miller, a member of the American team, had even told the Secretary of State that they supported giving the Palestinians no more than 90–95 percent of the territory. In meetings with Arafat they urged him, though, to insist on the 1967 borders, and on the implementation of Resolution 194 on refugees. Otherwise, "he would not be able to control the street." It was actually they who feared their own street, should they be seen exerting undue pressure on the Palestinians.

For the Americans, extricating concessions from these warring tribes of Israelis and Palestinians was never going to be a smooth exercise. The fundamental misunderstanding was that the Palestinians assumed that all the principles anchored in UN resolutions were agreed and settled and what was left to do was to finalize the details. While they weighed their options, the Americans conveyed to us the Palestinians' frustration at our refusal to apply to them the same principles we used in negotiating with Arab states. To us, there was an inherent difference in the nature of these conflicts. Here a state that never existed was being established, and we were endeavoring to resolve problems of a kind—refugees, a capital city, and the holy places—that went far beyond the mundane territorial, real estate issues at the center of Israel's peace with Egypt and Syria. With the Palestinians, Israel wanted to discuss a package within which mutual concessions could be balanced. If the Arab world ridiculed the Palestinians for being the only ones who had failed to negotiate a return to the 1967 borders, they would be able to respond, I said, that for generations Arabs had longed for Al-Quds and the Holy Places of Islam, and now these were resolved to the benefit of the entire Arab nation. The Palestinians would also be able to say that the refugees had been held in camps throughout the Arab world for decades and now the problem was resolved.

True, on arrival in Washington, on June 12, we met an encouragingly upbeat American team that had just seen a businesslike Abu Ala willing to even formulate a joint document with us that would enable the Americans to offer their own bridging proposals. But our first session with the Palestinian team brought us all down to earth. Abu Ala reverted to making speeches about "UN resolutions" and "international legitimacy." I told him that it was the logic of all negotiations that our respective positions at the end of the summit were bound to be different than those we held before it. They arrived to this point by virtue of their struggle, not by virtue of UN resolutions. "Make up your mind now. Do you want more UN resolutions or do you want an agreement?" Abu Ala was not impressed and was uncharacteristically patronizing: "We shall not demolish the Western Wall, even though President Arafat's property there was confiscated," he would say to Dennis Ross.[1] My idea of negotiating on the "assumption" of our acceptance of the 1967 lines meant that Israel would not rule out acknowledging them as the basis for a settlement. But Abu Ala chose to "forget" that he had already endorsed that idea when I raised it in our last meeting in Tel Aviv.[2]

The house of one of the generals at the airbase had been put at my disposal, and I decided to go there with Abu Ala for a heart-to-heart. The atmosphere between us changed immediately, as was always the case when we met in private. He wanted me to spell out again "the *real* percentage" of land for the settlements blocs that Barak would ultimately be willing to accept. I assured him that an earnest negotiating dynamic would eventually bring us to considerably lower figures than the guidelines we got from Barak. He also went to great lengths to convince me that he would give Arafat a balanced report of our negotiations to allay his fears of the summit. He even tried to find arguments in favor of a summit, by conjecturing that Barak had not given me enough leeway because he wanted to make the big, breakthrough decisions himself at the right moment.

The affable Abu Ala did not prepare me for the belligerent mood in which Arafat arrived in Washington on June 14. Egged on by the Egyptians, he had come ready for a fight and to tell the president that Barak lacked all credibility as a partner, especially, though not exclusively, in relation to the scheduled third-phase redeployment, and his failure to transfer the Jerusalem villages. This was the trap in which the two leaders were now tragically caught. Barak was constrained by his shaky political support, while Arafat's demand for the implementation of the interim agreements was substantive, not just tactical. He simply doubted that a final settlement was achievable. It was, then, in our interest to restore Palestinian confidence in the process. Hence, on the eve of the Arafat-Clinton meeting, we, Gilead and I, submitted a written exhortation to the prime minister for confidence-building measures, such as the release of a significant number of prisoners and an explicit commitment to transfer the Jerusalem villages. "If I had a coalition I would do it," replied Barak, when I impressed upon him in a telephone call the same points. In an attempt to improve the atmosphere, the Americans reconvened the teams for a joint meeting at the end of which Dennis urged the parties to go along with my suggestion of hypothetical "basic assumptions," something which Abu Ala again refused to do. We were deadlocked. I telephoned Barak to tell him that Dennis would certainly advise the president that the summit should not yet be convened. Ehud was up in arms: "What more is there to talk about!?" Barak clearly lived in a fantasy world.

Over at the State Department, Madeleine Albright described Clinton's meeting with a belligerent Arafat as particularly difficult. It was "the worst meeting they had over the past seven years," Sandy Berger, the president's National Security Adviser, would later proclaim. What particularly insulted Arafat was the previous day's stupid decision of the Israeli government back home to release only three prisoners. But not all was bad news. Arafat had climbed down from his demand for a third redeployment in return for an American guarantee that if there was no agreement at the summit, he would get his third redeployment. Barak's miserable gestures to the Palestinians had hit the American mediator hard, and it was a painful humiliation for Arafat. Sandy Berger rightly pressed us to be initiators and innovators and to show sensitivity to the Palestinians' situation.

On a stormy rain-soaked night typical of Washington in June, we arrived at the VIP lounge at Andrews Air Force Base for a tense meeting with Arafat, who was about to leave for home. It started, though, with laughter when I said jokingly to the Chairman that the purpose of the meeting was to "discuss how the release of the three prisoners was to be phased." But Arafat was rightly hurt. "Barak humiliated me," he complained. I explained the political pressures the prime minister was under and suggested that he allow Abu Ala to negotiate the chapter on security, which would make it easier for us to define the border. "The worst that can happen to you," I added, is that "you would expose the weakness of Israel's argument to control the Jordan Valley." He again spoke to me with longing and envy of Hezbollah's success in driving Israel out of Lebanon. There was more than a hint of a threat that he would set the Palestinian territories on fire, as Hezbollah had done in Lebanon. "They were our students," he told me proudly. Arafat had also Syria's Assad as a compelling model. With Assad's death only four days before Arafat became the sole remaining guardian of Arab orthodoxy, the last in the long line of historic Arab leaders, steadfast and uncompromising in dealing with Israel. He was not "asking for the moon," as he liked to say. In Arafat's thinking, a Syrian peace would have killed the prospects of a Palestinian deal, but the death of the Syrian dictator raised the price of a Palestinian peace, for it was only in Palestine that both Barak and Clinton could now secure their legacy.

Arafat's mindset was clearly shifting. He needed to keep the revolutionary fire in Fatah, and emulating Hezbollah's way was becoming a realistic option to him. This did not preclude allowing his men to explore the limits of Israel's concessions. On the contrary, fighting and negotiating at the same time were what all national movements of liberation which Arafat embraced as a model—e.g., Vietnam, Algeria—had done. The *ra'īs*, as it seemed, did eventually instruct Abu Ala to give negotiations a chance. The change in the atmosphere was indeed palpable. Previously forbidden areas were suddenly open to debate. The "generic" issues pertaining to a final peace agreement—water, the economy, the environment, policing the borders, cooperation in law enforcement, and more—all suddenly became open to discussion. Abu Ala also agreed that Mohammed Dahlan should lead the Palestinian team in the security talks. Abu Ala never ceased to surprise. He now suggested asking Dennis to present us with an American draft of the FAPS (Framework Agreement on Permanent Status).

We responded accordingly. To maintain the momentum, we gave the Americans an elaborate paper brilliantly drafted by Gilead Sher. Prepared as possible American "bridging ideas," it provided us with the opportunity of hinting at possible Israeli flexibility. We proposed, inter alia, that the border "would be based on the 1967 lines with changes to conform to the reality on the ground and the needs of the two sides." Our paper also offered Palestinian sovereignty in the Jordan Valley provided Israel was satisfied with the security arrangements there, and got her three blocs of settlements. Our paper got Dennis excited. Taking me aside he asked, "Does Barak know?" I assumed that Gilead Sher, Barak's chief of cabinet, who was throughout more genuinely representative of Barak's positions than I was, would not unnecessarily compromise his boss, but it turned out that he did, and Barak eventually asked him to remove the paper. I insisted, though, with Dennis on not working on the basis of Barak's denial. Our paper had its effect. Saeb Erakat, then in Washington, confided to Dennis a highly promising set of ideas for a peace deal—a state on 92 percent of the land with equal swaps, defining the number of refugees that Israel could admit as the implementation of UN Resolution 194, and accepting Israeli neighborhoods in East Jerusalem as part of Israel's Jewish capital side by side with a Palestinian capital in the city's Arab parts. Our non-paper and Erakat's surprisingly flexible ideas suddenly gave us a sense that should we both stick to that kind of attitude, the summit might still not be too wild a gamble.

Born in 1955 in Abu Dis, on the southeastern edge of Jerusalem and, until his death of the Corona virus in an Israeli hospital, a resident of Jericho, Saeb Erakat was a most eloquent spokesman of the Palestine cause. I first came across him at the 1991 Madrid Peace Conference where he was the only member of the Jordanian-Palestinian delegation defiantly wearing a keffiyeh. He held a doctorate in political science from an English university and had US citizenship after having lived for many years in the United States. He had no political standing in the Palestinian system or any revolutionary-military credentials, which could, paradoxically, be an advantage. None of the different factions suspected him of rival loyalties, and his outstanding communication capabilities made him an asset for all. He was a true man of peace and a most committed negotiator, sometimes irritatingly uncompromising and occasionally candid in exposing the inconsistencies of his own side. He was a family man always willing to socialize; it was at his initiative that our wives got to meet.

Our paper and Saeb's ideas helped produce a momentum that needed to be seized in order to dynamize the negotiations, even if that meant defying the prime minister. Still at Andrews, in a separate meeting with Dennis, I even went beyond our paper on both territory and Jerusalem. Neither I nor Saeb knew of each other's initiative, nor did we have at that point the support of our respective leaders; but we both gave the Americans if not the outline of a possible deal, then certainly the encouragement our leaders were unwilling to offer for convening the summit. Barak would eventually hear from Dennis my ideas as well as those of Saeb, and in his always convoluted way when he did not want to be interpreted as having made an irreversible commitment, he did not reject them out of hand. A few days later, both President Clinton and Sandy Berger would try over the telephone to get from Barak a sense of whether he indeed upheld the positions Dennis had discussed with him. Barak chose the same foggy style from which they could draw their own conclusion that if that was the price for an agreement, he would go for it.[3]

A Conceivable Endgame?

The coming days would further nourish President Clinton's conviction that venturing to a summit might not be that wild a gamble. Inter-Palestinian squabbles created a momentary opportunity for more substantive progress. Relaxed and approachable, Abu Ala met me in a Jerusalem hotel on June 21 to offer a return to the "Swedish spirit." He again agreed to discuss borders on the basis of "working assumptions," and reiterated his acceptance of Israel's annexation of 4 percent of the West Bank as well as our concept of "phased withdrawal" from the security areas. What could have caused this sudden display of flexibility? He explained he had been motivated by the fear of a different government coming to power in Israel, and also by uncertainty over the effect of Clinton's imminent departure from office. His proposals were also intended to provide me with arguments to persuade Barak to drop his opposition to another round of secret talks, this time in Cairo.

But rekindling the Stockholm spirit ahead of the summit was what Barak dreaded most, particularly now that our Andrews' talks had dragged him into a corral where he was forced by his own team to further erode his positions ahead of the summit. Nor was he wrong to assume that he could persuade Clinton to host us for a two-week stay in the enchanting mountains of Maryland without having to make additional concessions. Rejecting Abu Ala's proposal was, however, a fatal mistake. Peace, not the summit as such, was supposed to be the strategic objective. We lost in Abu Ala a vital ally in the preparation of the summit, and when it was finally called, he proved to be ill-tempered and a totally unhelpful negotiating partner. He had provided us with a window of opportunity to make the summit a success which we chose not to open.

But despite the prime minister's reservations, we persisted in our search for a more reasonable pre-summit outline. The American peace team was now back in Israel, and I shared with them tentative proposals on Jerusalem which I planned to present to Arafat a few days later. The idea was that the Palestinian capital, Al-Quds, should include Abu Dis, Azariyah, A-Sawara, and other Palestinian areas beyond the municipal boundaries of present-day Jerusalem, as well as

Palestinian neighborhoods along the eastern edge of the city, such as Tsur Baher Shuafat, and Beit Hanina. For the inner Palestinian neighborhoods I proposed that (a) municipal affairs be in Palestinian hands under overall Israeli sovereignty; (b) planning and zoning issues would be decided on the basis of the legitimate development needs of the Palestinian residents; and (c) "functional sovereignty" in areas of civilian life would be transferred to the Palestinians. The Americans admitted that this was the first time they had heard us present a significant change to the status quo in Jerusalem. Dennis Ross claimed he had indications that the Palestinians would accept having the inner Jerusalem neighborhoods under Palestinian functional sovereignty, as I had suggested.

Arafat was the ultimate authority, though, and we needed to co-opt him into the process. On Sunday, June 25, Gilead Sher, Yossi Ginnosar, and I attended what was slated to be a crucial meeting with Arafat at the home of Bassam Shakaa, the mayor of Nablus. The Chairman was joined by Abu Mazen, Abu Ala, Saeb Erekat, and Nabil Abu Rudeineh. In a long meeting stretching into the night, I made a detailed presentation of our positions on all the core issues. In contrast to his taciturn demeanor on many previous occasions the Chairman was alert, talkative, and responsive. As always, he regarded issues of security and borders as mere technicalities unseemly for an historic personage of his stature to deal with. His task was to deal with questions of eternity, religion, and ethos, and, in other words, Jerusalem and the refugees.

"I am not denying the morality of your demand for the right of return," I told him. Nor did I deny the fact that a solution to the problem was vital for his capacity to swing public opinion behind the agreement. But I exhorted him to see the historic meaning of the peace package in its totality. I invoked the mechanisms of compensation and resettlement of refugees we had agreed on with Abu Ala as a possible way forward, for, I said, there would never be an Israeli government that would agree to more than just a symbolic return of refugees. Arafat's automatic response came in a rhetorical question: "Do you think that the hundreds of thousands of Palestinians in Chile want to return?" What he wanted, he said, was to find a solution to the problem of the approximately 300,000 refugees in Lebanon, a country where they were particularly badly treated and marginalized. I could sense, however, that Arafat would consider sacrificing refugees on the altar of Jerusalem. As far as he was concerned, his emphasis on the refugees in Lebanon was his "compromise."

Jerusalem was to him in a totally different category. I assured him that no agreement would downgrade the current status quo established by the then Minister of Defense, Moshe Dayan, in 1967 that gave exclusive administrative authority to the Palestinians on the Temple Mount's upper esplanade. He reminded me of Shimon Peres's letter to the late Norwegian foreign minister, Johan Jørgen Holst, in which Peres had undertaken to recognize the status of the Palestinians in

East Jerusalem. I assured him that we did not deny that status, only that the holy places were a category apart that should be accorded "a special status." "We want," I added, "mutual recognition of Jerusalem as a capital for both parties."

Arafat was not willing to accept any part of the proposal I had earlier presented to the American team, and now to him. He was willing to agree to Israeli sovereignty over only two sites: the Wailing Wall—he reminisced about his childhood spent with his aunt who lived nearby—and the Jewish Quarter of the Old City. Everything else was to be under Palestinian sovereignty. To my proposal for functional autonomy under Israel sovereignty for the inner Palestinian neighborhoods, Arafat reacted with a cutting rejoinder: "You're not willing to recognize the refugees' right of return, yet you're willing to annex 300,000 Palestinians to Jewish Jerusalem." That was a brilliant comment to an avowedly monumental paradox in Israel's traditional position on Jerusalem. By annexing East Jerusalem, Israel had also annexed its 300,000 Palestinian inhabitants; in other words, she had already offered the right of return to 300,000 Palestinians.

I also felt the need to assure the Chairman that, even though Camp David would be a negotiating summit, he himself would not be expected to negotiate but rather to make decisions. "I make decisions; I don't negotiate," he admitted; he also boasted that he was a general and a politician, and, what is more, "a general who has never lost a war." "No, no. I am a politician; you are a statesman," I replied, in a not very subtle attempt to flatter him. While we were talking, a call came through from President Mubarak. He updated Arafat on his conversation with Minister of Justice Yossi Beilin, who, in a parallel move to my meeting with the Chairman, had been sent to Cairo to lobby for the summit. Egypt had changed the equation from "Jordan-Palestine" to "Egypt-Palestine," and this obliged her to act as a proactive mediator, thus also ingratiating itself with the Americans. The offensive against Arafat was, indeed, like a forceps movement that left him no escape from the summit that Barak wanted so much.

I was in the domain of practical arrangements; Arafat was flying higher into categorical statements and Muslim mythology. He mentioned to me the Covenant of Omar, signed in AD 638 between the conqueror of Jerusalem, Caliph Omar I, and the Byzantine patriarch, Sophronius, which set out the terms for the Christians' surrender to their Muslim conquerors, with the stipulation that Jews should not be allowed to live in Jerusalem. Arafat concluded, "Would any Muslim Arab accept what you are proposing? That the Al-Quds al-Sharif issue remain unresolved? Forget it. They would kick me. I cannot be left with nothing in Jerusalem." He also categorically rejected Barak's idea of postponing the discussion on Jerusalem for a few years. "Not even for two hours," he replied.

The meeting ended with Arafat falling back on his obsessive fascination with Hezbollah's success in evicting Israel from Lebanon, and with a tirade against Barak, who, he said, "is laughing at us." He accused him of marking time until

Clinton ceased to be relevant, and then another year would pass until Bush or Gore settled into the White House. The abysmal lack of trust between these two was indeed becoming a pivotal concern. What could come out of a summit with two leaders who at no stage even tried to reach an understanding on principles. There was no shared vision between them that the negotiators could have turned into an agreement. Without a meeting of minds and an adjustment of expectations at the leadership level the teams were in the dark as to how flexible they could be, or how best to meet the wishes of their respective leaders.

"The good news from your meeting with Arafat," Dennis Ross told me, "is the high regard that he has for you and your approach. The bad news is that he is still not convinced that there should be a summit." I disagreed. Arafat's performance in our meeting was one of his typical exercises in showmanship, and he clearly was also posturing in his message to Dennis. Overall, my impression was that Arafat, always a compulsive complainer about what one still owed him, was satisfied with taking note of the progress made so far. Indeed, immediately after we left the meeting, both Arafat and Abu Mazen, according to Abu Ala's own account, were quite upbeat and concluded that there had been progress on all the issues, including Jerusalem, so much so that Abu Ala felt he was no longer on the same wavelength as his superiors and handed in his resignation, which Arafat turned down on the spot.

Abu Ala's resignation had to do mainly with internal Palestinian power struggles. But it was also his way of saying that the summit would be "a vain enterprise" if only because there was a limit to how far we could stretch Barak's positions, which was what we did there, he assumed, by "moving from one topic to the next with precision and professionalism." Abu Ala sensed that I was going beyond Barak's positions. Indeed, as I saw it, our task as negotiators was to drag the leaders along by taking personal initiatives, and stretching their willingness to compromise to, and beyond, the limit. That much was graciously acknowledged by Abu Ala in his memoirs. My presentation to Arafat, he believed, was a way of "revitalizing Barak's negotiating positions," part of my ongoing effort aimed at "dragging Barak forward, one small step at a time." He credited me for constantly explaining "the Palestinian position to Barak and urging him to respond positively."[1] But, Abu Ala could also see the limits of my capacity to "deliver" Barak, and he doubted that Barak could eventually assume the high price of an agreement. Losing Abu Ala became the unwarranted price of our rush to the summit. In a series of telephone calls I made to him after our meeting with Arafat, I found he was becoming too hostile to the process. He was not cut out for "crowded summits." His métier was discreet long-drawn-out negotiations which allowed him to "cook up" agreements and then submit them to the leader for approval. "You twisted our arm," he told me. He cynically advised, "Maybe we should send Sheikh Yassin (the leader of Hamas) to the summit."

The American decision to go ahead with the summit was reinforced in a stop-over in Cairo on their way home. The Egyptians assured them that a deal was possible if the Palestinians got more than 90 percent of the territory, and "creative" solutions were found to the Jerusalem and refugee issues. It also seemed that Albright had taken Arafat to task, saying that his team "was not as open with us as the Israelis are." To which he responded that he would instruct them to change their approach and exhorted her to get back to him "if they showed no flexibility."

For the second time within just a short period, President Clinton would go with Ehud Barak to a summit whose chances of success were inevitably uncertain. But the Americans could claim to have some openings from the parties to build an endgame upon. Barak had mentioned to Secretary Albright that he might accept a Palestinian state on 90 percent of the West Bank. From the young Palestinian guard—Mohammed Dahlan and Muhammad Rashid—the Americans heard that Arafat might be satisfied with a state on 92 percent of the West Bank with land swaps. They were also aware of our changing thinking about the Jordan Valley, where we were coming to terms with the need to transfer it to Palestinian sovereignty. Barak also hinted to the president that he might accept his idea of a division of Jerusalem along ethnic lines with the Old City under a special regime, provided Palestinian sovereignty in the inner neighborhoods was limited.[2] Barak's memoirs put it in typically nebulous terms: "limited, symbolic moves on both land swaps and Palestinian sovereignty in part of East Jerusalem."[3] Barak must have been encouraged by ideas he had heard from Jerusalem's Mayor, Ehud Olmert, a Likud member by then still in his hard-line phase (he would later transform into a dovish prime minister), who suggested to him a plan for a sovereign Palestinian capital in Jerusalem's outer Arab neighborhoods while the inner Palestinian districts could be under shared Israeli-Palestinian sovereignty. Barak had also made clear to his coalition partners that he saw no chance that Arafat would accept Israeli sovereignty on the Temple Mount.

Clinton hoped to go down in history as the president who had achieved peace in Palestine, but he was in no way a calculating cynic. His desire to leave such a historical legacy did not interfere with his rational assessments. He was basically an enlightened man who cared more about peace between Israel and the Palestinians than about any other international issue. He genuinely believed that "it was now or never." And he was just as apprehensive as we all were about the alternative of a return to the path of confrontation and war. Connecting all the dots as they emerged in recent proposals, assurances, insinuations, and ideas on spaces of compromises from different actors—Israelis, Palestinians, and Egyptians—Clinton could conclude that the summit was not a suicidal political exercise and that he had a reasonable chance to orchestrate a successful endgame.

It remains a mystery to me, though, why it did not occur to Clinton to cali-brate expectations through a tripartite meeting with Barak and Arafat ahead of the summit. Barak came to Camp David with mistaken assumptions about what would Arafat agree to, and Arafat came in a defensive mood, highly suspicious of Israeli-American collusion. That would eventually make his stay at Camp David seem like a return to his bunker in the battle for Beirut, where his sole duty was to dig in and get out unscathed. Arafat was the carrier of Palestinian orthodoxy and, to his credit, he spelled it all out in a letter he sent to Clinton ahead of the summit. He wanted a Palestinian state on the 1967 borders ("I can agree to nothing less." The settlements created by the Israelis are their problem "not mine to resolve"); "a just settlement for the refugee problem" based on UN General Assembly Resolution 194; "reasonable security arrangements . . . with American presence"; Jerusalem as the capital of the two states, and if this proved impossible, "it could be an international city," as envisaged by the terms of the 1947 partition resolution.[4]

But, was Arafat's letter a bargaining position, an understandable display of his optimal conditions from which he would deviate as the compelling logic of negotiations would eventually require? Would he follow Charles de Gaulle's dictum that "a true leader always keeps an element of surprise up his sleeve which others cannot grasp"? He eventually would have such a surprise, but only on real estate issues—that is, territory and borders—not over the Palestinian national narrative, refugees and, above all, the "killing point" of Jerusalem, as Muhammad Rashid had defined it to me.

7

The Promise of an American Steamroller

Sunday, July 9. A night flight to the United States, first for a preparatory meeting with Secretary Albright and then to the summit, while back home the government was falling apart. Typical Israeli political dysfunction that was soon to be met with severe Palestinian political constraints. I wondered who it was exactly that we were representing in this grueling political undertaking. We were approaching this historic moment like a front line without a rearguard. Our disparate coalition did not assemble the qualities required for peace. Right-wing and right-of-center parties—Natan Sharansky's Yisrael Beiteinu, Yitzhak Levy's National Religious Party, and Shas, the Sephardi religious faction—now announced their withdrawal from the government. The government returned to its most basic political foundations: the left. It was a delusion to assume that these parties could muster the necessary audacity required for confronting their constituencies with a policy of disengagement from Judaea and Samaria. If all this was not dispiriting enough, Ehud Barak no longer commanded a majority in Parliament; his loss of a Knesset vote of no confidence moments before his departure for Washington added to our sense of political gloom. Here were the politicians deserting the battlefield one by one and barricading themselves behind their political power bases, and here were we associating ourselves with compromises that would inevitably alienate wide sections of the public. But leadership is not to be confused with the popularity that emanates from hiding behind an inoffensive consensus and avoiding painful decisions.

The Palestinians were not free of political constraints either. They were expected to represent all the factions of the Palestinian political family, moderates and extremists alike, which meant they had not much leeway. Much depended on whether Arafat, instead of being a hostage of his political system, would lead it to a divisive deal which, as he always feared, could even usher in civil war. The American president Andrew Jackson once said that "one courageous man can constitute a majority." Egypt's Anwar Sadat was such a man. Was Arafat cut from the same cloth? Was Barak such a man? The question was, then, to what extent would the two leaders be capable of rising above the myths that were perpetuating this conflict and claiming so much blood? To what extent would they be prepared to clash with their political systems to the point of triggering an earthquake that would rewrite the political fabric of their respective nations?

The signals from the Palestinians were mixed. Arafat had prepared all the heads of the political factions—among them the Marxist-Leninist Democratic Front for the Liberation of Palestine, the Palestine Communist Party, and the radical Palestinian Popular Struggle Front with its strong connections to the Syrian regime—for the negotiations. But, he had also been warned by them that their support was subject to the condition that he not make concessions on the Palestinian core narrative.[1] Co-opting Hamas was mission impossible; its discontent with and attempts to derail the entire peace process were manifested in terrorist activities throughout the life of our government. Nor was it clear that Arafat truly wanted to co-opt them. The option of "armed struggle" was one he always needed to have in reserve. Intelligence reports needed to be taken with a grain of salt; now they offered some encouragement. Arafat, they said, wanted a comprehensive agreement. He would not be able to permit himself to slam the door rudely in Clinton's face, a president who had done more than any other president before him to foster the Palestinian quest for deliverance. "I'm fed up. I want to reach an agreement and get it over with," Arafat was reported to have said to his personal physician, Ashraf al-Kurdi. Even the fact that he had brought all the faction leaders from Fatah with him to Camp David did not necessarily have to be interpreted as an attempt to tie his own hands. They could express his desire to reach an agreement with a broad domestic legitimacy.

Not an outstanding politician, but a thoughtful military man, Barak prepared his own fallback strategy. The Prime Minister's Office had put together emergency plans in case of a unilateral Palestinian declaration of an independent state, a threat that constantly loomed over our heads. It was proposed that Israel should respond by unilaterally disengaging from the bulk of the West Bank while annexing territories that were deemed to be vital for her security. The Peace Process Administration, headed by Colonel (res.) Shaul Arieli, defined this as "the painful alternative to the peace process." I cannot discard the possibility that, deep in his mind, Ehud Barak knew that the gulf that separated him from Arafat's position was unbridgeable. This made the American role so vitally central. If only because of the harsh legacy of the failure of the Geneva Summit on the Syrian front, Clinton, I said to myself, will not be able to take another failure. The success of the summit would depend on his aggressive leadership.

One and a half days' work in the State Department facing the Palestinians and the American team led by Madeleine Albright was supposed to hone our senses regarding the Palestinians' state of readiness and the expectations of the American mediator. Secretary Albright opened with words of praise for the commitment to peace of both sides. My thoughts went to statesmen like Rabin and Peres, as well as visionary pioneers like Aryeh Lova Eliav, the late Matti Peled and many, many others who had fought for, and dared to spell out, the steep price peace would entail, for which they were ostracized as incurable leftists. Also Palestine had its peace heroes, of course. PLO official Issam Sartawi paid with his life in 1983, when an Abu Nidal squad shot him for his peace efforts. Actually, this entire peace process would not have come about if it were not for Arafat's historic decision to accept the two-state solution in 1988.

"This is an historic moment," says Secretary Albright. Contrary to what the Palestinians had hinted, that Camp David was but one summit in a series of meetings, she stated, "We are only talking about one summit, not a series of summits." She warned us all that the alternative was collapse, violence. The Americans, she added, intend to determine and control the order of the day, and be involved in the negotiations down to the smallest detail. She guaranteed the president's absolute commitment and involvement. Abu Ala reacted in the usual style he reserved for public meetings—bureaucratic, legalistic, and terse—a style that would provoke President Clinton to anger, to the point of a violent outburst, at one of the sessions at Camp David. Gamal Helal, an affable Christian Egyptian-American who served as the American team's translator, would tell me several days later that this style, which brings to mind Palestinian speeches in the UN forums, "made the Secretary and her staff's blood boil." Abu Ala insisted on making distinctions between the issues and on negotiating each topic separately. This was typical of the wily old wolf. He wanted to prevent a trade-off between the issues at all costs, which was our basic approach and which was supposed to enable us, or so we expected, to concede on a given point in order to gain a Palestinian concession on another issue. From Abu Ala's point of view, any Israeli compromise stood for itself, and was not binding on other issues. He also reminded us of the sword of Damocles of the unilateral declaration of statehood planned for September 13.

Addressing Albright's estimation that we were likely to deteriorate into violence if there was no agreement, I acknowledged the seriousness of the moment, but also said that we came "with neither a messianic, nor with a Doomsday mentality, but yes with a realistic resoluteness." I asked that our government's political troubles be ignored for the sake of these negotiations, for Ehud Barak had a direct mandate from the people to make peace, and even if we had a wider coalition, we would still have to bring the peace accords to a referendum. The Secretary concluded by standing behind my approach to the methodology of negotiations in parallel tracks. The timetable she proposed was lightning; the summit had to conclude by the time Clinton left for the G8 summit in Japan in a week. Her "sense of emergency," as she put it, and Dennis Ross's talk of a concentrated effort "like nothing any of us has ever done in his life so far" unsettled the Palestinians. "What's this, an ultimatum?" responded Hassan Asfour to the American promise of a pressure cooker summit. The threat of an impending steamroller and the need for swift decisions prompted Saeb Erakat to moderate the Americans' enthusiasm. The deep distrust between Barak and Arafat, he pointed out, would make it impossible to reach an agreement within a week. The Palestinians emerged stunned from the meeting with Madeleine Albright. They felt as if they had navigated themselves into a trap. In retrospect, it turned out that from then on they were more concerned with the question of "how to get out of it" than with how to reach an agreement. How were they to evade what appeared to them to be an American-Israeli ambush?

Surprisingly, that same night, the American team shared with us their assessment that an agreement was definitely possible. Dennis said that the president would not have initiated the summit unless he had seen the potential for an agreement. He claimed that they had discerned unmistakeably clear Palestinian flexibility regarding security issues. He even thought that, up to a certain percentage of annexation for the purposes of the settlement blocs, the Palestinians would not even claim an exchange of territories. As regards the Jordan Valley, he estimated that the greater the dimensions of Palestinian sovereignty along its length, the greater their willingness would be to agree to security arrangements. As for Jerusalem, Dennis had discovered that the Palestinians had "interesting ideas." and were willing to consider different approaches regarding the Old City. Dennis's evaluations were based, of course, on what he had heard from some Palestinian representative or other, but certainly not from the man with the last word—Arafat—who was always close-mouthed when the talk turned to "flexibility." There was always only limited significance to what various Palestinian spokesmen said, especially when talking about what Arafat considered the holy of holies—Jerusalem, refugees, and the holy sites. Did the Americans reveal here faulty political intelligence or just exaggerated optimism? They also calmed us down regarding the criticism that had been leveled at them for not creating a web of support among Arab leaders for tough decisions on the part of Arafat. Dennis detailed to me the thorough work, as he alleged, that they had done on this. But the Arab reality was more complex than that. With Arafat, Arab leaders tiptoed on eggshells. No claims, no pressures lest the "Arab street" rises up against them. More than Arafat's patrons, they were his hostages. The burden of proof rested on Israel.

Dennis supposed that "dealing" with Arafat would indeed be a major task here. Clinton would work to change the Chairman's emotional state and try to free him from his sense of being a victim dragged like a sacrificial lamb to the summit, and make it clear to him that he stood to gain rather than lose from the agreement. Dennis hung much hope on some of us whom Arafat trusted to help melt the ice between Barak and Arafat. But even if there was trust, would Arafat compromise on Jerusalem? Waive the right of return? Waive his claim for full sovereignty in the Jordan Valley? And would we, the Israelis, find the courage to reshape and moderate not a few of our positions on these very matters?

This long day that had begun at 1:00 a.m. with our departure from Ben-Gurion Airport was still not over. In the early hours of July 10, I reported to Ehud Barak by telephone before he left for Cairo and the United States. I concluded from his comments that Barak was still at the stage of not internalizing the depth of the compromises we would need to make. Notwithstanding the hints he had given to both Dennis and the president in the wake of the Andrews pre-summit meeting,[2] his formal standpoints, which I hoped were just bargaining positions, were still utterly unrealistic.

For a moment, on the eve of the summit, it was possible to think that the director of the play that was about to be performed at Camp David had written an inflexible script and had developed a scenario for progressing to the play's denouement, and would not let anyone on either side disrupt the proceedings. I truly wanted the Americans to pursue their promised resolute course, persist in what looked to me now as shock treatment, exercise the skill of the arbitrator, and, with the sand running out of the hourglass, show the parties that the window of opportunity for reaching an agreement would not remain open forever.

Regrettably, I was wrong and Saeb was right. One dense summit could not resolve our profound differences. The leading actors at Camp David II could not rise to the occasion as did those at Camp David I, twenty-two years previously. To do Barak and Arafat justice, the issues they were asked to compromise on were weightier and more difficult than giving back the Sinai Peninsula. Our negotiations, it would immediately become apparent, were not a real estate deal. They were about cracking the genetic code of the Arab-Israeli conflict and perhaps even the Jewish-Muslim one: holy sites, Jerusalem, the biblical lands of Judea and Samaria, and the moral, not merely political legitimization of the establishment of a Jewish state in the Arab Middle East were all at stake here.

8

Inauspicious Beginnings

July 10. This epochal event is finally happening. We are at Camp David, an extensive area of wooded hills, full of paths leading to beauty spots and breathtaking vistas. This beauty is supposed to have a calming effect, but it does not. I am staying in Walnut, an ascetic cabin where Sadat's physicians slept twenty-two years ago. There is no contact whatsoever with the outside world. None of the delegates' cabins, apart from Arafat's and Barak's, has a telephone or any other means of communication. It looks like a summer camp, or a sanatorium for tuberculosis patients in the Bavarian Alps taken from the books of Thomas Mann. Tellingly, my Palestinian partner Abu Ala, who felt he had been dragged into an Israeli-American ambush, saw the place more as "a guarded citadel."[1]

Already at the official opening, basic differences could be discerned. Arafat, even though he was there under the exclusive aegis of the president of the United States, actually called for an international conference. Arafat never liked to walk alone in the darkness of difficult decision-making. He always preferred a forum for the big show, to escort him down the aisle of an agreement, or to the lack of it. He was also convinced that America was in Israel's pocket, and that negotiations sponsored exclusively by it would take him farther away from his fantasy model of an agreement, and that any international involvement would bring him closer to it. But if it had to be this summit, he expected an agreement "like the one between Egypt and Israel at Camp David," that is, where the Arab side got all its land back.

Clinton preferred to exude a practical, businesslike attitude. An effort had to be made to finish by the time he left for the G8 summit in Japan, for he intended to return with massive financial aid to pad out the peace agreement, mainly over the refugees problem. He wanted an agreement "here and now"—as he put it—before the election campaign in the United States heated up and certainly before, although he did not say it, he became a lame duck with the election of a new president in November. Barak's speech, short and assertive, invoked Rabin's legacy.

Later, at a meeting of our team, I advised that this was going to be the "Jerusalem summit." Barak showed an encouraging understanding of the Palestinian dilemma. "There won't be an agreement," he said, "if it doesn't provide answers to the really hard core of the Palestinians' claims and interests." "Jerusalem," he acknowledged, was "not just a Palestinian concern, but an all-Arab one." Typical Barak zigzagging. For, in a later meeting that very day, he still dreaded tackling the issue of Jerusalem. "We all agree it's wisest to leave Jerusalem to the end," seconded Elyakim Rubinstein, a brilliant right-of-center jurist who served in the past in both Labor and Likud governments and would later become a Supreme Court Justice. I disagreed with the sequence, for breaking taboos in Jerusalem was the decisive factor for changing the Palestinian standpoint in other vital areas.

Indeed, as Clinton could gather from his meeting with Arafat that same day, the issues that truly mattered were those that lay at the core of the Palestinian narrative, Jerusalem and refugees. The president confessed to not having a clue how to resolve them. But Arafat had: "It's simple. East Jerusalem goes to us, West Jerusalem to the Israelis. It will be the capital of two states, and will have a joint committee for solving problems like water, electricity, etc." He also hastened to mention the centrality of the Temple Mount to Islam. As for refugees, "The Israelis should recognize the right of return, and we'll then discuss the details." Abu Mazen, unlike his boss, always more focused on refugees than on Jerusalem, added that "substantial numbers of refugees should be able to return, and that return should be implemented systematically."

What the Americans did not appreciate was that what they heard from Arafat on the narrative issues was not opening positions; it was his endgame. Where did the Americans expect to lead the talks, then? Dennis Ross and Martin Indyk met Gilead Sher and me to present their working paper, which was basically a trade-off between sovereignty for the Palestinian State on its eastern border with Jordan and changes in its western border with Israel to accommodate 80 percent of the settlers. Border changes would require land swaps. On refugees, the formula was "reconciling the Palestinian need for the refugees to have the right of return with Israel's need to control admission to its territory." On Jerusalem, they offered two capitals in an "indivisible" city with mutual access to the holy sites under appropriate security and jurisdictional arrangements.

The American paper looked to me a reasonable basis for negotiations. It is true that it endorsed the principle of the 1967 borders, but there was no reason to disapprove of this since it came with the principle of blocs of settlements where 80 percent of the settlers could be accommodated. It was, therefore, surprising that Barak returned from his meeting with Clinton breathing fire and brimstone. He had sued for "significant" settlement blocs, attacked Arafat's approach as that of one "who is not prepared to be flexible and does not negotiate," rejected the principle of land swaps, and claimed that the security zone in the Jordan Valley should remain under our sovereignty for many years and thereafter be divided between the parties in agreed-upon proportions. Barak's harsh reaction to these innocuous parameters—it is sufficient to flash forward to the future to see the Clinton parameters of December 23 and the Taba talks—was utterly unhelpful. But more surprising was how quick the president was to remove his paper. Hardly one day into the summit and the negotiating strategy of the mediator collapsed. Barak had suggested that the American paper be framed as Israeli versus Palestinian positions, not as American ideas to steer the summit forward.

The Americans would eventually revise their paper. They replaced their proposed principles with a definition of what they perceived as Israeli and Palestinian positions, and added to it their "alternative solutions." But, even here, Barak was scandalized when he found that the chapter on Jerusalem did not mention the gaps between the parties, and simply stated that "the Jerusalem municipal area will host the national capitals of both Israel and the Palestinian state." His protest led to a correction of the clause; it now said that "the expanded area of Jerusalem" would be the home of the two capitals, a euphemism for having the Palestinian capital in some of East Jerusalem's outer villages. There was evidently no way the Palestinians could be convinced that the document was not drafted in collusion with the Israelis. They rejected it outright. Secretary Albright, to whom the Palestinians returned the paper at 3:00 a.m., calmed her excited guests by dropping the paper altogether. No paper, no compass for the summit.

Barak's confidence in his negotiating strategy was possibly boosted by the high degree of empathy that Bill Clinton had for his political predicament. To the Palestinians, the president sounded at times as Israel's advocate. On the third day of the summit, for example, Clinton tried to convince Arafat that, by ceding occupied land, Israel was setting a precedent in international relations. "For years," he told him, "I tried to convince the Russians to return to Japan the islands they took from her in World War II. To no avail."[2] Strange that Clinton, a former Rhodes scholar at Oxford, could see this as being in any way relevant to the Israel-Palestine situation.

Significantly, when the president invited me to his residence, he did not ask for my view on what the solutions that could produce a deal were. Rather, he wanted to know what peace parameters could gain acceptance in Israel. I mentioned three principles: settlement blocs to absorb 80 percent of the settlers, no right of return, and "non-partition of *Jewish* Jerusalem," making it clear that there would have to be an *Arab* Jerusalem. Regarding the Temple Mount, I told the president, one could propose Israeli sovereignty and effective Palestinian jurisdiction. Bafflingly optimistic, Clinton believed that the principle of 80 percent of the settlers demanded an annexation of 10 percent of West Bank territory by Israel. Utterly unrealistic would also prove to be his conviction that he could coax President Hosni Mubarak into offering Egyptian territory for the extension of the Gaza Strip into Sinai, thus saving the Israelis the need to offer land swaps for their blocs of settlements in the West Bank.[3] When the president gave me a ride in his golf cart to the dining room, I could not help but think that, in light of what we were hearing from the Palestinians, the president was appallingly naive. He was blessed with many endearing qualities, but lacked the bulldog-like attitude that had allowed Jimmy Carter to strike an Egyptian-Israeli peace. He would not twist arms à la Bush senior, or be brutally assertive like James Baker and Kissinger. The man I was sitting next to was a pleasant, genial, smart, even brilliant, warm person. But his Middle East clients with their tribal feuds required a particularly malicious and manipulative mediator to coax them into some kind of settlement.

But here the American patron lost control of the event he was supposed to orchestrate almost from day one. Instead of presenting a working document based on, say, the broad outline of an endgame as it emerged after our pre-summit Andrews talks,[4] the Americans resigned themselves to the parties' dread of such papers and left the summit to practically run itself leaderless, at the whims of the parties. The absence of American working papers throughout the entire summit was to be the most monumental blunder Clinton and his team could commit. Camp David I should have taught them the vital importance of such elaborate negotiating texts. The Jimmy Carter team produced throughout their summit no fewer than twenty-three drafts and kept "cleaning" and honing them until they could come out with an agreed text. In Camp David II, Clinton's team capitulated under the pressure of the parties, removed its working papers, and let the summit evolve without a guiding compass. Israelis and Palestinians came to the summit in the hope of taking advantage of each other's weaknesses, but the first thing they discovered was the feebleness of the superpower one could humble without paying a price. "We didn't run the summit; the summit ran us," observed Aaron Miller,[5] nor did the Americans develop a strategy to maximize success, or a backup plan to minimize the impact of failure.

With no binding guidelines, the negotiating groups into which the summit split could only tread water. The Americans summoned the three delegations to a meeting chaired by Secretary Albright. She presented the central topic in the territorial issue: how to reconcile the Israeli claim for three settlement blocs with the Palestinian insistence on the principle of the 1967 borders? Abu Ala, who had heard in Sweden my claim for 8 percent annexation to accommodate settlement blocs without falling off his chair, and who had himself agreed, in a closed meeting with me in a Jerusalem hotel, to blocs of up to 4 percent, now declared before this gallery that "no one on the Palestinian side has ever confirmed that he is prepared to have settlement blocs." For my part, I described the Israeli view as a swap, not necessarily of territory, but of values and assets. The historic change, I said, lay in the creation of an entirely new situation, which included a Palestinian state, a solution to the problem of the refugees, and a capital in Jerusalem. I proposed that we address the details of the border issue, "assuming that the 1967 line is the basis." But the Palestinians would not budge on the principle.

Our working group was in a better state than the one on refugees. Aaron Miller was despondent. "The Palestinians," he said, "were very extreme. We are regressing as compared to what you achieved in Sweden." It turned out that Abu Mazen insisted with Clinton that the principle of the right of return be endorsed as the basis of any further negotiation, to which the president responded that that would mean the Israelis giving a blank check on a matter that was existential to them. But Arafat, who came to Clinton that same night to air his feelings, made it clear that peace should be based on the principles of "international legitimacy," not on Israel's fears and concerns. "Did you invite us to Camp David to put the responsibility of failure on us?" he asked, and lashed out against Barak: "I remind you that that man voted against Oslo, and he wants to establish a unity government with the Likud."

We were at the beginning of the summit, and the atmosphere was one of a mutual digging in of heels and lack of communication between the leaders. At a staff meeting, Barak said that we had reached our red lines, which I thought was a premature assertion. That was what Amnon Lipkin-Shahak and I would come to tell him in a separate meeting. We challenged his unrealistic proposals on key core issues, and urged him to address the Jerusalem question. The solutions, we said, lay in the traditional vision of the Israeli left, not in the delusionary dreams of the right. Barak's answers did not make us any wiser. Had the Palestinians only been more flexible, he would have had the incentive to enter into a dynamic of greater compromise. He was still the prince of vagueness who wanted an agreement, but did not want to be caught in far-reaching concessions as long as Arafat's intentions remained unclear to him. "A Jewish prime minister cannot transfer sovereignty on the Temple Mount to the Palestinians, because the Holy of Holies lies beneath it."

But, we still had the Americans on our side; Sandy Berger would tell me that they were furious at the "seminar of principles" that the Palestinians gave us all. "They are being abstract, while you are being practical; it can't go on like this," he said. For Arafat, the "seminar" focused mainly on the irrevocable "principle" of Jerusalem. He claimed to be constrained by the Muslim world's uncompromising stance. He himself was, as he repeatedly reminded Clinton, the vice president of the Al-Quds Muslim Committee. In retrospect, one cannot resist the temptation of wondering how steadfast the Arab leaders' commitment to

Jerusalem is when they have been so stunningly sanguine about Donald Trump's unilateral recognition of Jerusalem as Israel's capital.

Still on the same day, at 11:00 p.m., I went with Yossi Ginossar to a meeting with Arafat and Abu Mazen. The latter was a monumental disappointment. Throughout the summit, he behaved like a guest who was just passing through. Always polite, courteous, and pleasant-mannered, but utterly extraneous and distant. "Why are you prepared to go back to the 1967 borders with the Arab countries and not with us?" Arafat asked me defiantly. I replied:

> *Because no Arab party gets a state it never had, a solution to the problem of refugees it doesn't have, and a capital city of global significance it doesn't have either. Between us and the Arab countries there is only the issue of land. With you we are talking about additional assets. The sense in the agreement lies in compromises that balance all these categories.*

The abyss between our conceptual attitude to peacemaking could not be greater. How could an agreement emerge from this, particularly as the two leaders who came from totally different cultural latitudes did not even communicate with each other. The one, Barak, made his positions more flexible, that is, as compared with his previous standpoints, and saw with frustration how his counterpart refused to budge an inch. In this war of nerves Arafat was better capable of maintaining his composure, not to mention the fact that, as is normally the case in asymmetric peace processes between a cumbersome democratic government and an autocracy, Arafat enjoyed a marked political preponderance. Unlike us, he did not have to contend with popular or coalition pressures back home to deliver an agreement. He had the tactical advantage in every sense.

9

Clinton: "We have Exhausted the Beauty of This Place"

Barak's decision to put Dan Meridor, an enlightened, statesmanlike former Likud minister, into the discussion group on Jerusalem was "a destructive signal," according to Rob Malley. Dennis Ross would tell me that putting Meridor with Jerusalem and Rubinstein with the refugees meant "that nothing will come out of these negotiations." Malley, for his part, believed that the president saw possible parameters for an agreement on the various issues, but that, regarding Jerusalem, he was at a loss. The best that Barak was willing to offer the president as an opening to work with was a vague idea he mentioned at a July 14 team meeting of "two capitals," with Palestinian "special status," but no sovereignty, on Temple Mount, and "special arrangements" in various parts of the city. He still resisted, though, my advice to give Clinton a "deposit" on the 1967 borders[1]; nor was he willing to help revitalize the working groups, now all a redundant, futile exercise, by proposing a leaders' meeting to agree on rules and principles. A meeting with Arafat was to Barak not an instrument for breaking the ice; it was a reward for good behaviour.

I shared with my colleagues the view that an agreement could only be made on the basis of a definition of our interests that was reduced to the very core of our existential concerns, not beyond that. An example of such a "core" agreement was the peace with Egypt. Menachem Begin, on his way to Camp David, professed he would build his house in Yamit, a city Israel had built deep in Sinai, and ended up giving back Sinai to the last grain of sand. He had to define Israel's interests in "core" terms by meeting our security needs through the demilitarization of the Sinai Peninsula, and the deployment of a multinational force. The international legitimacy of our borders was an additional, even vital shield of our "core" interests. General Yanai, who had a flair for picturesque language, would often explain that what is defined as security interests was like an onion whose outer layers one is forced to peel off in order to get to an agreement which was in fact the innermost, most basic core from which you could not retreat. It was for this inner core we had no choice but to strive if we desired an agreement. No Arab side ever gave us an agreement on the basis of a multilayered onion.

Elyakim Rubinstein opposed my presentation. "The State of Israel has an ethos, and it doesn't have to divest itself of it," he said. Barak's reaction was music to the ears of most of us:

> *We have to reach a decision on parting from control over another people. We all remember that it was possible to establish a smaller State of Israel (before 1967), with greater unity, and we must make the distinction between our justice and the clear perception that without a certain kind of satisfaction for the other side there will be no agreement.*

This Ben-Gurion-like spirit was in him, but its translation into real proposals was still hard to come by. Amnon Lipkin-Shahak—gentle, self-effacing, and devoid of populist mannerisms, a treasure trove of wisdom, and ever the calm, quiet voice of reason—determined that Arafat would not let things progress "until he gets what he wants on the core issues." He sharply criticized our meaningless mumbling about Jerusalem, and proposed defining for ourselves what our Jerusalem was. Did the Kalandia neighborhood and Shuafat refugee camp— both were never part of historical Jerusalem—and the Temple Mount all mean the same, he asked rhetorically. "I am not prepared to fight for some outpost settlement, Talmonim, for example, that only set up its caravans a year and a half ago," averred the former Chief of Staff. He even went one step further in a penetrating observation, not consensual in this forum, let alone the whole of Israeli society: "We are not getting near to a discussion amongst ourselves on red lines. Three hundred thousand non-Jewish Russians have been absorbed in Israel. Is this moral, as opposed to the Palestinian refugees we are not prepared to absorb?" he asked.

Barak was not yet willing to translate his Ben-Gurion like rhetoric into an "onion" metaphor. Nor were the Palestinians yet willing to budge from their "principled" positions. It was, therefore, no surprise that the session on territory ended in an explosion. The ammunition we were given failed to get the wheels of negotiation rolling. And it was not as if the Palestinians were particularly cooperative either. Abu Ala was clearly spoiling for a fight over the 1967 border principle. To my proposed formula of negotiations on border changes "on the assumption" that the borders were those of 1967, the Palestinians responded that the 1967 borders were not an "assumption," but a binding principle that had to be agreed upon first. We were treading water, as Barak wrongly assumed that he would break the Palestinians by a demonstration of strong nerve. The fact that we were at too great a distance from the area of Palestinian compromise did nothing to encourage them to budge.

As for Arafat, he sat in his cabin surrounded by his people as if he were in a bunker under heavy enemy fire, a replay of the battle for Beirut. But, unlike in Beirut, here he was in no rush. "I already have a state," he said to Albright, "I do not care if Barak and the world would recognize it in twenty years from now. Our situation is like South Africa's; the entire world supports me." And so did all those who surrounded him. Admittedly, one could discern a line dividing the two Palestinian generations. The Old Guard—Abu Ala, Abu Mazen—refused to deviate from orthodoxy to the smallest extent. The young ones—mainly Dahlan and Muhammad Rashid—were more intrepid. These two young Turks used to complain to us that the old leadership shirked responsibility and was entrenched in a mood of indifference. Abu Ala acknowledged the disorderly split in their camp: "We split into three factions that looked like three separate delegations in terms of their position . . . (while) Arafat was in a realm of his own, with his own private calculations that had dimensions of which we were unaware."[2] Palestinian delegation members, noted Abu Ala, were separately attempting to gain access to Arafat, to win him over to their own views on Clinton's proposals, "so much so that internal rivalries and personal calculations were leading us to lose our focus."[3]

Arafat's office was a court, and his men were courtiers, myrmidons whom he could always either overrule with an argument or bully into silence. It was not a question of paucity of talents, but of the stifling of dissent even within the tiny cabal around the leader. Essentially, the intergenerational struggle was over the political succession and access to the leader, not necessarily over the nature of the agreement. The Palestinian Young Turks carried no curse of Oedipus, for not even metaphorically were they willing to slay their leader-father or challenge his unfettered power. They would always end up falling into line with him. During a heart-to-heart into the night in which our interlocutors said they were willing to get their feet wet and face Arafat, they also reiterated all Arafat's red lines. Rashid emphasized that if he did not get Jerusalem as he demanded, Arafat would prefer to die like Nasser and remain a saint in the eyes of his people rather than follow in the footsteps of Sadat. In light of Barak's extravagant idea of building a system of overpasses and tunnels between Atarot and the Temple Mount in order to avoid giving the Palestinians unbroken sovereignty in Jerusalem, Rashid rightly pleaded that we "stop building a peace of overpasses."

In times of stalemate, Muhammad Rashid would show up with a formula for salvation that was more a trial balloon than a Palestinian position. One such moment was when, following one of Arafat's outbursts against Barak, he joined us at Yossi Ginossar's cabin and suggested 8 percent annexation by Israel of the West Bank in return for 4 percent exchange of territory plus safe passage under full Palestinian sovereignty which would cover an additional 4 percent. The Jordan Valley would be entirely theirs. Regarding Jerusalem, he proposed conferring on the Palestinian inner neighborhoods "administrative sovereignty," whereas in the Old City, the Muslim and Christian quarters would be in Palestinian hands, the Jewish quarter in ours, and the Armenian quarter would be common to all. The Temple Mount would be under Palestinian sovereignty. That was at long last a practical endgame proposition, and I told him that if this were official, the summit could still end in glorious success. This is where he became evasive: "I think I'll be able to promote it." He was not. Admittedly, Barak was not there yet either.

The central effort was, then, the American way: discussions in working groups. At 7:30 p.m., the territorial teams met with the president and his team. We immediately got bogged down in a futile discussion on the Palestinian 1967 "principle," and our 1967 "assumption." The president accepted our view and instructed both parties to discuss the issues of borders and security in a practical manner. Sandy Berger, generally a man with a short fuse, lashed out at the Palestinians in front of all of us—"Even on such a petty matter you are not prepared to do as the president asks." The president also adopted the strategic swap that I had always advocated in our internal deliberations, modifications in the western border in return for Palestinian control of the eastern border, that is, the Jordan Valley. Transferring of the Jordan Valley to the Palestinian state would also strengthen our claim that they implement the refugees' right of return within their own borders, for the valley was the only real land reserve that could meet that need. The Palestinians did not entirely reject that strategic swap, but we differed radically on the kind of border changes in the west, where they were ready for only minimal adjustments even under a land swap arrangement.

We continued tediously to spin our wheels in the working groups. The only result that came out of a Saturday morning's meeting on borders and security would be Clinton's rage at Abu Ala's rhetoric, which "finished off" the chief Palestinian negotiator and took him out of the game until the end of the summit. From then on, he would be frequently seen walking purposelessly through the alleyways of Camp David. I had proposed at the start of the session that we act according to the president's directives to deal with the practical needs of the parties without getting bogged down in the principles. But Abu Ala was adamant. The Palestinians then went out to consult. Rob Malley joined us to say how stunned he was by the "unhelpful" Palestinian attitude. Surprisingly, the Palestinians came back expressing a willingness to negotiate according to our approach: practical needs. The tactic was as simple as it was clever. They wanted to prove there was no salvation in our method either, for they would not accept our needs as legitimate anyway, which was exactly what happened. They charged us to come back with a more modest map.

At this stage, the president joined the meeting just to "listen in," but got dragged into the debate. Abu Ala complained about the "fingers" of Israeli settlements tearing up Palestinian space. I clarified in response that the Palestinian state must be considered as one piece, for it would also include, in addition to the West Bank, the entire Gaza Strip, the safe passage, and the swapped territories that had not yet been discussed. Abu Ala insisted now that I leave with him the map on which we made our presentation, which prompted an angry outburst from Sandy Berger at Abu Ala: "You want the map because you are preparing for the failure of the summit and want to point your finger at the reason it failed." At this point, the president suggested we work on three subjects: security problems in the Jordan Valley, how to reduce Israel's security areas in the West Bank, and how to lessen the size of the settlement blocs. This was his way of saying that the map we had presented was unacceptable, that it would not produce an agreement, and that a more modest map must therefore be proposed. Abu Ala could have used Clinton's advice to steer the discussion in his direction and claim a more modest map from us. Instead, he again opened with a programmed, declarative speech about the eternal principles of the Palestinian cause. Clinton was in front of me, and I could see how he was becoming flushed with anger, his red face fuming. Next thing I knew, he lost his patience and burst out:

> You Palestinians are not keeping the promise I got yesterday from Arafat. You are behaving with a lack of integrity. You are not acting in good faith. If you want to make speeches to the street or to the gallery, don't do it here. This is not the Security Council. This is not a United Nations General Assembly. Make a summit meeting there if you want and don't waste my time. I am the president of the United States. I am ready to pack my bags and take off. You are an obstacle to negotiation. You do not raise counterproposals. I, too, am risking a lot here. The meaning of a summit is to talk in good faith, as I concluded yesterday with Arafat. You have not come to this summit in good faith.

Everyone was struck dumb by the president's outburst. A tense, embarrassed silence filled the room, and we followed him as he rose and left the room, red-faced with anger.

The Palestinians showed negligible room for maneuver to the point of despair. But we too were not exactly constructive. The map we presented was definitely worse than our earlier ones; it was brought by Gilead Sher straight from Barak, and I myself had no foreknowledge of it. Barak had added an additional 3 percent of annexation to this map, and had stuck "fingers" of annexation in the heart of the West Bank in order to include settlements such as Kdumim, Eli, Beit-El, and Ofra. He probably thought that by showing the Palestinians what they would consider a tougher map, he would make them agree to our earlier one.

This was trying to be too clever. Barak also had throughout the summit the extravagant and truly expendable idea of keeping part of the Northern Gaza Strip.

Indeed, despite the fact that Clinton seemed as if he had supported us at that stormy meeting, both he and his aides were furious with Barak. Sandy Berger and Indyk later told me that Clinton warned Barak that if there was no progress by the next day, the Americans would put forward their own paper, "which you'll hate." During dinner later on, the president passed by me and commented with surprising equanimity, "I screwed up your meeting this morning, didn't I"? Clinton's irritations and outbursts of temper tended to disappear as quickly as they came. Sandy's attitude was less amusing. I was standing with Barak when he joined us to say in a threatening tone that he would stop being a peacemaker and would focus on defending his president. He even threatened to go to the media and put the blame on Barak. His rage continued to boil over after Barak left us. He was livid: "I don't care if the president fires me, but I intend to give Ehud a piece of my mind, which will have grave implications on Israel-US relations." He was angry, and justifiably so, about the map we had presented to the Palestinians. "That map was shocking," he said.

The Americans had arrived at a crossroads. "We've exhausted the beauty of this place," the president threw at me as we left the dining room for a staff meeting at Barak's. Dennis Ross would tell me later that night that the president was in a state of total despair. He had lost confidence that an agreement could be reached in light of Barak's positions on Jerusalem, and was deliberating whether to put a new paper on the table or to minimize the damage already done by putting a dignified end to the summit. If there was to be a paper, "it would be a hard one for Barak," Dennis Ross warned.

10

A Game Changer (or So It Looked)

What, then, were the American ideas that Dennis Ross had told us would be "hard for Barak." Two capitals in Jerusalem—the Palestinian one in only two outer neighbourhoods; in the rest, "functional autonomy"—with one municipal umbrella; "shared responsibilities" in the Old City and Palestinian "jurisdiction" on the Temple Mount. In the matter of borders, Israel would annex between 4 and 13 percent of the West Bank in exchange for "unequal swaps" that would include territory as well as assets (harbor rights, the safe passage, etc.), while the Jordan Valley would be a sovereign part of the Palestinian state. There would be no right of return, the solution being practical, in the spirit of our Stockholm talks. I would have run for the first pen around to sign such a document. But, with typical Barak posturing, he did not embrace it when Clinton spelled it out to him. What was utterly unrealistic was to assume that Arafat would go for this.

The poster image of military resoluteness, Barak was capable of harrowing vacillations in the domain of peace diplomacy. The paradox lay in the distance between his awareness of the price needed for an agreement he eagerly wanted and his unwillingness to actually pay it. "We have arrived at the moment of truth. History versus politics, on both sides. In our fight for Israel's Jewish image, time works against us. The separation of our two nations that can be made today might not be possible tomorrow." Well said. He even accepted Clinton's idea of a secret channel (Gilead Sher and I opposite Saeb Erakat and Mohammed Dahlan). But, at 00:45 on Sunday July 16, while we were preparing for nightlong secret talks, he ran to the president to warn him against putting forward an American paper waiving Israeli sovereignty in any part of Jerusalem.

"Bring up ideas; I pray you'll arrive at a joint paper," the president told us before we started our backchannel on Sunday after midnight. Gilead Sher went with Saeb Erakat to the president's study to work on a draft agreement that would naturally contain many discrepancies that could be bridged through American proposals. Gilead Sher was an ingenious drafter versed in the most arcane legal aspects of a peace treaty, but I did not envy him. His partner in the task thought that now was exactly the right time to renege on promises that were given in Sweden limiting the

Palestinian state's right to enter into international military treaties and make huge financial claims against Israel for the long years of occupation. I was left with Dahlan when Yisrael Hasson, a former head of Shabak in Jerusalem and an authority on the topography of the city, joined me. I took it upon myself to break the Jerusalem taboo. I harboured no illusions that what I was going to propose would meet Arafat's wishes, but I felt it necessary to co-opt Barak into the Jerusalem process and unleash a dialogue with the Palestinians thereof. My proposal to Dahlan was:

(a) **Transfer of the outer Arab neighborhoods to full Palestinian sovereignty**. These outer neighbourhoods included some in the northern outskirts of the city (Hizma, A' Zaim, Samiramis, Kafr 'Aqab, the part of Kalandyia within the area of Jerusalem, Al Matar in the region of the airport, the Jerusalem part of A-Ram, the Jerusalem part of Dahiat al' Barid, Beit Hanina, Shu'afat, the Shu'afat refugee camp, New 'Anata, and Ras Hamis), and others in the south like Ras Al Amud, Jabel Mukhaber, Sawahara il Gharbiya, Tsur Baher, Um-Tuba, Beit Safafa, Sharafat, and Al-Walaja.

(b) **The very inner Arab neighbourhoods, the core of Palestinian Jerusalem**—Wadi al-Joz, Sheikh Jarrah, the commercial region of Salah-ad-Din, and Sultan Suleiman, the As Sawana neighbourhood, A-Tur, Abu Tor, and Silwan (apart from the City of David)—would gain full municipal autonomy under Israeli sovereignty. It could be defined, I said to Dahlan, as "functional sovereignty."

(c) **The Old City** would remain under Israeli sovereignty, but a special regime for the different quarters would apply there in a way that would dilute the very concept of sovereignty.

(d) **The Temple Mount.** The status quo (by which Israel's overall sovereignty is limited by the full autonomous administration of the Palestinian Waqf) would be given an international legal basis in the form of Palestinian custodianship.

Our offer amounted to a complete peace outline that represented an improvement on our earlier proposals. We proposed a Palestinian state on the entire Gaza Strip, and on 89.5 percent of the West Bank and additional territory within Israel to compensate for the annexation by Israel of 10.5 percent of the West Bank needed for the three settlement blocs; Palestinian sovereignty in the Jordan Valley, while a security area, including three warning stations, would be kept by Israel for a period of ten years. A safe passage linking Gaza to the West Bank would be under Israeli sovereignty, but with "undisturbed and unlimited use" by the Palestinians, and, together with a wide array of infrastructure facilities within Israel, would be put at the service of the Palestinian state as part of the overall calculation of land swap percentages.

We broke up at around noon, and I went to report to Ehud. He reacted by saying that my Jerusalem offer was not to his liking. I understood this, however, to be an outward pose so that he could dissociate himself from the concessions if they proved insufficient to reach a breakthrough. Danny Yatom, who was with Barak when I gave my report, admitted that Barak was not taken aback by my proposals.[1]

Two hours later, the president convened the teams to hear their reports. He was clearly satisfied and for the first time saw a chance of a momentous shift in the course of the summit. "There's been some real movement here," the overly exhilarated president said. "Today, the Israelis have set a precedent in this matter of Jerusalem." He was so upbeat that he stressed that we, the Israelis, deserved now to know that "This leads to the end of the conflict." But there was nothing in Saeb Erakat's demeanor that hinted he was ready to join the general sense of an approaching breakthrough that the president wanted to inspire. Instead, he had nothing more brilliant to say than that the Palestinians intended asking for compensation for the years of Israeli occupation. "Saeb was being idiotic," Secretary Albright would tell me later.

I left the meeting with mixed feelings. On the one hand, we had popped the cork, we'd given breathing space to the summit, and we'd placed the onus on Arafat's shoulders. But, on the other hand, the Palestinians' chilly reaction did not leave room for much optimism. In Barak's mind, this meant that his worst fears were confirmed: we made moves and concessions, and the Palestinians simply pocketed them as a line of departure for additional bargaining. I tried to reassure him that we had taken the pressure off him and laid the burden of proof on Arafat's shoulders. Indeed, Sandy Berger later told me that there was a tough meeting between Clinton and Arafat—"Clinton really gave it to him"—and that Arafat received an ultimatum to come with answers that would prove that he was accepting the challenge we had set.

More than his negotiators' ideas, what truly made Barak hate these situations was his sense that the Palestinians were not truly responding. Struck by Palestinian inertia, he again lost his composure and hastened to send Clinton an angry letter stating that my proposals on Jerusalem "went too far." He also unfairly and unnecessarily lashed out at people "around the President"—meaning mainly Sandy Berger, a longtime supporter of "Peace Now"—who, he said, were serving as "defense counsel" for the Palestinians. Barak considered himself, and wrote thus to the President, "the first prime minister to come close, in such a daring and unprecedented way, to making decisions on heart-wrenching issues that touch the very soul of Jewish history and spirit." He could not bear with equanimity his willingness to break such taboos while Arafat remained still stubbornly entrenched behind his eternal myths. He ended his message in apocalyptic terms: "There is no power in the world that can force on us collective national suicide."

A professional lawyer and a close friend of the president, Sandy Berger enjoyed a proximity to Clinton that gave him an edge on Secretary Albright, with whom inevitable tensions emerged throughout the summit. Albright was the chief diplomat consumed with her many tasks as Secretary of State, while Sandy Berger tended to see things through the prism of the president's political interests. His own aides on the Middle East, Rob Malley and Bruce Reidel, were brilliant and highly knowledgeable professionals, with the former more attuned to the Palestinians' sensibilities and the latter a more centrist, national security adviser. Barak refrained from a heart-to-heart talk, as would have been appropriate, with Sandy Berger. But Sandy did speak to me. That was a touching, yet bizarre, even surrealistic situation, where the National Security Adviser of a foreign nation had to defend his Zionist credentials against a smear from an Israeli prime minister. He belonged, Sandy told me passionately, "to a family that has been connected to Zionist activity and the struggle for a just peace in the region for four generations."

More importantly, he told me now that, under the pressure of our move during the backchannel and after talking with the president, Arafat "feels himself on the edge of an abyss," so much so, that for the first time since the beginning of the summit, Arafat raised "counterproposals that contained what could be construed as a basis for resolving all the issues." What was the breakthrough that was allegedly about to happen on the basis of Arafat's counterproposals? From my conversation with Sandy, which the president himself joined (the meeting was in Clinton's office), it seemed that Arafat had agreed to settlement blocs in the West Bank of between 8 and 10 percent in return for symbolic exchanges of territories in the region of the Gaza Strip. Arafat even said to Clinton, "I have full confidence in you, Mr. President, and I leave the decision regarding the swap percentages in your hands."

How to explain this sudden Arafat largesse? First, he needed to get relief from Clinton's pressure. Second, and more importantly, he wanted to shift the entire summit onto one single issue, Jerusalem. Al-Quds was predominant in the mind of the old warrior, which was the reason for his indifference during an earlier meeting that day with his team where Abu Ala, Yasser Abed-Rabbo, and Nabil Shaath supported only meager percentages of Palestinian land for Israeli blocs of settlements. Arafat then made his own historic choice, acquiescing to even 10 percent to accommodate blocs of settlements, provided he got Jerusalem. Arafat was visibly annoyed with his people "for wanting to take a tougher line than he had with President Clinton."[2]

As for security arrangements, Arafat, according to Sandy, was willing to go along with "what will be decided," but expressed a preference for an international force in the Jordan Valley. The end of conflict, he said, would happen only after the full implementation of the agreement, not upon its being signed. Overly optimistic, neither Sandy nor the president anticipated any problems on the subject of refugees either. From now on, everything stood on a solution to Jerusalem "Arafat could live with." But the crux of the matter was that Arafat had brilliantly managed to wriggle out of a dire dilemma by putting the entire onus on Israel to give him the kind of solution to Jerusalem she was incapable of offering.

Apparently, this was all truly sensational, beyond our expectations. But the powerful in this summit did not listen carefully to the powerless, who just proved to be smarter. Arafat's zeal to appease did not last beyond the moment. He was a master in the art of walking out of a tight corner, through ephemeral promises, if necessary. Not only did he send later in the day a letter to the president in which he insisted on "an exchange of territory of a reasonable size on a reciprocal basis,"[3] but his entire move was also a brilliant ploy that would eventually doom the summit, and presumably shift the onus for its failure onto Barak. For what he did was to make his extraordinary generosity on all "real estate" issues, to him always of secondary importance, conditional on a solution to the Jerusalem question on such terms as were beyond Barak's wildest assumptions.

Indeed, both Sandy Berger and the president agreed that my Jerusalem proposals still fell short of meeting Arafat's expectations, and that further progress needed to be made.

Clinton told me that in the peace process in Northern Ireland a distinction had been made between the principle of unity and actually partitioning. He asked whether in my opinion one could apply the same principle in the Old City of Jerusalem. I told him that my proposal for a special regime under "light" Israeli sovereignty would be an attempt to do just that, since actually there would be an internal partition of jurisdictional areas in the four neighbourhoods without actually dividing the Old City. But the president was looking for a verbal formula that would satisfy the Palestinian claim, and wondered whether it was possible to talk in terms of "super-sovereignty" and "sub-sovereignty." He asked whether it was not worth opening another secret channel to discuss this issue alone. I replied that this was indeed desirable. I suggested, though, that the legal aspects be negotiated on our side by Elyakim Rubinstein, the government's legal adviser. Sandy Berger was taken aback: "This man is an extremist." But Clinton accepted the logic that a man of the right would put his seal on an agreement in Jerusalem's Old City.

I advised the president, though, that a no less central task for him was to see to Barak's mood. He needed to "reprogram him," I told him, by persuading him that Arafat was indeed ready for a real turning point. The president lost no time in going to Barak's cabin, where I joined him a few moments later. He reported "Arafat's concessions" and added that "Shlomo has some interesting ideas," referring to the one I raised on the subject of the Old City, and the one about continuing the negotiations to crack issues connected to the legal status and definition of sovereignty in the city's sacred basin.

At that time, I had a feeling that things were moving. The mood in the American delegation had shifted 180 degrees. You could smell the big breakthrough in the air. Rob Malley, Dennis Ross, and others were practically euphoric. It was one of those moments when I believed that an agreement was within reach. The problem was less in the positions of the sides and more in the extent to which they grasped that the other side was moving, initiating, compromising. The obstacle was not the extent of the compromise, but the sense of a lack of movement and entrenchment. It seemed to me that we had managed to break this feeling. We suddenly felt that the "package" was perhaps beginning to fall into place. Clinton invited Elyakim Rubinstein for a talk.

Oh Jerusalem! (and Its Lies)

Since 1967, the Israeli discourse on Jerusalem has been a pile of accepted lies. What exactly is Jerusalem?[1] For, in the megalomaniac spirit that drove the policies of Israeli governments after 1967, the city's boundaries were extended from about 10,875 acres to more than 31,000, thus swallowing into its new boundaries a chaotic amalgam of Arab villages, and even one gigantic refugee camp, Shuafat. Jerusalem, a modest city linked to the rest of Israel by one single road that went no farther than its border with Jordan, suddenly became a gigantic metropolis inhabited by two conflicting national groups living under two different legal systems. For us to claim that this vaingloriously extended Jerusalem was the millennial capital of the Jewish people was a travesty of history.

In 1966, a year before the unification of the city by Israel's elite paratroopers, the iconic composer Naomi Shemer sang in her "Jerusalem of Gold" of "the city that sits solitary, and in its heart a wall." But the wall dividing the city was now no longer made of concrete or brick; it was an invisible line that marked the hugely unequal living standards in the Jewish and Arab neighborhoods. How hollow our rhetoric about the "eternal united capital" was also reflected in the abysmal gap between the level of services and infrastructures in the Jewish and Arab parts of the city. In the year 2000, there were 1,079 public parks in the West as opposed to 99 in the East; 1,451 playgrounds in the West, 72 in the East; 32 mother-care stations in the West, 5 in the East. Without planning and zoning, the Arab neighborhoods were thrown by Israel's decision to freeze the registration of land in the eastern part of the city into a bureaucratic maze that denied them the right to build legally. In such a Kafkaesque situation, the bulk of new buildings in Arab East Jerusalem are to this very day actually "illegal," and could be demolished under Israeli court orders. Roads, sidewalks, sewerage, public lighting, school classes—in all of these, East Jerusalem was then more backward than Communist East Berlin on the eve of her unification with West Berlin.

Today, fifty-four years after the city's "unification," the underlying reality prevails of two separate communities deeply divided along lines of identity, religion, political aspirations, and socioeconomic disparities. Eighty-two percent of Jerusalem's Palestinians live now below the poverty line, 40 percent of its children drop out of school, and only 10 percent of the municipality's budget goes to the east of the city. The division of the city is also reflected in its demography. Demographic growth for the Palestinians stands today at 3.5 percent per year; that of the Jews is 1.5 percent. In 2017, 97 percent of those living in West Jerusalem were Jewish, and in the Jewish neighborhoods of East Jerusalem only 4,200 Arabs lived with 209,000 Jews, while only 1,770 Jews lived with 338,000 Palestinians in the Arab districts. And in the Old City, only 11 percent of the population is Jewish. The drive of "Judaizing" Jerusalem has not been an edifying success either; its Jewish population declined from 74 percent in 1967 to 62 percent in 2017. A total of 38 percent of the city's inhabitants are, then, Palestinian non-Israeli citizens who do not recognize it as Israel's capital. As residents, they have the right to vote in municipal elections but not to be elected. They also enjoy Israel's advanced social welfare system, but it has been their choice not to opt for citizenship. Otherwise, a massive participation of the Jerusalemite Palestinians in municipal elections, something they have always shunned doing lest this was seen as legitimizing Israeli rule, would shift control of the city to a Palestinian mayor and a city council with a Palestinian majority.

Since 1967, more than $20 billion was spent by Israeli governments of all political shades in order to "Israelize" Jerusalem through a network of new Jewish neighborhoods in the Palestinian eastern part of the city. This national project could not secure a solid Jewish majority not only because of the high Palestinian birthrate, but mainly because, since 1967, more than 200,000 middle-class liberal Israelis have abandoned this tense, embattled nest of irreconcilable cleavage between Jew and Arab, and between secular Jews and fanatical Orthodox congregations (30 percent of the population) waiting for the Messiah to redeem them from the rule of the Zionist liberal sinners. The massive investment in politically motivated Jewish neighborhoods in East Jerusalem denied governments the funds needed to develop a coherent investment strategy in growth-creating industries in the western, Jewish part of the city. This should help explain both the desertion of Jerusalem by the liberal middle class in favor of Tel Aviv, Israel's capital of modernity and high-tech-driven growth, as well as the fact that Jerusalem is today the poorest city in Israel.

While we were in Camp David defending our patriotic discourse on Jerusalem the eternal, an Israeli former police chief in Jerusalem, Arieh Amit, sent me the following comment:

> *Our grandiloquent claims about Jerusalem being our eternal capital in all of whose corners we are fully sovereign are devoid of any true content. Neither Israeli governments nor the Jerusalem municipality have ever dealt with the eastern part of the city and its Palestinian population*

the same way they treat its western parts. . . .The Israeli police has never
served the Arab population, did not interfere in their lives, and did not
solve their problems. . . . And so, over the years, a Palestinian autono-
mous governance developed in the East, which includes, among other
areas, an independent educational system, a health network with two
hospitals run exclusively by the Palestinian Authority, a welfare system
run not only by the PA but also by Hamas, a politico-religious admin-
istrative complex that runs proudly and openly the holy sites in the Old
City and outside it, and a security and police network that has full inde-
pendence in the eastern parts of the city.

This was also true with regard to the Temple Mount. In 1967, the Palestinians
were allowed by the Israeli occupying power full administrative control of the
area of the mosques both because it was a sacred Muslim site and because of
the Halachic prohibition against the presence of Jews on the Mount. Israeli
governments were consistently careful not to impose planning and zoning
regulations on the Temple Mount area, or any other Israeli laws that could challenge the authority of the Muslim Waqf in the holy site.

Significantly, this was an arrangement that continues to be widely supported
today by the Israeli public, who, contrary to the politicians' working assumption,
have never seen the Temple Mount as that central to their lives. The Halachic
prohibition against Jews going onto the Mount fully concurred with the wide
public's wish not to drag the conflict with the Palestinians into the religious
realm. For the Palestinians in Jerusalem, the Haram al-Sharif was since 1967
the only place in the city, and actually in the whole of Palestine, where a sort
of exclusive Muslim-Palestinian rule prevailed. This explains their hypersen-
sitivity to any Israeli move, however discreet and minor, to change the status
quo on the Mount. Before coming to Camp David, Arafat had personally appointed Akram Sabri as the new Mufti of Jerusalem. Significantly, it was during
the Netanyahu government (1996–99), not a left-wing pacifist government, that
the Palestinians built on the Temple Mount the El-Marwani Mosque, the biggest
mosque ever built in Palestine. That was clearly the most blatant departure from
the status quo in the Temple Mount in favor of the Muslims since the Crusaders'
Kingdom of Jerusalem in the twelfth century.

While we were in our Camp David bubble, the Palestinians were already
enjoying practical sovereignty over the Arab neighborhoods of Jerusalem.
Their national and political institutions in the city had all the makings of a surrogate Palestinian capital, with Orient House being its practical headquarter. It
hosted Faisal Husseini's Palestinian Agency for Jerusalem Affairs, the Center for
Cartography and Geography under Khalil Tufaqghi, the Office of International
Relations headed by Sharif al-Husseini, the Center for Civil and Social Rights

under Azmi Abu-Saud, and the Office of Religious Affairs, where Hassan Tahbub practically acted as the minister in charge of the Waqf's property in Jerusalem. The Committee for the Protection of Palestinian Prisoners also operated from Orient House.

Moreover, there was no effective control by Israeli governments of the entire Palestinian welfare system in East Jerusalem. Health, education, environment, and public transportation were all run autonomously. About five hundred buses and minibuses regulated exclusively by the Palestinian Authority served Palestinian commuters within the city and from it into the West Bank. The Palestinian Authority was also in full control of the entire educational network in the city. This included the curriculum even in schools that were funded by Israel's Jerusalem municipality. The final exams in high schools were all prepared either by Jordan or the Palestinian Authority itself. Arafat's brother ran the Al-Muqased Hospital that served the bulk of the Palestinian population. In East Jerusalem, the Higher Council for the Palestinian Tourist Industry also operated, as well as the Al-Quds University, which functioned outside the regulating control of Israel's Council for Higher Education.

Palestinian quasi-sovereignty was a reality also in what was for Israel the most sacred cow of all, security and political affairs. The Palestinian security services controlled safety and security throughout Arab East Jerusalem. And a political and judicial office in Abu Dis was run by the "Governor of Jerusalem," Jamil Othman Nasser, who was appointed directly by the Palestinian Authority to oversee, among other domains, a whole judicial system aimed at circumventing the authority of the Israeli courts. An independent police force—the Presidential Security—was responsible for the implementation of the Palestinian courts' decisions.

While we were resisting in Camp David the division of Jerusalem with a sense of awe and concern for the domestic political backlash, the city was for all practical purposes already divided. A member of the Palestinian Council, Khatem Abdul-Kader, would later comment that "already today, our rule over East Jerusalem is bigger than what we were offered at Camp David." There should have been, therefore, neither a municipal logic, nor a national one to insist in Camp David on Israeli sovereignty in the Arab neighborhoods in the city's outskirts and even in the inner districts, closer to the Old City. Paralyzed by right-wing slogans about a "united and eternal capital," we resisted offering a fair deal to the Palestinians in Jerusalem until the very last days of the process, that is, through the Clinton Peace Parameters of December 2000. This was too late, and for Arafat not enough, as it turned out.

* * *

However innovative and, at points, daring the ideas we toyed with during a marathon debate of our team on July 17, which were essentially aimed at continuing the momentum of the backchannel, they still exposed the abyss between the Jerusalem of our imagination and its crude reality. The good news was that, finally, Jerusalem was no longer out of bounds; we were no longer filled with fear and trepidation at every warning by political demagogues threatening us that we had "divided Jerusalem." The debate was exciting, even stormy at times, and we all had a palpable sense of the significance of the moment. Yet none of us had gotten as far as to go over the edge, to the point that we instinctively knew would be the only way to satisfy Arafat.

But the general opinion in this loaded debate, perhaps the first of its kind ever conducted by an Israeli delegation in a "live exercise," was that one could not remain in a rut and get bogged down in obsolete slogans. Yisrael Hasson, a veteran General Security Service man who knew Jerusalem down to its remotest alleyways, thought that using the term "functional autonomy" for Arab neighborhoods would perhaps help make it acceptable to the Palestinians. In the Old City, he proposed "a mutual suspension of the claim for sovereignty." Oded Eran, who was also impressively knowledgeable about Jerusalem and its history and archaeology, warned us that just "some kind" of sovereignty would fall short of Arafat's expectations.

Agonized and tense, Dan Meridor, a prince among the princes of the Israeli right, dared to voice an ambiguous willingness to partition the city. The question was just "how much," he said, for if we breached the line we had held until then, it was important we knew that that was the last step that gave us a permanent agreement. A prince, I said? But of the Hamletian sort. Later in the meeting, Meridor asked to further qualify his assertions with a statement of " 'No' to partitioning the city, 'No' to transferring sovereignty." He only meant, he said, a division of municipal faculties, boroughs London-style.

Gilead Sher opted for cruel realism. With all the innovations in our discussion, he said, it could be that a meeting between the core of our and the Palestinians' standpoint on Jerusalem might not be possible at this summit, and then one could forget about the end of the conflict and a permanent agreement. Gilead also assessed that it would not be right to make concessions on Jerusalem till the last minute, and even then one should leave it for the prime minister as a last breakthrough move. Danny Yatom, far more independent and creative than his public image suggested, advised breaking taboos. Jerusalem's municipal borders were not holy, from either a religious or a national point of view; these were borders that had received more glory and pomp than content, he said. He suggested, therefore, sharing sovereignty with the Palestinians on the Temple Mount, with the addition of adjectives defining its limits. Regarding the Old City, he believed the Palestinians should be given "signs of sovereignty."

"The State of Israel was built by practical Zionism that was prepared to make compromises all along the way," began Amnon Lipkin-Shahak. "What is Jerusalem?" he asked. "Large parts of Jerusalem today are not my Jerusalem. I have no problem not being in (the Arab neighborhood of) Tsur Baher." The Israeli interest was to transfer as many residents as possible to the Palestinians and to be left with fewer Arabs under Israeli control. But sovereignty on the Temple Mount must not be waived, for "we cannot give Arafat the Temple, the cradle of Jewish history." Regarding the Old City, he believed that the Palestinians should get a demarcated area in the Muslim Quarter. He was sufficiently frank, however, to admit that it might not satisfy Arafat, and then, "We go back to square one."

For Elyakim Rubinstein, this debate was very difficult. He was happy to include as few Arabs as possible both in Jerusalem and in the settlement blocs by freeing ourselves of the villages surrounding Jerusalem. On the Temple Mount, he supported maintaining the status quo of administrative responsibility residing with the Waqf, and the creation of a prayer area for the Jews. Sovereignty could not be transferred in the Old City, but an office representing the Palestinian State could be offered there. General Shlomo Yanai, like most of the participants in the debate, believed that the outer layers could be peeled off the city for the benefit of the Palestinians and we would thus be divested of the control over 300,000 Palestinians "who do not belong to Jerusalem."

Alluding to those who thought that the whole Jerusalem issue should be put off, I made the case for making a decision "today." There will be no permanent settlement, I said, if we only relate to the territorial aspect of the agreement and ignore the historical and mythological aspects connected to Jerusalem, which were so crucial to Arafat's political persona. I spoke of "a certain kind" of Palestinian sovereignty in the Old City or part of it. If we freed ourselves of Arab neighborhoods, where in any case our control was questionable, I said, it would then become clear that never in our history had Jewish Jerusalem been so big, and our control of it never so real. I explained that the Zionist movement had made good use of the time since 1967, and the Arabs had lost, but there could be no agreement by fixating on our achievements and their defeats. On the Temple Mount and holy sites, I proposed a noncompulsory, Israeli supreme sovereignty tempered with the upgrading of the current status quo of Palestinian administrative responsibility with new legal definitions. On the Palestinian neighborhoods, my view was that any agreement must change the status quo to their advantage, and this also referred to "the inner neighborhoods." With all this, the neighborhoods were a banal issue for Arafat, and there would be no agreement without a reference to Palestinian sovereignty, possibly attaching adjectives to it, in the Old City.

Typically, the Prime Minister summed up the debate with enlightened rhetoric offset by crude realism:

We are at the moment of truth in the historical process. The Zionist move-
ment created and joined two nations here, and we must not assume that the
Palestinians' national drive will just disappear, while ours remains a leading
motif. We are talking here about a decision similar to the one taken in the
debate on Partition, or the establishment of the state, or perhaps the crisis
of the Yom Kippur War at its height ... There is no longer any possibility of
postponing this process.

But Barak, like Barak, needed a protective shield of caution and ambiguity:

I don't see Rabin or any other prime minister transferring sovereignty of the
First and Second Temples to the Palestinians. Nevertheless, without a sepa-
ration of our two nations, and without an end to the conflict, we are heading
for tragedy. We must find, during this summit, the place between "There is
no agreement" and what our people absolutely cannot concede on. We are
coming to the end of the road; we cannot put off the moment any longer and
avoid making a decision.

He was always capable of inspiring, but still reserved and equivocal. Clinton was
eagerly waiting for the outcome of our debate; timid and cryptic positions were
not exactly what he expected from us.

Saeb Erakat: "Arafat Is Interested in a Crisis"

Disappointment awaited the president. "My negotiating team moved beyond my red lines," Barak complained at the start of our meeting—Barak, Danny Yatom, and I—with him that very night. Barak downgraded my Jerusalem offer (he would only allow Palestinian sovereignty in one outer neighborhood), refused to change the status quo on the Haram al-Sharif, denied any Palestinian sovereignty in the Old City, and asked for 11.3 percent annexation instead of our 10.5 percent. There would be Palestinian "control" of the Jordan Valley "with an Israeli security zone for a period of twelve years." As for refugees, the right of return would only apply to the Palestinian state.[1] Understandably, Clinton exploded in rage:

> You kept us and Arafat waiting all day and you want me to present something less than what Shlomo presented as our idea? I won't do it. I just won't do it. I would have no credibility. I can't go see Arafat with retrenchment. You want to present these ideas directly to Arafat, you go ahead and see if you can sell it. There is no way I can. This is not real. This is not serious. I went with you to Shepherdstown [Israeli-Syrian negotiations] and was told nothing by you for four days. I went to Geneva [a Clinton-Assad summit] and felt like a wooden Indian doing your bidding. I will not let it happen here. I will simply not do it.

The president also challenged Barak's claim that Arafat had so far not made any move or concession, for he was willing, he said, to concede 8–9 percent of the land for "your settlement blocks," and had even left the final decision as to the proportion of land swaps in the hands of the president.[2] Barak did not quite realize that the summit was now trapped in connected vessels: Arafat would concede land only if he got all he wanted in Jerusalem. Clinton then turned to me as if he wanted to be sure the backchannel proposals were still alive. I also got a written note from Sandy Berger: "What is exactly the brilliant idea here?" The only way out of this clearly embarrassing situation I could think of was to say to the president that Barak's ideas did not deviate from the principles of my proposals; he only translated them into sovereignty in fewer Arab neighborhoods. I added that, although Barak asked that the status quo in the Haram al-Sharif be maintained, the significant change he offered was to shift the authority in the site from the Waqf to the Palestinian state. I answered Berger in a note that "I have no doubt whatsoever that Barak stands behind my proposals, but he wants to come to them as the endgame, not as the basis for further concessions." I also added a suggestion that they should try to work with Barak on Palestinian sovereignty in East Jerusalem "with adjectives," which would be easier for him to digest. Barak responded to Clinton's harsh comments in a serene tone. He could not go beyond the mandate he got from the people and lose his moral and political authority, and he could not put at risk the most fundamental values of the Jewish state that his predecessors had created with such sacrifices.

But, Barak finally got the message. His tactical acrobatics risked not only his relations with the president but also the entire purpose for which he dragged us all to these Maryland hills. He needed to level with the president and could no longer evade facing Arafat with a credible comprehensive offer. A few hours later, at 3:30 a.m. on July 18, Barak went back to the president, this time alone. His report of the meeting was reserved and typically opaque. "I gave the president a maneuver space for his contacts with Arafat." What happened was that Clinton drafted a more forthcoming proposal, "consistent with what Shlomo and Gilead had proposed," to which Barak agreed. It was, then, again Palestinian sovereignty over all the outer neighborhoods, as well as the Muslim quarter of the Old City and a Palestinian "custodial role" over the holy sites.[3]

Barak was perhaps trapped in his penchant for tedious tactical maneuvers, but Arafat was in a straitjacket of myths and historical delusions that kept him incapable of moving. Barak could conveniently realize by now that the ra'īs would always be there to relieve him of his anguish. In his meeting with the president, Arafat turned down each and every concession made by Barak, which were presented to him as an American proposal. "I cannot go back to my people," he said, "without Al Quds al-Sharif; I would rather die as one that had been occupied but did not surrender." He wanted, he said, a peace deal along the lines of the Egypt-Israel agreement as well as the Israeli withdrawal from Lebanon. The Egyptians insisted, he said, and got back everything to the last grain of sand in Sinai, and with Lebanon, Israel was still engaged in a discussion over the last house in a border village, Radjer; and here Clinton was asking him to give up Jerusalem.

The president had then to go back to the drawing board. His improved Jerusalem proposal was anticipated to me by Dennis Ross:

- Palestinian custodianship of the Temple Mount;
- Palestinian sovereignty in the Old City's Muslim and Christian quarters;
- Full Palestinian sovereignty in Jerusalem's outer Arab neighborhoods and self-rule in the inner ones, which would include planning and zoning rights as well as policing and law enforcement.

I lost no time in conveying this to Barak. It was now clear to him that his tactical ploys had backfired, and he had to recover the initiative. He first started, though, with the idea of a partial settlement that would not include Jerusalem, but, as Sandy Berger and Rob Malley told him, Arafat might consider this only if he got to have custodianship of Temple Mount, and a sovereign office in the Old City. This was a strange proposal for a partial agreement that "postpones Jerusalem." Moreover, there was no chance that Arafat would give us the "end of conflict" without a complete Jerusalem deal, nor would he stick to the territorial concessions he had made, for they were linked to a full solution to the Jerusalem question. In his despair, Barak suddenly discovered the wonders of my Jerusalem proposal, and he asked Yossi Ginossar to see Arafat and present them as an official Israeli offer. Ginossar answered that it would be better done by the Americans. It was then, after he had exhausted all other escape routes from the agonizing need to put forward a truly generous offer, that Barak decided to finally leave his comfort zone and make his boldest move in this summit.

Following Rabin's way in the Syria negotiations, Barak presented his proposals as a "deposit," something I had pleaded with him to do on various occasions. He offered a Palestinian state over 91 percent of the West Bank and the entire Gaza Strip, a security zone in the Jordan Valley that Israel would keep for less than twelve years, while the Palestinians had sovereignty over 85 percent of the border area. His offer on Jerusalem was practically a copy of the American proposal as it was conveyed to him through me: Palestinian sovereignty over seven out of nine outer Jerusalem neighborhoods, while the inner ones would be under the Palestinian civil authority, including planning and zoning, and law enforcement. On the Temple Mount, he proposed a shared custodianship to include the state of Palestine, and Morocco as the chair of the Muslim Higher Commission on Jerusalem. He also agreed to Palestinian sovereignty over both the Old City's Muslim and Christian quarters. Regarding refugees, he spoke of a solution that could be "satisfactory to both sides."

Clinton was impressed. He believed the package had the potential of a fair endgame. It certainly reconciled him with Barak's intrepidity. "I have never met a man as courageous as Barak," he would tell me later. Clinton now exuded a renewed confidence in a peace agreement. That same evening, walking with Martin Indyk along the sidewalks of the place, we both felt that Barak had given the summit its decisive test. "We are on the path of a final agreement," he said. The president had decided to postpone for a day his trip to Japan, and might cancel it altogether if he saw the chance of a breakthrough. Back in my cabin, I woke up Gilead Sher to share with him the general enthusiasm for the approaching agreement.

But the wings of history flew only over our heads; the Palestinians remained unimpressed. Barak's move was revolutionary only with regard to his own old positions, and was not exactly the measure of Arafat's expectations. Our innocent euphoria dissipated with the news of the early morning. It turned out that Arafat again poured cold water on the president's enthusiasm. His reaction to Barak's move—conveyed to him by Clinton as "a basis for further negotiations," not as a take-it-or-leave-it deal—was "shitty," as Gamal Helal confided to me later in the day. Perhaps, but it was also stoic: "I cannot go back to my people without Holy Jerusalem. I prefer to die under occupation rather than give concessions or accept servility," said the Chairman. Arafat saw this as "Israeli occupation replaced with Israeli sovereignty." Nor was he impressed by an additional proposal to have the UN Security Council confer diplomatic status on the State of Palestine for the Haram al-Sharif. Clinton's pressure was truly bullying, but Arafat resisted it. He would not be, he insisted, the Arab leader who would give up Jerusalem. He would also reject an American suggestion to resolve everything, including in Jerusalem, but defer the Temple Mount issue, an idea that Hassan Asfour had come up with in a conversation with Clinton.

Snubbed by Arafat, Clinton did not give up. He came back to him later in the day to press, ardently I was told, an improved deal that offered a state in 92 percent of the West Bank plus 2 percent swapped land within Israel, and a Jerusalem solution based on the partition of the Old City. Arafat again flippantly dismissed the offer. There was no map attached to Clinton's last offer, but Map 1 is a reflection of what can be seen as the final Camp David proposal (it understates the offer, though, for it does not show the location of the 2 percent land swap).

It was all to no avail. The best Clinton could get from Arafat was a demand to interrupt the summit so that he could consult his people and Arab leaders free of the suffocating pressure of Camp David. Clinton rightly saw it as an escape, and turned him down. Barak's knee-jerk reaction to this demoralizing setback was to ask us all to get prepared for flying back home. That was the worst of all scenarios, returning home empty handed when all our concessions were exposed to the public. As for the Palestinians, their recurrent pattern of behavior was truly a cause of despair. Whenever a major offer was on the table, even as just a "basis" for further negotiations, as indeed was the case with Barak's ideas, they would ask for "clarifications," and then turn down the whole thing.

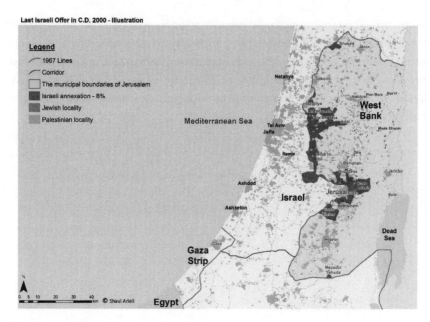

Map 1 Last Offer at Camp David, July 2000

At a working meeting Gilead Sher and I had later in the day with the Palestinian team, Saeb Erakat responded in an apocalyptic mood to our urging that they seize Barak's proposals as *the* opportunity in this summit. "Maybe the lights are turning down. None of us knows when they will be put on again. It is entirely possible that Arafat is interested in a crisis," he said. Arafat was getting ready for the crisis, for he now came to the conclusion that Israel's most far-reaching proposals would never meet his most fundamental requirements unless he forced her to through a confrontation that would "put on the lights" again.

Back home, friends and rivals would later accuse us of not having a Plan B, such as a partial agreement, for example. But it was Arafat who led the summit into the mortal path of either a comprehensive settlement that met all his expectations or a confrontation. Now, in his effort to convince us to stay, Clinton was acting to prevent the war that he felt would ensue from a disorderly collapse of the summit. "This is terrible, we are going from here to war," he told us during a brief exchange before he arrived, for the first time at the summit, smartly dressed in a suit, to see Barak before taking the flight to Japan.

Barak finally understood that it was wiser to stay, but he would not allow substantive negotiations before the president's return from Japan. He only allowed an exception for the search for a formula on Jerusalem's holy sites. To Clinton he said that if Arafat accepted Barak's deposit as an agreed starting point, formal negotiations could resume. Clinton accepted this formula. But it turned out that he did not mention to Arafat his understanding with Barak about the agreed ground rules for further engagement.[4] And so, with the president's departure, the summit became trapped in a bizarre, Rashomon-like set of differing perceptions. Secretary Albright was left with the ungrateful task of untying the imbroglio.

Albright's Intermezzo, Clinton's Last Push

With Albright at the helm, Barak was not prepared to address a series of requests by Arafat for "clarifications" of his peace offer. The prime minister secluded himself in his cabin and would respond in combative style to any American approach for engagement:

> *I am not prepared to sit down with Arafat, he said to the Secretary, just so that he can say he had sat down with Barak and told him no. We have used an entire arsenal of ammunition and Arafat hasn't fired a single shot . . . negotiations aren't just a matter of asking questions . . . Arafat has to be forced to negotiate because after eight months, eight weeks, and eight days he hasn't even started to negotiate in any real way.*

Arafat would respond in kind, although it is not clear at what point exactly he did it. Did Dennis Ross get it wrong when he reassured me that Arafat's pledge of 8–10 percent of Palestinian land for Israeli blocs of settlements was fully documented, and Arafat could not "wriggle out of it?" His aides actually claimed that Arafat did wriggle out of it either immediately after he had offered it or at some other moment in the summit.[1] But, Clinton was not impressed, and to the last day of the summit he acted on the basis of Arafat's 8–10 percent pledge.

Albright's interlude was not entirely uneventful, however. Barak allowed me to discuss with the State Department's legal adviser Jonathan Frankel possible wording with respect to the Temple Mount. After discussing a wide variety of options, Frankel put together an American paper, essentially built, he said, on the principles upon which US rule in Guantanamo Bay and British rule in Hong Kong were based:

- There would be an agreement between Israel and the UN securing legitimate Israeli needs, such as prayer on the Mount, a prohibition on excavations, recognition of Israel's control over the Western Wall, and international supervision of the Palestinian Custodian.

- The United Nations would appoint the Custodian and determine the ground rules upon which the Custodian would be authorized to operate.
- Palestinian law would apply in cases where Israelis were not involved.
- There would be a Palestinian office and a Palestinian flag on the Mount, as well as protected access to the Haram al-Sharif.
- A reasonable area for Jewish prayer would be established under the protection of the Government of Morocco and the Palestinian authorities.

Barak agreed with the paper's approach, but he ruled out any possible use of the term sovereignty as in any way defining the status of the Palestinians on the Mount, no matter how qualified it was. He refused to accept that the adjective "custodial" restricted and limited the term "sovereignty" as Frankel had suggested, and he protested that sooner or later we would have a full Palestinian sovereignty in the Mount. As usual, however, Barak did not have to worry too much. Arafat would turn down any formula that was not clear, unequivocal, adjective-free Palestinian sovereignty.

Against so many odds, we resorted again to our backchannel with Muhammad Rashid and Mohammed Dahlan with Dennis Ross's presence. Rashid weighed a number of options on the Haram al-Sharif, from sovereignty for the parties to sovereignty for none or for a third party. For the first time I raised the possibility of Palestinian recognition of Israel's "symbolic" link to the site, not necessarily sovereignty, an idea that I would develop further six months later in negotiations with a Palestinian team ahead of the presentation of the Clinton peace parameters.[2] A glimpse of hope appeared with the arrival of the Director of the CIA, George Tenet, who also managed to get from Arafat his acceptance of the Clinton/Barak ideas "with reservations." What were they? Arafat also wanted the Armenian quarter and full Palestinian sovereignty over the inner neighborhoods. Brilliant, and typical Arafat style. His qualified yes was always, in practical terms, a resounding no. He would repeat that very tactic when presented six months later with the take-it-or-leave-it Clinton peace parameters.

Secretary Albright did her best in an impossible situation. She interspersed the few discussions about the issues with social occasions, among them a festive dinner she arranged to warm the frosty atmosphere. But, tactless and unbecoming, Barak refused to exchange a single word with Arafat, whom he looked at disdainfully. He sat with arms tightly folded, highly irascible, and looking as if this was the very last place in the world that he wanted to be. Arafat's attempts to be amiable and connect, in effect to butter him up, proved utterly futile. Gentlemanly deference and urbanity were clearly in short supply at this summit. Barak claimed that there was only one test of Arafat's intentions: a positive answer to the president's ideas. Without this "no amount of eating baklava together will help," he said to the Secretary of State. Albright, an American of Czech origin, was unlikely, I thought, to ever have come across this sticky sweet. I was standing beside a wall clock in the dining room when Barak, who was known for his technical dexterity, approached me to wager that if an agreement was reached with "that character," Arafat, he would make the broken clock on the wall work. Barak's aides could also make fake news fly. First thing the following day, July 21, the early morning news in Israel carried what sounded like a deliberate briefing planted by Barak's people. It said Amnon Lipkin-Shahak and I were pressuring the prime minister to make concessions on Jerusalem. Someone was looking for scapegoats responsible for the ultimate political sin, the division of Jerusalem.

The contradictions and twists in Barak's mood never ceased to surprise. His self-imposed two-day seclusion proved to be the prelude to a revitalized and vigorous approach to the negotiations. Full of fire and determination, he suddenly became avid for re-engagement. He looked fully revived and assured us that if Arafat were to accept Clinton's proposals, he would find himself facing an open-minded Barak willing to extend even further his boundaries of compromise on Jerusalem as well as on other core issues, and join the *ra'is* in an historic agreement. He also offered Secretary Albright a reshaped version of his earlier proposal, in which he fell back on my idea of a special regime in the Old City, and was more generous with regard to Palestinian sovereignty in the inner Jerusalem neighborhoods. If Arafat turned down his new ideas, he would be left with only one option, uniting the people of Israel around him for the inevitable showdown. Torn as he was by these two very different possible outcomes, Barak instructed the delegation to continue drafting an agreement, to make progress on the legal aspects of a possible settlement, and even to examine the schedule for dismantling the settlements if an agreement was reached.

We (Amnon Lipkin-Shahak, Yossi Ginossar, and I) were now also allowed to respond to the Secretary of State's invitation to what she termed a "substantive" meeting with Arafat. We found the Palestinian leader humiliated and indignant. "Why is this man Barak behaving toward me as if I am a slave?" he had asked Secretary Albright. I tried to convince him of the wonders of custodianship over the Temple Mount. I told him that such an arrangement would greatly enhance his international status, to an extent unprecedented in the history of the Palestinian people. Within the Islamic world, I told him, he would hold a position equivalent to or perhaps even more central than that held by the Saudi royal family as the custodians of the Kaaba, the most sacred site in Islam. But, why would I succeed where Clinton failed? "Making concessions that I am forbidden to make would lead to a rebellion against me and possibly to my assassination," he claimed. He also advised me that Israel should be satisfied with being sovereign over the Jewish quarter while the Palestinians would have sovereignty over the Christian, Muslim, and Armenian quarters.

Encouraged by Barak's newfound dynamism, we made on the morning of Sunday, July 23, a further effort to grapple with the issue of Jerusalem. But, Erakat lost no time in pouring cold water on our enthusiasm. He was not truly willing to engage; he spoke in funereal tones warning of the demise of the Palestinian peace camp, should the summit fail. Gamal Helal described to me in dramatic terms the American view of Palestinian conduct in the negotiations: "They are stupid for not accepting the deal as it stands. They are missing an historic opportunity. They will forfeit a strategic asset gained over recent years, namely, their special relations with the United States."

The accumulation of bad news coming from our meetings with the Palestinians made Barak's resurrection a short-lived affair. The rift in his mind, his erratic oscillation between negotiations and disengagement, became his working method. One moment he would promise an alternative package of Palestinian sovereignty in "one and a half neighborhoods outside the wall," the next he would threaten that "there must be a price for Arafat's hesitations." He also fell back on his dream of setting up a government of national unity and returning to Washington with Natan Sharansky and Ariel Sharon. It was, of course, a delusion to assume that a change of government would change the Palestinians' price for peace. To this very day in 2021, although they had been battered and defeated by long years of Intifada and an extraordinarily effective Israeli occupation, there had not been even a slight crack in the positions they had been defending with such vigor at Camp David and after. It looked as if Barak was driven by resentment and anger at Arafat for having gotten the better of him tactically. The Jerusalem question had persistently gnawed at him, and now that he had finally made a proposal which he considered an unprecedented gesture of magnanimity, Arafat exposed him as a clumsy gambler, ignored the proposal, and moved on. Unlike Barak's spasmodic attitude to the negotiating process, Arafat was remarkably consistent in his objectives and moves. His delaying tactics and his fundamentalist positions played into the hands of Barak's other personality, the one that could not come to terms with the far-reaching compromises he had agreed to. And, indeed, minutes before Clinton's arrival from Japan, Barak shocked the Secretary of State when he resiled from his proposals on Jerusalem in a way that downgraded the status of the Palestinian neighborhoods and also replaced his offer of partition of the Old City with a special regime under Israeli sovereignty. That was Barak's way of punishing Arafat for his stand, but it was also his attempt to cut his political losses and avoid increasing the stakes, given that, as it turned out, all his previous proposals were leaked by the Palestinians to their press back home.[3] He felt that Arafat's tactics had dragged him into a politically prohibitive drift toward surrender which he needed to stop.

* * *

Indeed, once Clinton was back from the G8 in Japan, Sandy Berger informed him that Barak's peace offer, his Old City initiative included, had been withdrawn. Barak would also personally brief the president of his reduced proposal: "These are the limits of what I can make the Israeli public accept so long as Arafat insists on the right of return. If he gives it up, I will make further concessions. This is not about tactics. This is the simple truth."[4]

The summit was, then, again left without an organizing principle. But in spite of the recent contretemps, Gamal Helal assured me that the president was in a determined mood and would not allow speeches to the gallery stating maximum demands such as a return to the 1967 borders or Resolution 194 about refugees. If there was no agreement at the end of all the coming rounds, he said, the Americans would present their own position on all the issues on a take-it-or-leave-it basis. If only the Americans had put this threat into action! If only the president of the world's only superpower had ruthlessly twisted arms and forced the two sides into a decision! If it was to be done, it had to be done decisively and unambiguously, and that was not Clinton's way. But, to his great credit, he never gave up. All through the night of July 24–25, from just before midnight until 6:00 the next morning, neither he nor CIA Director George Tenet left the room in which the Israeli-Palestinian security working groups had convened.

Four hours later, in a testament to his indomitable vitality, Clinton was already sitting down for a lengthy disquisition with the groups dealing with refugees. "I am ready to do all it takes," he told an Israeli delegation amazed by his determination despite him having to listen to things that would quickly drive any ordinary mortal to utter despair. In the debate about refugees, Clinton asked Nabil Shaath for his estimate of how many refugees they would demand be allowed to return to Israel. "10–20 percent" replied Shaath. The incredulous president jumped up as if bitten by a snake: "It is your intention that between 400,000 and 800,000 refugees would return to Israel?" Others were more determined than Shaath. "An insistence on the right of every refugee to return home," was how Akram Haniyah, an Arafat confidant at Camp David, would define the Palestinian position in a series of articles in the Palestinian Authority's newspaper *Al Ayyam* after the summit.[5] Elyakim Rubinstein was unmovable in rejecting the principle of the right of return, questioned the legal basis of the entire concept, and focused on the creation of an international compensation fund and the return of small numbers on a humanitarian basis. He also raised a counterclaim, which I never understood why it should be a Palestinian concern, of compensation for the hundreds of thousands of Jews expelled from Arab countries in the wake of the 1948 war. The discussion on refugees got trapped in the same paralysis that affected the negotiations on territory. Just as Israel could not accept the principle of the 1967 borders and only then get down to discussing the details, Israel could not endorse the even more compromising right of return and only later discuss the numbers. Once the principle of return was accepted, Israel would find herself debating numbers she could never accept.

Conversely, the working group on security, on which Gilead Sher and Shlomo Yanai faced Abu Ala and Mohammed Dahlan, made some progress. Dahlan did not object to early warning stations being manned by Israelis, provided there was a symbolic American presence. Abu Ala did not entirely reject the Israeli Air Force's use of Palestinian airspace on the condition that it did not affect their commercial flights. Clinton noted the significance of demilitarizing the future Palestinian state and left open for debate the composition of the Palestinian force and the weaponry that it would carry. The Palestinians insisted that their state be described as having "limited armaments" not as "demilitarized." Gilead Sher officially informed those present that Barak accepted an international force being stationed in the Jordan Valley. The Palestinians, however, resisted invasive Israeli security requirements such as supply bases in the Jordan Valley, three roads across their state for emergency access to the valley, and Israeli control of Palestine's electromagnetic spectrum and its border crossings with Egypt and Jordan. "Your security theories are suffocating us," exclaimed Dahlan. Nor would he be convinced by General Yanai's offer that the Palestinian state get security guarantees from both Israel and the United States as an integral part of the peace agreement.

In the team discussing borders there was a novel development. For the first time ever, the Palestinians presented Gilead Sher with a map outlining their suggestions for the settlement blocs. This was a proposal for isolated "spots" connected to the 1967 line by links that were like flimsy shoelaces. Gilead Sher told Abu Ala that, apart from being geographically and politically unacceptable, the Palestinian proposal could not accommodate more than 30 percent of the settlers. The blocs were mere isolated and narrow enclaves that could be disconnected and cut off any time there was a random outbreak of violence. The Palestinians had tried to close the gap between our positions and theirs over the territorial issue when their cartographer, Samih el-Abed, presented us with a map of counterproposals. But it only allowed for settlement blocs of 2.5 percent of the West Bank that could accommodate no more than 35 percent of the settlers. We responded with an improved Israeli proposal that reduced our claims to 8.8 percent annexation from our previous 10.5 percent. The Palestinians could note at this stage that they had been offered about 91 percent of the West Bank and the entire Gaza Strip. They turned down the idea.

Given the polarized positions on borders and territory, it was decided that each party would present its views to the president separately. When it was my turn, Clinton wanted to know whether the settlement blocs would also be able to absorb additional settlers in the future. My reply was that once the territory ceased to be "occupied" and became an integral part of the sovereign territory of

Israel, it would be open to all Israelis. The same applied, I said, to the Palestinians wishing to live in territories they would get inside Israel as part of the land swaps. Dennis Ross went back to exploring the idea that reducing the size of the blocs would make it possible to forgo swaps altogether. That was an exceedingly optimistic supposition. Since Sweden, the Palestinians had insisted that annexation by Israel would have to be compensated for by an exchange of territories equal both in size and in quality.

I wondered how Dennis's optimism and the renewed vigorous involvement of the president could be reconciled with Martin Indyk telling me that very evening that Clinton was "in a state of despair." I again pleaded that the Americans, who knew what the positions of the two sides really were, should have defined those areas of disagreement that could realistically be bridged and drawn up a plan of their own. My advice to Indyk was made in the form of an improved proposal on Jerusalem which I handed to him on my own initiative in the hope that this could bring us closer to an endgame: full Palestinian sovereignty in the outer neighborhoods and "limited sovereignty" in the inner ones, a special regime for the Old City, and Palestinian "sovereign jurisdiction" or "sovereign custodianship" on the Haram al-Sharif. I gathered that Barak, who did not oppose the ideas of the State Department's legal adviser, Jonathan Frankel, would reconsider his rejection of an adjective being added to Palestinian sovereignty in the upper esplanade of the Temple Mount, assuming, of course, that this made a deal. Clinton would eventually see Arafat to discuss these ideas. Arafat turned them down again.[6]

Our Faintest Hour

In Saeb Erakat diary's vivid description of Clinton's meeting with Arafat on the morning of July 27,[1] Arafat's resistance to Clinton's and George Tenet's stampede was nothing less than heroic. His stamina was truly remarkable. Somber and acerbic, Clinton reviewed all past missed opportunities by the Palestinians from 1947 to the present, pleaded with the already peevish and temperamental *ra'is* to accept compromises in the pursuit of the greater cause of peace, and then threatened to cut off US relations with the Palestinians, end all financial aid, and declare the PLO a terrorist organization. "You will become a pariah in the Middle East, and be the reason," he shouted at him, "that the Haram will stay under Israeli sovereignty." To no avail. Gravely defiant, Arafat refused to be prodded, nor was he overawed by the president. He claimed to be the defender of the rights of both Muslims and Christians in Jerusalem, and he had no intention of betraying them. He would rather die than accept such proposals. "Do you want to come to my funeral?" he asked the president for the umpteenth time this summit. "Even if you offer me a state, and Haifa, and Jaffa I would not accept it unless it includes sovereignty on the Haram." Four years later, Arafat allegedly made a similar reflection: "Had they given me Al-Quds and the Al-Aqsa Mosque, I would have given them everything."[2] To Clinton's amazement, Arafat told him that the Israelis should be thankful to him, the real owner of the holy city, for conceding to them both the Western Wall and the Jewish quarter, even though the Western Wall had the status of an Islamic trust. "I cannot give them one more square meter," said the *ra'is*. "Are you asking me to sell the Christian holy places, such as the Church of the Holy Sepulcher and the Via Dolorosa, as well as the Islamic holy places?" The man truly saw himself as a cross between Saladdin and Richard the Lionheart. With such delusions of grandeur, the only thing left for the exasperated Clinton to do was to bring down to earth his elusive interlocutor. He had no right to speak on behalf of the Pope, he told him. Nor did he deserve an encomium for his access of generosity with assets he did not own. "Do you think you should get a medal for saying they can have the Jewish quarter?" he asked acidly.

But did we, who accused Arafat of being trapped in his own mythologies, not miss here a historic opportunity for not being hostage to our own myths? For what Arafat was proposing here was a truly grand historical bargain: Arab Jerusalem and Islam's holy sites in exchange for all the rest.

Jerusalem clearly weighed too heavily on our conscience and overcame us. A compelling counterargument is, of course, how long it would have taken the Palestinians to rebel against a peace based on Arafat's betrayal, for the sake of his Jerusalem fetish, of the entire Palestinian patrimony. Everything now converged, then, on a last attempt to crack the question of Jerusalem, which would make or break the entire summit. Barak agreed that I and Saeb Erakat should meet that same evening with the president and his entire team for a final try.

It was 9:00 p.m. when we started our meeting at the president's residence. Erakat's opening remarks indicated that he did not come to negotiate; for him the summit was over. He talked about the achievements of the summit, the "excellent atmosphere," and the possibility of continuing the talks after we dispersed. The deadline for an agreement, he said, was September 13, the date on which the Palestinians had threatened to declare unilaterally a Palestinian State. To his credit, Erakat was consistent. This was the position he had defended in the pre-summit meeting at the State Department. An agreement, he then said, could not be reached in one leap. Camp David was merely one phase in a longer journey.

My opening statement went through the series of moves and proposals on Jerusalem we had advanced at the summit, including our acceptance of Clinton's partition of the Old City into two sovereignties. I ended in an ominous tone:

> We are going from here into a catastrophe. You will forge an alliance with Hamas. On our side, the peace camp having been battered and diminished, we will opt for national unity. In the next phase you will confront us with your weapons of terror, while the West Bank will have been filled by even more settlements. It will take many years for the Israeli peace camp to recover from this defeat.

Erakat presented the Palestinian position on Jerusalem, which amounted to a clear-cut partition of the city and unqualified Palestinian sovereignty over the Temple Mount. I raised in response the ideas I had presented earlier to Ambassador Indyk.[3] The proposed Palestinian custodianship of the Temple Mount, I said, elevated Arafat to the status that the House of Saud had in the holy shrines of Mecca, and would make him the defender of the faith of a billion Muslims. To facilitate the debate, Clinton put a map of Jerusalem on the table. I asked Erakat whether, if, in the context of a wider agreement, I could bring Barak to agree to the Palestinians having qualified sovereignty over all the inner neighborhoods, not just the two he had in mind, he could get Arafat to agree that there be a special regime in the Old City, instead of it being partitioned. I actually proposed a conditional full-fledged partition of the city into two sovereignties along ethnic lines while keeping the Old City in a special regime. Strangely, Erakat understood this as implying Israeli sovereignty, and I had to correct him that a special regime meant that the two parties would have qualified, "soft sovereignty."

It was clear that Erakat was not authorized to negotiate. He preferred to focus on the issue of the Temple Mount, where he could more conveniently claim that Israel's position was lacking. Dennis Ross suggested a formula of a Palestinian "custodial or religious sovereignty" on the Mount and leaving Israel with the "remaining sovereignty." Erakat suggested that both sides concede sovereignty. That was an interesting proposal, but entirely unrealistic, for not even Erakat really believed that Arafat would agree to concede sovereignty over the Temple Mount. Erakat then engaged in what was always the response of my Arab interlocutors whenever I mentioned Jewish millennial roots in Jerusalem, particularly on Temple Mount. In his fanciful strategy of historical manipulation, Arafat would sometimes claim that the Jewish Temple Mount was actually in Nablus, or perhaps, he once said, in Yemen or Saudi Arabia. Our learned friend Erakat claimed that the whole story of the Temple was just a Jewish invention with no historical basis. Everyone knew, I said, the basic archaeological fact that in the course of history holy places, cities, and settlements were built in successive layers, one upon the other. Hence, just as the Al-Aqsa Mosque was built in that location because the Temple was underneath, the original Jewish Temple was probably built on the ruins of a pagan holy site.

Clinton intervened and, quite emotionally, exclaimed that not only did all the Jews in the world believe that the Temple was there but so did most Christians as well. In an exchange of written notes, the president asked me, "Did you mean to put the sovereignty of the Muslim and Christian quarters back on the table?" To which I wrote back: "If Arafat will accept this as a solution, you will have a strong argument with Barak. Although he had asked the idea to be taken off, he nevertheless wanted you to get an answer from Arafat." The president then proceeded to make practical proposals:

- "Qualified sovereignty" for the Palestinians in all the Arab inner-city neighborhoods.
- A division of sovereignty between Israel and the Palestinians in the Old City, two quarters to each side.
- The Palestinians would be accorded custodial sovereignty over the Temple Mount.

• All the outlying Arab neighborhoods of Jerusalem would come under full Palestinian sovereignty.

Even though Clinton had gone here a step closer to the *complete* partition of Jerusalem, his was a proposal that we could accept. It was not substantively different than the one I had defended earlier. While I spoke of a special regime in the Old City, the president preferred his original idea, which Barak had anyway already accepted, of dividing it in two. As to Clinton's "qualified sovereignty" for the Palestinians in the inner neighborhoods, Barak had agreed to two such neighborhoods, and earlier in the meeting I had taken the liberty of saying that extending the concept to the rest of the neighborhoods was a possibility as well. "Qualified sovereignty" for the Palestinians for the inner neighborhoods and "custodial sovereignty" for the Temple Mount were proposals I had made earlier to Martin Indyk, and Clinton went with these to Arafat only to be rebuffed by him.[4] Though they were not easy to digest, I had no doubt whatsoever that Barak would not turn these ideas down if Arafat accepted them as the ultimate breakthrough, or even as a basis for further talks.

Yet, when the President asked me to address his proposal, I told him that that was the time for the Palestinians to be the first to answer. I had no right to maneuver Barak into yet another situation where he accepted a proposal, as he did with his idea of splitting the Old City, only to be rebuffed by Arafat and be exposed back home to a political lynching, while Arafat pocketed yet another Israeli move without this leading to an agreement. After we had accepted his proposal to divide the Old City, I said, the only thing we got from Arafat was the cold shoulder. I needed now to be in a position to say to Barak that I had a yes from Arafat. The American team could safely understand my statement as a conditional yes. There was no reaction from Erekat. Sandy Berger and Madeleine Albright addressed him bluntly. Sandy: "How come you don't understand that at last you will have a credible state, and the problem of the refugees will be resolved?"

The president and his team then consulted briefly among themselves in a side room. When they returned, Clinton presented two alternative packages for us to choose between. The first was the one he had suggested earlier, but with the Old City in a special regime and Palestinian custodianship on the Haram al-Sharif; the second was about postponing for five years just the question of the Old City, while the status quo was maintained. During this period the Palestinians would not relinquish their demand for sovereignty.

Erekat rejected the idea of deferral and, in a kind of throwaway line he suggested that, if so, we could also defer the issue of the refugees. But, although postponing these two thorniest of issues meant that Israel would give away more than 90 percent of the land, while the Palestinians and the Arab world kept up the pressure on the two most potentially destabilizing issues, I did not object to the deferral or to a variation proposed by Sandy Berger of postponing only the issues of the Old City and the Temple Mount. But the discussion was becoming entirely academic. On countless occasions Arafat had said categorically that he would not accept leaving in abeyance the Jerusalem question under any formula whatsoever. He did so again in a written reply to Clinton's proposals only a few hours after the president presented it to him at the end of our meeting. From Arafat's point of view nothing that anyone had said during this debate had made the slightest difference. It should have been clear to all in that meeting that had Arafat agreed, Israel would not have blocked the adoption of any of the president's proposals. Clinton would indeed telephone Barak that same night with his Jerusalem proposals. Barak did not oppose them.[5]

It was now close to 1:00 a.m. Erekat was sent off by Clinton to get Arafat's reply. The president's assistants retired to their own rooms, and for a few minutes I was left to talk alone with him. In front of me, I saw an exhausted president having to face the probable failure of the main foreign policy objective of this last phase of his administration. I found myself in the role of comforter. I reminded the president how Jimmy Carter spent eight months of his presidency completing the agreement after his summit at Camp David. He went to the region, appeared before the Knesset, tied up loose ends, applied pressure, and twisted people's arms. Admittedly, not a brilliant analogy. In fact, at that moment, Clinton had precisely eight months left as president. Although he insisted he would fight until his last day in the White House, the truth was that with each passing day he was becoming more and more of a lame duck, with his ability to be effective diminishing by the day. Camp David I came in the middle of Carter's term of office. Clinton got there at the end of his second term and had to work with what little political capital he had left. One could only feel compassion at the sight of the president of the world superpower as he stood, dressed in a pair of ragged jeans, exhausted and helpless, venting his anger at Arafat. As his level of fury soared, so did his appearance of helplessness. Before I left the president's cabin, Clinton sent the Director of the CIA, George Tenet, in a final attempt to avert the *ra'is*'s habitual response. He pleaded with him that even if he rejected Clinton's ideas, he should make a counterproposal of his own to allow the negotiating process to continue.

But, when Erakat returned with a written reply just before 3:00 a.m., it was officially confirmed that Arafat, who had given the thumbs down to each and every Jerusalem proposal throughout the summit, had now studiously ignored Clinton's last ideas, repeated now his basic positions, and made no counterproposals. Clinton described this to Barak: "Erakat almost cried, and told me 'Arafat would be 72 next month; he is incapable of making a decision, although I myself think that an agreement is possible.'"[6]

Arafat had not come to Camp David to *negotiate* about Jerusalem. He had come to impose his one and only solution, and did not make the slightest move from that position throughout the entire proceedings. Real estate assets—borders, security—did not really matter to him, not even refugees that much. Only through Jerusalem could he express both his Muslim and his nationalist purity. Jerusalem and refugees were two battle cries that produced a great deal of passion in the Muslim world. Arafat used this passion as a weapon, but at the same time was shackled by it. He did not have the courage needed to break free, nor did he really want to. Only later did I learn that three days before this last meeting with President Clinton, Al-Aqsa's imam had issued a statement warning that:

> what is being debated at Camp David is the illegitimate existence of a Jewish state on Islamic soil. This debate is a total betrayal. We must not forget that during the Crusader conquests, when the Al-Aqsa Mosque was used as a stable for the conqueror's horses, the Muslims did not dare to compromise with the invaders on the eastern part of the city.

During the final hours at Camp David, Akram Sabri, the Mufti of Jerusalem, issued a fatwa that completely rejected the idea of "religious sovereignty" over the Temple Mount. "In Islam," he stated, "separation between religion and state does not exist. Muslims cannot accept religious sovereignty while Israel maintains political sovereignty." He claimed that the whole of Palestine was holy to Muslims and any compromise would be tantamount to the sale of Islamic soil. He also rejected any compromise on the right of return or its "purchase" by means of compensation. He went so far as to insist that, on the same strict religious principle, refugees who did not want to return would not even be entitled to compensation.

There was no agreement at Camp David because of these two fundamental issues, refugees and Jerusalem. Arafat could not move because he had entrenched himself in an uncompromising fundamentalist ethos. At times, it looked as if we were negotiating with an imam or mufti possessed by credal dogmas rather than the leader of an essentially secular national movement. "It's hopeless," said Dennis Ross, throwing up his hands to signify defeat. "Arafat is simply unable to make a decision on Jerusalem." Clinton would later share with Barak his own interpretation of the Palestinian predicament: "Arafat lives in a virtual world, not in the real world where we are all forced to explore alternatives and take decisions, With the Palestinians this works differently because they had been living for so many years with a heavy sense of victimhood."[7]

Our last team meeting at dawn was a bitter, somber occasion. Yossi Ginossar, who came back from a meeting with the Palestinian "young guard," reported that they were not siding with Arafat. Assuming this was true, what difference did this make right now? The subtleties of relations within the Palestinian delegation had worn me out. What did the notions of "majority" and "minority" mean in an organization that lacked any form of democratic governance? Our efforts have been halted because the other side has insisted that they had to have complete sovereignty over the Temple Mount, said Barak. Amnon Lipkin-Shahak, representing possibly the far left in our delegation and normally a critic of Barak's zigzagging tactics, also believed that we had done everything possible and that the sad outcome was the result of Arafat's utter inflexibility on Jerusalem. But even as Barak wanted to warn us of the awfulness of imminent catastrophe, he lingered on a peroration of resolve and statesmanship. We needed, he said, to avoid a complete rift. He believed that, in the course of the summit, we had been able to narrow down and focus on the issues that represented the real nucleus of our position. He thought that by doing this we had made it easier to achieve national unity in the event of confrontation.

I seconded the prime minister's attitude and advised not allowing frustration and anger to blind us to the summit's achievements. Despite everything, the Camp David summit had signaled a breakthrough in Palestinian thinking. The Palestinians were the only Arab side that had been willing to compromise on territory, agree to invasive security arrangements, and even indirectly recognize the legitimacy of the settlements, by accepting the principle of the blocs, although, admittedly, in a nonviable, meager shape. We had to maintain the momentum and avoid a descent into violence. We had no interest in seeing the total collapse of the Palestinian Authority, or in passions being inflamed. "We should not leave this place with a feeling of catastrophe and simply don our steel helmets and battledress." I also spoke of the gains we had made in our relationship with the United States. It was now clear that they supported our demand for changes to the 1967 borders and accepted that the settlements must be considered in determining the new border.

At 1:00 p.m., the president, the Secretary of State, and Sandy Berger came to say farewell to Barak. Everything needed to be done to prevent the area from sliding into conflagration and disaster, said Clinton. But it was clear that his main concern was how to help Barak politically. Clinton shared with Barak the same political pollsters (Stanley Greenberg, James Carville, and Robert Shrum) and the president was well aware of Barak's political predicament. His objective was shielding him and the Israeli peace camp from the domestic political fallout of the summit's failure, which trapped the Americans in a quandary. Condemning Arafat, as they eventually did, was against the rules of engagement they had agreed to ahead of the summit, nor did it exactly fit in with the need to protect the peace camp in Israel, because Arafat was, in a sense, that very camp's partner. Barak had a suggestion as to how the president could mitigate his political trouble. "Transfer the US Embassy to Jerusalem," he told him. That was a bridge too far, for Clinton still hoped to revive the process and would need the help of Arab states to do so.

Could something still have been salvaged from the five-minute-long farewell meeting of the leaders? Yossi Ginnossar claimed that during the night Arafat had promised him he would rethink his answer to the Jerusalem proposals. But Arafat did not come to that farewell meeting to say anything new. He remained mute on the issue; shyness was definitely not one of his characteristics.

Barak had been the one pushing for the summit, and it was he who now stood up to bear his responsibility with composure. "I carry the ultimate responsibility for the outcome of this summit, and for the fact that we still do not have an agreement and will have to continue to work to achieve it," he said, leaving a hopeful opening for the future. "Arafat's positions on the issue of Jerusalem prevented an agreement," he concluded. Jerusalem was clearly a major hurdle, but it also turned out to be a politically convenient tree to hang all sins and blunders on, theirs and ours.

Arafat: "Barak Has Gone beyond My Partner Rabin"

We returned with mixed emotions to a divided country. Some were disappointed by the outcome of the talks; others, especially on the right, were relieved. Our affliction was their *Schadenfreude*. The left wanted us to pursue negotiations even though the government was rapidly falling apart. Paradoxically, the Palestinians were the mirror image of the Israeli right; they left Camp David exuding a cheery sense of relief and liberation from a nightmare. "We did not miss an opportunity," wrote Abu Mazen. "We survived a trap . . . it was a prison,"[1] Abu Ala stated: "As soon as we passed through the gateway of Camp David, we began to joke foolishly amongst ourselves, like prisoners feeling the relief of release from their confinement . . . We were laughing with relief . . . it was like a celebration for our escape from a trap."[2] "The Joy of the Poor" is how the Israeli poet, Nathan Alterman, described the happiness of the wretched.

The lessons of Camp David were complex, filled with inconsistencies. Our official post-summit discourse was untrue, for the Palestinians did make concessions. But the discourse of pundits and political opponents who denigrated Barak was likewise unfair. Arafat himself would later demythologize his supposed belief in Rabin as a peacemaker. At Camp David, he confided to Dennis Ross that Barak had gone "beyond my partner Rabin."[3] A man of powerful convictions and reasoned statements, Barak had, however, no exceptional communication skills to help him prevail in the upcoming political battle, where he had to defend his concessions against the hawkish right without losing the left that blamed him for not going far enough.

We had returned home like dishonored prophets, while Arafat, by contrast, was welcomed as a national hero in the squalid sidestreets of Gaza. But Dahlan was right to tell him that "back in Gaza, you will be hailed as a Saladdin, but remember that Saladdin street in Arab Jerusalem would still be in Israel's hands." He returned empty-handed, with no state and no promise of a life of dignity for his people; yet they saw him as the sagacious leader who had faced up to an

Israeli-American conspiracy and prevailed. Akram Haniyah, a regular producer of paeans to Arafat, portrayed him in "The Camp David Papers" in the oleaginous terms befitting a persona almost transcending the boundaries of human history:

> In those sun-drenched days, Arafat fought one of the hardest campaigns of his life. He realized the extent of the trust that had been placed in him, and which committed him as the leader of a nation whose strength and pride derived from the fact that it was the protector of the holy places on its soil. This was not the pride that goes before a fall. Rather, it is a pride that imbues him with a sense of the weight of responsibility he carries as the leader of a campaign for the Palestinians, the Arab nations, the Muslim nations, and the Christians. It was his historic duty to defend the city linked to such great historical figures, beginning with the Khalif Omar al Khatib to Salah a-Din Alayoubi. It was his obligation to fight this battle alone.[4]

But amid the defiant rhetoric, a constant flow of intelligence reports spoke of "second thoughts" within the Palestinian camp, and a mood in favor of "being more flexible." A few days after our return, I met Mohammed Dahlan in Gaza. He lashed out at the "old guard," particularly Abu Mazen. "That man," he told me, "cannot be Arafat's successor." He reminded me how, following the Wye Agreement of October 1998, a few stones thrown outside Abu Mazen's house in protest at his failure to fight for the release of Palestinian prisoners had been enough to frighten him. In Dahlan's view, the tension that had emerged at Camp David between the "young guard" and the "veterans" would be a central factor in deciding the future of the process, and that it was his intention to take Abu Mazen to task. At Camp David, Dahlan told me, Arafat had lashed out at Abu Mazen for his focus on the refugee issue, saying, "Don't pester me with your nonsense about the refugees. I want Al-Quds." In response to my criticism of Arafat's conduct on Jerusalem, which had torpedoed the summit, Dahlan blamed the Saudis and the Egyptians, who had told Arafat to pay attention to Al-Quds but were unwilling to help him accept a compromise. I learned from him that Arafat had recruited him to appear before Palestinian audiences and express support "for the gains made at Camp David." In one such meeting he was quoted by an intelligence report as saying that during all the interim phases, the Palestinians gave nothing to Israel and only received from her. "We are not entitled to expect 100 percent of the territory," he told his audience. We were also heartened by news from the Vatican rejecting Arafat's pretensions to represent Christianity with regard to the holy places in Jerusalem. A few weeks after the summit, Vatican Foreign Minister Jean-Louis Tauran would confirm this to me in a meeting at his office.

Indefatigable and in full control of every nuance of the entire process, Gilead Sher recorded thirty-eight negotiating sessions between the parties from the end of the summit to the start of the Intifada. At the beginning, the Palestinians were uneasy and wanted to find a way out of the impasse. Muhammad Rashid went so far as to say that "when the Arabs understand what was offered to Arafat at Camp David, they will not be able to understand how we could reject it." Nabil Amr, a future minister of information who was to become one of the most articulate voices in opposing Arafat's recalcitrant approach to peace, said the Palestinians "had achieved a great deal at Camp David." Abu Ala agreed with Saeb Erakat's view that "at Camp David 80 percent of the problems had been resolved."

However, in the autocratic Palestinian system, all decisions were taken by Arafat in his own foggy way. In one of their meetings after Camp David, Saeb Erakat told Gilead Sher that he had "no idea what Arafat wanted," and didn't know "what the limits of my mandate in these talks are."

Arafat was in a real quandary. On the one hand, he wanted the peace talks to continue. At the same time, his acolytes were busy building his image as a modern-day Saladdin, a savior of all that was sacred to the nation of Islam. Sometimes he would pretend to be flexible; sometimes he would cling to a rigidly archaic fundamentalist position that Israel could never accept. Eventually he found himself stuck in a hopeless situation from which the only escape he could find was to surf into the violence of the Intifada that erupted at the end of September 2000. Arafat's embrace of armed resistance was also the result of the rough time he had during his tour of world capitals after Camp David. He had expected that Arab leaders would close ranks around him and tie his hands by subscribing to his red lines. He wanted a pan-Muslim summit that would arm him with a letter to Clinton stating that the Arab world would not allow him to concede the holy places. He got no such letter. The Arab leaders opted for staying on the sidelines, pleasing everyone by pleasing none. Arafat was anxious to gain the seal of approval for his maximalist positions from the guardians of anti-Zionist orthodoxy in Damascus, but Syria did not even agree to receive him.

For our part, immediately upon our arrival in Israel, Barak instructed me to work on the question of sovereignty in Jerusalem with a committee of experts. His determination to make progress was also shown by his willingness to sacrifice political credit to an extent that was clearly undermining his ability to keep the government together. That is not to say that everything was sweetness and light with our colleagues in the Labor Party. At a Labor faction meeting at the Ministry of Defense a few days after our return, Minister Haim Ramon, together with Shimon Peres assuming then the role of the disgruntled, attacked Barak in the most scathing terms for having even attempted to deal with the issue of Jerusalem. Peres believed we went too far in our concessions: we should have offered, he said, a Palestinian state in just 80 percent of the land, which, he claimed, he had checked out with the Palestinians.

But we were encouraged to pursue our peace efforts by Camp David's surprising impact on public opinion. For years, Israelis had been subject to hollow rhetoric, sheer wishful thinking, as to the price of peace. Camp David's shock treatment, as shown in a poll conducted by Dr. Mina Tzemach, increased support for the division of Jerusalem from only 5 percent to over 30 percent. I now suggested to Barak that he ask the Americans to record all that was agreed at Camp David so as to avoid denials and have an agreed platform upon which we could relaunch the process. But he even went further and asked Ambassador Indyk that the Americans offer bridging proposals. Meanwhile, we went about testing the credibility of the new diplomatic approach that seemed to be emerging in the Palestinian camp. Dr. Menachem Klein and Professor Ruth Lapidoth—the Jerusalem experts we worked with—offered us a wide array of concepts with regard to the more sensitive parts of Jerusalem. An idea that was toyed with was that of offering custodianship or sovereignty over Islam's holy places to a sort of *Dreikaiserbund*, a pact of the three kings of Jordan, Morocco, and Saudi Arabia.

The Egyptians were especially active. Dahlan and Muhammad Rashid worked in Egypt on an interfaith conference about "divine sovereignty" on the Temple Mount, where each side could be a custodian acting on behalf of the "divine sovereign." Amr Moussa would surprisingly suggest to Dennis Ross during a meeting in Cairo in the third week of August a qualified sovereignty—"sovereign jurisdiction"—for the Palestinians on the Haram al-Sharif and a similar status for us at the Wailing Wall. And at a meeting with me in Cairo on August 24, Moussa praised the progress made at Camp David, and even made creative proposals. His position on the Old City was not far from ours—a 2:2 division of quarters—which Arafat had rejected. He also tried to be positive about the refugee issue: he supported our concept of "family reunification," provided the number of returnees was "at least 100,000." He should surely have known that that was precisely the number that Israel had agreed to accept at the 1949 Lausanne Conference, and which the Arab delegates had then turned down. Alas, this hypercreativity was all immaterial; Arafat would turn down all these ideas when Dennis Ross later met him in Ramallah.

Sandy Berger was, however, rightly skeptical of the Egyptian role. They were merely trying to please the United States, but, said Berger, "They have disappointed us more than once." Berger's was an attitude not uncommon in Washington. Trent Lott, the Republican majority leader in the Senate, would reaffirm this to me during the UN Millennium General Assembly in September. "Egypt is mainly trying to make an impression on the United States," he said. And, as if to emphasize that Egypt was indeed a broken reed, Omar Suleiman, Egypt's minister in charge of the security services, told Yisrael Hasson on a visit to Cairo that Egypt would never accept Israeli political sovereignty over the Temple Mount, and, if necessary, Egypt would lead the whole Arab world in a struggle to prevent it. The creative ideas that had been conveyed to me in my meetings in Cairo with both Moussa and Mubarak on August 24 were later shifted under Palestinian pressure to unqualified Palestinian sovereignty. "No Muslim in the entire world would forgive Arafat if he lets the Israelis have sovereignty over Islam's holy sites," was now Mubarak's standpoint. That was a volteface that would not surprise Sandy Berger. That was their real position, which they would nuance whenever they needed to placate the Americans. Thus, on August 29, when Clinton met Mubarak in the VIP lounge of Cairo's international airport while his plane was refueling on its way to another destination, the Egyptians suggested entrusting the Temple Mount to the UN Security Council, an idea that was accepted by neither us nor the Americans, nor by the Palestinians for that matter.

The Temple Mount Rashomon was becoming an unremitting soap opera. Arafat would surprise Clinton at a meeting in Washington on September 7 with the idea that sovereignty could be vested in the Committee of Islamic States, which could then devolve jurisdiction to the Palestinians. According to Dennis Ross, who called to inform Barak of the meeting, Clinton, who was not happy with leaving this whole explosive issue in the hands of only Muslim leaders, suggested instead a consortium of the five permanent members of the Security Council plus four key Arab Muslim states: Saudi Arabia, Egypt, Morocco, and Jordan. The consortium would accord Arafat jurisdiction, with certain limitations on matters such as archaeological excavations. Barak rejected the Egyptian ideas with regard to the Temple Mount, but sounded to Dennis rather ambiguous with regard to the solution he might accept. He interpreted Barak's refusal to "surrender sovereignty over the Temple Mount to the Palestinians" as implying that he might not demand exclusive sovereignty for Israel, and might even waive it altogether. It was essential, though, as I had advised Sandy Berger, that the Al-Quds conference due to be held in Agadir under the chairmanship of the king of Morocco, Muhammad VI, would not block an agreement on Jerusalem. The Director of the CIA, George Tenet, would try to do just that, said Berger.

Another problem impeding progress was the fact that, oddly, the Americans had no written record of Camp David's deliberations and understandings. That much was admitted to me by Madeleine Albright, Sandy Berger, and Dennis Ross. Their mismanagement of the summit was such that they did not even have reliable, official records of it, as Dennis indeed confided to us. "We only have impressions drawn from non-official meetings with the parties," he said. The Egyptians then had their own version of the Camp David package. In my meetings with Amr Moussa in Cairo and later in Ismailia with President Mubarak, Moussa summed it up to me in a way that matched my own understanding of the proposed deal: a Palestinian state over 94 percent of the land, which was the 92 percent plus 2 percent of swapped land in Israel which Clinton had unilaterally offered Arafat.[5]

Not recording the Camp David package became, indeed, a serious source of trouble. The Americans realized that the constant Palestinian evasion of prior understandings, coupled with Arafat's penchant for globetrotting were combining to destroy all that had been achieved so far, which meant that our attempt to pursue the negotiations from some agreed point of departure became impossible. The Palestinians simply began to backtrack on practically every subject, an attitude that reached its peak during a negotiating session on August 16, when Dahlan repudiated Clinton's summary of the security issues, all of which had been recorded at the time by Gilead Sher. We fared no better on every other issue. During a negotiating meeting on August 27, Erakat brought up an extravagant "deal" whereby, in exchange for an end to conflict, Israel should accept the unrestricted implementation of the right of return. In other words, the disappearance of the Jewish state in exchange for an end to conflict with a state that had ceased to exist.

The Palestinians' behavior looked like an attempt to exploit our political distress. Our political time was clearly running out. We and the Palestinians were operating on the basis of two different timetables. Arafat did not need to make a deal until he was satisfied he had obtained everything he possibly could. Our political calendar was far shorter. We were also working under the threat of a possible Palestinian unilateral declaration of independence, which Barak defined as the ultimate attempt by Arafat to have a state while avoiding the price. If we needed some comfort, we got it, for a change, from the international community.

16

Reaping the Fruits of Success

My European trip started in Turkey on Thursday, August 10, immediately after Arafat had concluded his own visit there. The professionalism of Foreign Minister Ismail Çem and his team was impressive. During a three-hour meeting in Çem's house, we delved in detail into the issues under negotiation. We then moved to Prime Minister Bülent Ecevit's office. A sick man who looked older than his age, Ecevit had demonstrated a remarkable ability for political survival. He was an educated, broad-minded man who had actively supported the Palestinian cause all through his political career. I expected, though, that my line of reasoning about the dangers inherent in Arafat's espousal of Islamic extremism would resonate with the Kemalist, secular Ecevit. Both he and Minister Çem were adamant that Turkey would not allow her involvement in our peace process to interfere with the special ties between our two countries. That was a lot more than the European states, let alone our Arab neighbors, were willing to promise. The Turks were serious-minded and at all times ready to help by going into detail, which meant visits to Ankara were both rewarding and hard work. It was interesting to hear the undersecretary at the Foreign Ministry, Uğur Ziyal, confiding that they realized that it was not the Arab leaders who imposed on Arafat radical positions on Jerusalem, but the other way around. In particular, Arafat had asked the Turks to release documents from Turkish archives which would attest to the holy site's Islamic roots and the arrangements supposedly underlining predominant Muslim status in the site during the period of Ottoman rule.

My next stop was Barcelona for a meeting with the Spanish foreign minister, Josep Piqué. I also met Javier Solana, the EU's foreign policy chief. Solana, who had just moved from NATO to the thankless position of the EU's coordinator of foreign and security policy, tried to engage but did not have the support of a unified European foreign policy. He suggested that perhaps the Palestinians did not want to make tough decisions because they enjoyed the process too much. He also claimed that "the time has come for Arafat to step down." The problem, I advised, was that Arafat was the only one whose signature on a peace agreement could be seen as legitimate by his own people. From Spain

I journeyed to southern France for a meeting on August 13 with EU Foreign Affairs Commissioner Chris Patten at his vacation home in Albi. Patten was impressed by what had been achieved and the taboos, he said, that had been broken. The meeting was a particularly moving experience for me, not so much for its content as for its venue. This was the birthplace in the eleventh century of the "Albigensian heresy" and where the Inquisition had begun its activities. The visit to the magnificent Albi Cathedral was a refreshing trip in the time tunnel to my years as a student of medieval history. From Albi I went on to meet with the Italian prime minister, Giuliano Amato, who was vacationing in Tuscany. A man of refined tastes, with incisive observations and acute insights, Amato had no illusions about Arafat's nature. "You know, he comes here very often and cries on our shoulders," he told me. He pointed out that Arafat was a revolutionary leader who was incapable of making the transformation to becoming a statesman.

Tightening the diplomatic net around Arafat was also the objective in a meeting at the Vatican on the same day with the Holy See's foreign minister, Cardinal Jean-Louis Tauran. I told him that on the issue of Jerusalem, Arafat purported to represent Christians as well as Muslims. "Arafat's claim that he is the protector of the Christian holy places by virtue of an agreement with the Pope is without foundation," a civilized euphemism for a simple lie, the cardinal told me. "There never was any such agreement. What would happen tomorrow if Arafat were replaced by a fundamentalist Muslim leader? Would he be the protector of the Christian holy places too?" Cardinal Tauran had asked Nabil Shaath the same rhetorical question during Shaath's visit to the Vatican a few days earlier. Tauran did not think that either side should have sovereignty over the holy places. It would be better to allow "international bodies" to guarantee freedom of worship and access to the holy sites. When I commented that Israel did not like the principle of internationalization in Jerusalem, the cardinal retorted that the Holy See was not asking for internationalization, but rather wanted the holy sites to have a "special status."

Because Norway had a special connection to the process through the Oslo Accords, I thought it only right to telephone the Norwegian foreign minister, Thorbjørn Jagland, who updated me on Arafat's visit to that country. Arafat had apparently boasted about his extensive knowledge of Israeli politics. He assured the Norwegians that Barak had no problems in surviving politically and had room to maneuver in terms of concessions. This was true to an extent that was far more limited than Arafat's wishful assumptions. Arafat's utter insouciance about the political limits conditioning our peace policy would have a decisively adverse effect on the prospects of peace and would, moreover, usher in a calamity for the Palestinians as well. My Norwegian colleague understood this and suggested that pressure be put on those Europeans who were pandering to Arafat and "refusing to take him down off his high horse." Quite a few European leaders spoke in the same vein in private conversations, but they never brought themselves to truly force Arafat to accept the limits of what was possible. Germany's foreign minister, Joschka Fischer, a rare combination of a revolutionary who had become part of the establishment, an autodidact with a broad world view, and an eternally youthful spirit, was among the most empathic foreign statesmen we could dream of in Europe. He had outgrown the anti-Israel feeling common among his 1968 generation and had developed deep feelings of friendship for the Jewish State. In him, it also stemmed from a keen awareness of the unsettled account between Germany, the Jewish people, and Israel. Fischer was fully cognizant, though, of the limits of Europe's capacity for collective action on a foreign policy issue, Palestine in this case, in which the United States had a preponderant role.

Our globetrotting had to include the main Arab stakeholders, of course. The erratic behavior of the Egyptians reflected an oscillation between two opposed concerns, their need to endear themselves to the Americans and their fear of alienating the Palestinians. That placating America was now an immediate Egyptian concern was made patently clear to me when I met Mubarak in his palace on August 24. The president obsessively referred to a Thomas Friedman column in *The New York Times* harshly criticizing Egypt's ingratitude to America; she received generous US financial aid, yet cold-shouldered America when her support was needed. Mubarak could not conceal his fear of "street unrest" should Egypt be seen as imposing a deal on the Palestinians. Most of all, he dreaded turning the conflict into a religious one. Religious issues such as Jerusalem and the Temple Mount, he said, are a matter for the people. Governments could not dictate the people's beliefs. But why did only the view of Muslim peoples matter here, I wondered. The unwillingness of Arab leaders to even listen to the Israeli discourse on the holiness of the Temple Mount was a display of ignorance wrapped in conspiracy theories. The whole idea of a Jewish temple, they suspected, was invented to justify excavations that would cause the mosques to collapse. The Egyptian press joined in with a wave of contempt, ridicule, and ignorance. During one of my visits in Cairo, Moussa showed me a cartoon from an Egyptian newspaper with me carrying out excavations on the Temple Mount with a bible in my hand. Arafat's own rejection of any Jewish link to the Temple Mount was a reflection of his view of Zionism as a purely colonial movement with no roots whatsoever in the stolen lands of Palestine and its holy sites.

Two days before my trip to Cairo I had a meeting with the Jordanian foreign minister, Abdul Ilah el-Khatib, during King Abdullah's brief visit to Israel. Arafat, I said, wanted to represent Christianity as well; he wanted to be Saladin and Richard the Lionheart all rolled into one. Could he imagine, I asked, Ben-Gurion in 1948 refusing to declare independence and solve the worldwide Jewish refugee problem because Israel had no access to the Temple Mount or Rachel's

Tomb, let alone sovereignty over them? I differed with el-Khatib's assessment that Arafat would be able to compromise on Jerusalem or on the refugees, but not on both. Arafat showed no signs of willingness to compromise on Jerusalem, but seemed to accept a softer interpretation of the right of return than Abu Mazen's. Home to the largest community of Palestinian refugees, Jordan had a naturally keen interest in the refugees chapter. The Jordanian minister insisted that Israel accept the principle of the right of return and that the refugees be offered a choice between compensation and return. To assume that Israel would not only accept the principle of the right of return but would also engage in such an à la carte process was, of course, wildly far-fetched.

It was not only we and Arafat who went on pilgrimages round the region to seek support. Immediately after Camp David, Ned Walker, a former US ambassador to both Egypt and Israel, visited fourteen Arab countries in three weeks and returned with, as he put it, "a good feeling," quite an odd description of the content of his report. He did tell our ambassador in Washington, David Ivri, that wherever he went, the consensus was that a resolution on Jerusalem would lead to a solution of all the other issues. But he also admitted how fearful of their domestic public opinion his Arab interlocutors were. He mentioned Mubarak's obsession with internal security matters. Mubarak even asked Walker not to use the word "compromise" when referring to Jerusalem, because it made Muslims fear that they were compromising their religion. Unlike the Egyptians, the Saudis did not even try to pretend. "Of all the countries I visited, Saudi Arabia was the one whose position worries me most," Walker noted. Incidentally, as Sandy Berger would tell me in a telephone conversation on August 16, the Saudis, fearful of the fallout of divisive decisions on Palestine, were not at all enthusiastic about the Palestinian track having now been given priority. Like the Jordanians, they would have preferred Israel to have negotiated with Syria.

It was France's President Jacques Chirac who raised with Barak the need to co-opt Morocco into the process. The late King Hassan II, whom I had met in the early 1990s in Rabat, was a courageous and proactive statesman unapologetically committed to Israeli-Arab reconciliation. His heir was a more lukewarm player in that field. I arrived in Agadir on September 4 to meet with King Muhammad VI, who had been the leader of the Islamic States Conference held there a few days earlier. The king received me in his palace for a meeting at which a major role was played by his advisers, including two old friends of mine, Royal Counselor André Azoulay and Head of External Intelligence General Abdellah Kadiri. The foreign minister was Mohamed Benaissa, a native of Asilah, a city in northern Morocco that had at one time been a part of the Spanish protectorate. This had enabled us to speak in Spanish during our many telephone conversations.

Muhammad VI, Emir of the Believers and President of the All-Muslim Al-Quds Committee, could have played a vital role in reaching a settlement in Jerusalem, but his knowledge of some of the details was limited. He believed the Western Wall was tangential to the Al-Aqsa Mosque. I showed him an aerial photograph of Jerusalem, which I left him at his request. When I later shared over the telephone with Secretary Albright the anecdote about the location of the wall she replied, "Wait till I tell you about the Saudis; they know even less." Clinton himself realized when he tried to explain his Jerusalem deal to Saudi Crown Prince Abdullah that "Abdullah had never looked at a map of Jerusalem in his life." Egypt's Mubarak knew even less than Abdullah, as the American special envoy Ned Walker realized when he met him at about the same time.[1]

Muhammed VI's position was, "You must strive to attain parallel rights for the parties on the Temple Mount." I seized the opportunity to agree, saying that his formula of parallel rights might prevent dangerous wrangling over religion-based issues, and suggested that he invite spiritual leaders from the three religions to a meeting in Fez, in an attempt to depoliticize what was an essentially religious contention. The king took up this idea enthusiastically and instructed his people accordingly. On my return to Israel, I handed over this information to Michael Melchior, the Minister of Social and Diaspora Affairs, and he made contact with the Moroccans.

The entire meeting took place in a relaxed atmosphere and the king, in a gracious gesture, probably in tribute to my own Moroccan origins, escorted me out of the palace. I pleaded with him to help in facilitating an agreement before Clinton was gone. He thought, however, that it was unlikely a settlement could be reached during the Clinton presidency. Meeting the timetable imposed by the US elections and coping with the political situation in Israel might be harming the prospect of success in the talks, he said. He believed, though, that Arafat was not putting off making decisions "because he knows his time is running out." Eventually, the king's assessment was correct, but then so was mine. What other US President besides Clinton was going to delve so deeply into the issues? What other Israeli government would go as far as we had? And if such a combination of an engaged American president and a bold Israeli leader emerged again, would the parties have the courage to take the historic divisive decisions they are avoiding now? And what of all the blood that would be spilled in vain until then?

But, before the Second Intifada opened to us the gates of hell, the UN Millennium General Assembly would still allow us, for a very brief span of time, to continue savoring the flavor of international support. We would even move from it into a last attempt, sadly inconclusive, to break the deadlock in the negotiations just before the lights were turned off on us.

17

Moments of Grace on the Precipice's Edge

Abu Ala was right. Our "good behavior" on the Palestinian front was the key to our international standing, which was the reason Arafat lost his composure during the UN Millennium Assembly in New York, where he behaved as a megalomaniac no longer indulged by the organization that had repeatedly given way to him, but had now ceased treating Israel as an outlaw. He was aggressive and vainglorious, spectacularly so when he stormed out of a CNN interview with Christiane Amanpour, yelling in consuming vanity, "Do you know who you are talking to? You are talking to Yasser Arafat!" He also reprimanded Madeleine Albright for using the term "Temple Mount." He said that Israel had no more right to the site than Italy was entitled to sovereignty over the various Roman archaeological ruins in Gaza. Then he stormed out of that meeting too.

The change in Israel's international standing was, indeed, dramatic. One sign of this was that we, the only country not belonging to any block of nations, were at long last accepted as members of the UN block of West European and Others Group (WEOG). A meeting with UN Secretary General Kofi Annan was followed by a series of meetings with ministers from Arab States such as the Tunisian foreign minister, Habib Ben Yahia, and Morocco's Mohamed Benaissa. The latter was pleased at what he saw as Morocco's return to its rightful position "at the heart of the process." Business-oriented and living under the threatening shadow of predator states like Iraq and Iran, the Arab Gulf States were more willing to collaborate with the Jewish state. Not the ideological aspects of the conflict, but bilateral relations, commerce, the granting of business visas, and the like were high on the agenda in my talks with the foreign ministers of Oman, Qatar, and Bahrain. The improvement in Israel's international standing also made possible a meeting with Indonesia's foreign minister, Alwi Shihab. The world's largest Muslim country, Indonesia took an approach that was dictated by the wish to develop practical relations with Israel. In a second meeting in Geneva a couple of months later we agreed that Israel would open a commercial affairs office in Jakarta, Israeli businessmen would be granted visas for Indonesia, and Israel's representation in Singapore would be accredited to cover Indonesia while Indonesia's embassy in Amman was to handle her relations with Israel. Not very long ago, India, the engine of the Non-Aligned Movement, had spearheaded the international campaign to ostracize and isolate Israel. Now, as a result of the change in the global balance of power and our evident pursuit of peace, Foreign Minister Natwar Singh was open to all our suggestions for co-operation. Wise and refreshingly philosophical, Singh observed that "Israel and the Palestinians are not so much involved in solving a problem as they are in providing answers to fateful historical questions. This makes your task so especially difficult." He fully understood our opposition to the right of return. South Africa's Foreign Minister, Nkosazama Dlamini Zuma, thought, however, that Israel could and should accept at least four million Palestinian refugees. After all, she oddly added, "the entire world, Africa included, came to the rescue of the Jews during the Holocaust."

Of the Europeans, Greece had possibly always been the fiercest of our critics. But, unlike Former Prime Minister Andreas Papandreou, his son, Foreign Minister George Papandreou, thought in broader strategic terms of an eastern Mediterranean alliance between Greece, Turkey, Cyprus, Israel, and the future Palestinian state, a bloc that could also build special relations with the European Union. Also, Israel's always tense relations with the European Union was now going through the best of times, as I could see during my meeting with the Troika.

Russia's foreign minister, Igor Ivanov, exhibited a refreshingly creative attitude. It was not Palestine, but concern for Russia's global status, that moved Ivanov. His engagement had to do with Russia's post- Cold War drive to extricate herself from the passive role she was assigned by the United States, and become again a key actor in the international arena. Ivanov reshaped an idea he had already shared with me at an earlier meeting in Europe. He thought there should be two tracks: one, with the Americans as leaders, and the other somewhat akin to the "Dayton format," that is to say, a forum in which Russia, the United States, and the EU would work out solutions and lend broad international legitimacy to agreements arrived at by the parties. Not everyone was going to like the agreement that might be reached, and Ivanov thought it necessary to build strong international support so as to neutralize extremist challengers. Also, if there was no agreement, the involvement in the process of such a group of nations could be vital in order to prevent difficult regional crises. Ivanov made a great deal of sense. I myself was becoming increasingly convinced that only a strong international coalition could still salvage the process from our and the Palestinians' obstinate entrenchment in impossible positions. If America had really tried to form a strong international network to support the negotiations, it would have made achieving an agreement much more likely, and would have done much to limit the repercussions of the process's failure. But, US jealousy of her monopoly on the process excluded such otherwise truly useful Russian ideas. Ivanov insisted that he should not be understood as disparaging the Americans, for, he tried to reassure, the Middle East was not an area of competition between Russia and the United States. The Americans were not convinced, though, and we could not allow ourselves to bypass them.

* * *

While we were in New York, Gilead Sher and I had a series of meetings with the American peace team to discuss a "package" which the president could present to the parties as a nonnegotiable set of principles for a peace agreement. Barak was now on the same wavelength as us; he also finally wanted an American peace outline. But we were again struck by the inaccurate American assessment of Palestinian positions. "They have raised their expectations," Dennis Ross himself had been told in late August by Osama El-Baz, President Mubarak's foreign affairs adviser. And so, on September 12, we got from Dennis Ross yet another example of American misreading of Palestinian positions. He told us that the Palestinians were willing to accept a package of ideas that would make a peace deal a fair probability: on territory, a 7 percent annexation in exchange for only a 2 percent land swap; on security, three early warning stations, allowing Israeli Air Force flights in Palestinian airspace, and designated areas of Israeli Defense Forces emergency deployment within the Palestinian state. They would not agree, however, to any Israeli forces being stationed in the Jordan Valley, but would accept an international force. On refugees, the Palestinians could "live without" the right of return, provided that refugees living in Lebanon were given preferential treatment in the family reunion program. They would also accept, according to Dennis Ross's report, "qualified sovereignty" in the inner Arab districts of Jerusalem. On the crucial Temple Mount question, things remained difficult. Arafat's idea, which neither the Americans nor we could accept, was that sovereignty on the site be accorded to the Organization of the Islamic Conference. Were we then to have Iran, Malaysia, and Libya sharing sovereignty in the heart of Jerusalem?

To further advocate a final American peace proposal, Gilead Sher, Ambassador David Ivri, and I met Sandy Berger in his office the next day. We told him that the sooner they put an American paper on the table, the better, for we had not the foggiest idea who was authorized to negotiate on Arafat's behalf, and we had no confidence that what the Palestinians told Dennis Ross represented their real positions. Sandy replied that they intended to produce a document "reformulating" Camp David, and assemble within the next ten days a package that would be "very firm and nonnegotiable." That was two weeks before the

Intifada broke out. On September 21, a week before the Intifada began, I phoned Secretary Albright and urged her again to produce the package before the dialogue between us and the Palestinians fell apart. She told me they were making progress, but this effort was their "last shot," and they therefore needed make sure it succeeded. I advised that they involve the leaders of Arab countries so that there would be pan-Arab support from the beginning. All she could say was that the United States was still seriously considering its strategy. "When would the strategy be ready?" "By the end of the week," she replied. That was just about the time that Israel and the Palestinians slid into the bloodiest and ugliest war since 1948.

On my way back home from New York, I stopped off in Paris for a meeting with President Jacques Chirac. France's close identification with Arab and Palestinian matters gave her, we assumed, the necessary leverage to move things forward. Chirac was surprisingly creative. With respect to the Temple Mount, he elaborated an idea derived from maritime law known as "vertical sovereignty," which would mean that the area of the mosques would be under Palestinian sovereignty and what was below would be under Israeli sovereignty. Below, I asked, referred presumably to the layers of the Mount beneath the upper surface where the remains of the holiest of holies lay. Chirac said that that was also his understanding. In fact, this was also to be the view adopted by Clinton in his "peace parameters," which regrettably were only finalized and presented to the sides in late December, at a time when Clinton had already packed his bags and was preparing to leave the White House. I also talked to President Chirac about the king of Morocco's idea of "parallel and equal rights" of the two sides in the Temple Mount, Palestinian "jurisdictional sovereignty" over the surface of the Mount, and an Israeli parallel jurisdictional sovereignty over the lower levels.

Given that the round of talks that were still going on in Israel were at a dead end, the idea was now being toyed with in the White House of a negotiating track with me and Yossi Beilin for Israel, and Abu Ala and Abu Mazen for the Palestinians. They hoped to turn the 1995 Beilin-Abu Mazen understandings into a platform for a possible breakthrough. Beilin, an indefatigable, brilliant, and creative warrior for peace represented for Barak the kind of peacenik who might have dragged his government's public image too much to the left. I knew, however, from both Abu Ala and Abu Mazen that the latter was no longer, assuming he truly ever was, committed to the document carrying his name. It all led to the conclusion that talks between the two delegations had gone as far as they could and that only an American paper would be a barrier reef to end Arafat's surfing within a "process" that was becoming interminable. But Barak's disconcerting volte-faces brought him to again change his view and push for more negotiations with the Palestinians just before we got the American paper. I was skeptical.

Each side, I told him, would use the talks to impress on the Americans its own maximalist expectations.

There was nothing wrong, of course, in trying to break the ice between Barak and Arafat. The meeting we had always urged Barak to hold became, at long last, a reality. It was a dinner on September 23 at Barak's house in Kochav Yair with Arafat and his entourage. I arrived straight from a visit to King Abdullah in Amman. The king described the meeting that was about to take place as "important." The entire Arafat entourage—Abu Mazen, Abu Ala, Saeb Erakat, Mohammed Dahlan, and the Head of Arafat's office, Nabil Abu Rudeineh— came to Kochav Yair in a helicopter we put at their disposal. In his house, Barak had a truly transformative experience; he warmed up to Arafat and held out an olive branch to him. Of all the encounters between them that I had attended, this was the most pleasant and relaxed. The American-Jewish entrepreneur, Danny Abram, who orchestrated the whole occasion, moved happily among the guests like the best man at a wedding. In the middle of the dinner, a telephone call came through from President Clinton. Everything was sweetness and light. "I will be Arafat's partner no less than Rabin was," Barak told the president, in what I could only describe as an impressive character transformation. Barak and the *ra'īs* promised each other that the round of talks we were about to open in Washington would be decisive. "My delegation has a full mandate from me," said Arafat.

Off to Washington for yet another Israeli-Palestinian round of talks. Our first meeting with the Americans was held at the Ritz Carlton hotel in Washington on September 27, 2000. Dennis Ross confirmed my worst fears. Arafat's performance in Barak's house was his typical kind of posturing. By turning down American insistence that Abu Mazen and Abu Ala—those who truly mattered in critical occasions—join the Washington talks, Arafat indicated that he was not truly expecting substantive negotiations. The Americans had, therefore, reached the conclusion that only a peace package of their own could still change the course of the process. What happened now was that the US package was honed in a round of American shuttle diplomacy between us and the Palestinians. Dennis gave us the essence of his plan, which was not essentially different than the one he had introduced to us during our meetings in New York with him and Secretary Albright. I now raised an idea in connection with the refugee issue which would in due course be adopted by the Clinton parameters. The Palestinian refugees could return, I said, to the state of Israel by settling in those areas which had been sovereign Israeli territory and which the Palestinian state would be getting in the swap arrangements. By "Singaporizing" those areas, the Palestinians could settle hundreds of thousands of refugees there.

We left for home on the morning of September 29, right into the start of the Second Intifada. The leader of the opposition, Ariel Sharon, planned to visit the

Temple Mount in defiance not of Arafat or the Palestinians, but of the Barak government, which, he said, was conceding "the holiest of holies." The visit was planned for Thursday, September 28, while I was still in the United States. On Wednesday, September 27, when I learned about Sharon's plans, I telephoned Jibril Rajoub, Arafat's security adviser. He assured me that so long as Sharon did not venture into the area of the mosques, there would be no disturbances, and events could be kept under control. Sharon never stepped into any of the mosques. Yet, that same night, an intelligent report offered evidence of a Palestinian plan to use Sharon's visit as a trigger for violence after Friday's prayers. Both Danny Yatom and I called Madeleine Albright and Dennis Ross to contact Arafat and assure him that Sharon's move was not aimed in any way against the Palestinians. Dennis told me later that Arafat had promised the Secretary of State "to do all he could" to prevent a violent reaction. In the event, he did not lift a finger to prevent the disturbances.

PART II

A SAVAGE WAR FOR PEACE

18

"With Our Soul and Blood We'll Redeem Palestine"

We landed in Israel in the early hours of Friday, September 29, the eve of the Jewish new year. Sharon had visited the Temple Mount the previous day, but none of those present in Barak's security evaluation meeting—they included the head of Shin Bet, Military Intelligence, and ministers—mentioned the possibility of violence around the Mount or indeed anywhere else as a result. Confident that the worst was over, the Police High Commissioner, Yehuda Vilk, left the Temple Mount compound for his weekend break.

But, catastrophe lurked around the corner, and as Friday prayers in the mosques ended, upheaval came. The unfortunate concatenation of events that produced it started as the large Palestinian crowd became increasingly unruly and began to throw stones at the similarly big crowd of Jews who had assembled near the Western Wall to celebrate the Jewish new year. Not content with that, the rioters flocked in large numbers toward the Mughrabi Gate above the Wailing Wall, threatening to tear it down and then spill over into the concourse in front of the wall into the Jewish quarter. The Jerusalem chief of police, Yair Itzhaki, an experienced officer who always eschewed escalation in such ominous circumstances, was hit on the head by a stone and rushed unconscious to Hadassah Hospital. A moment or two later his deputy, a hotheaded and impulsive officer, ordered the police to storm the Mount. His aim was to push the rioters beyond stone-throwing range of the wall. But, his hasty decision ended with the deaths of seven of the rioters.

The Al-Aqsa Intifada had begun; it plunged us into a devastating ordeal. Only part of the broader trials and tribulations endured by both parties, the Intifada's human toll during the five years that it lasted would be around 3,300 Palestinians and 1,100 Israeli civilians killed and many more thousands injured on both sides. The first month reflected this disproportionality: 141 Palestinians were killed and 5,984 were wounded, while 12 Israelis were killed and 65 wounded. The shock on the Israeli side had to do, however, mainly with the appearance of a new, abominable brand of warfare: suicide terrorism in buses, public squares, schools, and kindergartens. The home front was exposed in a way it had never been in any previous conflict. The disturbances in the occupied territories gathered pace when, in the same day of the bloody Temple Mount incident, a serious clash developed at the Netzarim Junction in the Gaza Strip, where a twelve-year-old boy, Muhammad al-Durrah, was killed, apparently by crossfire. Thus, from the first day the Intifada had its very own martyr.

We sought assistance from Arafat, the Americans, and neighboring Arab states to help douse the flames. To no avail. I warned Jordan's foreign minister, Abdul Ilah el-Khatib, that Arafat was "riding on the back of a tiger he would not be able to dismount from, and the situation might get completely out of control, and affect you as well." I also pleaded with numerous European foreign ministers to help convince Arafat of the ominous consequences of this deviation from the path of negotiations. But was Arafat the man who stood behind the Intifada? Was he directly responsible for the bloodbath that engulfed us in what became the fiercest confrontation between our national movements since 1948, and on the way doomed irretrievably the Israeli peace camp? No less important a question is Israel's own role in fueling what eventually became a suicidal race by both parties into a crater that would engulf them in its infected waters.

The Intifada was not a bolt from the blue; its precursory signals were many. Earlier in July, a week after returning from Camp David, I made a telephone call from Mohammed Dahlan's office in Ramallah to Marwan Barghouti, leader of the Tanzim militia. In response to my brief summary of the summit, Barghouti mumbled that the Palestinian intention was to avoid violence until the end of September, when a reassessment would be made, depending on whether there would be "serious results in the field." He also warned that the bellicose statements of IDF Deputy Chief of Staff General Moshe Ya'alon, who also made no secret of his detestation of the peace process, were a potentially self-fulfilling prophecy.

In the early summer of 2000, while we were preparing for Camp David, it was not unusual to hear voices inside the Palestinian leadership threatening a renewal of the armed struggle. Freih Abu Madin, the Palestinian Minister of Justice, claimed that the riots of *Nakba* Day in May had merely been a "dress rehearsal . . . and if the Palestinians didn't get their rights, South Lebanon would be small fry compared to what would happen in Palestine." "Israel forgets," he said, "that her security is in the Palestinians' hands . . . It is not they who control us; we are those who control Israeli security, and we are willing to pay a high price for the defense of the fatherland."[1] Statements similar in both tone and content appeared in the Palestinian media. On the day after Camp David, the general manager of the Palestinian Office of Information, Hassan al Khashef, wrote in the Palestinian Authority's mouthpiece, *Al Ayyam*, that since the Palestinians were unable to accept the Camp David proposals "they must prepare for a pro-longed fight and even hoard food."[2]

On April 1, 2000, *Al Ayyam* quoted a speech of Arafat himself to a Fatah youth convention in Ramallah: "The Palestinian nation is likely to choose Intifada as one way of bringing about the establishment of a Palestinian state with Jerusalem as its capital." In a statement before our departure for Camp David, at the Fatah Congress in Nablus on June 25, the same place and date where I would meet him later in the day,[3] the Chairman made things even clearer: "We are fighting for our land and we are willing to sacrifice our lives for it. We are prepared to destroy everything and renew the armed struggle." He also announced his intention to "declare a Palestinian state" and, if necessary, go for another Intifada. "We can show resistance, as we did in the battle of Karameh (1968), Beirut (1982), and the seven-year Intifada."[4]

Clearly, since the spring of 2000, the Palestinian discourse on the transition to armed struggle had become a twin-track affair, the mounting of a military threat while pursuing negotiations. There would be a resort to arms as soon as it became apparent that diplomacy had not produced the hoped-for results. From the outset, Marwan Barghouti had assumed that there would be a military confrontation. In an interview on March 8, 2000, with the weekly *Akhbar el Halil*, Barghouti stated that:

> *Anyone who believes that it is possible to reach a final agreement on such issues as refugees, Jerusalem, the settlements and borders through negotiations, is deluding himself. We need to accompany negotiations with . . . armed struggle. We need dozens of struggles such as the Al-Aqsa tunnel . . . we are a movement of struggle . . . our minimum aim is a Palestinian state with Jerusalem as its capital, the right of return for the refugees, and the right of self-determination. If these rights are not realized all options are open.*

This was precisely how Arafat himself saw it. Palestinian goals were not achieved at Camp David; hence, as Sahar Habbash, one of Fatah's most radical ideologues, wrote in *Al-Hayat al-Jadida* on September 20, 2000, a week before the outbreak of the Intifada, that "after the summit, Brother Abu Amar (Arafat's nom de guerre) spoke in the language of a true believer who saw that he and the glorious Palestinian nation were facing the option of violent confrontation." On March 1, 2001, Mamduh Nufal, a prominent Palestinian commentator and occasional Arafat adviser, described to the French *Nouvel Observateur* the Chairman's decision to return to the armed struggle: "A few days before Sharon's visit to the area of the mosques, when Arafat asked us to prepare for war, I was in favor of mass demonstrations but opposed the use of arms." Nufal recalled that Jibril Rajoub had also, in vain, told Arafat that he was against the use of force. But, "Arafat was convinced that within two or three days, the imbalance between the forces of the two sides would be so intolerable that the Americans, the Europeans and the Arabs would force Barak to renew the negotiations," presumably on terms more favorable to the Palestinians, for since Camp David we had been anyway engaged in ongoing negotiations.

Arguably, the Intifada was also deeply rooted within the growing abyss between Palestinian society and its political leaders, whose guilt was compounded by their corruption and abuse of power.[5] Violence, as Barghouti had made me understand, was also the way the armed militias representing a new young leadership asserted themselves against the conservative establishment and their meager achievements in the peace process. The Intifada was, then, also an explosion of rage against the PLO's old guard, who had been responsible for the deceits of the peace process. As such, the Intifada presented Arafat with a way to resolve what became a crucial challenge for the internal cohesion of the Palestinian national movement. He had to manage the built-in tension between his two conflicting positions as the head of an institutionalized entity, the corrupt and unpopular Palestinian Authority, and the supreme commander of a presumably immaculate revolutionary national movement. The Intifada allowed him to heal the Palestinian Authority's rift with the Palestinian public and with the revolutionary armed groups which saw the conservative PA as a tool of Israel's occupation. It became his way to reconcile the PA and its institutions, which based their legitimacy (and their claim to the massive amounts of donors' money) on the peace process, with the revolutionary legitimacy of the militias, which, unlike the PA, were not a product of the vilified peace process and would not disappear if the process evaporated. As head of the PA and leader of the PLO and of Fatah, Arafat personified all the sources of legitimacy and authority. But these had been eroding constantly. The weakening of the PA weakened Arafat as a national symbol, and by the time he arrived at Camp David, he was left with a rather slim majority of public approval. An autocrat with no institutional legitimacy, Arafat was forced to embrace the Intifada to recover his revolutionary legitimacy.[6]

Fearful that they might lose the support of the street, the politicians around Arafat also rushed to acquire the revolutionary validity that could launder their tarnished image as officials of the corrupt Palestinian Authority. They went from one radio and television station to another to give their backing to the struggle. Hassan Asfour, a key peace negotiator and a voice of reason in normal times, declared in a broadcast on *The Voice of Palestine* on October 2: "We must unite against neofascism in Israel. We must overthrow these neofascists in order to restore the honor of Palestine to the Palestinian nation and defeat the occupation." Plunging back into armed confrontation with Israel turned out to be the old guard's best strategy for political survival. The truth is that if it had not been possible to turn their public's accumulated anger against Israel, it would have erupted in the form of a Palestinian Spring directed instead at Arafat and the entire Palestinian leadership.

In truth, the Palestinian armed groups, which together with the police were at least twice as large as permitted by the Oslo Accords, did not really need Arafat's explicit instructions in order to go to war. It had been always Arafat's way to engage in violence once he felt that politics and diplomacy had gotten stagnant and produced no results. His men interpreted his frustration at being blamed for the failure of the summit and his praise for Hezbolllah's successful resistance against the Israeli occupier as a green light for war. Nor was it entirely impossible that their preparations for war—as Sari Nusseibeh, the PLO's Minister for Jerusalem Affairs recalled, instructions were given through the local press for the hoarding of food, medicine, and vital necessities—were intended more as pressure on Israel ahead of the next rounds of negotiations than as operational moves.

The IDF high command was not composed of sisters of mercy, either.[7] They were willing accomplices in the task of fanning the embers of violence into large flames that would consume us all. Once intercepted by Israeli intelligence, all these Palestinian signals led, as Brigadier General Zvi Fogel, the deputy chief of the IDF's Southern Command, later recalled, to disproportionately robust war preparations. A belligerent, trigger-happy IDF was eager to "teach the Palestinians a lesson they should not forget." It was, General Fogel assumed, as if the trauma of the pullout from Lebanon could only be healed by another war.

The Intifada actually started not after, but before Sharon's visit to the Temple Mount. As Abu Ala himself admitted, the visit lasted for only half an hour and, as agreed with the Palestinian security chief, Jibril Rajoub, Sharon refrained from entering the colonnade fronting the Al-Aqsa Mosque.[8]

But a day earlier, an Israeli patrol escorting a group of settlers in the Gaza Strip was attacked by a Palestinian squad, which left one Israeli soldier dead and others wounded. The perpetrator was no other than Jihad al- Amarin, the man whose return to Gaza after the Oslo Accords Rabin had vetoed, but Arafat, in a typical breach of trust with his partner in "the peace of the braves," as he liked to boast, smuggled him in his car when he first arrived in Gaza in 1994. Dahlan's refusal to arrest him for the attack on the Israeli patrol was now interpreted by the Israelis as one more signal of the inevitable conflagration.

We clearly failed in mitigation, though. Barak's leadership as both prime minister and defense minister in these early days of the Intifada was lacking and deficient. His ambiguous instructions to the IDF and his poor control of the high command allowed the army to throw fuel on to an already highly combustible situation. He ordered "containment," but his political weakness forced him to show strength and determination; his political challenger was, after all, none other than Mr. Security, Ariel Sharon. Barak allowed the taking of odious measures that had never been taken before, such as air bombardments, serial targeted killings, and disproportionate firepower, which caused unnecessary civilian losses. The instructions to the army to "contain" the uprising bore little resemblance to what actually took place on the ground. The IDF released pent-up feelings of tension and anger accumulated during the First Intifada, the tunnel riots of 1996 in which sixteen soldiers had been killed, and the various Nakba Day related incidents. According to the Chief of Military Intelligence, General Amos Malka, Israeli troops shot a million bullets in the first days of the Intifada. Minister Amnon Lipkin-Shahak, an IDF former chief of staff, frequently shared with me his frustration at how the army conducted the war in contravention to the government's instructions. Goods that were clearly supposed to reach the Palestinian population were held up at roadblocks on orders from field commanders, while bulldozers uprooted hothouses, plant nurseries, and crops, presumably in the interest of security. The policy of collective punishment and economic hardship raised Palestinian anger to unprecedented levels and defeated the government's intention of restoring calm. The IDF wrongly believed that pressure on the civilian population would force the political leadership to restrain and control the militias. The opposite actually happened. The rage at Israel only increased, and the popular legitimacy of resistance was further enhanced. And, even when ministers repeatedly pointed this out to Barak, he failed to impose discipline on the high command. The army even avoided cooperating with the Peace Process Administration and frequently did not allow its head, Colonel (res.) Shaul Arieli, to gain access to sketch maps needed for our peace plans. All this exposed an inherent fault in Israeli democracy. The height of Chief of Staff General Shaul Mofaz's rebelliousness was reached when he later publicly attacked the Clinton peace parameters of December 23, 2000. He felt it his duty not only to criticize the proposal during a government meeting, which somehow it was his professional responsibility to do, but also to go to the media with this. He acted as if he himself were accountable to the public and the entire nation, rather than someone appointed by, and responsible only to, the government above him.

Israel's harsh response was determined to a great extent also by the fact that it was the hawkish argument that prevailed in the debate within the Israeli intelligence community over the question of whether the Intifada was explicitly initiated by Arafat. Shin Bet believed it was a spontaneous eruption, while military intelligence claimed it was a carefully planned war, a position that was wholly endorsed by both the government and public opinion. In this respect, the overwhelming influence of the eloquent and self-confident General Amos Gilead, the deputy chief of Military Intelligence, on our decision-making cannot be exaggerated. He had always warned that the Palestinians would resort to war if they failed to get what they wanted in peace talks, and he had also predicted with considerable exactitude Arafat's reaction to our Camp David peace proposals. He maintained that to Arafat, Israel was an artificial creature that was condemned to disappear. Arafat never wanted or expected a negotiated peace; he fought for a state without having to commit to the end of conflict or to the waiving of the right of return.

The claim that Arafat saw Israel as a temporary phenomenon and most self-convincingly questioned her claim to any historical or religious roots in the sacred Islamic land of Palestine is difficult to challenge. But the attempt by Israel's Military Intelligence to apply to Arafat's behavior a modern military logic based on planning and hierarchical chains of command was fundamentally flawed. If he gave instructions, it was through his silence and noninterference, and if he happened to call for restraint, his militias took it as Arafat's lip service to international pressure and did not abide by his call. Neither a great strategist nor a brilliant statesman, Arafat was an alley cat, proficient in the art of political survival, a man with a tactical cunning that frequently defeated his grand national vision. The failure of Camp David and Hezbollah's example did definitely stir in him a longing for the idea of a Palestinian state that could only be won in blood. He did not truly plan the conflagration, but he most willingly exploited it once it happened, and then he simply lost control and was incapable of stopping it. Tired of the peace process, which had not achieved the results he had hoped for, Arafat believed the time had come to impose on Israel terms that were more to his liking. He also saw in the war a worldwide public relations service to the Palestinian cause. He, therefore, had no intention of stopping the violence neither after the Sharm El-Sheikh ceasefire,[9] which he signed with us in mid-October, nor after the ceasefire he agreed with Shimon Peres on November 1.[10] Not only did he refrain from making a public call for an end to the violence, as stipulated by those agreements, but he also continued the transfer of funds to the militias, and gave his backing to Marwan Barghouti whenever he was challenged by opponents of the armed uprising such as Jibril Rajoub and Abu Mazen.

But Palestinians and Israelis behaved as the mirror image of each other; this war of deceit was a mutual affair. Knowing Arafat would not be willing or able to tame his militias, the Israeli high command ordered only a symbolic, minimal pullout of IDF units in contravention of the Sharm El-Sheikh agreement, which called for an Israeli withdrawal to the September 28 lines. Protests by thoughtful generals, such as Shlomo Yanai, and the Intelligence Chief, Amos Malka, in striking disagreement with his own deputy, at the disproportionate use of force were brushed aside by the Chief of Staff, Shaul Mofaz. The IDF defeated the government's containment strategy in the same way that Palestinian militia commanders mostly ignored the politicians' fear of a militarized Intifada. The escalating violence and the growing number of civilian deaths increased popular pressure for revenge, and weakened further the capacity of Palestinian politicians to rein in the militias.[11]

Jibril Rajoub was perhaps the only Palestinian strongman who resisted joining the wave of violence; he claimed that he would only act under explicit orders from Arafat, which conspicuously never came. In all the internal debates, Arafat would normally remain silent. That was his way not to alienate any of the competing groups around him. "Members of the Palestinian leadership would then leave Abu Ammar's office, each convinced in his own different way of (his) wisdom."[12] Also, the competition between rival militias acted as a combustible for war escalation. The creation of the Fatah-affiliated "Al-Aqsa Martyrs Brigades" in the first days of the Intifada was presented by Samir Mashrawi, Dahlan's deputy, as vital for saving Fatah from total breakdown in its competition with Hamas. "By letting it be known that it did not take a stand against these groups, the Fatah leadership was able to maintain some degree of control and regain respect," was how Abu Ala put it.[13] Suspecting that the Intifada was for Fatah just a means of improving its bargaining positions in peace negotiations, Hamas initially resisted any cooperation with it, but joined the war eventually mostly as part of its struggle for mastery with Fatah. A "division of labor" then developed, where Hamas fought inside Israel through suicide terror, while Fatah led a conventional armed struggle against the settlers and army units in the occupied territories.

On the Israeli side, the IDF high command was deeply apprehensive at Barak's insistence on pursuing negotiations under fire. The Deputy Chief of Staff, General Moshe Ya'alon, defined the Intifada as "the most important campaign since the 1948 war of independence," and he fought for a Palestinian defeat of such a scope that would be "burned into the Palestinian consciousness for long years to come." It was as if the army assumed not only the task of winning militarily, but also the political mission of defeating the legitimate Palestinian struggle for independence. The trauma of the First Intifada, a civic, essentially non-violent uprising that the IDF could not win, made the militarization of the Second Intifada an interest of the high command. A war was winnable; a civilian uprising was not.

Yezid Sayigh, a Palestinian scholar at the University of Cambridge, advanced his own sober interpretation of the Intifada.[14] What distinguished Arafat, he wrote, was the absence of any strategy. Maybe so. But the absence of a strategy was itself a strategy. Instead of taking the initiative, Arafat tended to shirk the responsibilities of leadership by surfing on the waves of his people's changing will. He would always stand above the fray and use his legendary standing among his people to accord legitimacy to their will. Conceivably, as Sayigh claims, Arafat's approach was improvised. But the improvisation was based on a simple logic. First, the Palestinians would prefer to achieve their aims by negotiation. Second, the threat of violence would accompany the negotiations. Third, if there were any hitch in negotiations, the threat could be reinforced by actual violence, as for example on *Nakba* Day in May 2000. Fourth, if negotiations failed to achieve the Palestinian aims, an all-out war would ensue. This was not a new Clausewitzian theory of warfare, but it was a page from the classical theory of anticolonial revolutionary struggle, ill-adapted now to the Israeli-Palestinian context.[15]

Professor Sayigh was right in blaming Arafat "for strategic mistakes whose serious consequences for the Palestinians are of an historical magnitude." Arafat erred in his assessment of the effect of his actions on both the Israeli public and its political establishment. In the final analysis, all his maximalist policies backfired and worked against the interests of the Palestinians. It truly did not matter one way or another whether Arafat instructed the Fatah activists. What was important was that in his own idiosyncratic way, from the moment the hoped-for eruption of violence broke out, he embraced and encouraged it because, as Sayigh puts it, it "released him from the political distress in which he found himself" in the wake of Camp David. It also offered him what Sayigh defined as a much needed "daily death toll" to put world opinion on his side.

Arafat's political distress was partly the result of his setbacks during the UN Millennium General Assembly. He had been accustomed to seeing Israel ostracized and shunned, a pariah state, always in the dock, always isolated, and always being voted down. Now, for the first time in a generation, Israel was being wooed and courted, and he was cornered into the role of the peace refusenik. This was an entirely new diplomatic situation for him, a new order which he had to overturn. The Intifada, wrote Abu Ala, "offered an opportunity to rid the Palestinian cause of the negative image it had acquired and to break out of the diplomatic isolation that Ehud Barak's government had tried to impose on us after Camp David."[16] Theoretically, the same objective could have been achieved through a bold diplomatic initiative that would put Israel on the defensive again. But the man of the eternal military fatigues needed the images of Palestinians soaked in blood and heroically facing the brutal Israelis to again attract international sympathy. Typically, in the first days of the Intifada, instead of staying put, Arafat went to two unimportant events abroad—a public demonstration in Tunisia and a seminar in Mallorca, Spain. By absenting himself, he was both escaping direct responsibility and giving the green light for the Intifada to proceed. He believed that the international and pan-Arab support produced by the Intifada would weaken American influence in the negotiations and enable him to drive a wedge between Europe and the United States, which was to him now, in the dying days of the Clinton administration, a paper tiger he could safely challenge.

In the short term, Arafat's strategy worked for him to a large extent due to the support he got from Europe and the Arab world. Arab satellite television offered daily scenes of bloody clashes that allowed, as Abu Ala put it, "the Palestinian issue to regain prominence . . . an inestimable advantage of publicity . . . with Yasser Arafat as our president becoming a focal point for diplomats, journalists, officials and politicians."[17] The prestigious Palestinian pollster Khalil Shikaki concurred. To him, Arafat "orchestrated and led" the Intifada "in order to gain popularity and legitimacy." These thunderous demonstrations of support also "translated into material and financial support as governments and peoples competed to offer assistance to the new Palestinian Intifada."[18] They all pointed the finger at Israel and gave a tailwind to Arafat's strategy of turning Palestinian suffering into a negotiating weapon. Arafat wanted to bring home to the Americans the message that if they chose not to end their "blind support" of Israel, it was within his power to drag the Middle East into a whirlpool of violence that would go beyond the borders of the region itself. Wholly intoxicated by the effects of his war with Israel, Arafat ran amok to his own and his nation's inexorable perdition.

Indeed, in the longer term, as even Fred Halliday, an old critic of Zionism's "suicidal obstinacy," explained, the Second Intifada was not at all an inspiring case of armed resistance; it was a political and moral disaster for a cause he, Halliday, keenly supported.[19] Arafat's monumental strategic blunder lay in his assumption that deliverance could be reached through an armed Intifada with salient jihadist traits. But the only thing it did was to push the Israeli electorate radically to the right and kill the chances of peace. Ours was perhaps a prosaic peace offer, not a messianic deal. But Arafat went away with neither. True, the talks would in due course be renewed, and the outline prepared by the Americans—the Clinton peace parameters—would be more generous than what had been proposed at Camp David. But Arafat would reject the parameters anyway, since he was always wrong in assessing the extent to which Israel was prepared to go. He woke up belatedly at Taba, but it was a limited awakening. He did not possess the power to bring the matter to a decision and was left only with the hope that his nemesis, Barak, would win at the coming elections. Arafat always pushed his luck too far, hoping to snatch victory from the jaws of defeat and ending with nothing but destruction and humiliation.

The outbreak of the Intifada allowed Arafat to use a tactic typical of the man: to escape by driving forward, but without having a clearly defined, achievable objective. He might not have planned the fortuitous Temple Mount incident, but from the moment it happened, he rode on its back and looked for ways to deepen and broaden its consequences, attempting to use the violence to reach political objectives which were not clear to him at all. What was the point in a revolt for a better peace deal when neither his negotiating team nor we the Israelis could ascertain at what point exactly Palestinian bargaining for a better deal would stop? "You have mobilized the entire Arab street on your side; you managed to recruit Al Jazeera to show very hard pictures. What, then, is your objective? Where are you going to?" These were the questions Jordan's King Abdullah told Ehud Barak, on a visit to Amman in December, he had put to Arafat without getting any response. What precisely did the Palestinians hope to achieve by the armed Intifada? What exactly was the meaning of the Intifada's call for "ending the occupation"? In Lebanon, Hezbollah's strategy was to fight for an attainable objective, Israel's unilateral withdrawal to the agreed international border, something both the Israeli government and Israeli society wanted to happen. But the Intifada could not have been expected to yield a similar outcome. It could neither drive Israel out of the territories nor compel it to accept the right of return for Palestinians. In effect, the Intifada was an attempt to twist Israel's arm without there being a clear objective, the achievement of which would mean the end of the fighting. All that the Intifada achieved was to stir up fierce popular passions and raise the embattled nation's expectations sky high, which made it all the more difficult to reach a reasonable compromise. That much was admitted by Abu Ala.[20] At no time either before or after the outbreak of the Intifada did the Palestinian leadership manage to expound realistic, conceivably attainable targets that might justify the continued spilling of blood.

The Intifada weakened the Palestinian case in an additional sense. It underlay their leadership's inability to strike a dialogue with the Israeli public. For the mass of Israelis had come to lose faith in the Palestinians' ability to stop the violence even if their nebulous goals were to be achieved. Poll after poll would show from then on that only a meager percentage of Israelis still believed that a signed peace agreement would mean the end of conflict. How could anyone in the Palestinian leadership have thought that the violence could do anything but cement a sharp swing to the right in Israel, a swing so radical and traumatic that it persists to this very day?

Twenty years after the Intifada, the Palestinians are today further from statehood and the fulfillment of their minimum demands than at any time since the Oslo Accords in 1993. The purposeless descent into bloodshed and destruction made of the Intifada a second *Nakba*, one that destroyed the spinal cord of Palestinian society and doomed who knows for how long the Palestinians' chances of redemption. At Camp David, Arafat dismantled the Palestinians' alliance with the United States for which the Oslo Accords had paved the way; in the Intifada he definitively sealed his divorce from America. A "general who never lost a battle," as he liked to define himself, Arafat had greeted the ending of the Cold War with a reckless strategic decision: he made an alliance with Saddam Hussein in 1990. The second Intifada was a far more consequential blunder. It was an all-out war that denied the Palestinians the glory of an unarmed civilian uprising, defeated the purpose of the uprising, and accorded Israel its victory. Armed resistance could be defeated, as Sharon would show in his Defensive

Shield Operation in 2003; a civilian uprising could not, as the first Intifada had shown. Like the 1936–39 Arab Revolt, the second Intifada turned out to be a blind explosion of rage and violence that brought the Palestinian community to the verge of collapse and dissolution, and buried for many years to come the dream of independence and statehood.

Diplomacy under Fire

In discussions I held with Terje Rød-Larsen, the Norwegian diplomat who, to-gether with his wife, Mona Juul, was the mastermind of the Oslo initiative and was now the UN envoy for the Palestinian peace process, we came up with an idea that could potentially get us out of the abyss. Pandering to Arafat's conviction of his own global importance, we proposed that three summit meetings be held in quick succession. The first two—one in Paris hosted by President Chirac whose country held the rotating presidency of the European Union, and the second in Cairo—would focus on stabilizing the situation. The third in Washington would allow President Clinton to present his final plan for a settlement. Barak did not hesitate for a moment to give the green light. He also agreed that we attempt to resolve the Temple Mount issue in the Paris meeting, hopefully along the lines of Chirac's idea of "vertical sovereignties." Jealous to preserve their monopoly on the negotiating process, the Americans insisted, however, that the first two summits deal solely with ceasefire issues, not with substantive negotiations. In a telephone conversation with Dennis Ross on October 2, I advised that Arafat would accept a ceasefire only if it was linked to progress in the negotiations; he needed to make sense of the Intifada's bloodshed.

The meeting with Chirac at the Elysée confirmed Secretary Albright's assess-ment. "Don't delude yourself," she had told us. "We in America understand you, but we're alone. You'll see it for yourself when you talk to Chirac." In a cold, in-hospitable atmosphere, Chirac announced that the main task of the meeting was not only to bring about a ceasefire, leading to Israel's withdrawal from positions it had taken since the outbreak of the Intifada, but also to establish a UN-mandated international committee to investigate "Israel's grave responsibility." He argued that the disproportion between Palestinian and Israeli casualties meant that Israel would never get anyone to believe that it was the Palestinians who were the aggressors.

Washington's skepticism with regard to Europe was not ill-founded. Europe's fascination with the Palestinian underdog, which had always precluded a more nuanced interpretation of the conflict, and her unqualified tolerance for Arafat's misconduct made her a problematic partner. Trapped between her Jewish guilt complex and her responsibility as a former colonial power for the Middle East's maladies, she was rendered an utterly ineffective player in the resolution of our conflict. The United States, Henry Kissinger observed, had at the time nothing to gain from involving European nations that were always reluctant to ask sacrifices of their Arab friends.[1] Overtaken by a post-historical mood, Europe was now Mario Andrea Rigoni's old lady, who, after she had allowed herself all liberties and a great number of horrors, expected us all to deal with her poisoned heritage in line with her need for repentance and moderation.[2] We had to deal with an anarchic Palestinian structure that defied all principles of governance and accountability. We were a government without a parliamentary majority that, against all political logic, was going further in its attempt to reach a settlement than any government had in the past. And all the Europeans, who had been nurturing Arafat for decades, could ask of us was "gestures" that would further undermine our already precarious political existence. In response to Javier Solana's question about Arafat's strategy, I referred him to a conversation I had had with Terje Rød-Larsen, certainly no enemy of the Palestinian cause, who believed that "Arafat wanted to use Palestinian blood to regain international sympathy."

The meeting in Paris was more like a surrealistic film than a political summit. Within twenty-four hours, Ehud Barak found himself in a Europe very different from the supportive continent we knew immediately after Camp David. Neither did we deserve Europe's exaggerated praise then nor were we now the villains and the romanticized Palestinians the innocent victims. Israel was once again cast in the role of a colonial superpower oppressing a helpless people. This was precisely the effect Arafat was trying to achieve. And he most certainly did achieve it, not least through our own disproportionate military reaction. No wonder Barak was like a tightly coiled spring in Paris, where the French treated him in a disgraceful, imperious way. In meetings with Arafat and his team, now at the US embassy, Barak presented evidence that Arafat was orchestrating the Intifada. As the artist that he was, Arafat was not discomfited when he pretended not to even know who Marwan Barghouti, the Tanzim commander, was. "If Arafat can't control them, he's a gang leader, not a political leader," Barak told the Americans. "It's possible that we're looking at a decade-long failure initiated by the signing of the Oslo Accords," he said. He asked Albright to tell Arafat to stop the violence, accept one package or another from the Americans, and reach a reasonable agreement. That was a Barak somersault. He now (until further notice) abandoned his pretension to negotiate and simply asked the Americans for an imposed solution. His suggestion to Arafat a week earlier (it now seemed like an eternity ago) at his home in Kochav Yair that we should continue direct negotiations because any US package would be harder for both of us was fundamentally flawed and untenable.

At the US embassy, the parties managed to agree on a joint statement drafted by the Secretary of State; it was even decided to initial it that very night and sign the following day in Sharm El-Sheikh in front of President Mubarak. But here the script was given an unexpected twist. Out of courtesy to the host, all the delegations went back to the Elysée just before midnight. Acting as "best men," were UN Secretary General Kofi Annan and his envoy Terje Rød-Larsen. Albright opened the proceedings and declared that both leaders had already given their respective heads of security preliminary orders to calm the atmosphere. She also confirmed that President Clinton would host the sides the following week for the final, decisive stage in the negotiations. But, instead of celebrating the achievement and the US pledge to finally present its peace package, Chirac insisted that a committee of inquiry into Israel's responsibilities for the bloodshed was a *sine qua non* for any future move on the peace front. For Arafat, now back in the US embassy with all the others, that was the opportunity he had been waiting for to wriggle out of having to sign the document. In a typical exercise of evasion, he dispatched Nabil Shaath and Saeb Erakat to initial the agreement on his behalf. Albright was furious. "We won't go to Sharm until that man comes here to sign," she said. She even ordered the embassy gate's guard to prevent Arafat from leaving the compound. However, "that man" managed to evade the guard.

On the ground, there was not to be any letup in the violence, despite Arafat's assurances in Paris that the signing of the ceasefire was "a mere formality." They shot at settlements in the West Bank, at the tunnel road and the Gilo neighborhood in Jerusalem and at the Rafah terminal. They threw stones at Israeli vehicles, put constant pressure on Netzarim, the isolated settlement in the Gaza Strip, and murdered Rabbi Hillel Lieberman on his way to Joseph's Tomb. Then, a Palestinian mob, incited by the inflammatory religious broadcasts of the Palestinian media, plundered, destroyed, and gutted the tomb. Explosive devices went off along the roads of the West Bank.

Against the odds of the devastating impact of the Intifada and the waves of suicide terrorism that accompanied it, our minority government still resisted the temptation of a unity government with Ariel Sharon's Likud, which would have meant an end to the negotiating process. To add to our troubles, on October 6, a new front opened up in the north. Three soldiers were kidnapped by Hezbollah guerillas under the noses of UN troops. This was a few days before UN Secretary General Kofi Annan arrived for a visit to Israel as Yom Kippur came to an end. I told Annan that responsibility for the northern front rested solely with the United Nations. After all, we went with the United Nations to the very last centimeter to implement Resolution 425 calling us to withdraw from Lebanon. It was tragically ironic, I told Annan, that this entire Intifada should have originated in the Palestinians' interpretation of our withdrawal from Lebanon as a sign of weakness, and that they were now transferring Hezbollah's modus operandi to the occupied territories. We had been constantly criticized for not respecting UN resolutions, and here we were inviting aggression precisely because the implementation of a UN resolution is perceived as sign of weakness. Annan conceded that the United Nations had an obligation vis-à-vis the kidnapped soldiers. Good intentions of a noble man, but hollow rhetoric. The soldiers were eventually murdered, and we got back their corpses years later.

The inutility of the United Nations as a peace guarantor and the risk of diluting the centrality of the American role in the process were further underlined to me by Richard Holbrooke, then US ambassador to the United Nations, in a meeting on October 4. Holbrooke was highly skeptical of a UN Security Council role in any agreement over the Temple Mount. "Look at examples from around the world," he said. "In southern Lebanon, where the UN plays a role, there's a mess. In Bosnia, where the UN does not play a role, the situation is good. The Bosnian model should be applied to the Temple Mount. The role of the Security Council should only be endorsement, not mandate." Who said that Republican neoconservative hawks were the only ones who treated the United Nations with suspicion?

During the course of that bloodstained Day of Atonement, I continued my round of contacts with counterparts and world leaders. In talking to the French foreign minister, Hubert Védrine, I was pleased to learn he was distancing himself from the utterly unexplainable approach taken by Chirac. The Dutch foreign minister, Jozias van Aartsen, with whom I shared dismay at Arafat's rejection of Norway as a possible member in a proposed international committee of inquiry on the Intifada, was an empathic voice in the hall of darkness we found ourselves in:

> I've seen the pictures from Joseph's Tomb. It confirms what you're saying about the Palestinians' behavior . . . The Palestinians are making a huge historical mistake. I'm glad Védrine is distancing himself from Chirac. I also agree regarding the investigating committee. It was an excellent idea to make Norway part of the committee. If Arafat doesn't agree, it will be a clear indication that he's not interested in peace. I believe in all of you, in Prime Minister Barak and you personally, as well as in your peace policy. I can understand how you feel. This is the last chance for peace.

The shocking pictures of the desecration of Joseph's Tomb and the murder at the tomb of the Israeli soldier Madhat Yusef marked a turning point. Our claims were at last beginning to be heard. The UK foreign minister, Robin Cook, wanted to know, "What is Arafat trying to gain?" I answered by repeating what I had tried to explain to everyone in lengthy, tiring conversations: he was worried about the peace package President Clinton was preparing, and he wanted to destroy it before it was born lest it expose him yet again as a peace refusenik in the eyes of the international community.

The Joseph's Tomb incident, and the televised lynching by an angry mob at Ramallah Police Station of two Israeli army reservists on October 12 were the darkest moments in this early stage of the Intifada and truly defining events. Everyone I spoke to among European leaders shared my concern at the prospect that this kind of wicked incident might force us to form a national unity government with Likud, led by Sharon. I made it clear to all that if the violence did not stop, we could do nothing to prevent the rise of a right-wing government that would disengage altogether from the peace process. The sad fundamental fact of Israeli politics, I explained, was that political survival required *not* engaging in peace talks. These incidents further emboldened the Israeli right, for they ate away at the already dwindling stores of our peace policy's legitimacy. Reaching peace agreements and pulling out from occupied lands, which was now the right-wing narrative, was only the prelude to further onslaughts on Israel. This was to be the same discourse that, following the recurrent wars with Hamas after Sharon's withdrawal from Gaza in 2005,[3] would sustain Netanyahu's resistance to any peace move in the future. Hezbollah's kidnappings and the atrocious Ramallah lynching shifted the Israeli public from the belief that peace was possible into the mindset of a tribal feud of bloody retribution, a religion-based war of murder, blood, and vengeance. Yet the government still resisted giving in to the public mood. On November 9, the Knesset heatedly debated the matter. The opposition called for all-out war. To which I responded:

> *Let's assume for a moment that you defeat them, beat them down, and destroy them. Do you think that after that there will be no need for a political solution? Even if you win a military victory and spill rivers of their blood, you will have to go back to the negotiating table. That is what we should be doing now, as quickly as possible.*

In the face of calls for revenge and retribution and increasing public abhorrence of the peace process, Barak remained steadfast, turned down the now popular call for a national unity government, and refused to turn aside from the path that he still hoped would lead to a settlement. At times, he seemed to be seeking reassurance. "Tell us something we might not know," Barak ranted and raved, venting his frustration on the Secretary of State and the CIA Chief during the Paris meeting. "Tell us that the Palestinian violence is a tactical move that is about to end—a kind of corridor to an agreement. Please tell us." His hope was that this was just a savage war for peace, much like the final days before the 1962 Évian peace accord that led to Algerian independence. We all wished this to be the case.

Trapped in No-Win Conditions

In the cycle of violence between the Israeli regional superpower and a people in arms fighting for its independence, we could only reap international opprobrium. But it also made sense for Barak to say to Clinton in a telephone conversation that if a Middle Eastern government did not respond to such a lynching (of the two reservists in Ramallah), it risked losing all legitimacy in the eyes of its people and the peoples of the region. We were trapped in a no-win situation. When, in reprisal for the lynching, helicopters attacked the police station where the incident had occurred, the powerful images of the lynching were immediately erased from the public mind. Again, the burden of guilt fell squarely on Israel.

Our attempt to walk a fine line between war and peace, respond militarily, and yet make a supreme effort to return to the negotiating table was a balancing act almost beyond human capacity. We suspected that Arafat wanted to arrive at the planned Arab Summit on October 21 against a backdrop of continuing bloodshed, but we agreed, nevertheless, to go for yet another attempt to reach a ceasefire in the proposed Sharm El-Sheikh conference ahead of the Arab summit. On October 16, Mubarak, Jordan's King Abdullah, Ehud Barak, Kofi Annan, Javier Solana, and President Clinton joined in a concerted international effort to put an end to the violence and return to the negotiating table.

As expected, the Egyptian press was fiery in tone, rabble-rousing, and with a level of incitement against Israel that bordered on the disgusting. Mubarak, who in my presence had said some months ago to our ambassador in Cairo to stop complaining about Egypt's media since they were "all incorrigible liars," feared that the press could trigger mass demonstrations that would threaten the stability of his regime. It was for good reason that Intelligence Chief Omar Suleiman was so committed to extinguishing the Israeli-Palestinian conflagration. As expected, Mubarak opened the conference with a tirade against "this wicked aggression by the stronger side . . . and Israel's provocative attempts to break the Palestinian people." Thankfully, Clinton, as always, was a beacon of humanity, urbanity, and warmth. His heart went out to us. "I know that the past few weeks have been hell for you and I don't know how you've managed to cope with it," he told us during that early morning meeting at which he presented his ceasefire plans.

The proposed ceasefire called for a joint declaration on the cessation of violence, the resumption of Israeli-Palestinian security cooperation, the opening of the international border crossings, the withdrawal of IDF troops to their pre-September 28 positions, the lifting of closures, the collection of illegal weapons, the convening of a high-ranking joint security committee, and—at the end of this graduated process—the resumption of peace negotiations. We also found a way around the issue of an international committee of inquiry by agreeing that it be headed by an American public figure—former Senator George Mitchell would later be picked—while its other members were to be Javier Solana and the former Turkish president Suleyman Demirel. When the committee's findings were finally published, the behavior of both parties was portrayed in the wider context of an anarchic and vicious conflict. Wisely, the committee was mainly preoccupied not with "responsibilities," as Chirac wanted, but with the need to create a roadmap that would end the political stalemate. I had suggested to Senator George Mitchell in a long telephone conversation on November 22 that he not take on the role of the historian because, at the moment, the statesman's role was more important. I know how flawed our performance was, I told him, but this was a typical asymmetric conflict, and if he investigated an Israeli officer for opening fire, he could track a chain of command leading to the prime minister himself. But if he investigated a Tanzim fighter, he would not be able to follow such a route of responsibility. The very fact that Israel attacked targets of various Palestinian military organizations indicated that Arafat violated past agreements, for according to the interim agreement there was not supposed to be sizable Palestinian armed forces in the first place.

Gifted with the instincts of an alley cat capable of skillfully wriggling out of tight spots, Arafat came to Sharm El-Sheikh with an exit strategy; he would sign the agreement, but not carry it out. Arafat never said yes gladly. It always had to be squeezed out of him. "Go ahead and sign, you dog!" was how in 1994 Mubarak had forced a shriveled and obdurate Arafat to sign the appendices to the Oslo Interim Agreement. With Arafat, there always had to be a residual debt. At Sharm El-Sheikh, practically all foreign leaders had to plead with him to sign, but when Arafat nervously twitched his legs while sitting, it meant he did not want to sign, and if he was forced to, he would not comply. His own aides, Jibril Rajoub and Mohammed Dahlan told CIA Chief George Tenet that Arafat would not start fulfilling his obligations before the Arab summit that was to be held five days later. He needed to arrive there as the leader of a victimized people in the middle of a cruel war with a merciless occupying force. Only thus he would also be able to stir the passions of the Arab leaders and maintain the pro-Palestinian hysteria in the Arab streets. We did not find much consolation in Arafat's deputy,

Mahmoud Abbas, either. In Sharm El-Sheikh he told me that two weeks of ac-
celerated negotiations could lead to an agreement and an "end of conflict." But
he would not initiate anything, nor would he break ranks with Arafat. "What is
the magic formula that has eluded us?" I asked him. "You aren't negotiating with
the right people," was his astonishing reply. This was again Abu Mazen's way of
saying that both of us, Israelis and Americans, were miserably incognizant of
Palestinian politics by trying to circumvent the PLO's historical leadership and
negotiate with what we wrongly assumed was the future leadership of the movement. I was not aware that that was our choice, and we would have negotiated
with whomever the Palestinians cared to appoint. I actually never truly understood why Henry Kissinger singled out Israel as a state whose foreign policy was
actually domestic.

Our drive to maintain the flow of negotiations amidst the mayhem of a dirty
war, suicide terrorism, and diplomatic pressure was increasingly becoming unsustainable. When on October 22, a group of Israeli hikers came under attack
on Mount Ebal, north of Nablus, Barak succumbed to the pressure of public
opinion and suspended the talks. His decision, of course, gave Arafat reason
to rejoice: "We will continue our march to Jerusalem, the capital of the independent Palestinian state. Barak can accept it or reject it just as he wants. He
can go to hell." Our woes greatly increased when Arab governments supported
Arafat's war with hostile diplomatic moves. Tunisia and Morocco seconded
Egypt's withdrawal of her ambassador by severing diplomatic ties with Israel.
Years of painstaking efforts went down the drain. We could understand Tunisia,
but Morocco? King Hassan II had steered his country with Bismarckian insight by maintaining a special relationship with Israel, while at the same time
preserving his status in the Arab family. Morocco now removed herself from her
traditionally privileged position as a bridge between the parties. This much I said
to the Moroccan foreign minister, Mohamed Benaissa, who was now particularly concerned with the adverse effects of their move on their standing in the
United States, and he asked me not to be too harsh on them in our contacts
with Washington. If Morocco acted that way, why not Egypt? Amr Moussa was
quick to declare that the peace process had ended, and Egypt had to support the
Intifada. Egypt simply stopped pretending to please the Americans; it no longer
feared the Clinton presidency, now in its final days, and was looking forward to
the election of George W. Bush, whose name conjured a dream of a less "Jewish,"
less pro-Israel presidency.

It was all a desperate search for a way to reactivate the negotiating process. We
also used the fifth anniversary of Rabin's assassination to warn our public of the
danger of dropping the torch of peace. But the vacuum that was to be created by
the imminent end of the Clinton administration loomed over us. Desperately
helpless, the Europeans did not have a policy beyond the October 13 Biarritz

declaration in support of the Camp David framework as the basis for a final set-tlement. And even if they had one, they did not have the strength to implement it. As usual, all they could think of was, once again, to call on Israel for self-con-trol, restraint, avoidance of the use of undue force, and so on. Could friendly foreign statesmen be of any help? On October 24, I asked the Norwegian foreign minister, Thorbjørn Jagland, to look into the possibility of inviting both Barak and Arafat to the upcoming congress of the Socialist International. In a reflec-tion of his distress, Barak welcomed the chance. As expected, Arafat dragged his feet, and this initiative died a quick death.

With Tony Blair at 10 Downing Street on October 31, the discussion was deeper and more empathetic. Blair doubted that Arafat was actually capable of making a decision on such thorny issues as the refugees and Jerusalem, and he wondered whether an agreement without these two issues could be contemplated. But, I said, if in exchange for a comprehensive agreement, Arafat would not impose order among his militias, why would he do so in exchange for another interim agreement, which he in any case kept rejecting? Blair agreed that Arafat would act if enough pressure was put on him. He believed that Britain, Germany, and Holland in dialogue with France could engineer the adoption of a European policy that should tell Arafat "Enough is enough!" His remarks were music to my ears. But, like us, Blair would discover that when he needed them for a bold initiative, the Europeans proved to be timid, confused, uncoordinated, and riddled with complexes.

October 30 was a particularly violent day. Two security guards at the East Jerusalem branch of the country's National Insurance Institution were shot to death, the body of a Gilo resident was found with signs of violence and abuse, and shells were fired at the casino in Jericho. In retaliation, air force helicopters again attacked Palestinian militia positions in Nablus, Ramallah, and Khan Yunis. Barak responded to these incidents in a Knesset speech in which he stuck to the difficult policy of clutching at peace while retaliating with force.

The day after Barak's Knesset speech, Shimon Peres asked to be sent to Arafat. He wanted to put to the test Barak's statement that he had "turned over every stone" in the search for peace. Peres overcame Barak's initial hesitation with the help of Rabin's widow, Leah, who at the time lay dying on a hospital bed. So Peres departed on his mission to suggest what was a truly brilliant idea. The sides would declare a week without violence in memory of Rabin. Forty-eight hours later they would begin to reimplement the Sharm El-Sheikh understandings, in-cluding an Israeli troop withdrawal. Arafat accepted. However, Arafat's prom-ised public statement of a week-long ceasefire was never issued in spite of him and Barak having agreed, in a telephone conversation, on the principles of such an announcement. On the ground, business as usual. Shortly before 3 p.m. on November 2, a car bomb exploded near the Mahane Yehuda open-air market in Jerusalem. Ayelet-Hashachar Levy, daughter of the National Religious Party leader Yitzak Levy, and Hanan Levy (unrelated) were killed. Islamic Jihad claimed responsibility for the attack. The shooting resumed now with full force in all sectors. The Peres-Arafat understandings went the way of all flesh, just as our Sharm El-Sheikh ceasefire agreement had.

Barak was gradually losing his belief in an agreement, which exposed him to criticism from the left for his "zigzagging" approach. Barak's inconsistency had an effect also on Clinton, who yearned to end his presidency with a great historical act, but was getting mixed messages from the prime minister. To boost his shaking domestic political standing, Barak expected from Clinton an upgraded strategic agreement with the United States. On the basis of my briefing, the Israeli-American businessman Haim Saban, who hosted President Clinton in Los Angeles on November 2, asked the president for his reaction to Barak's demand. Clinton's response, qualified but with his unswerving support for Israel underlying it, read to me by Saban, reflected the Clinton administration's delicate attempt in its last days in office to maintain a balanced approach between its alliance with Israel and the fear of alienating the Palestinians and the broader Arab world:

> *The Prime Minister continues to ask me to make an effort to return Arafat to the negotiating table. It would be very hard for me to do that and, at the same time, act unilaterally on the matter of the strategic upgrade package. Barak has to make a decision because we cannot implement both things simultaneously. If I reach the conclusion that we can't move the process forward, which includes coercing Arafat to return to negotiations, I won't have any problem making unilateral gestures vis-à-vis Israel, including the upgrade. If we come to the conclusion that we cannot put Arafat back on track, we will line up with Israel.*

Neither Inspiring nor Intimidating

Echoing Palestinian demands for "international protection against Israeli aggression," UN Secretary General Kofi Annan shared with me on November 2 a plan for the deployment of an international force in the Palestinian territories. Such a force, I replied, could be deployed only after a peace agreement with the aim of overseeing its implementation. Annan's initiative was killed in its bud when neither the Russian foreign minister, Igor Ivanov, nor his French counterpart, Hubert Védrine, supported it. To my surprise, Védrine also told me in our telephone conversation on November 4 that the French media were beginning to understand that it was the Palestinians who were being provocative. Otherwise, the odds were not particularly good for Israel's case.

For one thing, the increasing impotence of the United States in the dying days of the Clinton administration was becoming apparent. Clinton's reluctance to present his promised, ultimate peace plan responded to an increasing preoccupation with US standing in the Arab world. Ambassador Indyk said they feared that such a plan might force them to yet again condemn Arafat as having rejected peace, and this "would damage US strategic interests." The strategic upgrading of the US-Israel alliance, as demanded by Barak, could have a similar effect, he said. Also, the financial package promised for Israel's withdrawal from Lebanon and for countering the development of the Iranian Shahab-3 missile and other promised transfers of military technology were all being delayed. Clinton also dropped his promised legislation for punitive action against the Palestinians if they unilaterally declared statehood.

Arguably, it made tactical sense for the Americans to distance themselves from Israel ahead of the presentation of an even-handed peace plan. If only it changed Arafat's response, but it would not. What it did was to weaken even further the domestic political standing of Barak's government precisely when it was called upon to accept the most divisive peace plan ever presented to an Israeli government. The United States also refused to veto a UN Security Council vote censuring Israel's use of force. In a charged conversation I had with Sandy Berger, he excused this, saying a veto could damage US standing in the Arab world. A weak, fearful, and toothless America chose now to use its leverage on our minority government whose capacity to sustain its peace policy against tremendous domestic odds was diminishing by the day. A few days later, I would report to the Knesset's Foreign Affairs and Defense Committee that "Clinton is paralyzed by the fear of shock waves across the Arab world and anti-American unrest that would affect vital US interests in the region." If that was America, what could we expect of Europe, for whom Israel had always been a state on probation? Chris Patten, the EU foreign affairs commissioner, even asked to apply sanctions against Israel. How could this help the peace process? One thing it could certainly achieve was to increase Ariel Sharon's chances to become Israel's next prime minister.

Predictably, at the Mediterranean Foreign Ministers Forum meeting in Marseilles on November 15, we were put back in the dock. Europe's patronizing ethos of forgiveness and guilt toward their former Arab colonies was again at play in determining her policies. I stood alone, surrounded by a solid phalanx of hostile Arab and European foreign ministers. Around me were ministers from human rights' beacons such Egypt, Algeria, Libya, Tunisia, and Morocco ranting about Israel's "violations of human rights." Amr Moussa sanctimoniously expressed outrage at what he called "Israel's make-believe concessions," and in the same breath proclaimed that there would be no Palestinian compromise over withdrawal from the territories or the right of return.

Nabil Shaath invoked the memory of Yitzhak Rabin, nostalgically describing him as a "hero of peace" in an attempt to contrast Rabin's "heroism" with the actions of Barak's government. I replied, recalling what I knew of Rabin's real positions, far less accommodating than ours. Rabin's widow had just declared in an open letter to the press that if her late husband knew of the concessions made by us, he would be turning in his grave. "It is in your hands," I advised, "whether to cling to an illusion about the dead or return with us to the track of dialogue."

The French presidency issued a concluding communiqué that tried to please everybody, but pleased none. It described Sharon's visit to the Temple Mount as "the mother of all transgressions," even though the Mitchell committee was still discussing that matter. It also referred to the "relevant Security Council resolutions" ignoring the fact that only Resolutions 242 and 338 were the agreed basis of the peace process. But this was not enough to satisfy the Arab side. Nabil Shaath condemned "the doctrine of neutrality" adopted by the Europeans, and Moussa's militancy got him hailed as a hero by the Egyptian media.

Our main concern remained, however, that the way the United States distanced herself from Israel was interpreted by the Palestinians as a strategic blow that would force a weakened and abandoned Israel to assume that the Intifada was a Palestinian and all-Arab victory for which Israel would have to pay with more concessions. This was not good news for America either, for it exposed her as a panicking power desperately shifting her policies to please Arab autocracies. The United States itself thus raised the expectations of the Palestinians to such heights that, however even-handed her future peace plan might be, it would fail to convince them. If Europe inspired but did not intimidate, the United States in the dying days of the Clinton administration neither inspired nor intimidated.

It was somewhat embarrassing that against that background Igor Ivanov should have tactlessly, albeit fancifully, boasted of Russia's rising clout in the Middle East and the United States' declining status by showing me what he described as a desperate message he had gotten from Secretary Albright at the end of October in Paris. She described to him a grim Middle East scenario where Hezbollah, with the support of an emboldened Syria, was effectively challenging the Lebanese government; Iran was penetrating ever more deeply into Southern Lebanon and sending support to Palestinian terror organizations; and Iraq was reviving its military preparedness. In light of all this, the Secretary of State turned politely to the Russians and asked that they use their influence and weight in Iran.

We, on our side, continued to look for every possible opening. On November 19, Barak sent a message to Arafat that they agree on confidence-building steps, starting with a meeting with Israel's former President Ezer Weizman, who was known for his peace credentials. But the good intentions were cut short the next day by a roadside bomb that blew up a children's bus in Gush Katif. Two adults were killed, and three children, all members of the same family, had limbs amputated. IDF helicopters retaliated against military installations in Gaza. Another victim of the violence was a peace initiative we had agreed on with the Turkish foreign minister, Ismail Çem, who arrived for talks in Jerusalem and Gaza on November 22. We were supposed to start secret negotiations in Turkey as soon as the Palestinians sent a written document outlining their positions. But the violence continued—a large suicide bomb attack in Hadera—and so did Arafat's foot-dragging.

That same evening, a phone call from Albright dragged me out of a Cabinet meeting. She begged us not to retaliate because Arafat had contacted her and said he wanted to renew the negotiations. Was this a sign that the Chairman was coming to his senses? I rushed, then, to Washington again to discuss the possible way forward. At a meeting with Sandy Berger in his office on November 29, he suggested that a peace deal would be good for our electoral prospects. I begged to differ. War was also an electoral alternative. Begin won an election on the strength of having bombed an Iraqi nuclear reactor. Turning the Palestinian territories into a desert wilderness would have been, electorally speaking, a far better alternative than peace.

In parallel, Barak sent Gilead Sher to Cairo for secret talks with Intelligence Chief Omar Suleiman with a roadmap for returning to the negotiating table. On December 9, Suleiman himself arrived in Jerusalem to convey Mubarak's message that relations between the two states would not be affected by any incident. Now, Egypt was no longer driven by the need to please the debilitated Clinton administration, but by concerns of domestic stability and the fear of a Sharon electoral victory. Considering the alternative, Mubarak was interested to see Barak win the elections, for which the Egyptians even had their own peace plan. It called for an Israeli withdrawal from 90 percent of the land—including parts of the Jerusalem area—within six months. The negotiations for the final settlement would then proceed while Israel handed over another 5 percent of the land. If an agreement was not reached, an international conference would deal with the remaining issues, particularly refugees. Should the Jerusalem and Temple Mount issues not be resolved, they would be postponed for a number of years. To me, this sounded a reasonable way out of the impasse, but the plan apparently had not been coordinated with the Palestinians, nor were the Egyptians willing or able to coerce them into endorsing it.

The Egyptians were simply engaged in an exercise of diplomatic jugglery. To them, Clinton was now history, and it was not the prospect of an agreement that preoccupied Mubarak and even less so Omar Suleiman. Their concern was the stability of the regime. The Israeli-Palestinian blood feud unleashed waves of anger throughout the Arab world. Egypt genuinely feared that uncontrolled public outbursts of anger could force them to use repressive measures, and who could know where that would end? They wanted to have the best of all worlds: reduce the anger of the Egyptian street by recalling their ambassador, and retain their special links with Israel, which assured both their standing in America and their capacity to exercise influence over Israel's Palestinian policy. "The Palestinians always lie to us, which is why we would like to follow events in close contact with you," was how Omar Suleiman explained the motive of his visit.

By the first days of December signs were apparently accumulating that, as so often in the Middle East, war might still be the prelude to a settlement of sorts. On November 9, Arafat had come to the White House where President Clinton revealed to him the broad lines of his future peace plan. Territory, in "mid-90s"—Dennis Ross defined it as 8 percent Israeli annexation with 2 percent swap—Jerusalem, including the Old City, divided along ethnic lines, with Israel obtaining sovereignty over Jewish religious sites such as the cemetery on the Mount of Olives and the City of David; on the Haram al-Sharif each side would control its holy sites; with regard to refugees, a large compensations fund with no right of return, except for family reunifications of "a few thousand," mainly from Lebanon. The Americans claimed that the *ra'is*, surprisingly, did not object. A few days later, Dennis again confronted Arafat in Rabat, Morocco, with the Clinton plan, and again to his surprise, the *ra'īs* was positive.[1]

But this was all about Arafat's usual penchant for deception. Abu-Mazen, who had earlier seen this set of ideas, presumably worked out by Rob Malley and Hussein Agha, a brilliant Palestinian intellectual close to Abu Mazen, turned them down and anticipated that Arafat would do the same.[2] Barak's lukewarm response to the president's principles at a meeting in the White House on November 12 was by no means tantamount to a rejection of his ideas. Barak simply no longer set any store by Arafat's utterances or "qualified approvals." He saw his American interlocutors as well-intentioned, innocent Americans incapable of truly understanding Arafat's specious performances, his duplicity, and his alley cat mindset. Significantly, it was a man of the Middle East, the Saudi Ambassador in Washington, Bandar bin Sultan, who shared Barak's skepticism at the way the Americans interpreted Arafat's response. "If Arafat does not accept what is available now, it won't be a tragedy: it will be a crime," he said to Dennis Ross after he heard his report.[3]

His doubts notwithstanding, Barak was eager to seize any opportunity, however slim and uncertain, for a breakthrough. At a meeting of our peace team on December 6, he urged us not to give up on peace: "We have an historic responsibility to squeeze the process, even if at the end we are not successful . . . We are walking a tightrope, as we face violence and suicide attacks, but a comprehensive settlement however painful and difficult is in the national interest." Consequently, we tried to exert a positive influence over the process in any way we could. I went for a meeting in Paris with the Qatari foreign minister, Hamad bin Jassim Al Thani, whose country held the rotating presidency of the Conference of Islamic States. Qatar was the only Arab country to have the courage to allow the Israeli representative office to remain open during the Intifada and, with the aim of scoring points with the American administration, she did everything possible to tone down resolutions being passed in various Islamic forums. I reviewed with Al Thani the state of the negotiations, and was surprised when he confided to me that he fully understood our position on the Temple Mount. He also shared with me the wisdom accumulated by a small country in a hostile environment. He thought that Qatar's philosophy of survival could be a lesson for Israel too:

> *In fifty or a hundred years six million Jews will have to live in harmony with the Arab majority around them. Doing that will require a deal that you find hard to accept, but at least it will be a deal. Without a deal you may in another fifty years have to contend with a revival of Nasserism. I do not threaten. In Qatar what I do is clearly mark my boundaries. Your legitimacy*

in the region can only be achieved through a peace agreement that is accept-
able to the peoples of the region.

Still pursuing the elusive peace, I arrived in Gaza on December 14 together
with Gilead Sher and Yisrael Hasson for a late-night meeting with Arafat at
Muhammad Rashid's palatial house. The purpose was to find out whether the
news from Washington that Arafat was serious about reaching an agreement on
the basis of Clinton's ideas was indeed correct. I was encouraged to hear him say
that it would take a great deal of time for the incoming Bush administration to
master the issues under negotiation. For that reason, he concluded, "We have to
work quickly and seriously." But before departing, I went with him into a side
room for a private conversation where the all too well-known Arafat again repeated the old slogans. Assuming he had accepted the latest Clinton ideas, I told
him that on the right of return, the extreme right and the extreme left in Israel
spoke with one voice. Only he, I told him, could stand courageously before his
people and say that there would be no right of return to Israel, but that there
would definitely be a solution for each and every refugee, be it by way of resettlement or by way of compensation." Instead of replying, Arafat slipped his
trembling hand into his shirt pocket and took out a faded and tattered article
from the English edition of the Israeli daily newspaper *Haaretz*, in which it said
that over 50 percent of the immigrants coming to Israel from the former Soviet
Union were not Jewish. "Them you accept," he said, "but the Palestinians you
don't accept. What is the difference?" Many of them had Jewish roots that went
beyond the narrow definition of the rabbis, I replied. They were also willing to
serve the idea underlying the national Zionist project. "Do you expect that this
will be the case with the refugees from Lebanon? They should be Palestinian
patriots, not citizens in a predominantly Jewish state." I also discussed with him
the Temple Mount imbroglio. I assured him that we were conscious of his rights
in relation to the site, and that we were seeking to maintain "our religious and
historical link to this holy place, but we have no intention of doing anything of
substance such as changing the status quo, building or digging." I also explained
to him in detail the distinction we made between "Jewish Jerusalem" and "Arab
Jerusalem" in contrast to his demand that the city be divided between east and
west along pre-1967 lines.

At the end of the meeting, we issued a joint communiqué announcing the
immediate resumption of negotiations in Washington under US auspices.
Visibly moved, Dahlan saw us out, saying that at long last the time for a settlement had arrived. For the first time in a meeting with Arafat I got the feeling that
the Palestinian leader had finally grasped that he had to move, for his chances
for reaching a settlement were receding with the imminent change of presidents in the United States. Ambassador Indyk's assessment went along the same

lines: "Up till now Arafat's people have not been able to negotiate with you because they didn't know what Arafat wanted. Now they do understand," he told me. The discussion with the ambassador resonated with the feeling that this was decision time. We also discussed setting up an international umbrella for the agreement and mobilizing the G8 to work out an economic support system for the peace accord.

Before taking off on December 18 for a new round of talks with the Palestinians in Washington, we attended a meeting of the Peace Cabinet where practically everybody agreed with the assessment that Arafat wanted an agreement. Barak's instructions for the discussions in Washington were encouragingly innovative:

- In line with the spirit of the talks in Sweden we could agree to the definition of any agreement reached on refugees as implementation of UN Assembly Resolution 194.
- Regarding the Temple Mount, I made a mental note that Barak had not spoken about sovereignty but rather about "a form of words that would take proper account of our link to the site." It sounded as an echo of what I myself had said to Arafat during our meeting in Gaza a few days previously.
- On territory, he said explicitly that we must work for 95 percent of the West Bank for the Palestinians.

I would later be criticized for deviating from these instructions in the Washington talks. As a minister and leader of a negotiating team, I considered that it was vital that as the talks proceeded, I should be able to develop a degree of maneuverability. I did not believe that parroting a set of instructions without paying attention to their underlying *spirit* or to the dynamic of the negotiating process was the right way to conduct negotiations. Besides, Barak's sometimes oblique way of presenting his views always left you with the challenge of connecting the dots as best you could.

"Take It or Leave It": The Clinton Peace Parameters

On Wednesday, December 20, the two delegations arrived at the White House for a meeting with President Clinton, who explained to us the rules of the endgame. He would present us with a set of general peace parameters which he expected us to discuss over the following two days. Then, on the basis of our discussions, he would present us with a more tightly formulated set of parameters as a "take it or leave it" proposition. There would be no room for additional maneuvering or another round of negotiations; it would be decision time.

Immediately upon our arrival at Bolling Air Force Base, I sat with the head of the Palestinian delegation, Yasser Abed-Rabbo. As always, one-on-one meetings with Palestinian negotiators were refreshingly congenial and free of rhetoric. Abed-Rabbo even suggested territorial changes of a magnitude of 3 percent, with swaps, of course. I thought that 5 percent, not Barak's 8 percent, would be necessary if 80 percent of the settlers were to be concentrated in the settlements blocs, as stipulated by Clinton. The gap looked suddenly bridgeable. Alas, when the full delegations met later, things became more difficult. Saeb Erakat insisted that an end to the conflict could be offered only if and when Israel accepted the right of return and her "moral responsibility" for the *Nakba*. He was not impressed by my idea that the right of return be implemented with regard to the settling of refugees in swapped areas within Israel.

It was clear that, ahead of Clinton's presentation of his final plan, the parties wanted to impress on him their maximalist positions. That was not my approach, but it was Barak's. Gilead Sher presented the Palestinians with a provocative map showing a 10.5 percent annexation. Predictably, the meeting broke up in anger after twenty minutes. What was the sense, I asked my colleagues, of falling back on Camp David maps that extended beyond the president's broad parameters. I tried to see the broader picture that made all these tactical games look grossly inadequate. Clinton's administration was quickly becoming history. That the incoming administration would be in no hurry to follow in Clinton's footsteps was something I learned "straight from the horse's mouth": the Secretary of State Designate, Colin Powell, told me over the telephone that the new administration would honor any agreement we might reach as well as any commitment made by the Clinton team on behalf of the United States. But if we did not reach an agreement, "It won't be one of our top priorities to push the matter." I had heard much the same thing from the National Security Adviser Designate, Condoleezza Rice, during a dinner I hosted in her honor in Tel Aviv several weeks before the US elections.

Back to our talks. Even though it seemed that we had already tried every possible formula on the Temple Mount question, I attempted once more to push for a breakthrough. I proposed that Israel agree to Palestinian sovereignty over the Mount in exchange for their recognition of the site's sanctity to us. This meant a transfer of sovereignty over the Mount to the Palestinians without demanding for us "virtual" sovereignty over its substratum. But I stipulated that the Palestinians would spell out in the peace treaty the reason for not conducting archaeological excavations on the site in one of the following ways: "because the site contains the Jews' ancient holy Temple" or "because the area contains a Jewish holy site." I also proposed that the agreement be confirmed by the Organization of the Islamic Conference (OIC), which was tantamount to Islam's recognition of the Jews' "return to Zion." No sane individual in Israel thought we had to rebuild the Temple, and no one thought we had to dig into the depths of the mountain in order to reach the remnants of the shrine. Let that be left for the coming of the Messiah. Mine was an attempt to put the chances of a settlement to their ultimate test by seeing whether a solution to the Temple Mount imbroglio would make the other pieces of the jigsaw to fall into place as a Gestalt-like compromise for a comprehensive deal. The second part of my proposal concerned territory where I proposed reducing our extravagant claim for more than 10 percent annexation to 5 percent, excluding the area of the Jewish neighborhoods in Jerusalem. As they left the room to consult, it was obvious that the idea had caught the Palestinians by surprise.

It had been my way throughout these negotiations to translate ambiguous, sometimes convoluted hints I got from Barak into negotiating terms. Lately he had been using the need to have our "link," not sovereignty, to the Mount recognized. In mid-August, he had suggested to Ambassador Indyk that he was willing to cede sovereignty on the Temple Mount to God provided Arafat would do the same.[1] In fact, at Camp David, Barak did not rule out shared Israeli-Palestinian sovereignty on Temple Mount.[2] I was a politician, not a civil servant. When one has power, and I had some, one cannot sit on the sidelines or simply recite the positions of one's superiors. I had the obligation to push negotiations forward with new proposals or by a flexible interpretation of the prime minister's instructions. A possible reason he never reprimanded me was that the Palestinians did the job for him; anyway, they rejected my proposition, about which Amnon Abramovich, one of Israel's most respected journalists, said that "had the Palestinians accepted Ben-Ami's proposal, he would have to be protected [against Jewish attackers] by a team of bodyguards for the rest of his life." Yisrael Hasson, a member of our team, later said that if he had had a gun, he would have drawn it to discipline me.

Ambassador Indyk's account is misleading. I did not make this proposal out of domestic political considerations or, as he suggested, in order to thwart Shimon Peres's political ambitions.[3] No one ever thought that I was gifted with such Machiavellian capabilities. In fact, I wish I had them; politics is a complex art, and I am afraid I was too transparent and mission-driven to be sufficiently proficient in the craft. I do not claim, of course, to have been immune to the temptations of politics as the domain of intense, personal ambitions. That is why the idea that, in this case, I might have been genuinely motivated by conviction simply did not occur to the ambassador. If I was "possessed," as he claims, it was by the chance of a lifetime to push the quest for peace to its optimal limits. At Bolling, I was exactly the same individual as Indyk himself sought out at Camp David when the president was "exasperated" and was looking for "a last-minute ploy that might make a difference," because I had been, as he put it, "one of the most flexible and creative members of the Israeli delegation."[4] On the eve of my trip to Camp David, I had met Yael Dayan, whose father, Moshe Dayan, had been a mine of bold ideas and initiatives as Israel's foreign minister at Camp David I. Yael Dayan, an extraordinary, resilient woman who made Israeli-Arab reconciliation into her entire political life's project, pleaded with me to be the Moshe Dayan of our summit. That was too awesome a comparison, but she knew very well that I had not come into politics just to go through the motions. All this is over now, and a Palestinian peace is more remote than at any time since 1967. But to the end of my days I shall be haunted for failing to deserve Yael Dayan's overly generous comparison.

Our insistence on sovereignty beneath the Temple Mount ground based on the argument that the site contained remnants of the Temple was quite problematic. This belief has generally been typical of fundamentalist Christians and Jews, but has never been accepted by the Jewish mainstream, which believes that the Temple vessels are concealed in heaven and will be brought back to earth with the coming of the Messiah, which was exactly what the Chief Rabbis had told me and Barak at a meeting we convened with them ahead of the Camp David summit. The Temple Mount had hardly ever existed in Zionism's discourse and aspirations; it was the nationalist-religious hysteria unleashed by the 1967 victory that gave such prominence to the site which now held hostage a secular Israeli government. As the negotiations proceeded, I became increasingly convinced that Arafat's Palestinian nationalism needed to be understood also as a theological defiance of the Jewish claim of religious roots in Palestine. More than a national leader seeking a strictly political deal with Israel, he was there also representing Islam's historical claim as the religion that superseded all the religions that preceded it. He was Islam's *homo missus a Deo* to redeem its holy sites from the hands of the infidels, and he would under no circumstances betray his mission and go down in history as the one who surrendered the Haram al-Sharif to Jewish sovereignty. We and the Americans expected Arab leaders to coax Arafat into accepting qualified sovereignty on the Haram al-Sharif or sharing it in some form with Israel. But the Arab rulers feared that if they allowed Arafat to be the sole defender of a fundamentalist Islamic attitude to the Haram al-Sharif, they would expose themselves to popular rage, and Arafat would be the first to stir mass hysteria against them. I strongly felt that by defusing this central religious component of the conflict, we would open the way to a final settlement on the other issues under dispute. I was convinced that Arafat would not risk losing the offer by insisting on having his way on what was to him mundane issues such as territory and even refugees.

Our effective sovereignty over the Temple Mount had been limited anyway; it always hinged on the use of force, which was liable to ignite the entire region. For many years, we had been hostage to every Muslim stone thrower on the Mount. Sovereignty involves responsibility and requires judgment. Palestinian sovereignty, I believed, would ensure a more orderly regime than one based on the fear of Israeli security forces. Nor was rebuilding the Temple ever a Zionist vision; Ben-Gurion had declared independence with a divided Jerusalem and without even having access to the Temple Mount and the Wailing Wall. In proposing a solution to this pivotal issue I felt that I was putting the Palestinians to the ultimate test. Negotiating with the Palestinians was quite unlike anything we had ever experienced in our peace talks with Egypt and Syria, where no such awesome intangible categories were at stake. The question that needed to be answered here and now was whether, within the framework of a settlement, the Palestinians would be willing to recognize that our return to the land was not just a colonial conquest, but a return to age-old roots? Our Palestinian interlocutors failed the test. Their vapid reaction was that they would not admit that the reason for not conducting excavations was that the Mount contained a Jewish holy site. They were willing to sacrifice the national dream of a sovereign state and Palestinian/Muslim sovereignty over the Temple Mount, and not accept the Jewish "link" to the Mount, namely, the Jewish ancestral roots in Eretz Yisrael.

And yet both our intelligence assessments and the US team indicated that this round had created a dynamic of progress. Dennis Ross was upbeat: "The Palestinians are facing a political reality in which they are liable to face Sharon, and then all the achievements they have made thus far will evaporate . . . I believe Arafat wants an agreement now." My Temple Mount proposal, as well as my offer on territory, seemed to have, as Ambassador Indyk claimed, "a dramatic influence on Clinton's calculations." Clinton now felt he "could cut Jerusalem's Gordian knot," and that "the last piece of the puzzle had now fallen into place."[5] Clinton did eventually convey to Arafat the essence of my proposals. Ross interpreted Arafat's reaction in euphoric terms: "Arafat has decided to do it!"[6] Since the beginning of this tortuous process, I believed that there were here two clusters of issues, the tangible, real estate ones, and the intangible, narrative issues such as refugees and Jerusalem. Arafat would accept, I assumed, trade-offs within the clusters, not between them. That was precisely one of the aims of my proposal on the Temple Mount—to bring about a breakthrough on the refugee issue as well: sovereignty over the Temple Mount was not intended to be in return for the annexation of a cluster of settlements, but rather in exchange for a practical solution to the refugee problem that would exclude the right of return.

December 23 in Washington was a bright, snowy Saturday morning as I walked from the Willard Hotel to the White House. The rest of the Israeli team joined me from Bolling Air Force Base on the outskirts of town. Both delegations were received by the president, who was casually dressed, but looked purposeful and highly focused. He knew he was about to put his final and best effort on the table and there was nothing more he could do. He needed to marshal all the wisdom and experience he had gained since the start of this erratic voyage to the limits of our quest for peace. Ironically, as he was about to reach what could be the peak of his years in office, workers outside the White House were building the stage on Pennsylvania Avenue for his successor's inauguration. George W. Bush's victory, we assumed, signaled an end to the Clinton era of negotiations with the Palestinians; if there was no agreement now, we would have to wait a long time for another opportunity. Meanwhile, rivers of Israeli and Palestinian blood would have been shed. With these thoughts, I walked to the White House on the snow-covered sidewalk. I hoped that the bright day and blue sky portended good tidings.

The two delegations sat down on one side of the long table; the president and his people sat on the other side. Clinton read from prepared notes. He said he had already presented the two sides with general parameters; now he had narrowed them so that the leaders could make the final decision. "This isn't an American proposal," Clinton stressed. "These are ideas which, if you reject them, will not be there in the future. They go with me when I leave office." He said he was willing to receive both leaders immediately. This would not be for the purpose of further negotiations but in order to fine-tune his peace ideas. His deadline for our acceptance of these final parameters was Wednesday, December 27. These were Clinton's parameters for a Palestinian-Israeli peace.[7]

Territory: The Palestinian state would comprise the entire area of the Gaza Strip and between 94 and 96 percent of the West Bank. In other words, Israel would annex between 4 and 6 percent for the purpose of accommodating the settlement blocs. In exchange, Israel would hand over to the Palestinians between 1 and 3 percent of its sovereign territory; it would also provide them with a safe passage which, though under Israeli sovereignty, would be for Palestinian "permanent and unhindered usage." It should be possible to adjust the figures, if these percentages did not satisfy the parties' needs, by mutual leasing of land. Clinton repeated the principle of including "80 percent of the settlers" in blocs and the need to minimize the number of Palestinians who would remain "trapped" inside these blocs.

Security: The key lay in the presence of an international force along the Jordan Valley and Israel's phased withdrawal taking place within thirty-six months. For another three years there would be a reduced Israeli presence in specified locations. Three Israeli early warning stations, with a Palestinian liaison presence, would remain in the Palestinian state, an arrangement that could be revised by mutual consent. Zones would be agreed within the territory of the Palestinian state for the deployment of IDF forces in the event of an emergency, which was defined as "an imminent and demonstrable threat to Israel's security." And special arrangements would be made for the Israeli Air Force to use Palestinian airspace for operational purposes. The Palestinian state would be defined as "nonmilitarized" rather than "demilitarized."

Jerusalem: The city would be divided into two capitals along the principle that what was Jewish would be Israeli and what was Arab would be Palestinian. The same principle would apply to the Old City. As for the Temple Mount, the status quo had to be formalized to give the Palestinians de facto control, while respecting Israel's and the Jewish people's needs and links to the site. These principles could be implemented by means of one of the following arrangements: (a) Palestinian sovereignty over the Mount and Israeli sovereignty over the Western Wall and the holy of holies to which it is connected; (b) Palestinian sovereignty over the Mount and Israeli sovereignty over the Western Wall, with shared functional sovereignty over the issue of excavation under the mountain or behind the wall.

Refugees: Clinton squared the circle to the best of his ability. Israel would acknowledge the moral suffering and material damage caused to the Palestinian people. A proportion of the refugees would go to the Palestinian state, others would go to third countries, whilst still others would go to the territories which the Palestinian state would receive from Israel within the framework of territorial swaps. Many would remain in the current host countries. "There will be no specific right of return to Israel," but the Palestinians could claim that in going back to the Palestinian state they were "returning." Certainly that would be so when they "returned" to territory handed over to them by Israel as territorial swaps. The refugees would, in Clinton's terms, be returning "to historic

Palestine." A certain number would be granted entry to Israel "consistent with Israel's sovereign decision." Any solution, Clinton summed up, would be subject to the principle of "two states for two peoples." The agreement would be signed on the basis that it meant the "end of the conflict and an end to all claims."

"These are the ideas," he concluded. "If you don't accept them, they will be taken off the agenda." It had taken him a long time, but Clinton had learned to use the tactics that President Carter had used to achieve a breakthrough at Camp David. Carter had looked for the middle ground on each issue in contention. He had been able to come up with proposals he thought could meet each side's essential needs. On the last day of the summit, Carter presented his own document—not necessarily as an American proposal but as the mediator's understanding of the point at which a compromise could be made—thereby bringing both sides to agree. One surprising analogy between Clinton's plan and a peace plan on Palestine that the Carter State Department had prepared as early as 1977 was that both called for Israeli control of a 15-kilometer strip along the Jordan Valley and the Dead Sea, a Gush Etzion and Jerusalem bloc of settlements, and even Israeli surveillance stations on high points over the Jordan Valley. We did not invent the wheel if only because the precariousness of the security conditions in the area and its geostrategic map are built-in, compelling structural realities. Also the solution to the refugees was similar: compensation, resettlement in the West Bank and Jordan, and only token repatriation to Israel. The stipulation that Jerusalem would not be divided physically, but its Jewish neighborhoods would be under Israeli control and the Arab areas left to the Palestinians, is reminiscent of Clinton's division of the city along ethnic lines.[8] Alas, a crucial difference between the two situations was not only that Clinton's plan was an all-encompassing addressing of each and every core problem pertaining to the conflict, but that it was also the result of the longest and most arduous negotiations ever to have been conducted on the question of Palestine. Carter never offered his State Department's ideas to the parties; they were just internal working papers. The sad reality was that Carter's hyper peace activity, mainly focused anyway on the Israel-Egypt conflict, occurred during the first half of his term in office, whereas by the time Clinton produced his parameters, he was already a lame duck. His power had withered.

While listening to the president reading from his notes, I thought to myself that, considering the difficult nature of the conflict and the promise of peace, the proposals, which would be surely hard to digest for the Israeli public, were nonetheless right and fair. The terms proposed would most certainly safeguard our main values as a democratic and Jewish state. Some of the provisions would be hard to digest by the Palestinians as well. Their national narrative got only partial satisfaction. Still, I hoped that they would be capable of seeing the package in its totality. They were offered the end of occupation, statehood practically on the totality of the West Bank and the Gaza Strip, a safe passage linking Gaza and the West Bank under their exclusive control, a practical solution to the problem of refugees with a multibillion fund for reparations, a capital in all of Arab Jerusalem, including exclusive sovereignty over the entire Muslim compound in the Haram al-Sharif, and the opportunity to now unleash the qualities of the Palestinian people in order to occupy the place they deserved in the family of sovereign nations.

But, Yasser Abed-Rabbo, who sat to my right, and the other members of the Palestinian delegation had sour looks on their faces. But then, they always had sour looks, for either tactical or substantive reasons.

"A Crime against the Palestinian People"

Immediately upon landing in Israel on Sunday, December 24, Gilead Sher and I flew to an army base in the north to brief our inner Cabinet. This is the deal; it was now or never, we said. Everyone in the room, without exception, supported the parameters. Barak was unequivocal: "The alternative to this agreement is tragedy. If and when a peace agreement is signed the issues that are now causing us such difficulties will be swept away by the forward march toward peace." Three days later, shortly before the target date set by Clinton, the entire government, with two abstentions, approved the plan. Israel had now accepted a clear-cut partition of Jerusalem, and a Palestinian state on 97 percent of the West Bank and the entire Gaza Strip. The most outspoken opponent, though, was Chief of General Staff Mofaz, whom Barak challenged caustically for assuming that Israel could not exist "unless it controls the Palestinian people." Encouragingly, the Head of Mossad, Efraim Halevy, was supportive, but, he also passed me a note, wrong in its prediction, but right in its assessment of how unsettling for the Palestinians this entire peace adventure was:

> Within a year of the signing of the agreement, the violence in the Palestinian camp will reach peak levels, and there is a risk that Arafat will be assassinated by a Palestinian. What will happen then will pale in comparison with the settling of accounts that took place in 1936–39.

Mofaz's behavior was a pitiless indictment of the failure of Israel's military hierarchy to revise their calcified worldview on matters of national security and appreciate the significance of the nonmilitary components of security. I would later take issue with General Mofaz in a radio broadcast, when I reminded him that it was not the job of politicians to seek a peace settlement on the basis of security plans drawn up by the army; it was the army's job to provide answers to security problems stemming from plans decided upon by elected politicians after careful deliberation with the military, as we certainly did. One must also consider, I said, the danger to security if the occupation of an oppressed people continued.

But Barak, like Barak, even after the government had given its seal to the parameters, still made an utterly counterproductive move. He dispatched Gilead Sher and General Yanai to a meeting with Mubarak "in order to explain Israel's position vis-à-vis the Clinton parameters." I voiced my opposition to this mission and when Sandy Berger called me from Washington, he too expressed his reservations about it. The Egyptians had no wish to "understand the Israeli position" so as to pressure Arafat into accepting them. They had by now thrown their weight behind Arafat's attempt to beguile Israel into bilateral talks, thus helping him to eschew the straight answer Clinton had asked for. I told Barak that passing on messages to Mubarak would have the same effect as giving them directly to Arafat. No less grave was the fact that Gilead Sher had presented Mubarak, at Barak's request, with Israel's demand for the annexation of 8 percent of the territory, changes in Clinton's language on Temple Mount and refugees and so on. The parameters had already been endorsed by the government, so what was then the point in making a demand of Mubarak, of all people, that was close to being beyond the parameters when we were boasting that Palestinian reservations were outside the parameters and ours within them? That was giving Arafat ammunition for his delaying tactics.[1]

On Friday, December 29, Barak called me at home, admitted that my concerns were well founded, and asked me to calm Arafat's fears. I did so in a telephone conversation, telling the Chairman that we had no intention of deviating from Clinton's plan or ground rules for further engagement. I promised him that if negotiations were resumed based on the parameters, Yossi Beilin and Yossi Sarid, two emblematic doves, would be in our delegation. But the Palestinians went full tilt against Clinton's ideas. They were "worse than some of Israel's past proposals" was the general tone. A communiqué from the weekly Cabinet meeting in Gaza was explicit: "Our one and only position is that we insist on a full Israeli withdrawal, first and foremost from Jerusalem, without conceding our national rights." The Palestinians, and the Egyptians on their behalf, continued to call for preliminary negotiations in which we, rather than Clinton, would make further concessions. We were without parliamentary support, facing up to a fierce opposition and a confrontational army, and now the Palestinians wanted more improvements so that maybe—always only "maybe"—they would say yes to Clinton. The Americans sounded steadfast, as Sandy Berger assured me that same day. "We won't show flexibility. We won't answer their questions, and we won't get into any substantive discussions with them until they say yes." He also told me that Clinton was constantly lobbying Arab leaders to force Arafat to face his moment of truth. Dennis Ross gave me similar assurances that day: "We won't let them off the hook. We are being tough . . . the President is firm; he won't yield. The Palestinians are very edgy; they're asking for clarifications and meetings, and we're turning them down."

But, the Americans were not as tough as they said. In telephone conversations I had with Sandy and Dennis on December 31, they already sounded more hesitant and suggested that Clinton might after all meet Arafat "to clarify certain matters," without a prior Palestinian commitment to saying yes. Jordan's King Abdullah would later confide to Danny Yatom that if he had not stepped in at that point and put his full weight behind it, Arafat wouldn't have done anything at all, for the Chairman was in no hurry. During that same meeting in Amman, Foreign Minister el-Khatib said that Arafat believed the deadline for an agreement was not the end of Clinton's term on January 20, but rather the Israeli elections on February 6.

While busy procrastinating, Arafat also sent Clinton a letter spelling out the clarifications he asked for as well as his reservations.

Clarifications:
• What was the calculation of the ratio between the annexation and the territorial swaps?
• Was the principle of leasing land an option or a parameter?
• Did Israeli sovereignty include the entire Western Wall or only the Wailing Wall, and what effect would this have on Palestinian sovereignty over the Haram?
• Was the location of the IDF's emergency deployment dependent on Palestinian approval?

Reservations:
• Refugees should "return to their homes and villages," not just to "historical Palestine."
• The compensation for those who would not return should be made from Israel's Custodianship of Absentee Property.
• The thirty-six months proposed for the withdrawal of the IDF was too long and was an open invitation to the enemies of peace to torpedo the agreement.

It was revealing that Arafat should have mentioned "the return of refugees to their homes and villages," an assertion he would repeat a year later in a *New York Times* op-ed.[2] He also used as a reference the return of refugees in Afghanistan, Kosovo, and Timor Leste, all of them, however, cases which, contrary to the conditions in the Israel-Palestine situation, were subject to the accepted norm that return happened only when the returnees belonged to the majority ethnic group in the country they wanted to go back to. Arafat's position on a return, as I would find out some years later, when *Al Jazeera* invited me to Doha for a discussion of the Palestine Papers, an archive of leaked memos and other material pertaining to the peace negotiations, was a fundamental Palestinian standpoint.[3] They made a compromise over the territory, they argued, but the sacred right of return was inalienable; it was the very "heart" of the conflict and the Palestinian cause. By their insistence on the right of return, they were actually, they said, doing a favor to Israel. For this would help the Jews "to get rid of the racist Zionism."[4]

The Palestinian establishment declared war on Clinton's peace principles. A coalition of resistance organizations consisting of Fatah, the Tanzim, and Hamas known as the "Palestinian National and Islamic Forces," announced that any solution that did not guarantee the right of return would be "invalid and unacceptable." Speaking on the *Al Jazeera* network, Tanzim's chief, Marwan Barghouti, said: "These ideas do not meet even minimum Palestinian ambitions; they are essentially aimed at continuing the occupation, preserving the settlements, and denying the refugees their right of return." Speaking on the *Voice of Palestine*, Abu Ala announced that "the proposals do not meet Palestinian expectations or give us our national rights." He claimed that the danger of the parameters was that they purported to replace the "international legitimacy" of UN resolutions. The almost erotic attachment of the Palestinians to "international legitimacy" was what Clinton denounced on various occasions at Camp David. Peace, he maintained, was a reasonable balance between wishes and possibilities.

Arafat had surfed on the Intifida in order to force the United States and Israel to offer him a better deal than the one he had been offered at Camp David. The Clinton parameters were precisely such a deal; yet now he was held back by the sky-high expectations fueled by the Intifida, which, from the outset, had no clearly defined political objective which, if achieved, could be regarded as a fulfillment of the uprising's aims. Clinton would later say Arafat was the reason for "me having been such a colossal failure." Even Jacques Chirac was on record that Arafat's obsession to improve every "final" proposal presented to him was responsible in large measure for the catastrophe that has engulfed the peoples of the region. And at a dinner party I attended in the Club of Madrid together with Bill Clinton in 2003, none other than Egypt's then Arab League General Secretary Amr Moussa said that the opportunity missed by Arafat was not at Camp David, but in his refusal to accept the Clinton plan.

While the Palestinians kept on deluding themselves about getting a better deal, Barak was under unbearable pressure. Elections were around the corner, and opinion polls were anticipating a Sharon landslide. Even from our own ranks we were being criticized for "illegitimately and immorally" conducting negotiations when the Knesset had already been prorogued. The burden on Barak had simply become too heavy. Kicking and screaming, he wanted out so that he could focus on the war on terror and the election campaign. On Monday, January 1, 2001, Ambassador Indyk burst into my Knesset office, looking as white as a sheet. He explained that from the perspective of the international community the burden was now squarely on Arafat's shoulders and the president was engaged in a worldwide effort to get Arafat to give a positive answer to his Parameters. If we broke off the talks, Israel would be seen as the side that had never really wanted a settlement and was now conveniently disengaging from it. Nor did Barak find support in his peace cabinet, where he proposed unilateral disengagement from parts of the West Bank. Yossi Sarid warned that the loss of support from the left could be permanent. Peres said that whatever Barak did to quell the violence, he would never be able to make the public believe that he was tougher on terror than Sharon. Beilin crudely threatened that he would rally the Israeli peace camp against a prime minister who had betrayed the core message of the left, Barak's only political constituency ahead of the elections. Trapped in a cage of doves, Barak was forced to accept the logic of domestic and international reality.

Eventually, the Americans succumbed to Arafat's attrition tactics. He wanted to meet Clinton on January 2, just sixteen days before the president left office, and after a gathering in Cairo of the Arab Foreign Ministers' Monitoring Committee. Such a sequence would allow him to arrive in Washington in what was always his preferred bargaining position, presumably handcuffed by the support of the Arab family. With time running out, Clinton demanded that Arafat come immediately. This put the Chairman in a difficult position. He needed yet another excuse. Dahaniya Airport in Gaza, he blurted out, had been closed by the Israelis. He knew that, of all the hurdles, the closure of the airport was the easiest to deal with.

All of us took now part in an effort to induce world leaders to put pressure on Arafat. We made telephone calls to leaders ranging from the President of China to the Duke of Luxembourg, all of whom duly talked to Arafat. It is unlikely that the world has ever witnessed such an extensive effort aimed at trying to persuade the leader of a national movement to overcome his fears, pluck up his courage, and come to a decision worthy of a peacemaker. It was all in vain. In my dozens of calls to foreign ministers I proposed that once Arafat accepted the president's proposal, the settlement be "locked up" and get broad global legitimacy at an international summit. Canada promised through Foreign Minister John Manley financial assistance and the admission of Palestinian refugees. I was given similar commitments by Japan's foreign minister, Yohei Kono, and the Norwegian Thorbjørn Jagland. I talked candidly about the political earthquake and the dramatic social rift that Israel was likely to face if there was an agreement. But an Israeli yes and a Palestinian no would doom the Israeli peace camp for many years to come. Humbled by a recalcitrant Palestinian side, the Israeli left would lose any credibility in defending the case for a negotiated settlement.

Arafat arrived in Washington ten days after the deadline set by Clinton for a response to his proposals. Yet he had come not to give an answer but still to seek "clarifications." In Arafat's reply, as Bruce Reidel put it to me, "There was more divergence than convergence." Others in the administration would explain that Arafat's response had been "a small yes set against a large no." In practical terms it was a clear no. Indeed, as Arafat himself had said in the first sentence of his letter to Clinton, published in the Palestinian daily *Al Ayyam* on the very day of his meeting, the president's proposals "do not meet the required conditions for a lasting peace." Always cunningly alert, Arafat made a brilliant diplomatic move by making it look as if he and Barak were in the same position: they both accepted them "with reservations," and should simply negotiate their differences. This was how Barak's earlier wrongheaded attempt to renegotiate some of the issues in the parameters through Mubarak's "good services" had backfired.

For, in addition to a request for bigger percentages of annexed land for the settlement blocs, we also asked for a different definition of the parties' link to the Temple Mount, a revision of the mandate for the multinational force, more clarifications on the nature of the Palestinian security forces, mechanisms for the control of the demilitarization of the Palestinian state, a more assertive negation of the right of return, clarifications on what is meant by the Western Wall as opposed to the Wailing Wall, and also clarifications on Israel's sovereign right of admittance of refugees and the status of the safe passage. There was no way Clinton could address our reservations in a way that would not entirely destroy the already fragile possibility that the Palestinians would accept his parameters. And even though Arafat's reservations, involving fundamental issues such as the right of return, the Temple Mount, and territorial percentages, all largely outside the parameters, amounted to a big no—Dennis Ross defined them as "deal-killers"—he still could claim that we were on equal footing in that we too had our own reservations, though they were mostly inside the parameters. In our defense I should say that Barak's reservations were for all practical purposes eventually dropped and would not prevent us from defending the letter and spirit of the parameters when we went a few weeks later for a last-ditch attempt to save the peace in Taba. Taba did not produce an agreement precisely because we wanted to translate the parameters into a peace treaty and the Palestinians addressed them as a straitjacket they refused to work with.

Arafat's Washington trip was a typical exercise in diplomatic deceit, which he applied to his Arab allies as well. The Saudi Ambassador to the US, Bandar bin Sultan, had gone to Andrews Airforce Base to welcome Arafat, and both were later joined at the Ritz Carlton Hotel by the Egyptian ambassador, Nabil Fahmy. The two envoys tried to persuade Arafat to accept the parameters, telling him that they satisfied his own as well as basic Arab demands. Two years later, Ambassador bin Sultan gave his own account of their encounter with Arafat

before and after his meeting with the president.[5] Bin Sultan rhetorically asked
the *ra'īs*:

> How much longer are we going to continue on the same path that we have
> taken since 1948? Whenever a proposal is put on the table we say no.
> Sometime later we say yes. But by the time we have said yes, the proposal is
> no longer on the table. We then are forced to negotiate over a lesser offer. Isn't
> it high time we said yes?

Arafat assured the two ambassadors that he would accept the parameters if Saudi
Arabia and Egypt supported him. Bin Sultan and Fahmy promptly promised
to do so. Their understanding was that Arafat would get back to them immediately after his meeting with Clinton and that the three of them would then
call President Mubarak and Saudi Crown Prince Abdullah. Arafat was a born
survivor; the alley cat in him always defeated his sudden accesses of statesmanship. After his meeting with Clinton, he did everything he could to avoid the two
ambassadors. They chased him for an hour, and when they finally caught up with
him at the hotel, he told them a barefaced lie. "It was an excellent meeting," he
said. Yet from the expressions on the faces of the Chairman's aides, Ambassador
bin Sultan knew he had been lied to. In Arafat's presence, he called the White
House so as to hear from Sandy Berger that what he had been told was indeed a
lie. Berger said that Arafat had rejected Clinton's pleas and was admonished by
the president that "The clock is ticking fast," and that he was about to miss the
best, perhaps the only chance of redemption his people would ever have. "I hope
you will sremember," bin Sultan told Arafat, "that if we miss this opportunity, it
won't be a tragedy; it will be a crime" against both the Palestinian people and
the Arab nation. What it certainly was was a Palestinian mistake of historically
unforgivable proportions.

Immediately after Arafat's departure from Washington, Clinton was still ready
to engage in an almost suicidal political exercise. Two weeks before he left the
White House, he was willing to come to the region to clinch a final agreement,
provided the parties managed to bridge some of their key differences in a quick
round of talks involving Arafat and his partner in the Nobel Peace Prize, Shimon
Peres. Barak immediately embraced the idea. Arafat said he was too busy. He
had all kind of meetings with Arab leaders and trips and so on. "Let Peres meet
with Saeb Erakat," he said.[6] The *ra'īs* throve on crisis and adversity, and had no
problem also rejecting an Israeli initiative, warmly welcomed by the Americans,
to draft a Barak-Arafat joint letter summarizing areas of agreement that could
serve as the premise for future negotiations. And all this happened when buses
were still exploding in midtown Tel Aviv and Sharon's victory in the coming
Israeli elections was practically a given.

With Clinton's last-moment brave initiative dead, Sandy Berger admitted that the best that could be expected now was to keep the process alive, if only as a means of reducing the level of violence. We vainly looked now for European leaders to come up with their own insights. One such idea I immediately turned down as utterly counterproductive. Swedish Prime Minister Göran Persson raised the possibility that he, Tony Blair, France's Lionel Jospin, and Germany's Gerhard Schröder (the so-called "club of progressive leaders") could be mobilized to help in Barak's campaign for re-election. From Stockholm I went on to Berlin for meetings with Joschka Fischer. He was at a loss trying to comprehend the path the Palestinians were treading. I shared with him ideas I had raised in Sweden, a European push for the creation of an international coalition that would, in effect, coax the parties to negotiate along the lines of the parameters. Fischer saw the positive side of this, but was skeptical about the willingness of the Americans to permit an active European role. I also proposed that, if it all ended in failure, we work on a new joint Declaration of Principles to replace the Oslo framework, and serve as the basis for future negotiations.

Back from Washington, Gilead Sher reported that the Americans were thinking along similar lines, a presidential declaration in the presence of President-elect George Bush on the White House lawn. Barak, confusingly again in peacemaking mode, couched his remarks in positive terms. He wanted "a presidential declaration as comprehensive as possible." He also toyed with the idea of a summit on a US aircraft carrier that would determine most of the issues on which it would be possible to reach agreement. Desperation can be the mother of truly wild delusions.

Barak in a Cage of Doves

Clinton eventually gave up on his idea to come to the region even if it only was for producing a declaration of principle. "It would hurt me and it will hurt you too," he told Barak. "We cannot allow Arafat to trick us both." He suggested he send Dennis Ross instead. Right now, however, nothing less than a massive foreign, high-level involvement in the shape of a Euro-American rescue operation could salvage the situation. If only Europe were to cease being the bruised reed it was. It did not exactly respond to our pleas for a multilateral coalition in support of the parameters; the Swedish foreign minister, Anna Lindh, whose country held the EU rotating presidency at the time, was receptive but ineffective when I came to see her in Stockholm. On the same lightning European trip in the second week of January 2001, King Juan Carlos of Spain told me of his efforts with Arab leaders to impress upon Arafat a sense of urgency. His conversation with Muhammad VI had been particularly frustrating. "Yes, but what about the rights of the refugees to return to their homes. After all without that no agreement is possible?" said the Moroccan monarch. Still in Madrid, Prime Minister José María Aznar wondered whether the Palestinians' habit of making last-minute claims in search of an elusive "improved deal" was a carefully planned strategy, or a sign of chaos. I told him it was a combination of both.

After meetings in Paris with France's foreign minister, Hubert Védrine, and his prime minister, Lionel Jospin, a message reached me that Clinton had convinced Arafat to personally participate in renewed negotiations starting that very evening at the Erez Crossing in Gaza. I cut short my European tour only to discover that Arafat would not attend the meeting. Yet the meeting was not entirely uneventful; for the first time the Palestinians themselves, and not some third party, spelled out their reservations on the parameters. "We don't want Clinton's boxes: we want a free-wheeling debate," was the underlying motif in Saeb Erekat's presentation. The document he presented us was a radical amendment to each and every single chapter of the parameters. It practically annulled them:[1]

Jerusalem:

- Connecting roads between the Jewish and Arab neighborhoods are not feasible.
- Israeli sovereignty over the Western Wall is not acceptable.
- Happy with their sovereignty over the Temple Mount but rejected Israel's "virtual" sovereignty over the Mount's substratum.
- Rejected Israel's claim over religious areas such as Mount Zion, the Mount of Olives, and the City of David.

Security:

- An international force vitiates the need for Israeli emergency deployment zones.
- Categorically opposed to IAF use of Palestinian airspace as well as a thirty-six-month phased withdrawal from areas in the Jordan Valley.
- Accepted warning stations only if operated by the international force with no Israeli presence.
- Rejected Palestinian state as a "nonmilitarized state"; insisted on a "state with limited arms."

Territory:

- Rejected territorial deal. Land swaps only on the basis of equality "in size and quality." The settlements represented "only 1.8 percent of the West Bank," and that should be the basis for the new borders.

Refugees:

- The right of return must be established, and only then would they be prepared to discuss the details and the mechanism of return. Clinton's concept of the refugees return to "their homeland" or to "historical Palestine" is unacceptable. They wanted that the return be "to their homes." They also rejected the emphasis on the role of the international community in resolving the problem. This, they claimed, released Israel from her responsibilities. They also rejected the Clintonian definition of Israel as "the homeland of the Jewish people." Whether the refugees should return to the Palestinian state, as stipulated by the parameters, was "an internal Palestinian affair, not a matter of interference from outside." They accepted the return of refugees to areas in Israel received as part of the land swaps, but this did not answer the condition of a return "to their homes," that is "their right to choose where exactly in Israel they would want to live."

End of conflict:

• Should be linked to guarantees ensuring the implementation of the treaty.

We told Erakat that because these were not just "reservations," but an entirely new set of parameters, a dynamic was likely to be created in which we too would be free to make substantive changes to the parameters, which would return us both to square one. Gilead Sher described how, to judge from the American account, it was clear that the Palestinians were not frank with the Americans, for they were raising here reservations they had never mentioned to them. The Palestinians had gone along with Clinton until they had got all the concessions they could, and now they wanted yet another round of negotiations to substantively and radically change the deal in their favor. We decided it would be better to break the meeting at this stage, but before we left Erez, I telephoned Arafat. "Why don't you say clearly that you are rejecting the parameters?" I asked him. He mumbled his standard, tepid platitudes, such as "Where there's a will, there's a way," which, coming from him, meant that whoever he was talking to must provide both the will and the way. And when I asked him what sense it made to tell Clinton he intended to reach an agreement before the end of his presidency, he uttered a piece of typical Arafatian nonsense: "We will get there even before that."

With an eye to the elections, Barak's instructions now were not to give up on negotiations; this, he said, would help maintain a background of hope ahead of the upcoming elections, while at the same time giving the Palestinians an incentive to reduce the violence. We then scheduled a meeting in Gaza with Arafat and an Israeli team that included Shimon Peres. Over dinner, Peres asked Arafat to keep negotiating as a way to "mark time" and getting through the election period peacefully. Not for a moment did I believe that we could win the elections, and given Sharon's imminent rise, I was convinced that now was our last chance to reach peace. I said to Arafat that if he was prepared to return to the parameters, there would be no need to just "kill time." In his reply, Arafat recalled the peace agreement with Egypt when "at the last moment" Begin and Sadat reopened all the issues, and in the end reached agreement during the last three days of the summit. On the way back from Gaza, Peres complained to me that we had "gone too far" in our concessions. He still kept insisting that a territorial formula of 80 percent for the Palestinians and 20 percent for us would be something Arafat could very well live with.

No wonder that at the peace cabinet meeting on January 16 Barak talked despairingly about the prospects of an agreement. He suggested that we prepare a document summarizing our efforts to reach peace, and make it available to President Clinton and his successor President-elect Bush. At the same time, said

Barak, we should continue to prepare for unilateral disengagement from parts of the West Bank. But the embattled prime minister, now in the most strenuous moments of his premiership, found himself reined in by the peace cabinet he had put together. He was not allowed to cast away the supreme objective of his government for the sake of political survival. Amnon Lipkin-Shahak told him that disengaging from the talks would only fuel the Intifada. Peres was particularly scathing and lambasted Barak for leading to a catastrophe where Arafat "would turn this place into a living hell." In a strange volte-face, Peres suddenly spoke of negotiations "that will lead to a solution." Barak was infuriated. "You said yourself that we had gone too far toward the Palestinians and that now all we could do was kill time, and now you speak of an imminent agreement. You can't always have it both ways." In the end, Barak was practically blackmailed into accepting that the negotiations continue. There was a pistol on the table. The elections were a month away, and his peace cabinet threatened to deny him the little public support he still had.

I suggested that perhaps at this time the Egyptian president would realize, not for the sake of Israel but for his own interest, that Arafat's defiance was leading the region to destruction, and would therefore agree to put massive pressure on Arafat, even at the eleventh hour. Barak agreed that I should make a final attempt to enlist the Egyptian *ra'īs* to the task. On the morning of January 17, I set off on a hurried mission to Cairo. "I can be of no use vis-à-vis the Palestinians unless I myself am convinced," said the president. I went over the Clinton parameters with him point by point, and accompanied my presentation with a high-resolution map. He confessed to being impressed and said that, contrary to what he was led to believe, that was a rational Palestinian state with fully contiguous territory. He also responded positively to my explanations about the refugees, but his own comments were mainly about security matters. We did not need these emergency deployment zones, he told me, for anyway the Palestinians would not be capable of stopping us should we need to penetrate their territory. Mubarak was satisfied with my reasoning that we did not want every clash with a foreign force across the Jordan to turn into a war with the Palestinian state. He wisely suggested, though, that this particular clause should be part of a peace treaty between two sovereign states rather than included in the Framework Agreement for a Peace Settlement. "This is decision time," I said in a plea for his cooperation. Mubarak suggested then that I meet Arafat that very day in Cairo.

And so that very night, I met Arafat (and Abu Mazen) at the guesthouse that was permanently at his disposal whenever he visited Cairo. For the umpteenth time I went over the issues with him. He began by complaining that Qatar and the Emirates were not transferring funds to him, to which I responded that Palestine's future lay in an agreement with us, not in Arab charity. He also complained of the criticism being leveled for the concessions he had made, and oddly mentioned Edward Said's criticism in the American press. I replied that the fact that we both were under heavy criticism was the best proof that the parameters were fair. Now came the usual nonsense. "Who was it that destroyed the atomic reactor in Iraq?" he asked rhetorically, going on to argue that as a superpower Israel did not need such things as emergency deployment zones inside Palestinian territory. I suggested the idea formulated by Mubarak, that this Israeli demand be dealt with separately instead of being an integral part of the agreement. But he insisted that the stationing of an international force should make our security claims redundant. I went on to talk of the need for intensive discussions but added that the parameters would have to be the basis. He avoided any reference to the parameters, and just reminded me how, before finalizing the Oslo Interim Agreement, they had sat in Taba for ten days and concluded a deal. "We should repeat that model," he said, not before reminding me that the Palestinian issue was central to Israel's international standing: "After the settlement with Egypt, you didn't get anything. After you signed with us in Oslo, you achieved an improvement in relations with countries from Indonesia to Senegal. Even Hussein said in the Jordanian Parliament 'I signed after Arafat did.'"

He would not find, I told him, a single Israeli leader today to offer more than Barak is proposing, for even Peres had said that we were giving too much away. "Peres told me the opposite," he replied. Arafat was not a particularly trustworthy individual, and Peres was not immune to human weaknesses either. Arafat now told me of a fantasy which he clung to obsessively, according to which Rabin had promised him that following the third-phase redeployment he would be in possession of 91 percent of the West Bank. I said that even if this was true, he would not be losing anything by reaching an agreement on the basis of the Clinton plan, which gave him 97 percent, plus the safe passage, the Haram al-Sharif, a solution to the refugees, and other assets. Amr Moussa joined the conversation as I was summarizing what we had decided. There would be an intensive round with a separate working group dealing with the refugees. We would attempt to achieve a framework agreement by working on a modular basis, that is to say, if we were not able to settle all the issues pertaining to a permanent settlement, we would agree on a set of "guidelines" to an agreement in place of a full agreement. "For our people, a framework agreement is the minimum," he concurred.

In preliminary contacts with the Palestinian team ahead of our final attempt to save the peace in Taba, a ray of hope appeared in the form of a question they asked: What would happen if we reached an agreement and Sharon was then elected? That was the last of our worries, but Gilead Sher assured them that from every point of view the agreement would be valid. The harsh, topsy-turvy reality of our situation led Barak to write me a note about the red lines he did not want to be trespassed in the oncoming Taba talks. But with the elections as his central preoccupation, his note could not mask his sense of the government's coming downfall:

> Shalom Shlomo,
>
> Very prepared for a painful but not humiliating agreement (there is to be no right of return). It is vital to preserve hope (only with us closer than ever) side by side with sobriety. There is no agreement because we have been firm on those issues that are vital to Israel (no right of return, appropriate settlement blocs, Jerusalem, the holy places, security arrangements). The main thing: we must totally demolish Sharon's attempt to portray the government as being forcibly pulled by Arafat. In all our relations with the Palestinians, we must be assertive and say we are determined to reach an agreement—if that is at all possible—and resolve to be firm on the issues that are essential to Israel, as well as in our determination to fight against terror.
>
> Ehud.

The intelligence assessments on the eve of yet another round of talks were, as always, typically ambiguous. Arafat, they said, had given instructions to work for a settlement, but "There is no hint of new-found Palestinian flexibility." What were we to make of this apparent contradiction? Arafat had begun to understand that the cost of violence was greater than its benefits, they said. Given the uncertainty in the transition from Clinton to Bush, Arafat was afraid that if he did not get an agreement now, he might lose everything he had gained. According to this assessment, the Palestinian leader thought that even if Barak lost the election, an agreement would make it easier for Arafat to mobilize the international community to put pressure on any prospective Israeli government to fulfill its terms. Neither Israeli intelligence nor the National Security Council was under any illusion about the tough conditions that would be attached to any possible settlement. Yet they were consistently in favor of us pursuing negotiations, if only in the hope that they would serve as "a brake on violence."

The Palestinians had their own reasons for pursuing the negotiations. In Arafat's inner circle, voices could be heard expressing the fear that those "terror gangs," the militias, could bring about the disintegration of the Palestinian Authority. Arafat had manipulated the Intifada as a weapon for his own use, and it was now proving a double-edged sword. Tayeb Abdul Rahim, Arafat's bureau chief, told him that only a diplomatic solution could resolve the built-in tensions within the Palestinian camp. That was all in line with an influential analysis that had been made by Palestinian pollster Dr. Khalil Shikaki late in 2000 where he described how the "revolutionary source of authority" was gaining control over the "political source of authority." He argued that only a resumption of the diplomatic process could restore the power of the latter. The establishment of a Palestinian state by agreement was necessary to put an end to the internal disintegration of the entire national movement, he concluded.[2] Israeli intelligence concurred; one assessment stated that a renewed diplomatic process that would produce an improved settlement had become for Arafat an existential necessity.

Alas, the task at hand was inconceivably difficult. We were a minority government facing elections under the most adverse conditions possible, public opinion was hostile, the nation was irreconcilably divided, and we were at war with the Palestinians. As I made my way to Taba at the head of our negotiating team, the hysterical attacks of the settlers and members of the extreme right were ringing in my ears. Not that the left showered us with frankincense and myrrh; a deep rift was exposed in our own party, where key members condemned negotiations in such times as "immoral." We were left with a constituency that was not even willing to defend us against the heinous attacks from the right. Our predicament reminded me of Leah Rabin, Yitzhak's widow, saying to members of the left who had come to comfort her following her husband's murder, "Why didn't you come before?" I retold this story in a long and detailed interview I gave to the Friday supplement of *Yedioth Ahronoth* (January 19, 2001) on the eve of my departure for Taba:

> It is utterly surrealistic that Barak, who has led the left to the brink of the peace it had always craved, should now have to plead with that very left to give him their backing. This pattern in which the left's penchant for infighting makes way for the right to come to power is not new. There are plenty of examples of it in the history of other nations.

In what turned out to be a political swan song of sorts, I laid down the political philosophy that motivated us in this last-ditch attempt to save the peace from the jaws of possible defeat:

> We Israelis have turned the absence of borders into a definition of our identity. We need to understand that a normal country is not supposed to establish settlements beyond its legitimate borders. We established a state; we were accepted into the UN; we sought a recognized place in the international community. Yet we have remained stuck in a pre-state mindset. This government's tormented journey toward peace requires us as a nation once and for all to decide whether we are a state or a settler community.

The permanent agreement that we sought, I explained, "will make it clear that the territorial phase of Zionism has ended and the time has come for Israeli society to look inward once again." But, however unbearably heavy the price of peace would be, we did not harbor dreams of a heavenly peace:

I don't deceive myself that the end of armed conflict with the Arabs will mean an end to ideological conflict. My sole expectation is that peace will bring us legitimate borders and an end to all Palestinian claims against us. That, in my view, is the significance of an end to the conflict. My horizon does not include the dawn of a Messianic age.

And, if "legitimacy" sounded too theoretical and too distant a goal, there was, indeed, a more immediate reason for establishing ourselves within permanent borders before it was too late. In the year 2020 there would be 15 million between the Mediterranean and the Jordan river with an
Arab majority. "Have we still not understood that we must find diplomatic and political solutions to this problem before disaster strikes?" I warned that "Sharon's plans would reduce the territories to the level of Lebanon or worse still to that of Algeria." I concluded on a sober note:

In the perspective of history, the negotiating path we have chosen was unavoidable.... We now have to confront head on the most painful truths in our history. It fell to us to tell these truths. We have outlined the form of peace between us and the Palestinians for the years ahead. These are the only possible lines. If they are not supported now they will be missed in time to come.

‖ 25 ‖

Taba: "The Boss Doesn't Want an Agreement"

At Taba, the Palestinians revealed their strategy at once. At the opening session, Abu Ala said what he would later confirm to *Al Ayyam* (January 29, 2001): "The Israelis said that the Clinton proposals should be the basis, but we rejected them." We started, then, with no accepted working premise. To Abu Ala I explained that my proposal should not be read as annexing 6 percent of the West Bank, but of the Palestinian state. If the Gaza Strip were included in the calculation, we would be annexing only 4.5 percent, in exchange for which they would get 3 percent within Israel—their exact location was still to be determined (and is therefore not specified in Map 2)—whose infrastructures they would also be allowed to use. My proposal was in absolute consonance with Clinton's parameters. Admittedly, Barak gave different instructions to Gilead Sher; he expected us to calculate the passage within Israeli territory linking Gaza with the West Bank as amounting to 2 percent. I have no doubt, though, that my view would have prevailed if this turned out to be what would make or break the deal. I also said to Abu Ala that even though many settlers would choose to leave straight away, "as the *pieds-noirs* did in Algeria," the thirty-six months of phased withdrawal from defined areas were required for the evacuation of the settlements, which was bound to be a complex, traumatic affair. I urged him for the umpteenth time: "It's now or never. The day will come when you will bitterly regret not having accepted the Clinton parameters."

We then divided into two working groups. Yossi Beilin talked separately with Nabil Shaath on refugees, and I led the rest of the team to discuss territory, security, and Jerusalem. Abu Ala was now sounding more open, and was ready to look at a map showing a 6 percent annexation in the West Bank. It showed that we would have to evacuate 102 settlements and outposts. This was the first time since the beginning of negotiations that the Palestinians had given serious consideration to an Israeli map. Our optimism was boosted by an intelligence

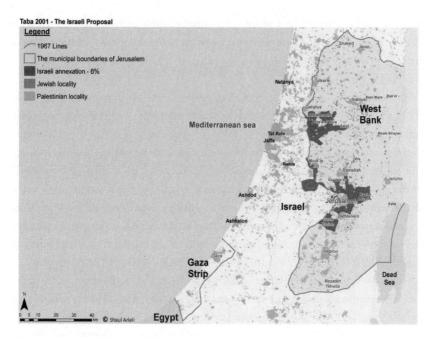

Map 2 Taba, 2001, Ben-Ami's Initial Proposal

assessment: "The Palestinian objective is a quick, purposeful negotiating process leading to a full agreement."

This was matched by the mood in our internal brainstorming sessions. Beilin
was optimistic that we could find a solution to the refugee problem without
deviating from the Clinton parameters. Amnon Lipkin-Shahak's impression
was that the Palestinians' attitude was becoming more mature, for which he
was willing to explore the boldest idea any of us would raise in Taba, giving up
Ariel, twenty kilometers inside the occupied West Bank, and building a new city
closer to the Green Line. He proposed drawing an alternative to the map we had
been "enslaved by." We all doubted that this could work in the current political
climate. "Has the proposition really been investigated properly?" he asked. "It's
what you could call intuition, Amnon. We both live in the same political environment, don't we?" I replied. Nor did we have a guarantee that this would
be seen by the Palestinians as the final concession. Political constraints also affected our attitude to Kiryat Arba, a hotbed of Jewish religious fanaticism on
the outskirts of Hebron, about fifteen kilometers east of the Green Line. The
Palestinians refused to accept a solution based on leasing it to us. Gilead Sher
thought that no government would ever agree to evacuate Kiryat Arba, if only
because of the sociopolitical earthquake, even civil strife, awaiting us if such a
move was tried. Barak too sent his own signals from Jerusalem. He wanted an
agreement so badly that in a note he sent me he spoke of land swaps in the ratio

of 5:5 with the remaining 3 percent he sought being covered by mutual lease arrangements. To all intents and purposes the Palestinians could have viewed this as an offer to swap territory in the ratio of 1:1. They categorically rejected the leasing idea, however.

This clarified a basic conceptual divergence. Israel's "narrow waist," the need to compensate for our withdrawal from the Jordan Valley, and the demographic changes that had taken place since 1967 all required a significant redrawing of borders for which we were prepared to offer real territorial exchanges. Abu Ala claimed that we could house all the settlers "in fifty high-rise buildings," for which we did not need the hundreds of hectares we asked for. The Palestinian view was no different from that of Egypt and Syria in their peace negotiations with Israel. Peace was not supposed to be based on Israel's national ethos or security strategy, such as settlements or improved military deployment capabilities. Even Sadat had categorically rejected an offer from Israel of significant territorial compensation for Egypt in the Negev, so that Israel could retain the Jewish settlements in northern Sinai. The purpose of peace in the Arab view was to return Israel to its "natural size" and deny any legitimacy to the territorial consequences of the 1967 war.

General Shlomo Yanai's report of the discussions on security was mixed. The Palestinians were prepared to discuss the deployment of an international force, to collaborate in a joint war on terror, and, provided their country was not defined as a demilitarized state, discuss the weaponry they would be allowed to keep. They were also willing to discuss the early-warning stations. Yet they staunchly opposed the thirty-six-month phased withdrawal, Israel's freedom to fly in Palestinian airspace, and her control of border crossings. In all those areas, they had stepped back considerably from the Camp David understandings. Yanai's assessment was that the Palestinians' serious approach had come too late and that a full agreement in the time we had left was impossible.

Gilead Sher was encouraged that though the extent of settlement blocs proposed by the Palestinians was entirely unacceptable, it was, nonetheless, the first time they had presented a map that included such blocs (see Map 3). They not only insisted, however, that not even one single Palestinian village be included in either of the blocs, but also totally eroded the three already shrunken blocs and effectively voided the whole bloc concept of content. According to their map, only a few isolated Israeli settlements would remain, which would be dependent on thin strings of narrow access roads. Leaving Jerusalem and the no man's land of Latrun out of the equation, the Palestinians were now willing to accept settlement blocs—they labeled them "colonial clusters"—amounting to 2.3 percent of the West Bank, in exchange for an equal area of Israeli territory. If Jerusalem and Latrun were to be included in the calculation, this figure would rise to 3.4 percent. The blocs would include only seventeen Jewish settlements with a total population of 32,000, whereas the Clinton parameters had provided for blocs holding 137,000 settlers in thirty-two settlements. The Palestinian plan entailed the displacement of around 140,000 West Bank settlers, more than three times the number contemplated by the Clinton plan. The solutions that had been proposed, Colonel Arieli, a distinguished professional and the most dovish military man around, told me, could not bridge the gaps in terms of the

Map 3 Taba, 2001, Palestinian Proposal

way both sides saw the blocs. But it was clear that the Palestinians had made a substantively constructive move. Arguably, the territorial chapter with its promising dynamic looked solvable if only a similar dynamic had existed in the Jerusalem and refugees' questions.

Beilin, focused and proficient, sounded characteristically upbeat when he reported on his negotiations with Nabil Shaath over refugees. They worked on a preamble that would provide "moral compensation" to the refugees through Israel's acceptance of her share of responsibility in the creation of the problem, but without her recognizing the right of return. They also discussed numbers of returnees, with Beilin offering 40,000. Shaath said that Arafat was interested in the return of 300,000 refugees, essentially the entire Palestinian refugee population in Lebanon, whom Arafat always referred to as "my brothers and beloved refugees of Lebanon." But, Shaath had truly no idea what the number would be that Arafat would say yes to, and he therefore added that *all the refugees* be allowed a year to decide whether they wanted to return to the Palestinian state or to Israel. The number of returnees could not be an exclusive, sovereign Israeli decision, as Clinton had put it. Beilin is a man of sophisticated political acumen and an inventive warrior for peace who never has hesitated to swim against the stream. His work on responsibilities for the *Nakba* was right and courageous. However, I really had a hard time understanding his optimism regarding the supposedly "earth-shattering" progress he had made in his talks with Nabil Shaath. The two issues—numbers and the principle of the right of return—left for the leaders to resolve were precisely the same that had remained unresolved at the end of the secret talks in Sweden.

On Jerusalem, we struggled with the eternal bones of contention. The Palestinians demanded exclusive sovereignty over Temple Mount and the Holy Basin with the surrounding area outside the Old City down to the Mount of Olives. They rejected our sovereignty over the entire Western Wall, as the Clinton plan suggested; they would only agree to Israeli sovereignty over the Wailing Wall. They turned down any suggestion of a special regime in the Old City, where they demanded sovereignty over 2.5 quarters with sovereignty over the Jewish Quarter and half of the Armenian allocated to us. Yossi Sarid proposed a solution worthy of King Solomon: dividing the burden; some of the problems would be solved according to the Palestinian approach, and some according to ours. "If you expect us to make all the concessions, forget it; it'll never happen." They turned down Sarid's biblical solution, which brought this most emblematic icon of Israel's peace camp during an internal team meeting to express his conviction that an agreement was beyond reach:

> It's clear that both sides have just about reached the limit of their ability to compromise. In the ten days before the general elections, it's no longer

possible to hold serious talks. There are a lot of things that might have been accepted earlier on, but are very problematic now. The three main issues are territory, refugees, and Jerusalem, and there are unbridgeable gaps in all three. Politically, any linkage between the word "Lebanon" and the matter of the refugees would be lethal.

Coming from Sarid, for many years the most outspoken, eloquent prophet of doom of the Israeli left, this judgment carried a special gravity. But Beilin argued that in the past, when making peace with Jordan and concessions to the Syrians, Israeli leaders did not consult with anyone. In the end, the people would decide, and we could hold a referendum. Lipkin-Shahak, who was not exactly an opponent of peace, rejected Beilin's comparisons. Beilin stubbornly insisted that if we gave in to them on Jerusalem, they would go along with us on the rest of the issues. Unfortunately, nothing we had seen till then supported this claim. The Palestinians looked at each issue separately and were never prepared to engage in quid pro quo negotiation. I had proof of this straight from the horse's mouth, when I had earlier mentioned to Abu Ala precisely that linkage. As the talks proceeded, it was becoming increasingly apparent that the Palestinians believed that the pressure we were under because of the elections gave them a chance to extract additional dramatic concessions from us, without giving any guarantee that this would clinch a deal.

We were all coming to the conclusion that the best we could achieve was a "non-paper" summarizing the stage that the talks had reached, and also work on a joint declaration to be made by the two leaders, somewhere in Europe. The Palestinians wanted this as a kind of inventory of our concessions, but this would pose no problem for Israel as long as the Palestinian concessions on settlement blocs, borders, Jerusalem, and so on were also documented. I immediately made a telephone call from Taba to the Swedish prime minister, Göran Persson, whose country held the EU rotating presidency at the time. "The penny has dropped too late for the Palestinians," he said. I suggested that he invite Barak and Arafat to a joint announcement of the outcome of our talks. Kofi Annan and Javier Solana, I told him, had agreed to be part of the support network. Persson was excited by the idea and promised to act.

But we all still resisted giving up, and without dropping the non-paper fallback idea, we decided to offer the Palestinians a focused brainstorming session in the hope of narrowing the gaps. Barak was surprisingly supportive but stipulated that only Yossi Sarid and I would represent our side, and said he was interested in "something dramatic; otherwise there will be no turnaround here." In the elections, he meant. At the first brainstorming meeting with Abu Ala, I suggested that none of us document the proposals expressed by the other, but the old fox could not resist writing it all down in his notebook. He simply wanted to record our concessions with the fallacious assumption that a future Israeli government would agree to see them as the point of departure in renewed negotiations. And this when Sharon was waiting *ante portas*. When we addressed the Temple Mount, he said, "It is only Arafat who is obsessed with Haram al-Sharif; none of us agrees with him about it." Nevertheless, he rejected the idea of Sarid's "Solomon-like" judgment. Barak often worked on parallel tracks. He also authorized Gilead Sher and Yisrael Hasson to hold a secret meeting with Abu Ala and Dahlan. Abu Ala defined this as an "attempt to keep the Taba talks afloat in the absence of the Israeli ministers."[1] Not much progress was made on either track, yet we defined our disagreements. When Gilead Sher offered to provide a helicopter so that the Palestinians could go to Arafat to wrap up what we had in our hands into an agreed memorandum, they replied, "The boss doesn't want an agreement."[2]

No wonder that shortly before taking office, George W. Bush asked the Saudi Ambassador to Washington, Bandar bin Sultan: "Explain one thing to me. How is it that this guy [Arafat] doesn't close a deal with two desperate people [Clinton and Barak]?"[3] Taba failed also because of the Palestinians' belief that with Bush they would get a better deal. A born-again Christian, and one of the best friends Israel ever had in the White House, Bush was wrongly perceived by the Palestinians as worth placing their faith in, as Abu Ala would later admit.[4]

The sun was setting on the negotiating process. There would be no agreement, either partial or full. Only a miracle could prevent Sharon from winning the election, and if he did, that would mark the end of the peace process. Our efforts were drowning in a sea of tears and blood. Yet another opportunity was missed. Who could tell when they and we would have another like it? A wretched people with a colossally tragic fate, they were dragging us into the abyss with them. But our plight was also the result of our own sins: the sins of arrogance and occupation, the folly of settlements and of ignoring the tragedy for so long that the way out of the imbroglio had become beyond human capability. What was shocking to me, however, was that there was no sadness in the Palestinian negotiators' faces, no sorrow over a lost opportunity. The refugees' right of return was a historical impossibility. Why did they themselves not encourage refugees to live in the Palestinian state? They even rejected the idea of settling hundreds of thousand refugees in areas received from us as part of the swap. This, they said, would prevent the refugees from choosing where they wanted to settle within the State of Israel. I asked myself, what kind of national movement dreams of establishing a state only in order to settle its exiles in a neighboring country? Why on earth were they willing to scatter their refugees to the four corners of the world (Canada, Australia, etc.)? How is it that a national movement does not build an ethos based on the ingathering of its exiles? They argued with us that not even one Palestinian would stay in the settlement blocs—their main argument against large settlement blocs—yet they were willing to leave their refugees dispersed all over the region and the world.

Abu Ala summed up Taba in a letter he addressed to Arafat. Though the blocs of Ariel and Jerusalem, he wrote, "still distort the geography of our homeland, the Israelis have produced a map showing both the north and the south with Palestinian territory fully contiguous and clear of settlements." On refugees, he stated, "Their latest paper was different from the Camp David one, yet still unacceptable." On security, he pronounced that "disagreement remains on those issues related to sovereignty." He found nothing new to say about Jerusalem. Miguel Angel Moratinos, the EU envoy to the region, prepared a fairer description of the Taba negotiations' understandings and remaining gaps.[5]

Once the curtain had fallen on the Taba talks, I went back to the task of arranging a leaders' summit that would cap our efforts with messages of goodwill, and form a basis for resuming talks in the future. I recruited the UN Secretary General Kofi Annan for the task, and he even promised he would try to bring on board the new US Secretary of State Colin Powell. Ehud Barak had no objection. But just as he was getting into his stride, disaster struck, as Arafat put yet another nail in the coffin of all our efforts for a decent ending. On Sunday, January 28, 2001, I could see the leaders' summit I had planned being consumed in the fire of Arafat's self-destructive actions. I had advance knowledge that he planned to lash out at Israel in the Davos World Economic Forum for, according to his wild imagination, attacking his people with uranium. I called Kofi Annan, who was also in Davos, and urged him to stop the chairman from uttering such blatant lies. Annan hurried to the stage, but it was too late. Arafat had already launched into his slanderous speech: "Israel is conducting a fascist war against our people. Israel is conducting a cruel, barbaric war against the Palestinians . . . Israel is conquering, destroying, and bombing the Palestinians with depleted uranium bombs."

Arafat was always emboldened in his appearances in international fora where the favorite sport was to put Israel in the dock, and where he could trade in Palestinian blood. Instead of defending the peace policy of the government of which he was a minister, Shimon Peres, for whom politics and courting popularity among such *bien-pensant,* but ill-informed international constituencies was his lifeblood, extended his hand "to my dear friend and partner Arafat." Later, he explained that "it wasn't the place for a public confrontation." Be that as it may, a despondent Barak decided things had gone too far. He announced that there was no point in a leaders' summit with "that man."

With the curtain falling on Taba, I called Ambassador Indyk to bring him up to date, and unfortunately the conversation became most unpleasant. He complained that we were trying to keep the United States out of the peace process. He had read in *Haaretz* a report of a lecture I had given at the Jaffe Center for Strategic Studies at Tel Aviv University, in which I had told the audience,

"We have to internationalize the solution. The emphasis should be placed on Europe and the UN." I reminded Indyk that he himself had told me that he had been instructed by Colin Powell to stay away from Taba. Nothing would have made us happier than to see Colin Powell attend a summit in Stockholm, which was exactly what Kofi Annan and I had spoken about, and if he wanted to lead it, even better.

But the hope of convening an international summit initiative was dead. Arafat was a walking embarrassment. On top of everything else, two Israelis were murdered in the territories that day, February 1. Public opinion gave Barak no choice: he announced that there would be no summit. Another day passed, and on February 2, four days before the elections, Turkey's foreign minister, Ismail Çem told me that Arafat had accepted the idea of a summit in Turkey. But now Barak was marching to a different drum. The opinion poll results could not have been worse. Every Israeli prime minister who had ever negotiated with Arafat ended up being defeated in the polls.

When it came to the crunch, the process was betrayed by everyone involved. With Clinton gone and an administration supposedly indifferent to a Palestinian peace about to assume office in Washington, the Egyptians revealed their real views. Or, perhaps, this was their way of staving off any Palestinian criticism of Egypt's *tactical* support of Clinton's peace ideas. While we were still in Taba, Amr Moussa gave a speech effectively rejecting the Clinton parameters, and asked for a better formula to be produced and for any form of agreement that amounted to a ruse for forcing a solution on the Arabs to be removed from the process. Given Israel's strategic superiority, he said, a solution based on "the objective criteria of international legitimacy" was needed. It was at the Egyptians that Clinton was directing his criticism when, in his farewell letter to the Palestinians, he warned that "there will always be those sitting comfortably on the outside urging you to hold out for the impossible more . . . They are not the ones who will pay the price of missing a historic opportunity."[6]

Back in the second week of January, both Amr Moussa and Osama El-Baz, Mubarak's foreign affairs adviser, had publicly announced in a conference at Cairo University that progress in the negotiations was "conditional upon Israel's acceptance of the Palestinians' demands" and "Egypt's balanced peace conditions." Among other things, this meant "the ending of Israel's military advantages, such as its nuclear capability." Moussa spoke unequivocally about what he termed "Israel's military advantages, which make regional peace diffi- cult to achieve." The flaw in the management of the process, he said, was the American mediation, which favored Israel. "We mustn't fear them," he said of the Americans. "Instead we must do what Arafat has done and openly express the Arab position." On the TV show *Good Morning Egypt*, El-Baz defined Israel as "an alien state in the Arab region in terms of culture, civilization, and politics."[7]

Righteous men had not vanished altogether, though. In moments of crippling decision for his nation, Arafat's self-destructive recalcitrance did not go unnoticed. Sometime later Tarek Haji, an Egyptian intellectual, wrote this on his website on August 8, 2004: "In Taba, Arafat thwarted the effort to achieve an acceptable, balanced framework for a final settlement . . . Who then is responsible for the waste of life, the blood, interest and time . . . or there is no one responsible for our Arab reality?"[8]

But Arafat, just like his Egyptian supporting choir, breathed a great sigh of relief at the end of the Clinton presidency. They all wrongly believed that the incoming Bush administration would be more favorable to the Arab cause. Arafat's official newspaper *Al Hayat al Jadida* heralded the end of the Clinton presidency as "the end of the era of the Jewish lobby," and an unnamed senior Palestinian official briefed reporters that the incoming Bush administration "will be a hundred times better" than Clinton's.[9] As Ambassador Ned Walker reported after his series of meetings in Arab capitals, they all believed that Vice President Dick Cheney's oil businesses and the presumably pro-Arab legacy of the new president's father would lead to a radical change in America's pro-Israel policies. Walker even assumed that the Saudis might have been those who advised Arafat to wait for a better deal from the new administration. His successors are still waiting.

Post-Mortem

The failure of the Camp David process has been the subject of heated debate. For the Israeli right, it is the ultimate vindication of its worldview; the left hangs on the contention that the two-state solution *is* possible, and that it was Barak who failed to produce it. Barak's claim that the Palestinians were prisoners of the mythologies of return, refugeeism, and Islam, and thus were unable to accept a compromise that recognized the moral rights of a Jewish state was applauded by the exhilarated right and is still denounced by the now dwindling left.

But Camp David needs to be looked at not just in such a binary perspective. The Palestinian negotiators were right when, from the outset, they suggested that Camp David be a stage in a chain of meetings leading to an endgame. Despite the litany of errors committed by all sides, the summit and its culmination in the Clinton parameters and Taba represented a signal leap to a balanced peace outline. Even if taken alone, the summit allowed us to break the taboos that had paralyzed all previous peace seekers and educate the Israelis about the Palestinian narrative. None before us had negotiated, as we did in Sweden and later in Taba, a joint text about responsibilities for the *Nakba* and mechanisms for the solution of the problem of refugees. This is also the case with Jerusalem. When we went to Camp David, opinion polls taught us that only 5 percent of Israelis were ready to contemplate a division of Jerusalem (three years earlier, Netanyahu had won a general election with the slogan: "Peres will divide Jerusalem"). When we left the summit, polls showed that 41 percent of Israelis contemplated such a division for the sake of a real peace.[1]

The significance of the Camp David process also cannot be exaggerated when it comes to the radical changes that it produced within the Israeli right. Without its taboo-breaking talks, key figures of the Israeli right would not have converted into the peace process. A Likud hard-liner such as Ehud Olmert, and one of the most salient princesses of the Israeli right, Tzipi Livni, would not have become such peace seekers if it were not for the hopes raised by the Camp David process. It helped turn the peace process into an enterprise no longer confined to the usual suspects of the left.

Thomas Macaulay, the great nineteenth-century British historian, believed that to distribute praise or blame is the true task of the historian. But history is not a court of justice; it is about understanding processes and seeking the truth. Arafat was genuinely incapable of reconciling the cosmic tragedy of his people with the poverty of the territorial solution and the betrayal of the refugees. Arafat could not extricate himself from the trap of his nation's core narratives. He was a complex, enigmatic figure, and this account of him should not be read as a philippic. If blame must be apportioned, Arafat would not be the sole culprit. We all faltered in that peace enterprise. Israeli settlements, the sins of occupation, and the flaws and blunders of our own government are certainly no less to blame. Barak allowed the Palestinians to reject his proposals for the simple reason that they turned out not to be red lines, but tactical moves. What is a Palestinian negotiator expected to do when his interlocutor starts by proposing a Palestinian state on 66 percent of the land, and then moves to 87 percent in order to settle for 92 percent, and a few months later accepts the Clinton parameters" of 97 percent with land swaps? Among themselves, Palestinian negotiators referred to Barak as "the lemon" to be squeezed. With the Palestinians understandably keeping up the pressure for more Israeli concessions, it was clear that Barak's grudging, piecemeal surrender of positions was flawed tactics yielding dramatically diminishing returns.

The Clinton parameters, which were a considerable improvement on Camp David, are the best proof that Arafat was right to turn down the summit's offers. He proved to be a shrewder negotiator than the other two leaders. I myself am on record as having said, "If I were a Palestinian, I would have rejected what was offered at the Camp David Summit."[2] This book stands by this assertion. But the general preoccupation with the summit, as opposed to the entire Camp David process, seriously distorts what exactly the proposals were that Arafat refused to accept. At one point in September Clinton considered presenting his final peace package. It is perfectly plausible that Arafat surfed on the fortuitous eruption of the Al-Aqsa Intifada as a way of either impacting the peace plan or blocking its presentation altogether, for he knew that, however improved in comparison with the Camp David proposals it might be, it would fall short of his expectations and only serve to expose him again as a peace refusenik. Arafat's fatal blunder lay in his historical flights of fancy into an imaginary deal that neither he himself ever lent substance to, nor could his Israeli interlocutors fulfill. He had an innate incapacity for stopping bargaining, in not gauging the limits of Israel's capacity for compromise. He never accepted that in such a peace enterprise, politics and strategy were one, and a deal that would break the political spinal cord of his Israeli interlocutors was like not having a deal at all. It is there that he doomed his people's chances for redemption. The discussion of whether or not the Camp David process was a missed opportunity derives, of course, particular relevance when seen from the perspective of the utter loss of the prospects of a Palestinian peace since then and for the foreseeable future. A common Palestinian claim was that Camp David had failed because the summit was not properly prepared. But the exposure of the secret talks in Stockholm by the Palestinians themselves made such preparation more difficult. Dennis Ross, who was in the area just prior to the summit, confirmed that "nothing was done on the Palestinian side to make preparing for the summit any the easier." Arafat kept all his cards, if he had any, close to his chest. The Annapolis process under George W. Bush that ended with a daring peace proposal by Prime Minister Ehud Olmert that in some key aspects went beyond the Clinton parameters and Taba was presumably better prepared, and it also failed. Is it not about time for pundits and would-be peacemakers to assume the defining nature of such failures and, hence, revisit the entire two-state vision upon which the peace process was built? Others, particularly in Israel, argued that attempting to reach a permanent settlement had been a hopeless mistake and that another interim agreement should have been preferred. But it was Arafat who kept pressing the Americans to "solve all the problems." He was right. Seven years after Oslo, not only could the Palestinians see no end in sight, but their situation was going from bad to worse under the yoke of Israeli occupation.

Ed Abington, a former US Consul General in Jerusalem who was now the lobbyist for the Palestinians in Washington, passed on August 15, 2000, to the Palestinian leadership a review given to a closed forum by a senior American official (Clinton himself or a surrogate?) on July 28, immediately after the end of the summit. In a typical American overestimation of the role of Arab countries, the official admitted America's dismay at the Arab leaders for being unable to help coax Arafat into a settlement. But these leaders had no incentive to risk a domestic backlash and an always looming fundamentalist threat to their rule by imposing on the Palestinians concessions on such pan-Islamic values as Jerusalem and the Temple Mount. They also probably shared Arafat's and Hezbollah's reading of Israel's panicked withdrawal from Lebanon, as well as her concessions to Arafat amidst a bloody Intifada, as signals of political and spiritual breakdown. Nor did it seem that Arafat was particularly interested in the involvement of his Arab "brethren," unless it was just in order to have them as a shield against American pressure or as the ultimate alibi for not being able to accept proposals that presumably affected the entire Arab family. The main regional actors were simply not willing to offer the regional envelope of support for an Israeli-Palestinian peace without which a settlement looked impossible. The 2002 Arab Peace Initiative came after, not before Camp David; and it might not have been produced without it.

What the "American official" could not bring himself to say was that an Israeli-Palestinian peace was perhaps a sentimental cause and a political obsession for the Clinton presidency, but not a vital national security priority. To be sure, it did elicit broad nonpartisan support even though Clinton was already a lame duck, as I could witness myself in meetings on the Hill with Republican heavyweights such as Senators Trent Lott and John McCain. The winner of the Cold War and the undisputed global hegemon, America did not address the Palestine question as one where failure was simply not an option. It is otherwise difficult to understand how, in the dying days of the Clinton administration, the United States allowed itself to be exposed as such a toothless tiger with no ability to intimidate or coerce. In 1991, George H. W. Bush did not hesitate to confront head on Israel's friends in America when he decided to coerce Israel's prime minister, Yitzhak Shamir, to come to the Madrid Peace Conference. At Camp David, Clinton's care for the political standing of Ehud Barak overrode the logic of peace negotiations that required exerting pressure on Israel, not just on Arafat. Nor was the Clinton administration willing to forge a solid coalition for an Israeli-Palestinian peace with its European allies, as she would have done perhaps in a matter of paramount national security urgency. Denied America's backing, Europe, always full of good intentions, lacked even a semblance of a coherent foreign policy, so that she too failed to impress, let alone intimidate.

Camp David failed because of the two sides' conflicting interpretations of the terms of reference of the peace process. The Israelis came to the negotiations with the conviction inherent in the letter of the Oslo Accords that this was an open-ended process where no preconceived solutions existed and where every one of the core issues would be open to negotiation so that a reasonable point of equilibrium between the needs of the parties could be found. The Palestinians saw the negotiations as a step in a journey where they would get their rights as if this were a clear-cut process of decolonization based on "international legitimacy" and "all UN relevant resolutions." Constructive ambiguity facilitated an agreement in Oslo at the price of creating irreconcilable misconceptions with regard to the final settlement. Oslo created the false impression among Israeli negotiators that the PLO had shifted the emphasis of its struggle to the territorial domain. But the Israeli negotiators at Camp David and Taba who came to solve the problems created by the 1967 war discovered eventually that the intractable issues of 1948, first and foremost that of the refugees' right of return, were now high on the Palestinian agenda. Akram Haniyah, a member of the Palestinian team at Camp David, pretended to act as Arafat's surrogate when he later defined the Palestinian strategy as that of righting a historic injustice and issuing a moral verdict against a state that was born in sin. The issue of refugees, Haniyah wrote, is the story of "massacres and terror campaigns", a story of mass expulsion and "wholesale destruction of villages" that the Israelis wanted to silence. It therefore stood "at the root of the conflict," and "was ruled by history . . . It placed Israel in front of her direct victims, in front of the witnesses of its crimes." But throughout the deliberation, the Israelis, he wrote, persisted in "a complete denial of their crime ... despite all the evidence."[3]

The return of refugees was, indeed, a central Palestinian demand. A Palestinian poll showed at the time that 68 percent supported Arafat's position at Camp David that Israel recognize UN Resolution 194 and the return of "hundreds of thousands of refugees," while 20 percent thought even this was too much of a compromise.[4]

Throughout the whole process, Arafat was in the grip of a dilemma from which there was no way out. He hated the interim agreements and the disappointments they had brought, and therefore wanted a comprehensive settlement. But he could not bring himself to end the conflict either because, a man of permanent struggle for whom the concept of "end" was utterly alien, he was incapable of forgoing the ultimate and inexpiable sins of the Zionist entity against his people or because Israel fell too short to meet his minimum requirements, which he had otherwise not been able to spell out in an orderly manner or as an articulate peace proposal. To the end of his life, Arafat refused to acknowledge that he was indeed offered a settlement that would have given him a state with 100 percent of the Gaza strip and 97 percent of the West Bank, a capital city in Arab Jerusalem, sovereignty over the Temple Mount, and unrestricted return of refugees to a Palestinian state and to territories transferred from Israel in territorial exchanges. The offer also included financial compensation for every single refugee and every family in the refugee camps via massive funds. Yet, to this very day, the Palestinians and their friends talk of a "humiliating settlement" and a "state of Bantustans."

Above all, Arafat never thought of the Camp David process, or any other American-brokered peace enterprise for that matter, as his "last chance." He perceived himself as an almost mythological figure engaged in a long historical struggle against a Jewish state that was born in sin and would disappear sooner or later, defeated by its own contradictions. Indonesia's foreign minister, Alwi Shihab, whom I met in New York during the UN Millennium General Assembly in September 2000, told me how his president, Abdurrahman Wahid, had insisted that Arafat strike a deal with the Barak government, to which the ra'is responded: "In a hundred years Israel will disappear. Why rush to recognize her now?"

Arafat's willingness to come to the negotiating table did not mean he had given up on his historic mission. Any agreement that did not conform to the core narrative of the PLO was for Arafat a surrender. The right of return, which has become these days the banner of the BDS (Boycott, Divestment, Sanctions) movement, is a euphemism for the end of the Jewish state which not even a fanatic critic of Zionism's unpardonable sins such as Noam Chomsky—"sadistic," defined by "criminality" and "moral depravity" is how he describes Israeli society—would support. Neither is the right of return supported by international law, nor can Israel be forced to accept a Palestinian population it does not want, Chomsky wrote in 2014.[5]

At the September 2001 anti-Israel orgy, otherwise known as the Durban World Conference against Racism, where *The Protocols of the Elders of Zion,* a 1903 notoriously fabricated antisemitic text purporting to describe a Jewish plan for global domination, was freely distributed, Arafat reminded the excited audience that Israel was nothing but the "result of the rivalry and conspiracies of the colonialist forces in the region at that time." Given the colonial paradigm he worked with, it was understandable that he should not think that it was up to him, the head of a colonized nation, to advance creative ideas on how to end the occupation. This was why the pattern throughout the entire process was one where Arafat would never make a counterproposal and Israel would go on bringing him one idea after another until he eventually could be satisfied. This was a pattern Arafat and his people stuck to throughout much of the peace process. When Rabin asked Arafat during the negotiations in 1995 on Oslo B to make a proposal, his answer was: "No, no, no, you are a general. I'm an engineer. You have the upper hand and therefore you should propose."[6] To me, it always seemed, however, that Arafat never really defined to himself what *exactly* that final peace outline he could endorse was, which was why the Israeli side felt it was being constantly dragged into a black hole with no walls where all this was supposed to end. It is true that some in the Palestinian delegation supported compromises such as acceptance of the principle of the settlement blocs, even if in their maps the blocs were so small as to have no significance, and Israeli sovereignty over the Jewish neighborhoods in East Jerusalem. But at no stage did any of us, or indeed the Americans, hear Arafat approve of these compromises. This is how his second in command, Abu Mazen, described the validity of these compromises: "We told them [the Israelis], have you heard these things from President Arafat? So long as you don't hear this from him, then whatever you heard [from other members in the delegation] is a lie."[7]

Our mistakes were partly the result of the conceptual defects of the Oslo process; others were entirely of our own making. Barak pretended to solve a century-old conflict within a very short, rigidly restricted period of time, and with a government that was a witch's brew of right and left. Achieving a *permanent* peace, which would inevitably carry a heavy price tag, was an impossible task for such a ragbag of assorted odds and ends. Barak appointed Yitzhak Levy, the head of the Religious Nationalist Party and the settlers' advocate in the government, as the minister of housing who administered the growth of the settler population in the occupied territories by about 26,000 new settlers. Not exactly a confidence-building gesture in the middle of peace negotiations. The government was like a multistage rocket whose component parts dropped off one after another as it came closer and closer to its target. At the end of the process it was left with only the control module at the top, a front without a rearguard. The Barak government sought lofty targets with inadequate political resources, and by the end of the negotiating process, the government was left with barely 40 seats in the 120-member Knesset. That was all like squaring the proverbial circle. We also wrongheadedly expected the Palestinians to come to terms with the deficiencies in the conduct of our government. That is to say, the Palestinians had to be prepared to ignore the nonfulfillment of Israeli undertakings and to trust in the Israelis' good intentions that "all would be well" when it came to a final settlement. They also had to take action within the Palestinian areas and to quieten down the mounting agitation and anger and to suppress the terror militias. With the Palestinian territories becoming a tightly wound spring threatening to uncoil, Arafat refused to, or was unable, to follow the scenario that Barak had prepared for him.

The task was overwhelming, but Barak's political gifts were inadequate. He had a grand strategic vision but lacked the requisite political skills of a national leader. In the absence of internal political organization even the greatest of visions is destined to fail. A prime minister seeking peace has to be brave and inspirational, but his entire peace vision will be defeated if he behaves like an irresponsible political adventurer. Not becoming hostage to the imperatives of politics is one thing; ignoring them altogether is another. Proverbially maladroit as a politician, Barak went too far in his mismanagement of the rapid shrinkage of his domestic political base. Seeking a final peace with the Palestinians was perhaps the most audacious diplomatic initiative undertaken by any government since the establishment of the state of Israel. It was a titanic task for any government, much more so for one whose public support was dwindling by the day. It is true that war unites nations and peace divides them, and that seeking a broad national consensus can sometimes be the negation of leadership when divisive decisions must be taken. History has cases where "one man with courage makes a majority," as US President Andrew Jackson suggested. David Ben-Gurion, Anwar Sadat, Menachem Begin, Yitzhak Rabin, Charles de Gaulle in Algeria, Richard Nixon with China, and de Klerk in South Africa were such decisive leaders. But, though Barak was at least as brave and audacious as most of them, he had neither their political skills nor the popular touch without which it became impossible to garner the necessary domestic support for the politics of peace. Barak and his team were a group of political suicides utterly indifferent to considerations of political survival who, nevertheless, believed that history would be kinder to them.

In the struggle for peace, a leader must also be a mentor and teacher to the nation. Barak lacked that pedagogical instinct, so important particularly as the civil population did not trust the enemy that Barak was trying to turn into a friend. His was a daunting task, though, for he also had to pursue it against the background of mounting public displeasure with previous peace enterprises. Peace with Egypt had been bought at a very high price and was seen as disappointingly cold, even hostile. The withdrawal from Lebanon had left Hezbollah as a continuing threat on our northern border, and the peace talks with Syria had just broken down after Hafez al-Assad rejected Israel's concept of normalization and security while at the same time insisting on having not only the entire Golan Heights, which Israel had taken in a war of self-defense, but also part of the eastern shores of the Sea of Galilee, Israel's only and last water reservoir.

We also failed in a decisively vital task, that of getting our peace policies accepted by the army command, which operated on a different wavelength. The army's top brass did not share Barak's peace strategy and appeared to be looking on ironically at the freneticism that had seized their leader. Throughout the Intifada, it operated with an intensity and force that defeated the government's purpose of striking a difficult balance between the compelling need to respond to violence and the need to leave open the chances of peace. From October 2000, the bloody sights of the Intifada fatally weakened, if not completely destroyed Barak's ability to persuade a skeptical nation. The Intifada struck a terrible blow at the public's faith in the Palestinian partner that perdures to this very day, twenty years after Camp David; it also uncorked a hard strain of Israeli rejectionism of the very idea of a two-state solution, and, worse, made it into a national consensus.

Our political predicament was mirrored on the other side of the hill. The Palestinians' disenchantment with the peace process and their suffering under the curse of occupation partly explain why their leader never ceased to mobilize them in a campaign for Jerusalem and the right of return. Arafat never delivered an unequivocal message of peace. He never tried to prepare the Palestinians for the painful compromises that peace would require. If Barak was an awkward peace pedagogue, desperately poor in political skills, Arafat was an incorrigible warrior. The institutional chaos in the territories, Arafat's arbitrary personal rule, and his insouciance about reaching out to the Israelis fed their mistrust of his final intentions. He never truly represented for the Israelis the promise of reconciliation. In a Palestinian system lacking a free, democratic discourse, the Israelis were left only with Arafat's penchant for double talk and ambiguities to guess what the real Palestinian strategic objectives were. In a way, Arafat embodied the built-in trait of authoritarian regimes where leaders, as shown by the case of Egypt's Abdel Nasser after the debacle of 1967, are more capable of surviving a military defeat than the inevitable sacrifices made by the peacemaker. He certainly did not model himself on Egypt's Anwar Sadat; he preferred the example of Nasser and at times even Saladin, and Omar ibn al-Khattab. Such comparisons are not a figment of the imagination. Arafat compared himself to these historic figures in a conversation with me in Nablus on June 25, 2000. The tragic fate of Anwar Sadat and Jordan's King Abdullah I—both assassinated for making peace with Israel—was always in Arafat's mind; he even spelled it out to Clinton— "Do you want to come to my funeral?"—on many occasions during the summit. Arafat, it became clear, was not prepared to be the first and only Arab leader to recognize the unique historical and religious roots linking the Jews to their millennial homeland. The result was that he, who was proud of his education as an engineer, proved to his people that, when it came to building a state, he was certainly no architect.

Not unlike Barak, Arafat had behind him a fragmented political community ranging from the Islamist Hamas, for which the two-state solution was secondary to values such as the right of return and Al-Aqsa, to the communist George Habash's Popular Front for the Liberation of Palestine, for which liberation and social revolution were intertwined. Neither of these groups had accepted the very notion of a "peace process" with the "Zionist entity," nor did they endorse Arafat's 1988 renunciation of terror, which to them meant armed struggle. Things were not simple within Arafat's own Fatah either. Even his own foreign minister, Farouk Kaddoumi, boycotted the summit and kept his distance from the entire peace process. Indifference and aloofness were Mahmoud Abbas's way as well. More than once he made it clear to us that he had no confidence in the Palestinian negotiating team and defended throughout fundamentalist positions on the issue of refugees, whom he suspected Arafat might sell out if he got an acceptable deal on Jerusalem. Nor was Arafat's closest entourage monolithic. Cliques, rivalries, games of honor, and political struggles characterized his Byzantine court. There were militia leaders and warlords such as Dahlan and Jibril Rajoub, a "young guard" of Dahlan, Hassan Asfour, Muhammad Rashid, and others, and veterans such as Abu Mazen and Abu Ala. All these groups struggled for ascendancy, with tensions and competition between and within. Yasser Abed-Rabbo, Saeb Erekat, and others ran between the camps and jostled for favorable places round the Chairman.

Unlike Barak, however, Arafat was a historic persona, the embodiment of the Palestinian cause, capable of rallying behind him the myriad disparate political groups and factions. He was also a man of political acumen, an effective politician who was able to keep control of his organization internally in spite of its internal contradictions. With his most immediate political court, his aides and negotiators, Arafat was like the sphinx; his real intentions and the direction he wanted to take remained unknown to everyone else. In negotiations, rather than acting on instructions from him, his negotiators vied among themselves to extract more gains from Israel so as to impress their leader. Not one of them had the remotest idea as to what the goal of the negotiations really was. Arafat was always the final arbiter, and more than once we saw him repudiate proposals his representatives had made. Sometimes, when agreement seemed close, he would create a last-minute crisis in order to improve his positions and make progress toward his greater "vision." I myself experienced this when I negotiated in October 1999 the safe passage connecting Gaza to the West Bank. When all was settled and signed with his minister, Jamil Tarifi, Arafat called me to renegotiate a number of clauses, a demand which I simply could not accept.

Arafat was the only one with the stature required to lead the Palestinians to their promised land. But rallying majority support for a controversial decision on a peace deal that looked inadequate to him was something he could not or did not want to do. We undertook that journey in the hope that at the moment of decision Arafat would seize the historic opportunity and bring into the negotiations an element of surprise, as great historical leaders always did in such conjunctures. But Arafat expected a settlement for which his public then and there would applaud him or at any rate not rise up against him. He was never willing to accept that peace, as John Maynard Keynes explained to the statesmen at the 1919 Versailles Conference in his *The Economic Consequences of the Peace*, was not about justice and retribution, but about stability and regional equilibrium. The head of a movement driven by an historic injustice, Arafat could never concur with Israel's notion of a "reasonable solution." But nor is peace about forcing the enemy into servitude, as was contemplated by our initial peace offers. Only after Arafat had lost all trust in him did Barak internalize that a crippled Palestinian state was a bad idea for Israel's own interest in regional equilibrium.

Arafat's overriding concern with the unity of the Palestinian national movement was not particularly helpful in producing a settlement with Israel. Had Anwar Sadat looked for national consensus in Egypt ahead of his dramatic trip to Jerusalem, Israel and Egypt would still today be in a state of war. All the disparate Palestinian groups did meet Arafat ahead of his trip to Camp David and, as Israel's military intelligence informed us, they acquiesced with his decision to join the summit, but only on condition that he did not make concessions. Negotiating without making concessions is a self-defeating oxymoron. The thread that connected the factions and subfactions, Arafat was the one who made the difference between a Palestinian society united around a common objective and a civil war of all against all. Sanctification of the consensus and the avoidance of internal strife were always the pillars of his success. But this was also precisely why he was forced to shun a compromise with Israel that might have shattered that "holy" consensus. Knowing that he, and only he, had the power to make the decision that would legitimize an agreement, he raised the price of peace to a level beyond our reach. To him, no Israeli government had presented him with the kind of settlement that would confront him with the real dilemma: reject the settlement or defend it in an all-out war with Hamas. We believed, though, that, unlike our political predecessors, we presented Arafat first with the challenge of an apparently inadequate settlement at Camp David, but then with a more equitable one through the Clinton parameters and Taba. But he preferred the warmth of the national unity that had been forged in the years of struggle to the unbearable disruption that would have arisen from a peace under, to him, imperfect terms.

Personalities, indeed, need to be central to our interpretation of leaders' summits. The encounter between Barak and Arafat was quintessentially a Hegelian exercise in mutual destruction. In Friedrich Hegel's conception, conflict, which is the essence of tragedy, arises out of the tragic hero's unyielding conviction of his rectitude and the stubborn fixity of will that leads him to a one-sided attitude, or action, that violates another legitimate right. If he backs down, the drama might not end in tragedy, but if he refuses to yield, he would be destroyed by the very powers he refuses to recognize. This Hegelian denouement of the tragedy was almost built into the irreconcilable clash of characters and the radically divergent national ethics that defined the two main heroes in this story. It is hard to imagine two people so utterly unlike each other. The first saw himself as a historic and legendary figure, the embodiment of an irreparable national tragedy of biblical dimensions, rather than as a politician operating in the real world. He was a rare combination of megalomania and inferiority, compulsively jealous of his honor and status. He was as different from the Cartesian rationalism that characterized Barak as it is possible to imagine. Barak was a sophisticated systems analyst who made his decisions in a precise, calculating way after orderly staff discussions. On the negative side, he lacked emotional intelligence and was utterly blind to cultural nuances. He was the quintessential Israeli brought up in a belief in the unqualified justice of his nation's case and was utterly insouciant with regard to the plight of the nation we had disinherited. Peace is more about respect than about trust, and Israelis congenitally suffered from a lack of both empathy and respect for the plight of the Palestinians. Barak would negotiate with the Syrians out of respect for their power; he had no such regard for the Palestinians. "He treats me as though I am a slave," Arafat complained to Madeleine Albright at Camp David. Hard to believe, but these two men never had one real meeting during the entire summit. When Begin and Sadat met at Camp David I, the degree of trust between them was no greater than that between Arafat and Barak; yet they managed to reach a settlement because they respected the political weight and the strategic value of each other's country.

The first Camp David summit was attended by an emotional, romantic Israeli prime minister and a daring, extraordinarily prescient Egyptian leader, Anwar Sadat, whose peace move had isolated him in the Arab world and whose people and political class were incredulous about, and split by, his trip to Jerusalem. Also, his willingness to sacrifice Palestine on the altar of Egypt's superior interest was a bold and controversial move. At Camp David II, the Arab leader, Arafat, was a fearful and obstinate man with a mind focused on not deviating from his nation's narrative. Throughout the summit he seemed to be dreaming of the adulation of the masses in the squares of Gaza for standing up for their rights and defying the mighty United States. "We will march unimpeded to Al-Quds and realize the right of the 1948 refugees to return to their stolen homes and lands," he would tell them. In Camp David and in his rejection of the Clinton parameters, Arafat captured the imagination of his people but left behind him unfulfilled dreams of redemption.

Barak's failing tactics with Syria repeated themselves on the Palestinian front. He initially got immersed in tactical maneuvers that lost him the confidence of President Assad and, months later, when Assad was no longer interested, he sent Clinton with his real red lines to a Geneva summit with a Syrian president who had by then completely lost respect for him. With the benefit of hindsight, the lost opportunity was Camp David, not Taba. At Camp David we lost the Palestinians when we got entangled in tactics that involved going one step forward and two steps back without clarifying either to ourselves or to them what our real red lines were. Our tardy and timid offers were interpreted as a desperate attempt to save the summit, which made them in the Palestinians' perception a basis for further concessions. The Americans accepted the heavy responsibility for steering the summit without knowing what the bottom-line positions of the man who pressed more than anybody else for the summit were. For their part, the Palestinians entrenched themselves behind intransigent principles and poured cold water on every suggestion from either Israel or the Americans. In Taba, as in Geneva, the clock could not be put back, if only because the Israelis had "formatted" the process as an incremental voyage in which their presumed red lines would always be broken. The Palestinian blunder lay in dooming their national cause by their compulsive indifference to the context, to the political and strategic environment in which we all operated, which made their gains no more than a mirage in the desert. They could never bring themselves to collect their gains and run before the whole edifice collapsed on their heads. They were possibly influenced also by Syrian President Assad's determination to receive the "full price," his insistence that everything including the most trivial of details be agreed on or else there would be no settlement at all. When Assad died on the eve of Camp David, Arafat saw himself as the last keeper of the seal of orthodoxy in the matter of a settlement with Israel. The difference, though, was that Assad only lost the Golan Heights; Arafat went for broke and gambled on the fate of a nation.

Also, placing all the blame for the failure of the summit on Arafat, as Clinton did, was unjust and extremely counterproductive. The Palestinians, of course, saw this as further proof that the summit was nothing more than an American-Israeli plot and that Arafat had done the right thing by removing himself from it. From then on, Arafat, already an unlikely leader for times of transition to peace, lost any trust in the negotiating process. But losing America proved to be strategically ruinous for the Palestinians. They were left without the support of the one power that could have helped them achieve their national aspirations. However "biased" and "unreliable," the United States is the only external power that brought the Palestinians, through Clinton's Camp David process first and George W. Bush's Annapolis process later, to the outer limits of the search for peace with dignity. From everyone else they got and will continue to get only words and declarations.

As for us, even our staunchest critics would find it difficult to deny that the process which we led set out the fundamental principles, inconceivably to be improved substantively in any future context, for an Israeli Palestinian settlement. With all his flaws and inconsistencies, Barak "proved to be the most daring and by far the most conciliatory Israeli prime minister in history."[8] With him, we defined the most realistically possible outline for a two-state solution. Realistic, perhaps, but not sufficiently reassuring for our interlocutors. Their expectations went far beyond what any conceivable Israeli government could ever meet.

PART III

2001–20: A STORY OF PROMISE AND DECEIT

The Conversion of the Hawks

The quest for peace did not die in Taba. But the ever unbridgeable gap between what it was *necessary* and what was *possible* for the parties to do attests to the built-in intractability of the conflict. Every peace plan produced since the year 2000 was a reshaped version of the outline approved by the Barak government in the form of the Clinton parameters. Trapped these days, twenty-one years after the Camp David process, in an ever deepening occupation, and denied any horizons of a peaceful political solution to their plight, the Palestinians might wonder whether the Clinton parameters were such a bad deal after all. Eighteen months after he had rejected them, a besieged Yasser Arafat, in a frantic attempt to save his political life, said he now "absolutely" accepted the parameters.[1] They are no longer on the agenda was the then prime minister Ariel Sharon's reaction.[2]

George W. Bush's Road Map (2002–4)

A born-again Christian who saw the world in Manichean terms of good and evil, with Israel being on the right side of the divide—his mother referred to him as "America's first Jewish president"—George W. Bush initially placed no priority on Israeli-Palestinian peacemaking. It was the War on Terror following the 9/11 attacks and the need to forge an Arab coalition against jihadism that drew him into the Israel-Palestine situation. But he would not pursue a peace process with Arafat, to him a devious politician and unrepentant terrorist, the embodiment of the kind of evil he was in a crusade against.

Bush's first-term administration was split between the believers in a proactive engagement on Palestine—chief among them Secretary of State Colin Powell, who pushed for a multilateral peace effort, for which he created the Quartet comprising the United States, the European Union, Russia, and the United States—and the skeptics headed by Vice President Dick Cheney and Secretary of Defense Donald Rumsfeld. In line with his broader regional strategy, however, Bush did make, in his April 4, 2000, speech a reference to the need for democratic reforms in Palestine and strict security arrangements as the *sine qua non* for the two-state solution.

It was eventually the Iraq War that made an Israeli-Palestinian settlement pivotal to Bush's Middle East designs. Europe, America's Arab allies, and his closest partner, Britain's Tony Blair, needed an American peace initiative as an antidote to the growing antiwar opposition. Osama Bin Laden and George Bush used the Palestinian plight for the same reason, the one so as to ennoble his war against the infidel, the other to wrap his questionable war in Iraq in a cloak of worldwide consensus. The vision of a Palestinian state became the way to launder America's sins as an occupying power on the banks of the Tigris River. The launching in April 2003 by the United States and the other members of the Quartet of the roadmap for an Israeli-Palestinian peace was a grudging admission by the Bush administration that Baghdad and Jerusalem were connected vessels. Recovering Europe's friendship became so vitally important to the Bush administration that, for the first time ever, the United States had let Europe define her peace diplomacy in the Middle East.

The roadmap stipulated that the resolution of the Israeli-Palestinian conflict and "the end of the occupation that began in 1967" should be based

> on the foundations of the Madrid Peace Conference, the principle of land for peace, UN Security Council Resolutions 242, 338 and 1397, agreements previously reached by the parties, and the initiative of Saudi Crown Prince Abdullah—endorsed by the Arab League Summit— calling for acceptance of Israel as a neighbor living in peace and security, in the context of a comprehensive settlement.

Based on incremental and mutual steps by the parties, the roadmap started with the call for democratic reform in the Palestinian Authority and the end of Palestinian violence in parallel with Israel's settlement freeze and withdrawal from the Palestinian cities it had taken over in her 2002 Defensive Shield Operation. The parties would then proceed to negotiate the creation of a Palestinian state in provisional borders simultaneously with the Arab states restoring the diplomatic links they had severed with Israel during the first stages of the Intifada. The roadmap's last phase would address all core issues pertaining to a final settlement.

Alas, too susceptible to procrastination and evasion, the roadmap was stillborn. Both the Palestinians and Israel's Sharon government paid it nothing but lip service with only one objective in mind: not to be perceived as being responsible for its subversion. Neither of the parties even started to implement its most primary provisions. Arafat grudgingly agreed to appoint his deputy, Mahmoud Abbas, as prime minister, but did not crack down on terrorism. And the Israelis, whose prime minister had accepted the roadmap with fourteen "reservations," returned to the targeted killing of terrorists and dragged their feet when it came to removing the "illegal" outposts, let alone stopping the expansion of the "legal" settlements. The fatal symmetry between terrorism and settlements that was born with the Oslo Accords and was eventually to wreck them was the same that subverted the roadmap from the first moment. The roadmap also shared with the defunct Oslo process some of its major fallacies. Both plans contained no binding third-party mechanisms for monitoring and enforcement. It was utterly unrealistic to expect the parties to genuinely engage once again in a process that, like Oslo, left wide open the precise contours of the final settlement. Both frameworks were a standing invitation for the parties to dictate the nature of the final deal through unilateral acts, such as the expansion of settlements by the Israelis and the wild campaign of suicide terrorism and armed uprising by the Palestinians.

Ariel Sharon's Gaza Unilateral Withdrawal (2005)

Prime Minister Ariel Sharon totally discarded direct negotiations as stipulated by the roadmap. He neither trusted the Palestinians nor wanted to be absorbed by a process that could only lead to a return to the borders of 1967 and to the partition of Jerusalem into two capitals, Clinton parameters-style. Weary of the chances of pushing ahead with the ill-fated roadmap, the Bush administration opted to unilaterally offer guarantees to Israel with regard to a future possible peace outline. It rewarded Sharon with a pledge that no negotiations with the Palestinian Authority would start before there was an end to terror. And since the chances that Palestinian terror might end without a political horizon in sight were nonexistent, this meant that the option of negotiations was, for all practical purposes, removed from the agenda. Bush went even further in compensating Sharon. In a letter he had written to him dated April 14, 2004, he pledged that in any future peace deal Israel should be guaranteed sizable blocks of settlements in the West Bank, and that the right of return should only apply to the Palestinian state, not to Israel. That was, essentially, Clinton parameters stuff, with one crucial difference. The parameters drew their legitimacy from the long and laborious negotiations that preceded them; they were not a whimsical gift. Sharon did promise his American benefactor that he would draw precise contours for the settlement blocs beyond which Israel would not build, but failed eventually to comply. Typically, the Americans did not follow up on Israel's pledge either.

Sharon's closest aide and confidant, Dov Weissglas, who used to say that "unless they converted into Finns," it was suicidal for Israel to offer the Palestinians an independent state, was now hilarious:

The significance is the freezing of the political process. And when you freeze that process, you prevent the establishment of a Palestinian state and you prevent a discussion about the refugees, the borders, and Jerusalem. Effectively, this whole package that is called the Palestinian state, with all that it entails, has been removed from our agenda indefinitely. And all this with authority and permission. All with a presidential blessing and the ratification of both houses of Congress . . . And we educated the world to understand that there is no one to talk to.[3]

Yet in his difficult balancing act between Jews and Arabs, Bush would later qualify his generous pledge to the Israelis. On May 26, 2005, he promised Mahmoud Abbas, who had succeeded Arafat—he died in November 2004 in a Paris hospital—as president of the Palestinian Authority, that his pledge to Sharon would not prejudice the outcome of final-status negotiations and that border changes would have to be "mutually agreed."

However spoiled and catered to, Sharon feared that, unless he did "something," his diplomatic inaction might invite the United States to impose on him an American peace plan that he would hate. He initially let his foreign minister, Shimon Peres, who had earlier forced a divided Labor Party to enter the political wilderness of service in a Sharon government, assume the unenviable task of negotiating peace under a prime minister averse to negotiations. Peres's talks with the then Palestinian prime minister, Abu Ala, on the roadmap's provision of a first stage creating a Palestinian state within temporary borders led nowhere. Abu Ala categorically refused, just as he did at Camp David, to accept a repeat of the old ambiguous formula in which the Palestinian state's final borders would be based on the ambiguous UN Resolution 242. He demanded the 1967 lines, an utter anathema to Sharon. "Constructive ambiguity" had run its course, and the Palestinians now wanted clarity and certainty.

Sharon preferred, anyway, his own "something," a something for which he got the surprising backing of President Bush. In mid-August 2005, he mustered his notorious ruthlessness and penchant for bold moves to execute a unilateral withdrawal from the Gaza Strip and a small area in the northwestern corner of the West Bank, which meant dismantling all the settlements there, most of which he had created himself, and evacuating their eight thousand settlers. That we, the peace-lovers on the left, had never had the guts to remove even one settlement is our own story of ineptitude and political cowardice. Ariel Sharon's disengagement and the barrier he started to build between the West Bank and Israel signaled the end of his government's pretension to pursue a negotiated settlement.

Unilateralism now became the expression of Israel's national consensus precisely because it circumvented negotiations which the Israeli public, traumatized by the Intifada and the failure of the Camp David process, simply abhorred. To

Sharon, negotiations were an invitation into a black hole leading to national suicide. He described negotiations as a corral at the end of which the cattle are in-
escapably slaughtered. A crafty and devious politician, Sharon knew that peace
negotiations with Arafat, as all former prime ministers since 1994 could attest to,
was the surest way to political perdition. And he was not one to walk that path.
Benjamin Disraeli's description of politics as a "greasy pole" became an enduring
truth for all Israeli prime ministers who earnestly negotiated a Palestinian peace.

Unilateralism was to have ominous consequences, however. Sharon's disengagement from Gaza ushered in, as some of us had warned,[4] the Lebanonization
of the Strip. We believed that pulling out from Gaza without coordinating it with
a Palestinian or an international body that could help secure stability would
open a new phase in the Israeli-Palestinian war of attrition. Nor was it that outlandish to assume that Hamas would develop, or acquire, long-range missiles
which could hit targets deep in Israel. Both Sharon and President Abbas were
not interested in coordinating the Gaza operation with each other for the same
reason, Sharon because he did not want to be drawn into a broader peace initiative that would inevitably require additional concessions, and Abbas because
he refused to be complicit in the burial of the peace process. A degree of coordination between the parties did exist, however, on a lower ministerial level.[5] But
what the Israeli prime minister failed to foresee was that, just as in the case of
Israel's withdrawal from Lebanon in May 2000, which allowed an emboldened
Hezbollah to claim victory over the occupier, the Gaza disengagement would be
hailed by Hamas as the victory of military resistance over Abbas's peace diplomacy. Indeed, Hamas's victory over Abbas's Fatah in the January 2006 elections
in Gaza was a direct result of the rise in Palestine of an emboldened Islamist
alternative to the corrupt Palestinian Authority and its failing peace diplomacy.

With direct negotiations no longer a viable option, and Sharon's plan for
further disengagements in the West Bank highly likely to usher in a state of
war more ferocious than that which already existed in Gaza, the international
sponsors of the roadmap had to admit that the entire diplomatic edifice they had
built had crumbled. Sharon's plans for a possible West Bank disengagement were
abruptly brought to an end when he suffered a stroke on January 4, 2006. He was
succeeded by his deputy, Ehud Olmert. Sharon would remain in permanent veg-
etative state until his death in January 2014.

Sharon's disengagement from Gaza reflected a momentous personal transformation. The unscrupulous and ruthless man of action had finally realized
the limits of force. His divorce from his old allies on the right and the political
courage he displayed in defying head-on the most sacred values of the settler
community was a show of extraordinary political courage and determination.
No one who knew his personal and political history would have imagined him
uttering a speech like the one he delivered on October 26, 2004, the day the

Knesset approved his disengagement plan. Addressing the settlers, those whom he had spoiled and cultivated for years, he said:

> As one who fought in all of Israel's wars, and learned from personal experience that without proper force, we have no chance to survive in this part of the world that has no mercy for the weak, I have also learned from experience that the sword alone cannot decide this bitter dispute in this land . . . We have no desire to permanently rule over millions of Palestinians, who double their numbers every generation. Israel, which wishes to be an exemplary democracy, will not be able to bear such a reality over time. The withdrawal from Gaza will open the gates to a different reality.

Sharon ended his speech addressing the agitated settlers, suggestively with a quote from late prime minister, Menachem Begin—"You have developed among you a dangerous Messianic spirit"—another rightwing hawk , who had dismantled all the settlements in Sinai as part of the peace he made with Egypt.[6]

The George W. Bush Annapolis Process (2007–8)

The good news for the Palestinian president Mahmoud Abbas was that President Bush, overwhelmed by his domestic and Iraq troubles and under strong pressure from his European allies, refused to endorse the Convergence Plan, a scheme based on Sharon's vision of a massive unilateral disengagement from much of the West Bank that Ehud Olmert had planned.[7] Bush made it clear that a unilateral Israeli move could not be allowed to determine permanent borders. Also, both he and Condoleezza Rice, who had replaced Colin Powell as Secretary of State in Bush's second term, shifted now to unusually blunt language against Israel's "continued occupation of the West Bank." The president, who had arrived in the White House with an ABC ("Anything but Clinton") philosophy, was now forced to come as close as he possibly could to endorsing Bill Clinton's peace formula by his affirmation that "the borders of the past, the realities of the present, and agreed territorial changes" would define his two-state solution.

The Annapolis Peace Conference of November 27, 2007, Bush's grand initiative on Palestine, was supposed to erase the bitter memories of the Camp David experiment. Unlike Camp David, Annapolis had the advantage of the support of practically the entire region and the key global players. In addition to the neighboring stakeholders, such as Egypt, Jordan, and Saudi Arabia, the conference was attended by representatives from most of the members of the Arab League, including Syria, Malaysia, Sudan, and Lebanon. Russia, the European

Union, and the United Nations represented, together with the host country, the Quartet.

Ehud Olmert assumed the role of peacemaker with bold determination. He was assisted by a robust and highly qualified negotiating team headed by Brigadier General Udi Dekel. He could not avoid, though, some of the typical flaws of the Israeli system. A meticulous study described how the Israeli side's performance was marked by "faulty preparation, inadequate management, and problematic guidelines," not to speak of the acrimonious tension between Prime Minister Olmert and his foreign minister, Tzipi Livni. The Israeli side came to the Annapolis talks unprepared: the protocols of the Taba and Camp David negotiations had "vanished," the defense establishment was uncooperative, and the negotiation team tried to reopen previous agreements reached with the Palestinians.[8] And as in the case of Barak at Camp David, Israel's reluctance to discuss Jerusalem throughout most of the Annapolis process fed Palestinian mistrust in Israeli intentions. Twelve Israeli subcommittees were assigned to negotiate "professional issues"—territory and borders and economic cooperation—none of which included Jerusalem. On top of everything, Israeli official and nonofficial channels stepped on each other's toes.[9] Also the divisions between two parallel inimical tracks, Olmert's and his foreign minister's, was an embarrassing exercise in typical Israeli chaos. For more than a year, Foreign Minister Tzipi Livni's track, with hardly any coordination with her nemesis, Prime Minister Ehud Olmert, got bogged down in inconclusive debates with the Palestinian chief negotiator Abu Ala. Also, the lack of coordination between the subcommittees drove an embarrassing wedge between the parties. And at the moment of decision when Olmert was about to present his final deal, his foreign minister urged both the Americans and the Palestinians "not to enshrine the prime minister's proposals," for, she said, "he has no standing in Israel."[10]

Indeed, the Israeli political context was not particularly conducive to a settlement. Olmert was under pressure to complete negotiations before corruption charges brought an end to his mandate. As in Barak's case in the final stages of his premiership, but for different reasons, Olmert was seen as lacking the necessary public legitimacy for pursuing such an historic peace deal.

The Palestinian Authority was not faring much better. Hamas had won the 2006 legislative elections, seized control of the Gaza Strip, and violently ousted what remained of the PA security forces in Gaza, the very forces that were supposed to implement the security aspects of a peace agreement with Israel. Annapolis was throughout paved with doubts as to President Abbas' ability to implement such an agreement. And, as at Camp David, the Palestinian side too arrived at the talks with inherent barriers to progress. The Palestinian negotiator Hiba Husseini candidly admitted to me at a Track Two meeting in Madrid that while everyone on the team knew the red lines, no one was clear about what room for flexibility there was on core issues. Also Hamas's rise made former American peace negotiators such as Aaron Miller wonder whether "an Israeli prime minister (could) make existential concessions to a man [Abbas] who doesn't control the guns?" Robert Malley, another Clinton aide, concurred: "All this is a fantasy unless internal Palestinian divisions are healed."[11] Abbas definitely lacked Arafat's incontestable stature as a leader capable of rallying behind him the disparate Palestinian political community.

Nor did the fact that settlements' expansion in both the West Bank and East Jerusalem continued unabated offer the Palestinians any sense that the peace talks were tied to reality. Typically, Israel's dysfunctional politics prevented Olmert from reining in the settlers, the traditional spoilers of the peace process. In order to further an agreement, he needed, as he explained to President Bush, quiet on the settlers front. "If I have to choose between freezing construction and serious negotiations that may result in an agreement, I prefer the latter," he said.

This inauspicious political context also explains the conceptual confusion that existed as to the purpose of the Annapolis process. The apparent premise was that, given the fact that Palestine was in a state of war with itself, the chances of finalizing a peace deal before Bush's last year in office ended were slim. Accordingly, a framework agreement was set as a realistic goal; at times, a "shelf agreement" was mentioned, which would not be implemented while Hamas remained in power in Gaza. That was how President Bush saw the objective, as he stated before the Israeli Cabinet in January 2008: "The goal now is to lay out a vision of a state, not to move to a state right now." Also, the negotiating process was conceived by the Americans differently than any other previous process. There was not to be active American mediation, or "bridging proposals," only monitoring from afar.

Against such an uncertain background, Ehud Olmert's perseverance and bold creativity stand out with exceptional salience. A former hard-line Likud member now imbued with an access of statesmanship, Olmert had, against all the odds, shifted to dovish positions. He now wanted to achieve, in his words, a "big bang" on Palestine. A man of real warmth and social interaction, he believed that Israel should fight her "implanted DNA . . . the idea that we are lords of the manor." "Without some basic humility there will not be any negotiations," he said.[12] He, therefore, disengaged from Livni's tedious negotiating tactics and developed his own personal track with President Abbas at the end of which, on September 16, 2008, he would offer his final peace proposal, the core of which, in essence, reshaped, and on the territorial issue upgraded, Clinton's peace parameters.[13]

Olmert was willing to go to the outer limits of Israel's capacity for compromise, knowing all too well that this might not suffice. His plan B was to take unilateral steps in line with his 2006 Convergence Plan. At first, though, Olmert's acceptance of the 1967 lines as the basis for his territorial deal made the Palestinians "ecstatic," according to Secretary of State Condoleezza Rice. But here the enthusiasm ended. Olmert's proposed annexation of 6.5 percent of the West Bank to be swapped for 5.8 percent of Israeli territory was met with an adamant Palestinian position throughout the entire process of only a 1.9 percent land swap. The Palestinians in Taba were more forthcoming with their 2.3 percent offer. But in both Taba and Annapolis, despite Israel's emphasis on security and defensible borders, when drawing the maps, "the Israeli side gave precedence to political and settlement considerations over security concerns."[14] And as in the Clinton parameters, Olmert proposed to quantify in percentage terms the safe passage—admittedly in more realistic terms, 0.7 percent, than our 2 percent—linking Gaza and the West Bank in order to wrap up a deal of a Palestinian state on 100 percent of the land. Olmert's proposal would have left in the blocs of settlements, including Jerusalem, about 87 percent of the settlers, a somewhat higher figure than the one discussed in Taba. But it all again came to nothing. Bones of contention such as the territorial quantification of the safe passage—the Palestinians also wanted full sovereignty over it, thus cutting Israel in two—and the Palestinian demand that settlements located too deeply in Palestinian territory, such as the urban centers of Ariel and Maale Adumim, be removed remained undecided. Secretary Rice was right. Ariel, she said, was a "knife in the belly of the Palestinian state."[15] The Gaza Strip was practically left out of the negotiations, for the PA had no effective control over it, and Israel saw it as a Hamas enemy state that would never accept Israel's existence. Map 4 is a representation of Olmert's proposal.

On security matters, there was "a profound gap"[16] between the parties' attitudes, and they failed to resolve any of the problems left open by Ehud Barak's negotiators. Israel has always insisted on a long-term military presence in the Jordan Valley as well as on land and air freedom of operation in the entire West Bank even after the creation of a Palestinian state. In Taba we agreed on a Palestinian state with limited arms, but in Annapolis the Palestinians rejected Clinton's old idea of Palestine becoming a "nonmilitarized" state. They would not accept any security arrangement that would infringe their sovereignty. To Israel's insistence on the IDF's deployment in the Jordan Valley they responded that peace in itself was the guarantee of security, and that whatever force might be deployed in the Jordan Valley would have to be international. Olmert responded with the idea of an international-Jordanian force, but the Jordanians opposed it. Peace for Israel was always about separation. Hence, the Israelis in Annapolis opposed the Palestinian idea of open borders between the two states. At Taba, the Israelis asked for three early warning stations located within the Palestinian state. But in Annapolis, Olmert's team asked for five such stations, while the Palestinians were willing to concede only two. The parties also differed on the management of the stations—the Palestinians wanted them to be manned by an

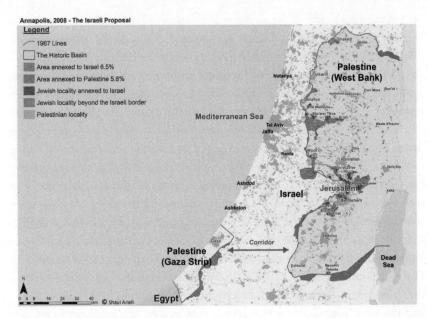

Map 4 Annapolis, 2008, Israeli Proposal

international force. Disagreements also remained on Israel's insistence on controlling the airspace and electromagnetic space and all the border crossings of the Palestinian state. Israel also refused to allow the state of Palestine to have its own international airport.

It did not help that Olmert's defense minister, Ehud Barak, scarred by his own failure at peacemaking, was hostile to, and uncooperative with, the entire process. And so was the army under his responsibility. "Do you want a Palestinian state or a military base?" was how the Palestinians referred to Israel's invasive security requirements.[17] But Israel's perception of the security risks, the lessons of the Al-Aqsa Intifada, and the rise of what the Israelis labeled as a Hamastan state in Gaza increased the skepticism over the Palestinians' ability to guarantee security, which was understandable, but counterproductive. That the Israelis did not seek to promote Palestinian security capabilities, but rather to fully control security in Palestine practically amounted to the negation of the very idea of an independent Palestinians state. When it came to security, Olmert felt forced to concur with his ministry of defense. "I can sell this deal," he said, "but not if the IDF says it will undermine Israel's security. That's the one thing no prime minister can survive."[18]

On the Jerusalem question, Olmert's creativity brought him no closer to an agreement than the Barak team in Taba. As he himself explained in a *New York Times* column on September 22, 2011, he had proposed two capitals in Jerusalem on the lines of Clinton's ethnic division of the city. The "Holy Basin" was proposed as an international area to be administered by Israel, Palestine, Jordan, Saudi Arabia, and the United States, thus deviating from the Camp David concept of the division of sovereignty. The idea of a special regime, which I defended unsuccessfully during the Camp David process, was partly embraced by Olmert. I had the chance to hand him, and advocate for, the extraordinarily detailed program for an Old City special regime spread over three volumes which was prepared under the auspices of the Canadian University of Windsor.[19] It was the first time that an Israeli prime minister proposed the internationalization of Jerusalem's Holy Basin, and the relinquishing of even Israel's monopoly on matters of security. Alas, the Palestinians preferred the Clinton concept of splitting the sovereignty with Israel to Olmert's surprising resuscitation of an idea reminiscent of the *corpus separatum* for Jerusalem in the 1947 United Nations Partition Plan for Palestine. Also, the question of Palestinian sovereignty over the Temple Mount remained unresolved. Through the Clinton peace parameters, the Barak government had accepted Palestinian sovereignty over the Mount's esplanade, while in Annapolis, Olmert simply stuck to the old status quo.[20] Other unresolved bones of contention were the Palestinian request to have open borders between the two capitals—which Israel opposed for security reasons—and territorial compensation for Israel's annexation of her East Jerusalem Jewish neighborhoods.[21]

As for the refugees, Annapolis practically meant no deviation from the Clinton parameters. Olmert's position was that the Palestinian state was to be the home of the returning refugees, and only as a strictly humanitarian gesture "unrelated to the right of return," he agreed to a meager number of five thousand refugees to be spread over five years, a substantive regression from the forty thousand refugees that Yossi Beilin had offered Nabil Shaath at Taba. Olmert's foreign minister, Tzipi Livni, adamantly opposed the return "of even one refugee."[22] Taba also made progress with regard to a narrative preamble. In Annapolis, Israel refused to take responsibility for the creation and perpetuation of the refugees problem or for solving it, and it also rejected the right of return as well as UN Resolution 194 as the term of reference for solving the problem. The Palestinians also demanded that refugees be granted both return and compensation, rather than having to choose between them; and that compensation be given to the host countries as well. But Olmert did not deviate from Israel's traditional position with regard to the compensation mechanism for the refugees either. Always cherry-picking when the involvement of the international community suited her, Israel turned down the Palestinian demand that compensation should come from the refugees' abandoned assets in Israel, and asked instead for a strictly international compensation mechanism.[23]

The head of Israel's negotiating team at Annapolis, who lamented "the inability of the Palestinian leadership to take fateful decisions as well as their hesitation to bear responsibility," was commendably aware also of Israel's own difficulty in making decisions that involved historic responsibility, security risks, and even election considerations.[24] This peace process was victim of the ever unbridgeable gap between the enormity of the Palestinian tragedy and the most generous peace offer that Israel could ever make.

Be that as it may, once more the Palestinians got cold feet when faced with a bold peace proposal, however inevitably imperfect. How familiar to those of us who saw the Palestinians reject the Clinton parameters and then the Taba outline in the expressed hope that George W. Bush, a staunch believer in the Jews' return to Zion, would give them a better deal. "In the end," wrote Secretary Rice in her memoirs, "the Palestinians walked away from the negotiations" and from what she, whose childhood in segregationist Alabama had made her especially sensitive to Palestinian suffering,[25] defined as "extraordinary terms."[26] Excited at Olmert's peace offer, she wrote: "This is unbelievable. Am I really hearing this? I wondered. Is the Israeli Prime Minister saying that he'll divide Jerusalem and put an international body in charge of the holy sites? . . . Yitzhak Rabin had been killed for offering far less."[27] But Abbas, to whom Rice rushed to share her enthusiasm, poured cold water on it. "How would I explain to four million refugees that Israel is not willing to admit them?" he asked.[28]

The odd, perhaps even surrealistic anticlimax happened on September 16 at the prime minister's residence. Olmert finished his detailed presentation of his peace offer to the Palestinian leader, only to be met with Abbas's complete silence. At some point in the charged atmosphere, Abbas did ask Olmert to give him the map of his territorial plan, which the prime minister had drawn on a napkin but Olmert would not do it without Abbas's prior acceptance of his peace plan. Nor was Abbas impressed by Olmert's suggestion that they both travel to New York to present the agreement to the UN Security Council. Abbas finally promised that he would get back with an answer. He never did. He also proposed a meeting between aides, to which Olmert agreed, but he later simply canceled it. Saeb Erakat later explained that he and Abbas "forgot" they had an urgent trip to Amman, and he proposed a meeting for the following week, which did not happen.[29] Olmert later sent to Abbas two of the most emblematic doves around, Ron Pundak and Yossi Beilin, after they had both endorsed the plan. They both came back empty-handed.[30] Interestingly, there would be yet one more meeting, in mid-November 2008, between Olmert and Abbas, in which, according to the Israelis, answers were provided to "most of the Palestinians' queries." They also agreed to convene a bilateral group to discuss Olmert's map. But the Palestinians did not show up, and Abbas's chief of Cabinet, Nabil Abu Rudeineh, dismissed in a public announcement Olmert's plan as a show of a "lack of seriousness." For Saeb Erakat, accepting Olmert's plan would have amounted to a betrayal of the Palestinian people.[31]

At a meeting in the White House in December 2009, Abbas turned down George Bush's last-minute plea that he reconsider Olmert's offer. Abbas would later say that there was no point in striking a deal with a lame duck prime minister. The fact that we, Barak's negotiators, were also political lame ducks when we made our last offer in Taba should have taught Abbas a fundamental truth about Israeli politics. Making a bold peace offer to Palestine would always be the swan song of an Israeli prime minister. Olmert later lamented:

> I know all of their arguments. They say that Abu Mazen agreed with George W. Bush that Chief Palestinian Negotiator Saeb Erakat would meet with [my] diplomatic adviser Shalom Turjeman in early January [(2009) in Washington, but that was a few days before Bush left the White House and we received no such invitation. They claim that it was because I was finished politically, so Abbas hesitated. But that is an excuse after the fact. The Palestinians were very worried. Abu Mazen is not a big hero. They were afraid. Erakat was worried. In the end they thought that maybe after the American elections they would get more from President Obama.[32]

They were always fatally hanging their hopes on the next president. Olmert's political woes were a pretext; the real reason, as Abbas would later explain, was that the gaps were still too wide.[33] After eighteen months of negotiations and three hundred meetings between the teams, Olmert's chief negotiator also acknowledged the existence of "unbridgeable gaps."[34]

In conclusion, Olmert's peace offer was bolder than any previous Israeli peace proposal only with regard to the territorial issue. Contrary to the Israeli perception that the Annapolis plan was a dramatic improvement on previous Israeli proposals, it remained broadly within the same box of recent Israeli offers rejected by the Palestinians. To them, it still was too pusillanimous a plan to be convincing. But according to Saeb Erakat, there was a philosophy behind the compulsive Palestinian rejectionism: "First they offered us [in Menachem Begin's autonomy plan] the running of hospitals and schools. They were later willing to give us 66 percent of the land. At Camp David they went beyond 90 percent (and now "100 percent through territorial swaps"). Why should we then hurry after all the injustice done to us?" As for the refugees, he said, the Palestinians wanted both the right of return and compensation, not either of the two.[35]

No less responsible for Annapolis's sad denouement was the flawed American approach of minimal involvement. Contrary to Clinton's overwhelming engagement, the Bush team conveyed a sense of aloofness, even a lack of purpose and determination, that left the parties to be consumed by their domestic constraints and moral convictions. It again transpired that, for the United States, an Israeli-Palestinian peace was simply not such a paramount national security priority, an irrevocable purpose for which failure was simply not an option. Once again, a bold Israeli peace proposal became the political swan song of the prime ministers who made it. In seriously dealing with Palestine Prime Ministers were either toppled or assassinated. True, Olmert could not complete his peace journey because of the accusations of corruption that forced him to resign, but the truth is that he had no legal obligation to quit office. He was toppled by a rebellion within his own government, essentially led by his top ministers, Livni and Barak, and by the irresistible pressure from the opposition.[36]

The Impossible
Triangle: Obama-Netanyahu-Abbas

The Limits of Obama's Engagement

There is no single, exclusive explanation for America's persistent vindication of its commitment to Israel or for the vigorous resonance that Israel's cause has had in America. American presidents since Harry Truman have all embodied either the emotional or the realpolitik aspect—some represented both—of these relations. The suspicion that Benjamin Netanyahu, who succeeded Olmert as prime minister in March 2009, fed throughout his right-wing constituency was that Barack Obama was committed to neither and that he was about to change course in America's special relationship with the Jewish state.

Obama was a revolutionary phenomenon in American history; he certainly did not fit the traditional pattern of American presidents after World War II. He was shaped by far less profound religious and biblical teachings than all of them, and the narrative of Jewish history and of the heroic emergence of the State of Israel out of the ashes of the Holocaust was not the primordial formative sentiment in his attitude to the Arab-Israeli conflict. The Palestinian tragedy was certainly no less central in defining his Middle East view. As such, Obama was to Netanyahu the mirror image of the leftist, naive peace dreamers he confronted at home. He lost no opportunity, even in public, to question the president's infatuation with the two-state solution, and he refused to see the link that Obama believed existed between an Israeli-Palestinian peace and his capacity to curtail Iran's nuclear ambitions. After two Middle East wars that had shattered America's standing in the Arab and Muslim world, the thrust of Obama's Middle East policy was now that of reconciling America with Muslim civilization. He believed this to be the best way to address the challenge of Islamic terrorism and the specter of uncontrolled nuclear proliferation in the region. For this strategy to succeed, Israel had to behave: stop settlements and withdraw from the territories to allow the creation of a Palestinian state with East Jerusalem as its capital. Netanyahu was on a totally different wavelength. An ideologue of Jewish catastrophe, he imbued Israel's existence with all of the Jews' past anxieties, pains, and struggles. It did not matter that Israel possessed, according to foreign sources, a nuclear arsenal, as well as a robust economy and a strong alliance with the world's most powerful nation. To Netanyahu, Israel still was an old Jewish ghetto holding out against relentless pogroms.

To stress his commitment to an Israeli-Palestinian peace, Obama appointed, on the very morrow of his inauguration, the former senator and peace broker in Northern Ireland, George Mitchell, to be his envoy for the peace process. But the new envoy's negotiating strategy of bridging the gaps left by the sides in the Annapolis process was utterly unacceptable to Netanyahu. He would make it clear from the outset that, just like Sharon before him, he refused to be impressed by the Palestinians' way of registering the concessions they got from the previous Israeli government with the assumption that the next one, whatever its political color, would pursue the negotiations from the point at which they were left off. For Netanyahu, Olmert's and Barak's peace offers were null and void.

But these were still times when an Israeli prime minister, however inimical to the two-state solution, needed his own peace plan to placate his American patron and secure his own place in the international soirée. In his speech at Bar-Ilan University on June 14, 2009, Netanyahu offered the new American president space for peace diplomacy. He grudgingly accepted the two-state concept, but he established red lines that would make it practically indigestible for the Palestinians. He stipulated that they would have to accept Israel as the nation-state of the Jewish people, waive the right of return, and have a state that was completely demilitarized with iron-clad security provisions that were bound to infringe on their sovereignty. Later in October, Netanyahu also agreed to a ten-month freeze of new housing starts in West Bank settlements, which Secretary of State Hillary Clinton defined as an "unprecedented" move.

Israelis and Palestinians have a good record in the ceremonious launching of peace talks, less so in striking agreements. After a long failing exercise of proximity talks run by Senator Mitchell, the shift with much fanfare to direct negotiations did not fare any better. The summit convened in Washington on September 1, 2010, was attended by Netanyahu and Abbas, Egypt's Hosni Mubarak, Jordan's King Abdullah II, and Quartet envoy Tony Blair. But this was where it all practically ended. Later that month, Netanyahu and Abbas did meet in Jerusalem, where Abbas tabled a detailed peace plan, but the only thing he got from Netanyahu was a lecture on Israel's security needs.[1] The Palestinians insisted on an extension of the settlements moratorium, for which the United States was willing to compensate Israel with an exorbitant package of security incentives. Netanyahu managed to get a two-month extension approved by his Cabinet, but then the Palestinians asked that Jerusalem be included in the housing moratorium, and the whole thing crumbled. On May 13, 2011, George Mitchell resigned as special envoy. In the ineffective, intermittent contacts between Israeli and Palestinian delegations later in the year, Netanyahu's envoy, Yitzhak Molcho, refused to even look at a Palestinian position paper, but Abbas would anyway send one such peace proposal on April 15, 2012, to Netanyahu's office. He did not even get an acknowledgment.[2]

It was hardly surprising, then, that throughout the entire eight-year Obama presidency, Israelis and Palestinians could not agree on a common platform for peace negotiations. Netanyahu inherited an intractable enough process, but his own calculated contribution to make it even more so by raising the demand that Israel be recognized as the nation-state of the Jewish people was his way of negating the Palestinian right of return. Netanyahu should have known that by focusing on Israel's Jewish narratives, he was inviting the Palestinians to fall back on theirs. But by rejecting Netanyahu's claim that Israel be recognized as a Jewish state, Abbas vindicated a key inquietude of the Israelis, and fueled the fears of a mass of skeptics about the Palestinians' hidden grand strategy of phases leading to one Palestine with an Arab majority. But Abbas was anyway just too weak and compromised to accept a final settlement that Netanyahu could live with. Arafat had set the standard, and Abbas could not allow himself to deviate from it. As he admitted in an interview to the Palestinian *Al-Quds,* if pressured to concede on sacred Palestinian principles such as refugees, Jerusalem, and borders, he "would pack his suitcase and go away."

Obama wanted, nonetheless, to establish his own peace legacy, even if just through a declaration. In a speech at the State Department on May 19, 2011, he reiterated George W. Bush's support for Israel's requirement to be recognized as "a Jewish state and the homeland for the Jewish people," and he stressed that the two-state solution would be based "on the 1967 lines with mutually agreed swaps," and on strict security arrangements. He believed that solving the question of borders and security would create the foundation for a solution of the two greatest bones of contention, Jerusalem and refugees.

But Netanyahu would have none of this. The 1967 borders, he said, were a suicidal line Israel could not live with. He also wanted America to reaffirm George W. Bush's 2004 pledge to Sharon on Israeli settlement blocs and accept his Bar-Ilan condition that the refugee problem be resolved outside of Israel's borders. Netanyahu's response to Obama's speech was of such vehemence that the president simply gave in. Significantly, it was in a speech to Israel's lobby, AIPAC (American Israel Public Affairs Committee), that on May 22 Obama chose to assuage Netanyahu's fears. He now qualified his reference to the 1967 lines with an assertion that the new borders would have "to account for the changes that have taken place" since 1967, particularly "the demographic realities on the ground," a euphemism for settlement blocs to be annexed to Israel. Alas, any attempt to respect the sensibilities of one of the sides in this conflict has always ended up alienating the other side. Thus ended Barack Obama's first-term exercise in Israeli-Palestinian peacemaking. The president's energy was now consumed by the Arab Spring and the showdown with Iran over her nuclear ambitions.

John Kerry's Failing Bid

Reading about and discussing with participants this and earlier phases of the Israeli-Palestinian talks always made me wonder again why the Camp David process had been singled out for such a bad press. The Israeli team at Camp David was a monument to team loyalty, proper coordination, and orderly deliberations compared with the Israelis' behavior in the Annapolis and Kerry processes. The same Tzipi Livni who had dissuaded the Palestinians from striking a deal with Olmert ahead of his indictment worked now as Netanyahu's minister in charge of the peace talks to undermine the prime minister among his right-wing constituency. She confided to the Palestinians that she could not believe "Netanyahu was going so far." She would also veto Netanyahu's acceptance of the Kerry formula on refugees, which was practically a replica of the Clinton plan. Not even one refugee should be admitted, she maintained.

Netanyahu's performance in the Kerry-led process remains an intriguing affair, though. He headed a right-wing coalition; yet, as attested by a most reliable Palestinian negotiator, Hussein Agha, he "went beyond any other prime minister." I wonder. Yes, he agreed with formulae that were not normally identified with his political persona. But these were all negotiations about a framework, about principles. The parties never got down to dealing with a practical solution to the core issues. Also, Netanyahu knew from the lessons of the past that whatever peace formula, however bold, an Israeli leader would be able to accept would be rejected by the Palestinians. When Abbas went to the White House in March 2014 to get Obama's final proposal for a peace framework, Netanyahu knew that, however different from traditional official US standpoints and however tilted toward the Palestinian positions it was, Abbas would turn down Obama's formula.

John Kerry and his envoy to the talks, the former US Ambassador to Israel, Martin Indyk, were right to assume that the problem with the Camp David process lay in the fact that it lacked an agreed framework of principles upon which the negotiations could be conducted. Hence, they invested most of their diplomatic energy in negotiating such a framework agreement, whose details were later revealed by different participants.[3]

The work on the framework started in a secret channel that had been going on for some time in London between Netanyahu's envoy, Yitzhak Molcho, and General (res.) Mike Herzog, on the Israeli side, and Mahmoud Abbas's adviser, Hussein Agha, probably the most knowledgeable individual about the intricacies of the conflict. After a long, exhaustive brainstorming exercise, the group moved to the drafting of a framework, which they eventually came very close to finalizing. The Jerusalem issue remained unresolved, but the channel was in the hands of the best people around, and it was a gross mistake for Secretary Kerry to press for the creation of an open channel, which he eventually merged with the secret one.

John Kerry also wrongly assumed that the real problem he faced was Netanyahu's intransigence. He then dedicated most of his power of conviction to talks with him, and hardly engaged with Abbas. The result was that the Palestinian leader would eventually dismiss the final product as an Israeli document wrapped in an American flag. But the truth is that Netanyahu did venture "outside his natural comfort zone," or, as Martin Indyk put it, "We had him . . . in the zone of a possible agreement."[4]

The document that Kerry eventually presented to Abbas in Paris on February 19 as "a proposed American Framework" drew upon the lessons of both the Clinton parameters and Annapolis, but also corrected some of their ambiguities. The supposedly new assertion of the principle of "two states for two peoples, Palestine, the nation-state of the Palestinian people, living in peace with Israel, the nation-state of the Jewish people" was actually the underlying principle of Clinton's parameters. A novel element aimed at accommodating Abbas's opposition to the Jewishness of Israel was the framework's promise to Israeli Arabs of "full equal rights" and freedom from discrimination. Also, the territorial issue was addressed in a far more explicit way. Netanyahu accepted that

> the new secure and recognized international borders between Israel and Palestine will be negotiated based on the 1967 lines with mutually-agreed swaps whose size and location will be negotiated, so that Palestine will have viable territory corresponding in size to the territory controlled by Egypt and Jordan before June 4, 1967, with territorial contiguity in the West Bank.

The final borders would also take into account "Israel's security requirements and the goal of minimizing movement of existing populations while avoiding friction." In other words, the creation of settlement blocs where the overwhelming majority of settlers lived could remain. The chapter on Jerusalem was, however, somewhat nebulous. It stated that the city would not be redivided, but mentioned the possibility of two capitals. In practical terms, though, Netanyahu expected the Palestinian capital to be in one of the outer East Jerusalem neighborhoods, Beit Hanina, for example. Using different wording, the document followed the Clinton parameters on refugees by stating that "an independent Palestinian state will provide a national homeland for all Palestinians, including the refugees." The menu of options was similar to Clinton's parameters: resettlement in the State of Palestine, in the current host states, and "in third countries" around the world. In special humanitarian cases, admission to Israel "will be decided upon by Israel, without obligation, at its sole discretion." Security issues were addressed by US General John Allen along the same principles as were defined throughout Camp David and Annapolis. The Palestinian state would be demilitarized—Clinton had preferred the term "nonmilitarized"—but would have an effective internal security force. As always, Israel opposed, though, any presence of American forces in the Palestinian state, presumably in order to keep her undisturbed freedom to operate there and, above all, avoid friction with the Americans. A mention was also made of the presence of the IDF along the Jordan Valley *for an undefined period*. It also asked for the right to emergency deployment in the Palestinian state should an imminent threat appear from the East. Palestine, it was also stated, would have "permanent borders with Jordan and Egypt," meaning that both the Gaza Strip and the Jordan Valley would be a *sovereign* part of Palestine.

As expected, Abbas turned down the document when it was presented to him by Kerry on February 19 in Paris. The Americans needed to better square the circle with regard to Netanyahu's and Abbas's positions. They now prepared a different proposal, this time without negotiating it with the Israelis. It inevitably tilted toward some of Abbas's key concerns, particularly over Jerusalem. It was now stated that both Israel and Palestine would have "internationally recognized capitals in Jerusalem, with East Jerusalem serving as the Palestinian capital." It still, however, offered no clue as to how to resolve the problem of the Old City. Where the Americans could offer no concession to Abbas was on Netanyahu's *sine qua non* condition about the "Jewish state."

It was Obama in person who presented the new proposals to Abbas in a meeting at the White House on March 17, 2014. Abbas asked for time to ponder, but characteristically never got back to him. Obama pleaded with him "to see the big picture" instead of getting bogged down in "this or that detail." To no avail. The same Abu Mazen who bravely stood against the Palestinian strategy of terror was also more comfortable pivoting the public grievance than taking divisive decisions on peace.[5] The Palestinians would later claim that the problem was that Abbas had not been given a written proposal. But it was Saeb Erakat who had explicitly asked the Americans not to present such a written document so that Abbas could keep a degree of deniability.

The strict deadline imposed by Kerry combined with Palestinian politics gave the *coup de grâce* to the entire process. The nine-month straitjacket that Kerry had imposed for reaching an agreement responded to the Palestinians' impatience to get to the next stage in their strategy, achieving UN recognition and full membership for the State of Palestine. In the last two months of the Kerry process, the parties' energy was then exclusively consumed by negotiations over the extension of the deadline. As if negotiations were not a Palestinian necessity but a gift to Israel, they asked for incentives in the form of either a settlements freeze or a release of prisoners. This kind of situation, which in this case Secretary Kerry managed in a particularly clumsy way, was always a recipe for the contamination of the process. The Israelis agreed to the release of prisoners as being more politically digestible. But Abbas wanted Israeli Arabs to be among the prisoners to be released, an extremely sensitive issue for Israel, which Kerry promised to get for him. To appease the Israelis, the Secretary of State practically introduced a time bomb into what remained of the process by agreeing that Israel could balance the agony of each tranche of prisoners released with announcements of building in Jerusalem and in the settlement blocs. Any such announcement, understandably, met with a Palestinian outcry.

The talks over extension continued after the unsuccessful Obama-Abbas meeting, but they now turned into a bazaar, with the Palestinians asking for four hundred more prisoners. On April 1, while Netanyahu was still debating with his Cabinet the release of prisoners, Abbas handed the Palestinian request to be admitted to fifteen UN agencies. If this were not enough, while the parties were making a truly last-ditch attempt to agree on an extension at a Jerusalem hotel on April 22, where Saeb Erakat confessed to being impressed by an Israeli offer to allow planning and zoning rights to the Palestinians in parts of Area C, Abbas was finalizing his reconciliation talks with Hamas. Their agreement was signed on April 23.

Eventually, the Hamas-PLO agreement did not materialize, but it conveniently allowed Netanyahu to slip away from the process. He would not negotiate with a Palestinian government "backed by a terrorist organization that calls for Israel's destruction." He went even further, and imposed economic sanctions on the Palestinian Authority, and canceled plans for Palestinian housing in Area C. To Netanyahu, aligning with the radical parties of settlers and other messianic fanatics was an Israeli monopoly, but a similar alliance among the Palestinians was a *casus belli*.

If Netanyahu was posturing as a man of peace, then a sigh of relief and a comforting sense of *déjà vu* must have invaded him with Abbas's typical non-answer to Obama's proposed framework. That he had agreed to formulae so diametrically opposed to what he was known to believe, and which his political constituency rebelled against, can only be explained by his educated understanding that, as always, an agreement that he would barely live with would be with great certainty rejected by the Palestinians. Indyk was too kind to Netanyahu when he assumed that "the promoters of the settlement activity" in his coalition had undermined Netanyahu's peace drive. Throughout his long years as prime minister, Netanyahu has never operated outside his power base. Now he was back where he always loved to be, in the warm bosom of his right-wing constituency. For both Netanyahu and Abbas, it was now easier to engage in the blame game than go through the political nightmare of turning Kerry's framework into a peace treaty.

As was the case throughout the entire peace process, the domestic politics of both parties played a crucial role in defeating the chances of an agreement. Hamas and Islamic Jihad as well as the Fatah-affiliated militias, not to mention the impossible standards established by Arafat for a peace agreement, all weighed heavily on Abbas. He was always too weak and too lacking in popular appeal to make the historic leap to a divisive peace agreement. On the other hand, Israel's ever-present, irresistible penchant for *faits accomplis* could always be relied upon to undermine the Palestinians' faith in the negotiations. According to the Israeli NGO Peace Now, during the nine months of the John Kerry peace talks, Israel set a new record for settlements expansion with nearly fourteen thousand newly approved settlers' homes. Netanyahu's minister of housing, Uri Ariel, himself a settler of the annexationist party *The Jewish Home*, stood at the forefront of a settlement project that threatened to practically link the 1967 border with the Jordan Valley, thus the cutting in two the Palestinian territory. Ministers were also pushing bills to annex the Jordan Valley. A revealing exposure of the Netanyahu government's attitude to the whole process came also from Minister of Defense Moshe Ya'alon lashing out at Kerry for his "peace messianism" and cynically stating that the "only thing that can save us is that John Kerry will get a Nobel Peace Prize and leave us alone." A few days later, hardliners in Netanyahu's coalition threatened to withdraw from the government if he accepted the 1967 borders as a baseline for talks. Abbas's disengagement from the talks saved them the trouble.

Text and Context in Obama's Peace Initiatives

The fate of the text of peace proposals is frequently decided by the context in which they are produced. Distracted by more vital challenges to America, Obama now saw little sense in investing political capital in a hopeless peace endeavor in Palestine. He was particularly enraged by Netanyahu's attempt to undermine his Iran policy in his own political backyard, the US Congress and public opinion. The ultimate aim of Netanyahu's posture as a peacemaker, Obama realized, was to garner support for his challenge to the president's Iran policy.

The entire process was now exposed to and conditioned by two major regional dynamics, the Arab Spring and the Iran nuclear deal. In the eyes of Israel and America's Arab allies, the United States was now perceived as an exhausted power retreating from its commitments to her allies, appeasing their Iranian nemesis, and leaving behind an unstable Iraq, and an Afghanistan practically in the hands of the Taliban. US credibility suffered a major setback particularly with its vacillations on the Syrian front, where it practically offered immunity to Bashar al-Assad to continue slaughtering his people and opened the gates of the Middle East to penetration by Russia. With Obama's credibility so deeply tarnished throughout the region, Netanyahu was happy to cast himself in the role of the champion of a hysterical Sunni Middle East which, in its obsession with the Iranian threat and the rise of Islamic jihadism, had relegated the Palestinian question to a secondary position. ·

A conservative in revolutionary times, Netanyahu was unimpressed by the Arab Spring and by what others saw as the beginning of an era of democracy in the Arab world. He, therefore, preferred not to budge on any front, the Palestinian track included. But with Obama's Iran deal, Netanyahu faced what was for him a nightmare come true of Iran's possible integration into the international community without having to dismantle its nuclear potential. He dismissed as sheer lunacy the notion that the nuclear agreement with Iran that the Obama administration had reached in April 2015 opened a ten-fifteen-year window for creative statesmanship to reshape regional politics. A regional system based on a Palestinian peace and a collective system of security that would include nuclear nonproliferation was, he would argue, the agenda of naive dreamers.

As the living spirit of the Iran nuclear deal, John Kerry was in no position to further soften Netanyahu's position on Palestine. The Israelis' conventional strategic wisdom was based on an equation of "Bushehr versus Yitzhar," that is, an Israeli readiness to dismantle settlements in the heartland of Judea and Samaria if the Iranian centrifuges in Bushehr were dismantled. That this did not seem to be taking place was the reason that the tensions between Obama and Netanyahu over Iran now became the new underlying factor in Israel-US relations.

John Kerry's peace initiative became, then, trapped in a paralyzing power game. Should the process fail, Kerry warned, the United States would not be able to rescue Israel from the wave of international condemnation and sanctions that would be unleashed against her. But Netanyahu's playing card was more than a threat. His friends in the US Senate had already put together in January 2014 close to a majority of sixty for a bill imposing new sanctions on Iran, which was tantamount to torpedoing Obama's major foreign policy objective.[6]

It was this reality that led the Americans to endorse two Netanyahu positions— recognition of Israel as a Jewish state and intrusive security arrangements—that the Palestinians were bound to reject. Recognizing the "Jewish state" was a betrayal of the constituent ethos of Palestinian nationalism, while intrusive security arrangements were a standing invitation to radical groups to fight what would be seen as occupation in disguise. Peace and security in the desperately small geography of Israel-Palestine could never be reconciled, particularly against the background of an imploding Middle East. Israel's concerns were legitimate, but so too were those of the Palestinians.

Nor did the ill-fated Arab Spring, another Middle East moment that the Obama administration was identified with, make Netanyahu amenable to concessions on Palestine. He could now cite the anarchy on Israel's borders as a preoccupation that precluded any serious peace initiatives on his part. To create a Palestinian state when existing Arab states seemed to be crumbling and a part of Palestine was in the hands of Salafists and Hamas did not look to the Israelis a particularly brilliant idea. Another adverse effect of the Arab turmoil on the Israeli-Palestinian situation had to do with Jordan, which was forced by the fighting in Syria to give preference to her strategic relationship with Israel over the Palestinian issue. Jordan was a major Israeli concern, with Netanyahu's security advisers even being sceptical as to the chances of survival of the Hashemite monarchy. The possibility that at some time in the future, a hostile, probably jihadist, regime might rise in Amman was something that the Israelis had never ceased to be preoccupied about.

Palestine was, in any case, not central to Netanyahu's concerns. His strategic thinking was diametrically opposed to that of his Laborite predecessors. Rabin went to Oslo and Barak to Camp David not because they believed that the Palestinians deserved a state, but because they understood that Palestine was central to the chances of a broader Arab-Israeli peace. But Netanyahu maintained that any meaningful concession to the Palestinians needed to be preceded by the neutralization of each and every existential threat emanating from the outer circle of the region, namely, Iran, Iraq, and so on.

With such a strategic setup, the Kerry process was going nowhere. Left to his own devices, Netanyahu felt free to expand settlements, put security first, and neutralize Palestinians in cantons in what was termed as the "spatial shaping" of the West Bank. While the region was in flux and borders throughout the region were being challenged, Netanyahu's strategy remained that of trying to get away with what he could, and, if possible, redrawing borders, as was being done elsewhere in the Middle East by ISIS and the Kurds, and later Turkey, in northern Syria. Netanyahu conducted a similar policy of *faits accomplis* in Jerusalem, where the expansion of Jewish neighborhoods systematically eroded the applicability of the Clinton parameters to Jerusalem. In his obsession with the gerrymandering of Jerusalem into a Jewish city, he put 100,000 Palestinians beyond the city's municipal borders, which his far-right coalitions still expected to extend to Maale Adumin on the way to the Jordan Valley.

Nor was it helpful to the Kerry-led process that the Palestinians held the sword of Damocles of a UN-backed unilateral declaration of statehood over the head of both Israelis and Americans. The internationalization of the solution became ever since the main thrust of the new Palestinian strategy. Abbas assumed that from the moment his state was recognized by the UN Security Council, Israel would become the illegal occupier of a sovereign state (and a full member of the United Nations). But notwithstanding the damage that the Palestinian strategy was inflicting on Israel's fragile international standing, Abbas was embarking on what could, nonetheless, turn out to be a self-defeating diplomatic exercise. Negotiations have an implicit assumption of equivalence of demands between the sides. But the creation of a Palestinian state through an international body could embolden future Israeli governments to also enact unilateral steps in the West Bank and unceremoniously declare the death of the Oslo process. Another risk for the Palestinians was that unilateral statehood could reduce the conflict with Israel to a banal border dispute between sovereign states and sideline the major narrative issues—refugees and Jerusalem. Indeed, by unilaterally declaring a Palestinian state along the 1967 ceasefire line, Abbas could have put into practice Israel's vision of "two states for two peoples," a concept he recalcitrantly opposed during the Kerry-led process.

An Uninviting Concept

The Geneva Understandings as a Parable

"I'm a pessimist because of intelligence, but an optimist because of will," wrote Antonio Gramsci in one of his letters from prison. Humbly, my entire reading of current history, the Israel-Palestine two-state dilemma included, is exactly the opposite. I am an optimist because of intelligence and a pessimist because of will. Rationally and hence technically, the two-state solution is possible and is, moreover, the only formula of redemption for both the Palestinian and the Zionist projects before they turn into a monstrous empire built on apartheid. Alas, politically, its chances are as remote as one could possibly imagine. The two-state solution, arguably the most dauntingly complex divorce in history, has now become a religion by rote for liberals and genuine peace lovers. But, as with most routine articles of faith, it lost its link to reality.

The optimists believe that the two-state solution is still possible because the entire settlements enterprise has not been the historic success that it pretended to be. A moral obscenity and a political march of folly, the settlements, they say, are still not an insuperable obstacle for a peace based on land swaps. A recent report by Israel's Central Statistics Bureau has shown that 80 percent of the settlers, 334,000, are still concentrated in settlement blocs adjacent to the Green Line, consisting in all of no more than 4 percent of the West Bank. The Israelis certainly failed to reach demographic dominance in the West Bank, where 87 percent of the population is Palestinian—around 3,000,000 Palestinians and around 640,000 Israelis (Jerusalem included; without it, the number of Israelis descends to around 430,000, less than 5 percent of Israel's population)—and only 11 percent of the settlements have more than 5,000 inhabitants. Most of the settlers live in sixty settlements and in twelve East Jerusalem neighborhoods, all adjacent to the 1967 border. Thirteen out of the fifteen settlements with more than 5,000 settlers are also adjacent to the old border, and the two Orthodox settlements, Modi'in Illit and Beitar Illit—73,000 and 57,000 inhabitants respectively—both practically on the border, contain a third of the settlers in the entire West Bank. The two other urban centers are Maale Adumim and Ariel with 38,193 and 20,456 inhabitants, respectively. Settling in the territories, it turns out, is not the attraction it pretended to be for masses of Israelis; the demographic growth rate of the settlements dropped from close to 14 percent in 1995 to 3.48 percent in 2017. In spite of unprecedented assistance from Netanyahu's governments, only 92,000 Israelis live in the 75 religious-nationalist isolated settlements in the heartland of Judea and Samaria that were built to block the creation of a contiguous Palestinian state. These religious ideological settlers pretended to be the second wave of Zionist pioneering, but, unlike the earlier Zionists, they created neither inspiring social utopias nor an independent economy. The entire settlements project is mostly dependent on work in Israel proper and on the massive investments and subsidies from the central government.[1]

A two-state solution is always possible, of course, if one negotiates in a sand table, in laboratory conditions, that is, in a sociopolitical vacuum unaffected by political constraints. Such was the case of the 2003 peace game known as the Geneva Initiative,[2] where the wide room for maneuver the Israeli negotiators, headed by Israel's most indefatigable peace-seeker dove, Yossi Beilin, allowed themselves ended up producing a deal that broke all Israel's red lines. No peace plan, real or imagined, has ever gone as far as the "Geneva Understandings" in meeting Palestinian demands. The former US president Jimmy Carter, who attended the signing ceremony in Geneva, called on Israel and the PLO to adopt the understandings as a "bible." But its eventual rejection by both parties speaks volumes.

The Israelis in Geneva unlocked each and every part of the Clinton plan about which the Palestinians had reservations without receiving a single concession indicating that the Israeli position at Taba had been maintained, let alone improved. As shown in Map 5, the understandings devised the settlement blocs and the related land swaps, equal in size and quality to the blocs, in such a way that the Palestinians would get a state exactly equivalent to 100 percent of the Gaza Strip and the West Bank. In Jerusalem, it offered the three-quarters of the Old City that the Palestinians had always demanded; it also nullified Israel's sovereignty over the Jerusalem Wall Tunnel and while offering full sovereignty to the Palestinians over the entire Temple Mount area, it subtly diluted the formula I had proposed during our own talks at Bolling Air Force Base in December 2000 of full Palestinian sovereignty over the Temple Mount in exchange for a Palestinian acknowledgment of the site as "holy to Judaism."[3] At Taba, they rejected my proposal, and in Geneva, they diluted it by acknowledging the "unique religious and cultural significance of the site to the Jewish nation."

Map 5 The Geneva Understandings: Model for a Permanent Agreement

On the matter of refugees, Geneva is blatantly at odds with the Clinton parameters in both substance and spirit. Clinton made it unequivocally clear that "there is no explicit right of return to Israel," whereas the Geneva document allows the right of return essentially through the front door. It endorses UN Resolution 194, which asserts that "those Palestinian refugees who want to live at peace with their Jewish neighbors are entitled to return at the earliest possible opportunity." Yet UN Resolution 194 was never an agreed basis for peace negotiations. The understanding that negotiations would be based only on Resolutions 242 and 338 was part of the Israel-PLO Declaration of Principles of September 1993 and the Interim Agreement of September 1995. In December, 2000, I proposed that Palestinian refugees be allowed to return to the areas that their new state would annex from Israel in the swap arrangements. This notion was subsequently included in the Clinton peace parameters and, notably, in the Geneva document also. I was at the time motivated by a belief that such a provision would enable the Palestinians to claim that there had been an effective return of refugees to Israel proper. But in Geneva this particular clause had no such significance at all.

The Geneva document did state that any return was "at the sovereign discretion of Israel." However, the proposed rules for the operation of the international commission charged with implementing the solution essentially vitiated this assertion. For Israel was required to propose a number of returnees that was equal to the average number of refugees absorbed in third countries such as Australia and Canada. Moreover, the international commission was a sovereign body charged with "the full and exclusive responsibility to carry out all the aspects of the agreement connected to the issue of the refugees." In addition to the number of returnees, on such issues as compensation and Palestinian property Israel was also likely to regularly find itself in a head-on collision with the commission, to which "refugees shall have the right to appeal decisions affecting them according to mechanisms established by this Agreement." This right of appeal was likely to open a Pandora's box that would have made Israel's determination to obtain a pledge from the Palestinians on the "end of conflict and finality of claims" an elusive endeavor.

According to the Geneva document, Israel would essentially be dealing with two compensation funds, one relating to property and the other to "the situation of refugeehood." A panel of experts would value the Palestinian property on the basis of "the records of the Custodian for Absentee Property," thus creating a mandatory link between the extent to which Israel had benefited from Palestinian property and the matter of compensation. Israel would also be expected to contribute to the second fund, a "Refugeehood Fund," aimed at "commemorating the experience of refugeehood."

Notwithstanding these major concessions, I am of the view that by breaking all Israel's official red lines, Geneva created a peace offer based on reconciliation and healing that brilliantly addressed the core concerns and fundamental national narrative of the Palestinians without undermining Zionism's core values. Alas, the Palestinian signatories, headed by Yasser Abed-Rabbo, were dismissed, in the words of Palestinian pollster Khalil Shikaki, as having "little credibility in the eyes of their respective publics [which] . . . may be reluctant to approve a document associated with such individuals." Indeed, a poll conducted between December 4 and 9, 2003, by the Palestinian Center for Policy and Survey Research[4] found significant opposition to the document among those Palestinians familiar with it. Among those who had heard of or read about it, support reached 25 percent and opposition 61 percent. After informing the respondents of seven core elements of the document, support increased from 19 percent to 39 percent, opposition from 44 percent to 58 percent. Palestinian opposition groups managed to frame the whole Geneva document as a sell-out of refugees' rights. And despite provisions such as qualitative land swaps that would allow a Palestinian state in 100 percent of the land, and full Palestinian sovereignty over Temple Mount, none in the Palestinian national leadership applauded the deal. In practice, the Geneva Understandings turned out to be the swan song of Yasser Abed-Rabbo's political life. He left the political limelight, presumably in an act of betrayal of the Palestinian national ethos.

Besieged by Ariel Sharon in his Ramallah compound and in an attempt to reaffirm his political relevance, Arafat seemingly uttered a word of support for Geneva. It was, he said, "a brave initiative that opens the door to peace."[5] Eighteen months earlier, he said he "absolutely" supported a less generous offer, the Clinton parameters.[6] Arguably, in the utterly unlikely event that an Israeli government would have endorsed Geneva, Arafat would have seen the understandings as no more than a platform for further bargaining. In Arafat language, what he acknowledged here was the "potential" of Geneva, not its claim to be the final historic compromise. Arafat's obsession with improving every "final" proposal presented to him was a pattern he never deviated from.

Throughout the years, numerous unofficial backchannels have mushroomed alongside the Israeli-Palestinian peace process. The Palestinians used such channels to test the limits of Israeli flexibility without ever agreeing to endorse an outcome. A typical document in this mold was the one drawn up in 1995 by Yossi Beilin and Abu Mazen. When I suggested to Abu Ala during our secret "Swedish channel" in the spring of 2000 that the Beilin-Abu Mazen document become the peace agreement, he took the document from his briefcase and showed me the many tightly packed reservations that Abu Mazen himself had noted in the document's margins. I also had the opportunity to make a similar suggestion to Arafat at a meeting in Ramallah in 1997. His answer was that the Beilin-Abu Mazen document was "words, words."

Shaul Arieli, one of the initiators of the Geneva Initiative, would eventually distance himself from the territorial and border aspects of the understandings. Another emblematic dove, the former Shabak chief, Ami Ayalon, opposed Geneva for its chapter on refugees, which he saw as clear-cut implementation of the right of return. Using the criteria of Charles Fawcett's theory of the "good border," Arieli, as shown in Map 6, produced an optimal land swap in terms of the interests of, and costs that would be incurred by, the two sides. These included the consideration of issues such as land ownership, the number of agricultural farms along the border, the concerns of people who would be affected by the new lines, the commercial relations between villages on the two sides of

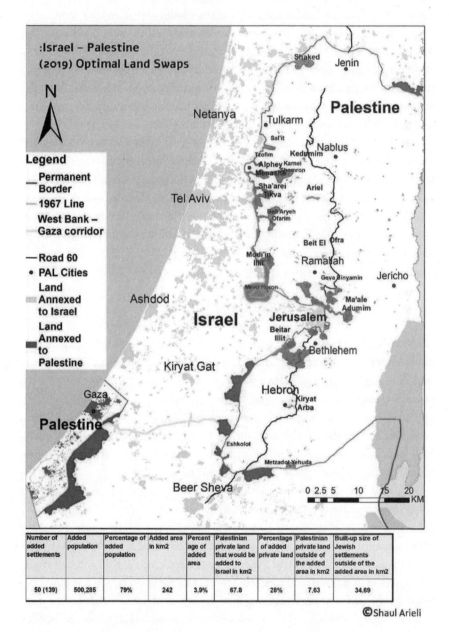

Number of added settlements	Added population	Percentage of added population	Added area in km2	Percentage of added area	Palestinian private land that would be added to Israel in km2	Percentage of added private land	Palestinian private land outside of the added area in km2	Built-up size of Jewish settlements outside of the added area in km2
50 (139)	500,285	79%	242	3.9%	67.8	28%	7.63	34.69

©Shaul Arieli

Map 6 Israel-Palestine: Optimal Land Swaps

the border, the problems of water sources, health services, industrial zones, and transportation routes.

Arieli's main challenger, Jan de Jong, is a genuine interpreter of Palestinian positions, for he is a former chief consultant of the Arab Jerusalem Rehabilitation Project, of the PLO Negotiations Affairs Department, and of the Office of the Quartet Representative in Jerusalem. De Jong, who found "critical shortcomings" even in the Geneva Understandings, acknowledged that Arieli's land swaps are equal in size, but repudiated them as "in every other aspect, radically unequal." For, he observed, what Palestine cedes to Israel is vital for its statehood, but what it would acquire in return is irrelevant to the Palestinian national project. Palestine sacrificed here, he wrote, "indigenous, socio-economically stable statehood." In Arab Jerusalem, where Arieli's plan is minimally different from Geneva's, de Jong found "a cluster of fragmented ghettoized quarters."[7]

But however important the disagreements over maps and percentages may be, it is the parties' lack of political will and their fundamentalist rigidity over their core concerns and national narratives that doomed the two-state idea.[8] The old concepts defining the problem and its solution, Geneva included (its leader Yossi Beilin has lost hope in the traditional two-state idea; he now advocates the idea of Two states, One Fatherland, an Israeli-Palestinian Confederation)[9] are no longer Israel's accepted compass.

Beyond the Parable

Notwithstanding Netanyahu's guilt, it would be wrong to dwell excessively on the weaknesses of the current leaders, for that presupposes that, with different leaders at the helm, a two-state agreement could be reached. Personalities are, of course, important, but so are also the unbeatable impersonal forces of history that have made the conflict into such an inextricable knot. It is not only Benjamin Netanyahu's dishonest attitude to negotiations and the Palestinians' fragmented and visionless polity that make a return to negotiations a pointless affair; it is the entire two-state idea that needs to be revisited.

Arguably, the two-state solution proved not to be particularly attractive to either side even before the current regional turmoil. There has always been a sense of anguish among both Israelis and Palestinians when they approached the moment of truth of a final decision on a peace deal. The gap between the colossal tragedy of the *Nakba* and the poverty of the territorial solution that would sandwich the demilitarized Palestinian mini-state between two major powers—Israel and Jordan—neither suffering from an excess of love for Palestinian statehood and deeply suspicious of its future evolution, was bound to remain an open wound. As Rob Malley and Hussein Agha rightly affirmed in their *New York*

Review of Books article, the Palestinians came to Camp David "more resigned to the two-state solution than they were willing to embrace it; they were prepared to accept Israel's existence, but not its moral legitimacy."[10] Also, any solution to the refugees problem that Israel is willing to accept would always be seen by the Palestinians as a betrayal of the constituent ethos of Palestinian nationalism, namely, the right of return. A Palestinian state that fell short of meeting the dreams cultivated over long years of exile and destitution would then suffer from a very serious deficit of legitimacy among the Palestinians themselves. Deeply divided between Hamas and the PLO, and lacking a truly profound demo-cratic ethos, the Palestinian factions are likely to respond with a civil war to any such peace proposal. Indeed, Fatah, the key component of the PLO, explicitly admitted that this had been exactly the reason that they had rejected the Clinton peace parameters. "The parameters," they said on their website, were "the biggest trick," for they were designed to shift the conflict from an Israeli-Palestinian dis-pute to "an internal Palestinian-Palestinian conflict."[11]

As for the Israelis, a two-state solution would mean a return to what Abba Eban, not exactly a hawk, defined as "Auschwitz borders." Moreover, a settlement that the Palestinians could accept would entail for Israel a sociopolitical earth-quake of untold dimensions, a massive evacuation of settlers, military disobedi-ence, civil strife, and all this in order to go back to borders very few have a special nostalgia for—80 percent of Israelis were born after the Six Day War—with a neighbor nobody truly trusts. The Israelis know the difference between a state and a movement, which explains the difference between the way they negotiated with Arab states and the suspicion with which they treat the Palestinians. Not one shot has been fired on the Golan Heights since the 1974 separation of mili-tary forces between Syria and Israel. But any progress, or failure thereof, on the Palestinian front was accompanied with flare ups and terror.

The Israelis do not believe the Palestinians would be able to prevent Hamas from taking over the West Bank and becoming an outpost of Iran a stone's throw from Tel Aviv. Also, the right of return question represents a major difficulty for ending the conflict and bringing about a finality of claims, two major Israeli prerequisites for acquiescing with the two-state solution. Also, neither side believes that Israel will be able to dismantle and relocate about 100,000 fanatical ideological settlers and dozens of outposts with their messianic defenders. And given the lessons of the Gaza wars, the invasive security requirements of Israel would be impossible to reconcile with the Palestinian idea of what exactly a sov-ereign state is.

Predictably, the Palestinian pollster Khalil Shikaki found a significant rise in the Palestinians' belief that the two-state solution was no longer feasible or even desired; support for a detailed nine-point peace package implementing it dropped from 62 percent in 2008 to 37 percent in 2018. Another 2018 poll by

Tel Aviv University's Tami Steinmetz Center for Peace Research and Shikaki's Palestinian Center for Policy and Survey Research found support to be the lowest in twenty years.[12] Also, mostly consistent across Palestinian generations was the rejection of permanent peace with Israel. Asked in a 2019 poll whether a two-state solution should be "the end of conflict with Israel," just 34 percent of young West Bank respondents answered yes; the proportion was even lower among older residents—25 percent.[13]

The younger generation's despair of the two-state solution is understandable. They watched as illegal settlements spread unabated—there were 220,000 settlers when they started school, there is thrice that number now—they saw the growing indifference of their Arab brethren to their plight, and listened incessantly to the unchallenged drumbeat of extreme-right Israeli politicians calling for a "Greater Israel." The Gazan youth lived through their own bloody civil war in which Hamas seized power, and they witnessed the destruction of life and property in successive wars with Israel and through Hamas's tyranny. Together with their West Bank contemporaries, they came of age during the Second Intifada, which left behind a broken Palestinian society and shattered any trust in the peace process and its stillborn child, the two-state solution. This looked to them definitely buried by the Trump administration's blind support for the Greater Israel ideology of the Israeli right.[14] The promise of the Biden administration is bound to be limited. It would work to improve life for the Palestinians, but would not invest the political capital required for the lost two-state cause.

Young Palestinians were portrayed in a *Newsweek* special issue[15] as highly educated and heavily underemployed (40 percent of West Bank residents under 30 are jobless). This generation is the most nonpolitical generation of Palestinians since the beginning of the Palestinian national movement. The Oslo years were for their parents times of high political activism, hopes, and dreams of liberation. Their sons and daughters have lost any illusion about the creation of a mini-Palestinian state next to Israel. Their goals are equality, dignity, freedom, and relief from joblessness. The end of occupation is what matters to them, and this does not necessarily have to mean an independent Palestinian state. This civic agenda makes this new Palestinian generation more open to embracing the one-state reality with its presumed promise of rights and opportunities.

The case for a two-state solution is not more promising among Israeli youth. The Rafi Smith Polling Institute[16] found that four times as many Israelis in their twenties support the annexation of the West Bank and the refusal to give citizenship to Palestinians as is the case with Israelis who are over 50. Younger Israelis are emphatically more right-wing and religious. Their formative years were influenced by the memory of the Second Intifada and the Gaza wars, all successfully framed by the only prime minister they have lived under for most of their lives, Benjamin Netanyahu. They were inculcated with the conviction about the

Palestinians' peace rejectionism and their dream of doing away with the Jewish state altogether.

What unites Israelis and Palestinians of whatever age in a tacit unholy alliance of inaction and inertia is the fear that bisecting the land might explode into a civil war in their midst. And so the creation of a Palestinian state is today a more remote possibility than at any time since the start of the peace process thirty years ago. The Palestinians are battered and defeated, while Israel is held hostage to messianic settlers bent on perpetuating the malignant grip of the occupation on the nation's life. Even mainstream leaders have despaired of the 1990s culture of conflict resolution, whose most emblematic icons, Yitzhak Rabin and Shimon Peres, anyway never truly thought that the peace process should usher in a full-fledged Palestinian state.

The Failed "Zionization" of Palestine and the Three-State "Solution"

A national entity struggling against the wicked occupier has made the Palestinian cause into one of the most widely acclaimed in modern history. It sometimes looked to me that the Palestinian elites with whom we negotiated were so enamored of their standing in world opinion that they preferred it to an always imperfect political solution to the conflict. Rejoicing at Israel's calamity for being seated constantly in the dock of the court of international opinion was the vengeance of the occupied, their way of defeating the occupier and gaining the moral high ground.

A state in the making is always in a more heroic condition than a full-fledged state. If and when such a state is created, it would inevitably fall short of the dream. It would not take long before the international image of the State of Palestine would be tarnished by its own policies and blunders. It would turn out to be one more state in an Arab region where the very concept of the nation-state has not yet been fully integrated. Palestine has the genes of a failing state. It would be a minuscule state with no natural resources, split between Islamist Gaza and a presumably secular West Bank, and lacking a convincing democratic culture. The PLO is no more democratic than Hamas; it rules the West Bank by decree, does not convene Parliament, postpones elections, and relies on the security services and on the bayonets of the occupier.

In practice financed by colossal contributions from donor states—data from *Global Humanitarian Assistance* show that the Palestinians get more financial aid per capita than any other nation on earth, nine times as much aid as the Sudanese and thirty-nine times the aid per capita that residents of the war-torn Democratic Republic of Congo receive, a level unprecedented in any other conflict since World War II. This level of aid exceeds the lifespan of other high-profile emergencies, such as Kosovo and Afghanistan, where aid peaked and waned.[1] The Palestinians' transition to statehood is bound to be a painful exercise in addiction treatment. The pre-state elites are now spared the many problems and challenges that come with statehood.

The pernicious effects of Israeli occupation have, of course, much to answer for, but the current institutional disarray in Palestine cannot be exclusively blamed on the occupation. Landrum Bolling, who served as a backchannel between US President Jimmy Carter and Arafat in 1977, described a situation that has not changed much to this very day. He described the PLO as an assortment of factions with extraordinary freedom each to go its own way. "It is a mad, mad situation," he said. He also described the general fear among Palestinians that Arafat and his team were not up to the leadership role required for running an independent state.[2]

While in office, Salam Fayyad, the Palestinian finance minister from 2002 to 2005 and prime minister from 2007 to 2012, set out to transform Palestinian nationalism's Byzantine polity and revolutionary ethos into one of state-building. He was eventually defeated by the forces of inertia. Fayyadism was about the "Zionization" of the Palestinian national movement, an uphill attempt to imbue it with an ethos of nation and state-building by superseding its paralytic obsession with a never fulfilled vindication of rights and justice. Fayyadism was also about isolating Hamas and modernizing the economy and the PA administration—it was Fayyad who ended Arafat's corrupt practice of paying salaries in cash, and tried ineptly to introduce a democratic separation of powers—as well as professionalizing the Palestinian security forces around the principle of "One Homeland, One Flag, and One Law." Not overly optimistic as to the chances of peace with Israel, Fayyad believed that a "de facto Palestinian State" should, nevertheless, be created and that it might eventually become a historical reality. But he was forced to resign under strong Hamas pressure and against a background of repeated, abortive attempts to create a Hamas-PLO unity government.

In Zionism, the ethos of state-building sprang from the Jewish pre-state community (the *Yishuv*) in Palestine being "a state in the making." The *Yishuv* was throughout the source of decision-making for the entire movement, with the Diaspora serving as a strategic backup. In the case of Palestinian nationalism, it was the ethos of the Diaspora, with the plight of the refugees and the strategy of armed struggle at its center, that acted as the beating heart of the national cause and the source of decision-making for the entire movement. The Palestinian community in the occupied territories was always subservient to the primacy of the Diaspora. And when the "inside" ventured to assume a leading role, during the First Intifada for example, it was suppressed by the Diaspora-based PLO. Even Oslo was a typical exercise in bypassing the leaders of the inside who were at the time negotiating peace with Israel in Washington.

I will never be able to erase from my memory my feelings in Taba. Here, I wrote in my diary, an outline of a reasonable settlement is lying on the table.

One would have had to be blind not to understand that these were also the last days of the Israeli left in power, maybe for many years to come. The political profile of an Israeli team consisting of Yossi Sarid, Yossi Beilin, Amnon Lipkin-Shahak and, if I may, myself, as the head of the Israeli team, could simply not be repeated in years to come. In other words, if an agreement was not to be reached then, there would be no agreement at all, and both Israelis and Palestinians would be thrown into a wilderness of blood, despair, and economic decline. Nevertheless, I did not succeed in discerning any sense of urgency or missed opportunity among my Palestinian friends. Zionism, admittedly principally up to 1948, would have never functioned this way against what is always and inevitably an imperfect settlement. It always functioned with its back to the wall, which is why it grabbed every partition plan that was proposed by the British colonial power or the international community.

The Palestinians, the presumed weak side of the conflict, never acted out of lack of choice. They stumbled over every road block, avoided no mistake, and always seemed to take the wrong path. Rarely—if ever—is modern history familiar with a similar case of a disparity between the extraordinary high degree of international support enjoyed by a national movement and the poor results of such support. For it was frequently interpreted by the Palestinian leadership as an implicit encouragement to persist in its almost built-in incapacity to take decisions and instead find satisfaction in Israel being put in the dock of the court of international opinion.

Another difference between Zionism and Palestinian nationalism relates to the ethos. Zionism was a social revolution, an attempt to change the patterns of existence of the Jewish people no less than it was a journey into an ancestral homeland. Though he admittedly never really abandoned wider territorial dreams, it would never have occurred to Ben-Gurion to delay the establishment of the Jewish state because he would not have access to the Western Wall or to the Temple Mount. To him, the ethos of building a new society was supposed to compensate for the poverty of the territorial solution, and science, in his words, would compensate for "what nature has denied us." The Palestinian leadership failed its people primarily due to the lack of will to temper the ethos of restitution through an alternative ideology of nation-building that could enable them to assume reasonable compromises at vital crossroads throughout their clash with the Zionists.

Seen from the perspective of the Palestinian tragedy of the loss of a homeland, dispossession, and exile, the Palestinian ethos of restitution is fully comprehensible. Alas, justice has been frequently the enemy of peace. The tragedy of the Israeli-Palestinian conflict stemmed from discrepant historical rhythms. The history of the Jews' modern national movement had been characterized by realistic responses to objective historical conditions. The Palestinians have consistently fought for the solutions of yesterday, those they had rejected a generation or two earlier. This persistent attempt to turn back the clock of history lies at the root of many of the misfortunes that have befallen them.

* * *

Zionism's pragmatic ethos has by now been superseded by many years of rule by messianic nationalists, fanatical annexationists, and dysfunctional politics. The chances of peace were too frequently defeated by Israelis and Palestinians being the mirror image of each other when it comes to their dysfunctional polities. Arafat, the ultimate legitimizer of a two-state solution, gave a sense of direction to Palestinian nationalism and was capable of creating a consensus around national objectives. This is no longer the case. "Back in Abu Amar's days we had a plan, there was a strategy, and we would carry his orders," was how a bitter Fatah militia leader in Jenin, Zakaria Zbeidi put it at a time when General Keith Dayton, the US security coordinator for Israel and the Palestinian Authority (2005–10), was effectively the viceroy of the occupied territories. Palestinian nationalism was in total disarray, shapeless and leaderless, Zubeidi said:

> *The political splits and schisms have destroyed us not only politically; they have destroyed our national identity. Today there is no Palestinian identity. Go up to anyone in the street and ask him, "Who are you?" He'll answer you, "I'm a Fatah activist," "I'm a Hamas activist," or an activist of some other organization, but he won't say to you, "I am a Palestinian." Every organization flies its own flag, but no one is raising the flag of Palestine. We are marching in the direction of nowhere, toward total ruin. The Palestinian people is finished. Done for.*[3]

Zbeidi's elegy on the demise of Palestinian nationalism was the reflection of the abyss that had opened between two major wings of the Palestinian national struggle, the "outside," the PLO apparatus that was brought from Tunis on the wings of the Oslo Accords, and the "inside," the local leadership that had led the First Intifada only to be marginalized and overruled by Arafat.

This was to a large extent the natural outcome of Arafat's attitude to the Oslo Accords. Arafat went to Oslo to save the PLO from declining into oblivion, not just in search of a peace formula. He needed to establish a foothold in Palestine at all costs, even at the expense of an agreement with Israel that did not secure vital Palestinian aspirations such as the right of self-determination and an acceptable solution to the issues of Jerusalem and refugees. Such was Arafat's eagerness to get a foothold in Palestine that he even agreed to Israeli settlement expansion during the five-year transition period and, later in the interim agreement, to the constrained sovereignty of a Palestinian Authority effectively subject to Israeli control. He bought his way back to Palestine at a far cheaper price for the occupier than that being asked by the Palestinian local leadership in the Washington negotiations.

What the Oslo years produced, however, was the constant decline of the "outside," that is, of those who failed to fulfill the promise of the peace process, in favor of the "inside," the young local leadership bent on the idea of "struggle" and "resistance." The "outside" further alienated the masses by their scandalous corruption. So long as Arafat was alive, he managed to harness "outside" and "inside" to a common objective. With his departure, the more radical forces in Fatah and Hamas went back in full force to challenge the decrepit clique of Oslo and the PA's conservative project in favor of revolutionary, maximalist positions on issues such as the idea of return and the liberation of Palestine. A facade of unity could be maintained so long as there was no peace process, but the moment a deal with Israel over the core issues of Palestinian nationalism seemed close—through the Clinton parameters and Taba—they declined into civil war conditions. Such a civil war also developed with Israel's disengagement from the Gaza Strip in 2005.

This most fundamental flaw in the Palestinian system was well understood by the architects of George W. Bush's roadmap, who, therefore, worked to democratize the Palestinian polity and turn it into a reliable partner for a negotiated peace. But the shift to a democratic system in Palestine remains to this day a very shaky enterprise. Soft-spoken and moderate in his manners, Abbas is as authoritarian a ruler as any of the incumbents in the neighboring Arab states. His personality cult has recently reached pathetic heights. Fifteen years since the last elections, the fear of a Hamas victory and the split within Fatah help perpetuate Abbas's dictatorial regime. A Khalil Shikaki poll in December 2020 found that an overwhelming majority of Palestinians did not trust that the loser in the elections would ever willingly respect the results.[4]

* * *

State-building was never the main motif of Palestinian nationalism, now split between pan-Islamist dreamers of a borderless Arab nation and secular nationalists who could never settle for Israel's optimal peace offers. The artificial existence of the Palestinian Authority perpetuates the status quo because it supports the illusion that the situation is temporary and that the peace process will soon end it. In their drive to end the occupation, the Palestinians also suffer from a major crisis of leadership. Yasser Arafat is no longer there to give a modicum of cohesion and sense of purpose to a movement that has lost its way, that is fragmented, and whose political spinal cord, Fatah, the party that led the shift to the idea of partition and statehood, is broken, practically nonexistent. The carriers of the two-state idea, the Oslo clique that still governs in Palestine, represent the monumental disappointment that came with the peace process. They definitely exhausted their already limited stores of legitimacy; for, like Hamas, they rule by decree, shun Parliament and elections, and rely for their political survival on the occupier's army.

The Israeli right's dream is finally coming true of a shattered and fragmented Palestinian national movement. The irreconcilable divisions within its two main branches, Hamas and PLO, are not uncommon in the history of national movements, only in the Palestinian case, the split is not just about tactics and means; it is about the very purpose of the struggle. Ghazi Hamad, a former deputy foreign minister of Hamas, wrote in January 2015 an extraordinarily candid op-ed in which he lamented the inbred incapacity of the Palestinian leadership to unite around an agreed national objective:

> *Because the Palestinians lost two of their national pillars, strategic vision and national consensus, their paths diverged. . . . They moved between temporary and permanent solutions, between the Palestinian Authority and resistance . . . between the statehood project and the liberation project. . . . Indeed, the lack of a strategic vision is a national disaster. . . . President Abu Mazen is rushing between capitals searching for signatures for a country . . . Hamas claps with one hand at its festivals, sings of its heroism, listens to itself and describes the other as faltering. . . . We tried a Fatah government and corruption was rampant in both the administrative and security services. Then came a national unity government, but it only took two months before it reached its demise. Then there was the Hamas government, accompanied by wars and a siege. . . . The tragedy . . . strikes at the heart of the divided nation. . . . We are rushing from failure to greater failure!! We only employ the language of rejection and doubt. . . . We complain and grumble . . . Then we complain and grumble again . . . As a result—after six decades—Palestine has vanished and its blood has been divided between the different tribes/ factions.[5]*

Conveniently for Israel, which like all imperial powers rules through *divide et impera*, the Palestinian fratricidal conflict has allowed her to bury even deeper the two-state dream, which has now given way to a three-state reality, Israel, the PLO's West Bank, and Hamas's Gaza. Hamas's persistent attempts to start a new Intifada and stage terrorist attacks on Israeli targets in the West Bank are a bid to shake the foundations of the PLO's rule in the West Bank by exposing its strategy of collaboration with the occupier. Indeed, the Palestinian president, Mahmoud Abbas, knows that security cooperation with Israel is his last line of defense against a Hamas takeover. Abbas's tools in his war with Hamas are the international legitimacy of his Palestinian Authority as well as the financial resources he possesses as the recipient of the world's donor money. But, unless forced by a resounding military defeat, Hamas would never surrender its territorial control of Gaza, where it has become an entrenched political and economic establishment. Hamas would not rule out a unified government with Abbas's PLO, but only as an avenue to the political takeover of the entire national movement. They would under no condition surrender their independent military capabilities and the freedom to use them. Hamas aspires to emulate the Hezbollah model in Lebanon of a political party with its own formidable military force that should eventually make it the ultimate political arbiter in Palestine.

Gaza is, for all practical purposes, an independent Sunni Islamic state with its own network of regional alliances—Hezbollah, Iran, Qatar, and Turkey. They are all anti-status quo powers opposed to the pro-Western Palestinian Authority. Theirs is an alternative model of Islamic democracy in defiance of the conservative regimes in the region, Abbas's Palestinian Authority included. Moreover, though vociferously upholding the Palestinian cause, Hamas's allies in Hezbollah and Iran are actually opposed to the two-state solution. An Israeli-Palestinian peace along the lines conceived by the liberal West would presumably get Israel off the hook, solve her major regional predicament, accord her regional legitimacy, and make her an overt central ally of the region's conservative Arab regimes. Hamas and the PLO represent, then, diametrically opposed strategies and objectives. The PLO wants the two-state solution and is not interested in any kind of interim settlement with Israel that, as past experience has shown, could become the new permanent reality of occupation in disguise. Hamas, for which statehood is secondary to the victory of Islam, is innately opposed to the two-state solution, and is ideologically incapable of admitting the existence of a Jewish state in the sacred land of Palestine.

This is paradoxically where Hamas and Israel concur. Israel, certainly under its far-right governments, is also ideologically incapable of making the necessary concessions required for a viable two-state solution. Just like Hamas, Israel could afford an interim settlement, not the price of a final peace. A *hudna* with Israel, a long truce that might, or might not, develop into full peace, is a concept from the Arab-Muslim tradition that Hamas has sometimes toyed with. Arafat himself referred to it in a speech he delivered in Johannesburg, South Africa, a short time after the signing of the Oslo Accords. He then mentioned the Treaty of Hudaybiyyah, signed in 628 between the Prophet Muhammad and the Quraysh tribe, and later broken by Muhammad, after he had acquired enough power to conquer Mecca. To the Israelis, that was a shocking speech, for it implied that Oslo would be broken the moment it suited the *ra'is*. Israel, in any case, could never accept a *hudna* whose price, as spelled out by Hamas many times, was practically the same as the PLO would ask for a final settlement.

Be that as it may, Benjamin Netanyahu struck an unwritten deal with Hamas against Abbas's Palestinian Authority, which his governments have consistently done all they could to weaken and humiliate. A Hamas Islamic fundamentalist state in Gaza offers Israel the ultimate pretext against peace negotiations, the best antidote to the two-state solution, as Netanyahu explicitly confided in 2010 to no less than Egypt's President Mubarak.[6] He also shared this strategy with his party colleagues in a close meeting in March 2019: "This is our way to thwart the creation of a Palestinian state," he said.[7] And while Netanyahu treats Abbas only as a subcontractor of Israel's security, he respectfully negotiates with Hamas through third parties on exchanges of prisoners and ceasefires. Netanyahu even allowed Qatar to keep the Gaza state functioning by paying the salaries of Hamas functionaries, thus undercutting Abbas's strategy of withholding salaries in order to coax Hamas into more conciliatory positions on national unity.

The PLO–Hamas struggle for mastery has consolidated the territorial division of the Palestinian lands into two warring, separate quasi-states. In Gaza, Hamas runs its own state institutions and services as well as a strong military force that has even been capable of defying Israel's IDF and terrorizing its civilian population. In the West Bank, Mahmoud Abbas's Palestinian Authority has its own parliament, government, and military and internal intelligence units, as well as a worldwide network of diplomatic missions. Israel, for her part, has secured the three-state reality through walls and fences separating her from Gaza and much of the West Bank.

Israel's own experience shows that a movement of national liberation cannot reach its objective unless it conduct its own "*Altalena,*" an Israeli euphemism for civil war. *Altalena* was in 1948 the ship loaded with weapons for Menachem Begin's dissident, radical Irgun that was sunk on David Ben-Gurion's orders. Like Ben-Gurion then, Abbas today is fully aware that a unified military command and one agreed strategy are indispensable if a united Palestinian state is ever to be achieved. But a Palestinian civil war when no political horizon is offered by the occupier, whose strategy of divide and rule is, moreover, edifyingly successful, would be for the Palestinians a monumental exercise in political stupidity or sheer national suicide.

Hence, Hamas and Fatah "states" remain bogged down in a competition over their level of commitment to the national narrative, always careful not to deviate from the dogma, which is why the moderate PLO, or its main component, Fatah, never officially gave up on the core Palestinian narrative, the ethos of dispossession and return with which Israel, even if governed by a left-wing coalition—these days, a fantasy scenario—could never acquiesce to.

The decisions taken in the sixth Fatah Convention held at Bethlehem in 2009 called explicitly for the refugees to "return to their homes and cities." The convention also reaffirmed its "absolute and irrevocable opposition" to the recognition of Israel as a Jewish state and asserted its commitment to fight for the rights of Israeli Arabs.[8] The seventh Fatah Convention in 2016 revoked none of these Fatah articles of faith.

The Region and the World: A Broken Reed

The Changing Regional Strategic Game

The window of opportunity for an Israeli–Palestinian peace that existed in the last two years of the Clinton presidency and later in the wake of George W. Bush's Iraq War has closed. Today, not only have the conservative Arab regimes relegated the Palestinian question in order to deal with their own existential challenges, but Israel is consumed by the more immediate threats from enemies more resolute than any she has faced in the past: Iran, Hezbollah, and Hamas. Israel's shift to the right and the betrayal of Palestine by the Arab states make a return to the old "civilized" way of peacemaking a simple delusion.

The dogged attempt to establish final and recognized borders between Israel and Palestine at a time when the entire Middle East lives in "interim" conditions —states are melting down, the century-old Sykes-Picot regional political order is challenged, and incumbent Arab regimes have exhausted their already limited stores of legitimacy—does not seem to the Israelis a particularly appealing idea. The fragility of Sykes-Picot's order was exposed when the ISIS Caliphate showed how Iraq's and Syria's borders were fluid, when Turkey fought the Kurds by invading and occupying northern Syria, when the United States arbitrarily recognized Israel's sovereignty on the occupied Golan Heights and Jerusalem, and when Israel pursued her crippling annexation of West Bank areas and still earnestly contemplates annexing the Jordan Valley. Israel acts today as a revisionist power happy to participate in the reshuffle of the old established Middle East border system.

Nor does the turmoil throughout the Arab world that followed the ill-fated Arab Spring and the civilizational crisis engulfing the entire Islamic universe counsel Israel's strategic planners to be sanguine about the security risks of a Palestinian state. Surrounded by imploding states (Lebanon, Syria, Gaza, Egypt's Sinai Peninsula, and farther away Iraq, Yemen, and Libya) and Sunni warlords always ready to fill the vacuum of authority in no man's lands, the anarchy along Israel's borders has made her rethink the entire two-state idea. To the now hegemonic right, creating a Palestinian state, yet one more Arab state whose viability is a priori doubtful, when existing Arab states are crumbling and the very concept of the modern nation-state is challenged throughout the Arab world, does not seem like a particularly appealing idea. The dwindling Israeli left's insistence on reaching a two-state solution with fixed and recognized borders when the entire region is in flux is ridiculed as anachronistic. Actually, the entire culture of "conflict resolution" is simply no longer looked on as a necessary component of Israel's regional strategy. Also, the breakdown of the region, which makes the emergence of a grand war coalition against Israel a remote possibility, ensures that Palestine would no longer be the trigger for a major regional war.

Furthermore, notwithstanding the 2002 Arab Peace Initiative, the Israelis perceive the Arab states as being lukewarm in their support for the two-state solution. Its prospects of success are too slim to justify the daunting political risk involved in getting bogged down in its quagmire. In the late 1970s, Sadat, not a great friend of a fully independent Palestinian state, was, nonetheless, willing to consider boosting the viability of the Gaza Strip by extending it into Northern Sinai.[1] When, in 2000, I made a similar suggestion to President Mubarak that included compensation to Egypt in the form of territory inside Israel—Professor Yehoshua Ben-Arieh, a geographer at the Hebrew University of Jerusalem, had prepared an elaborate plan along such lines—he took it as a bad joke. The response to such a proposal of President Al-Sisi, Israel's new ally in Cairo these days, would not be any different. To the incumbent conservative Arab regimes, a Palestinian state is an entity that would rise with a revolutionary, destabilizing genetic code. If anything, their fears have only increased since the then US president Jimmy Carter spoke in 1977 of their alarm at the prospect of a radicalized Palestinian entity led by "a Qadhafi-like leader."[2]

Some regions of the world have a tradition, however erratic, of regional cooperation. The peace agreements in Central America in the late 1980s and early 1990s were made possible by such regional cooperation. Also the peace in Colombia with the FARC insurgency benefited greatly from regional cooperation. The pressure these days on Nicolás Maduro's dictatorship in Venezuela from the "group of Lima," which comprises Latin American democracies, and from the Mercosur common market is still a key tool that could spur the military to rethink their loyalty to Maduro's regime. Latin America and the Caribbean are also the only region of the world that, as early as 1968, reached through its Treaty of Tlatelolco, an agreement on the prohibition of nuclear weapons. Africa too has an interesting record in regional politics. The African Union has been instrumental in resolving conflicts, sending peacekeeping forces to conflict theaters, and deterring dictators throughout the continent.

Alas, the Middle East can only dream of such a civilized regional architecture; actually, it has never been known for collective action. Sadly, the Arab Peace Initiative, born, one should stress, not exactly out of concern for Palestine, but as a way for Saudi Arabia to launder her tarnished image in the United States after the 9/11 massacre in which her citizens played a pivotal role, was unwisely overlooked by Israel and neglected by the international stakeholders. But its built-in flaws cannot be ignored either. The Arab League does not truly have any experience, or political capacity, to initiate a regional process based on her peace plan. It has never seriously tried to launch a convincing diplomatic effort for the solution of any of the region's problems, be it the Syrian civil war, the Yemen carnage, the Iran nuclear standoff, or the Palestinian conflict. In fact, the four Arab states that made their peace with Israel in 2020 through the Abraham Accords did it in defiance of the Arab Peace Initiative and while the Palestinian problem was still badly festering. The Arab Initiative can become a tool of peace-making only if and when it is actively supported by the United States. Security guarantees from Arab states would not have much traction among Israelis unless backed and reinforced by the United States and other global actors, which brings us back to the incapacity of the "international community" for collective action, more so on a matter as marginal to her concerns as Palestine.

Would America Save the Two-State Solution?

Israel's international standing reflects an intriguing dichotomy. Increasingly condemned and denigrated by public opinion and UN agencies for her policies on Palestine, Israel enjoys these days historically unprecedented global clout and improved relations with governments across the world. The same dichotomy is increasingly becoming apparent in the United States as well. These are changing times in America, and Israel has reasons to be concerned that her standing in US public opinion is no longer as solid as it used to be. The rise of new American generations for whom the inspiring old Zionist story about the resurgence of a pioneering Jewish state is now a distant memory and the emergence of an illiberal Israel tyrannizing a disenfranchised Palestinian nation have made the question of Palestine a polarized issue in American public opinion. Israel's citadel in America is no longer as impregnable as it used to be. A poll of December 2015 showed that 66 percent of Americans supported a more even-handed US policy in the Israel-Palestine conflict. This was particularly the case among 80 percent of Democrats under 35.[3] Israel's standing in America has further deteriorated in subsequent years.

Nor is AIPAC, Israel's mythological lobby in America, the unbeatable force that uneducated opinion thinks it is. Past experience shows that American presidents could force Israel to assume policies it had previously resisted. President Eisenhower forced David Ben-Gurion to withdraw from the Sinai Peninsula in 1956 a few days after the Israeli prime minister had announced the birth of "the third Kingdom of Israel." Henry Kissinger threatened Prime Minister Yitzhak Rabin in 1975 with America's "reassessment" of her links to Israel unless he assumed more accommodating positions in the negotiations on the Sinai disengagement with Egypt. Jimmy Carter threatened to use America's leverage against both parties if an Israeli-Egyptian agreement was not reached at Camp David. The George H. Bush James Baker tandem dragged Prime Minister Yitzhak Shamir against his will to the 1991 Madrid Peace Conference by withholding the $10 billion loan guarantees that Israel had requested for the absorption of a million Jewish immigrants from the disintegrating Soviet Union. President Bush did not even hesitate to denounce what he called in a press conference "a thousand lobbyists" working on the Hill against the president's policies. Arguably, Bush eventually toppled Yitzhak Shamir and facilitated the victory of Yitzhak Rabin in the 1992 elections.

Presidents always prevailed when they resisted being intimidated by the myth surrounding the Israel lobby. AIPAC was defeated when it feuded with Jimmy Carter in 1978 over his selling of F-15 Eagle fighters to Saudi Arabia, and again in 1981 when it challenged Ronald Reagan's supplying of AWACS reconnaissance planes to Saudi Arabia. AIPAC also reaped a resounding defeat when it battled with George H. Bush in 1991 for the linkage he made between loan guarantees for Israel and Shamir's opposition to the Madrid Peace Conference. Not unlike George H. Bush, President Obama won the day by publicly exposing the AIPAC lobby. In his American University speech on August 5, 2015, he called the critics of his Iran deal "people who would be opposed to any deal with Iran," and specifically targeted AIPAC and "the 20 million dollars that's being spent on ads on TV." Obama even put AIPAC in the same category as those Republicans who were "responsible" for America getting into the Iraq War. AIPAC's attempt to undo the Iran nuclear deal, an Obama central foreign policy legacy, was bound to be defeated as an insolent affront to the president in intimate complicity with his Republican enemies.

But here comes the paradox. Despite Israel's extraordinary levels of dependence on America's friendship, the Jewish state feels freer than at any time in the past to turn its back on the imperatives of a genuine peace process. The brave call of the late George Ball, an independent-minded American diplomat, "to save Israel in spite of herself,"[4] would not come to be. Despite the increasing gap between the pro-Israel consensus in Washington's political establishment and the deeper trends in public opinion, particularly among Democrats, American coercive diplomacy is not in the offing.

Israel has so far paid in America for her Palestine policy only in public opinion currency, not yet in the extraordinary levels of political and material support from Washington. America's commitment to Israel's "qualitative military edge," with the Obama and Donald Trump administrations breaking all historical records, continues to underwrite the annexationist policies of blatantly defiant governments in Jerusalem that resist using the military edge offered by American taxpayers to take calculated risks for peace.

One assumes that, with such a formidable leverage, it is only America that can make a difference in the Israeli-Palestinian equation. The progressive dreamers of such a scenario would have to realize, however, that American pressure, if and when it comes, would inevitably have to be exerted on both sides. Not only is the assumption that Israel is the only party that needs to change its positions wrong, but not even American pressure could force Israel to concede vital points or give in to each and every Palestinian demand, however legitimate and morally justified they might be. And if it comes, American pressure might be accompanied by a peace plan along lines that have already failed to produce a deal in the past.

It was one thing to force Israel to participate in the Madrid Peace Conference or even to withdraw from the Sinai Peninsula in 1956; it is another to force her to accept a Palestinian state a few miles from her major urban centers under conditions that even the most dovish governments deemed unacceptable. And with America's changing global agenda and priorities, it is utterly unrealistic to expect that any future president would invest the necessary political capital in imposing a solution on the recalcitrant Israelis and Palestinians. Henry Kissinger used coercive diplomacy in mediating an Israeli-Egyptian peace because it was key to the broader US strategic objective of unravelling the Soviet presence in the Middle East and eventually winning the Cold War. The Bush-Baker tandem forced Israel to come to the Madrid Peace Conference not only because they had to reward the many Arab states that had joined America in her war on Saddam Hussein, but also because they saw it as fundamental to the new global order they had fought for in the wake of the Iraq War and the dissolution of the Soviet Union. Today, with America's standing in the region and beyond shattered by the disarray it has left behind in Afghanistan, and practically leaving the Middle East in the hands of the Russia-Iran-Hezbollah-Turkey anti-Western axis, the responsibility she would be asked to assume in Palestine in terms of state-building, security risks, and political backlash would be too formidable for her to accept in a matter that is clearly no national security priority. Actually, America has never truly addressed the peace process as an enterprise in which failure was simply not an option. Sensing that this is the case, both parties would always prefer to resist the pressure, however painful, and fall back to their comfort zones and on their moral convictions.

It is clear, then, that Israel does not today have any outside pressure to depart from its conveniently cost-free occupation of Palestinian lands. The Trump presidency behaved more like the Likud branch in Washington than a power in search of a balanced settlement between Zion and Palestine. Israel got two major unilateral gifts from Trump, his recognition of the Golan Heights as sovereign Israeli territory and Jerusalem as her capital. Conversely, the Palestinians only got sticks, namely, the end of all American financial aid and harsh condemnations of their unrealistic political dreams.

The new Biden administration would not reverse Trump's gifts to Israel, but would have a more balanced attitude to the conflict. Alas, in Palestine, Israel's facts on the ground have moved faster than Washington's change of attitude, which would anyway stay within pro-Israel contours. The Biden administration would use its leverage to improve the conditions of the occupied Palestinians, but would be most careful not to re-engage in what all former presidents experienced as a lost cause, political negotiations for a two-state solution.

An Internationally Led Two-State Solution?

A month before his sad premature death from a fatal illness, Ron Pundak, the peace visionary who, together with Yair Hirshfeld, started the entire Oslo initiative, confided to me that the Oslo paradigm of direct negotiations was dead and that he was willing to advocate the idea of an international solution I had been defending since the failure of Camp David. Arguably, after each and every other peace paradigm has failed, referring the question that started in 1947 as an international enterprise to the international community makes compelling sense. A practical imposition of a peace agreement by the international community would also have the advantage of being "mutually unacceptable." Alas, this logic, like everything that has to do with the Israeli-Palestinian conundrum, is repeatedly defeated by reality. What follows is a hypothetical exercise about the tension between what can be a compelling logic for an international solution and the resilient reality that works against it.

The Compelling Logic

Ron Pundak agreed that the new paradigm means also that a peace plan based on the core principles that were understood time and again to be the foundation of a peace deal—two states along the 1967 borders with territorial swaps to accommodate the demographic changes, two capitals in Jerusalem, an agreed solution to the refugee problem, and security arrangements—could be turned

into a US-supported UN Security Council Resolution as the internationally accepted interpretation of what a fair deal in this dispute is. Turning a parameter
resolution into a binding document that would distill the work of countless negotiation sessions into a single set of established guidelines could be, indeed, a
gigantic step toward a possible settlement.

A robust international engagement would also be required for the creation of
incentives that would encourage the parties to accept the painful compromises.
The Palestinian state will require a major injection of financial aid to allow it
to absorb refugees and upgrade its infrastructures and educational system. The
United States might be required to compensate Israel through upgraded strategic cooperation and a robust financial package to facilitate massive military
redeployments and the convergence of settlers into the new boundaries. Europe
might also like to consider offering EU membership to Israel and upgrading its
economic links with the state of Palestine, and NATO might be ready to offer
membership to a democratic state finally lying behind fixed borders such as
Israel.

The logic of an international solution also stems from America's proven
failure to solve the Israeli-Palestinian conflict all by herself. Indeed, why would
the Iranian nuclear showdown need a P5 + 1 (the five permanent members of
the UN Security Council and Germany) forum of powers to resolve it, while the
Palestinian question remains an American monopoly in spite of Washington's
serial failures? In the last thirty years, the United States made the world used
to seeing her forming international coalitions for war in the Middle East. For a
change, America could now try an international alliance for a Middle East peace.
This would mean giving a greater role to the Quartet (the European Union,
Russia, the United Nations, and the United States) and to key Arab states.

Arafat always longed for an international solution to the plight of his people.
But where he got it wrong was in his assumption that the international community would give him the peace deal of his dreams. An international solution,
in which the United States would inevitably play a dominant role, would not
make the peace parameters any easier to digest for the Palestinians. Yet if the
all-powerful Arafat attributed such great importance to having an international
umbrella escort him to the altar of an agreement, does it seem probable that
lesser Palestinian figures saddled with such difficult terms of inheritance would
be able on their own to cast off the ethos of the right of return and the Temple
Mount without a tight-fitting envelope of support from the international community, especially from the Arab states and the Palestinians' allies in Europe?
Also, Israel would have to be coaxed into a sharp departure from the annexationist policies of successive right-wing governments and endorse again the
Rabin-Barak-Olmert peace legacies.

That a strictly bilateral approach is manifestly inadequate was well understood by the call of the initiators of the 2002 all-Arab peace initiative to regionalize the solution to the conflict. They also offered bait to Israel in the form of a broader peace with all the members of the Arab League. The Arab Initiative rightly assumed that the future Palestinian state would be in no position to offer Israel the security guarantees that she needs; these would have to be of a regional nature, and it is the surrounding Arab states that would put them in place.

Arguably, a broad international framework is also the way to coax Hamas into the two-state solution. The organization would be incapable of sustaining the isolation that the rejection of such a plan would condemn it to. Hamas is a radical organization, not a suicidal one, and an international initiative could also boost the pragmatic elements in its midst. As Muhammad Ghazal, a West Bank-based Hamas leader, put it in the wake of the movement's January 2006 electoral victory in Gaza, "Hamas' charter is not the Qur'an . . . we are talking now about reality, about political solutions."[5] But no Hamas leader has put in a more outspoken and courageous way Hamas's quest for a way out of the unsustainable dogma about the liberation of "all" Palestine than Ismail Abu Shanab, one of the founders of Hamas, and its second highest leader after Sheikh Ahmed Yassin. A staunch opponent of suicide terrorism and an advocate of a long-term truce with Israel, he said this not long before his assassination by Israel sealed the end of the 2003 ceasefire:

> What is the point in speaking rhetoric? Let's be frank, we cannot destroy Israel. The practical solution is for us to have a state alongside Israel . . . When we build a Palestinian state, we will not need these militias; all the needs for attack will stop. Everything will change into a civil life.[6]

There was even a moment when Hamas's former leader, Khaled Mashal, acknowledged the possibility of Hamas acquiescing in the two-state idea. In an interview he gave to the Palestinian mouthpiece *Al Ayyam*, which was utterly ignored by Israel, he reiterated Hamas's support for the May 2006 "prisoners' covenant," a peace platform that was brokered by Marwan Barghouti between Hamas and Fatah prisoners in Israeli jails. Khaled Mashal also assured that Hamas would abide by the will of the Palestinian people as this would be expressed in a referendum for the approval of the settlement with Israel. Not in vain did Al-Qaeda at the time continuously condemn Hamas as infidels who were ready to reach an agreement of coexistence with the Jewish state.

Precisely because of the split within the Palestinian national movement, the shift to Palestinian statehood cannot be an automatic affair; it requires a period of transition. In the last days of the Clinton-Barak experiment, and even more so subsequently, I advocated extensively the idea of an international mandate to oversee Palestine's transition to orderly governance, stability, and transparency.[7] Israel obviously will not consent if all the international mandate sets out to do is force her to end the occupation and limit her ability to counter Palestinian terror. The Palestinians will not consent if all the mandate does is disarm the militias and build institutions without any guarantee of a political solution that meets their minimum demands. The mandate will not be accepted as legitimate unless the outline of a final settlement can be determined beforehand; it must not be merely an aimless trusteeship. Also, Palestinian institutions cannot be reformed without the aid of a powerful international inspectorate to ensure the reforms are implemented. Even the March 2003 elementary reform required by George W. Bush's roadmap of the way in which a Palestinian prime minister was to be appointed would not have taken place had it not been for the enormous pressure brought to bear on Arafat from the United States, Europe, and Egypt.

Indeed, George W. Bush's roadmap did eventually recognize that elements of trusteeship were required in the Palestinian territories. John Wolf, Bush's representative in the region, was more like a high commissioner than the emissary that Dennis Ross once was. Wolf had in his hands powers, admittedly still flimsy and inadequate, to inspect and control and to apportion blame for any violations of agreements. He made, though, endless requests for his mandate to be given greater powers, more observers, and greater means of inspection and control. Voices could also be heard in the United States, for example that of John Warner, the then Chairman of the Senate Armed Services Committee, calling for the dispatch of NATO forces to the territories. General Wesley Clark, Commander of NATO forces at the time of the war in Kosovo, expressed a similar view.

The Demise of the "International Community"

In 2019, opening one of the UN Security Council's quarterly debates on the situation in the Middle East, Undersecretary General for Political and Peacebuilding Affairs Rosemary DiCarlo said the Israeli-Palestinian conflict remained "locked in a dangerous paralysis that is fueling extremism and exacerbating tensions." But her call for an international effort to resolve the conflict met with the same old worn-out rhetoric from all discussants, where lip service was being paid to the cause but with no sense of urgency, and no realistic or credible action plan. The Russians protested against the American monopoly of the peace process, but had no alternative suggestion. Speaking on behalf of the European Union, the representative of Croatia said the bloc's position called for direct negotiations and for carrying out economic projects that would contribute to the two-state solution. Arab representatives repeated the all too familiar condemnations of

Israel and so on. As might have been expected, the Israeli delegate put the blame squarely on the Palestinians and Iran's subversive regional strategy. The US representative advised everybody to hold their breath, put aside tired rhetoric, and wait for Trump's "Deal of the Century" to be revealed.[8]

The question is, then, whether there is truly an international community anymore, one capable of acting collectively for the solution of global and regional conflicts and upholding international rules of conduct. In the current age of a disintegrating world order, the demise of multilateralism, and a return to the Westphalian system of nation-states and the balance of power, one has every reason to doubt the capacity or, indeed, the will of the major international players to get together in a concert of powers to restore order to the Middle East, certainly the most dysfunctional part of the planet. The faltering "international community" is now overwhelmed by an ominously changing global agenda that is triggering what George Orwell would have defined as the fear of "catastrophic gradualism."[9] This is a short list of the world's more urgent worries: the risk of collapse of the post-Cold War strategic nuclear agreements, the US-China trade war and global competition, the EU's existential struggle amidst the rise of political extremism, economic stagnation and the fallout from Brexit, the North Korea nuclear showdown, Russia's revisionism and Vladimir Putin's hybrid war on Western democracies, the mounting challenge of uncontrolled mass migrations, the approaching global ecological holocaust, and the unceremonious death of multilateralism that has plunged the world into global disorder where national egoism prevails. Such an "international community" is in no mood to spare any energy for a combined effort in Palestine. Palestine is simply not such an important item in her concerns; this is so even with regard to the Palestinians' "brethren" in the Arab world. A major Middle East war involving Iran, Hezbollah, and Israel; a broader Israeli-Palestinian conflagration that might emerge out of the kind of flare-up we saw in May 2021 between Hamas and Israel; or a sudden change in America's ways from unilateralism to a concert of global powers might perhaps change that, but even this is not guaranteed. Meanwhile, goodwill, lofty speeches, continued financial assistance for the Palestinians, a growing weariness on the part of the Arab world with the Palestinian ulcer, and routine condemnations of Israel would persist. Israel has learned to live with all of this.

The Occupation's Traits
of Permanence

Twenty-one years since President Clinton failed in his painstaking attempt to broker a peace deal, one cannot avoid the conclusion that the Israeli-Palestinian peace process has been one of the most spectacular disappointments in modern diplomatic history. Leaders in both Ramallah and Jerusalem know only too well that a two-state solution to be reached through direct negotiations and American mediation has by now been unceremoniously buried. Israel's decline into an ethnocentric reality and the rise of the nationalist-religious worldview at the expense of the peace culture of the more secular and modern Israel make it utterly impossible for an Israeli government to repeat two-state peace proposals such as those made by prime ministers Ehud Barak and Ehud Olmert.

But ours was a defining failure that stemmed from the built-in intractability of a conflict that transcends negotiable categories of land and security—the stuff of diplomacy—and gets irremediably stuck in issues of narrative, religion, and legit-imacy—the stuff of theology. No magic formula could reconcile the Palestinian ethos of dispossession and return with the Israelis' inbred spirit of settlement and possession, and their obsession with total security. Too poor in geography, the Israeli-Palestinian space does not allow much room for accommodating vital interests; too rich in history, it is replete with conflicting narratives that defeated time and again the most devoted peacemakers.

The intractability of the conflict is strongly linked to the resilience of na-tionalist atavisms—the eminent historian Fernand Braudel wrote about the "mentalities (that) are prisons of long duration"—to the dysfunctional nature of the parties' respective politics, and to the poverty of leadership. But the ab-ject submission of the Palestinians and the ever deepening system of occupation and discrimination in the territories are Israel's sole and exclusive responsibility. As brilliantly explained by Michael Sfard, this is a system built on three pillars: the gun, the settlements, and the law that formalizes the network of coloniza-tion.[1] Under the mantle of security claims, the Jewish state has created in the

Palestinian territories one of the most efficient occupation regimes in history, which is, moreover, also cost-effective, for it is the international community's donor money to the Palestinian Authority that saves the occupier the burden of having to directly administer the territories. This leaves Israel free to cater to its insatiable security needs with draconic measures, such as limiting the Palestinians' freedom of movement, erecting walls that separate communities, dotting roads with checkpoints where innocent people are manhandled, activating sophisticated intelligence mechanisms that control the lives of an ever growing number of suspects, conducting surprise searches of private houses in the middle of the night, and carrying out arbitrary administrative detentions. If this were not enough, vigilantes among the settlers, some known as "the Youth of the Hills," constantly harass Palestinian communities, destroy orchard trees, and arbitrarily apply a "price tag" of punishments to innocent civilians for whatever terrorist attack might have been perpetrated by a Palestinian squad. Underlying this very serious problem of the unpardonable depravity of settlers' extremism is the even more serious problem that has to do with the involvement of the entire Israeli body politic in maintaining and continuously expanding a regime of dominance in the territories. For too long, the peace process has served as a curtain behind which the policy of practical annexation has flourished.

Israel's Quest for *Lebensraum*

As early as 1984, when only 1.3 million Palestinians and about 30,000 settlers lived in the West Bank—now the numbers are 3 million and about 650,000 respectively—Meron Benvenisti, a brilliant scholar who also served as deputy mayor of Jerusalem, shocked Israeli liberals with his thesis about the irreversibility of Israel's occupation of the West Bank and, hence, of the inevitability of a one-state, binational reality. The Second Israeli Republic, as he called it, that was born in 1967 was a binational state stretching from the Jordan River to the Mediterranean. Years before Jimmy Carter warned of Israel's apartheid system in the territories, Benvenisti described Israel's unstoppable decline into a morally troubling South African reality.[2] Benvenisti spoke of how Israel's colonial policies—expanding settlements, controlling roads and water links, subjugating the Palestinian economy to a dependency status, purchasing or confiscating land for military purposes and for the development of suburban Jerusalem and Tel Aviv, institutionalizing a dual system of law that protected the settlers but denied the Palestinians fundamental civic rights—were converging into a point of no return. That was a state of affairs where there was not even a need for formal annexation, Benvenisti argued.

Reality in Benvenisti's time was still manageable, and Professor Sari Nusseibeh, a Palestinian intellectual of noble convictions about peace and coexistence, could still challenge Benvenisti's disturbing dystopia. "I don't think it is irreversible yet. Maybe if it goes on another five or ten years," he said. Well, Nusseibeh waited another twenty-eight years before he finally endorsed Benvenisti's dystopic vision.[3] Now, reality and its perception finally coincided. Seven years after Nusseibeh's surrender to Benvenisti's 1984 logic, the occupation's traits of permanence have only deepened.[4]

Israel is a small country with the highest birth rate (3.17 per woman) in the West. According to data released by Israel's Central Bureau of Statistics, the total fertility rate in 2018 marked a demographic shift, with an increase in fertility rates among Jews and a decrease among Muslims; the total fertility rate for Jewish women hit then a forty-five-year high.[5] Also, Israel's population density of four hundred per square meter is among the highest in the world. Accordingly, real estate is Israel's most precious and diminishing commodity. This is where the West Bank comes to the rescue of the country's saturated land space. A country essentially concentrated around two major urban conglomerates adjacent to the West Bank—Tel Aviv and Jerusalem—Israel's natural expansion since 1967 has been eastward, with parts of the West Bank practically becoming suburbs of Tel Aviv and Jerusalem. Settling five minutes from my hometown Kfar Saba, on this side of the border, as the government's propaganda publicizes it, has been a tempting attraction for lower-income settlers.

It is precisely this agrarian hunger that should explain how the low-income ultra-Orthodox prolific population that was sent to settle in new townships in the West Bank—Beitar Illit, with a population of 57,000, and Modi'in Illit with more than 73,000 are the most populated settlements—is moving further and further to the political right, becoming almost one with the nationalist settler movement. Traditionally, ultra-Orthodox sectors were a-Zionist, if not anti-Zionist; now they are reinforcing the ultra-Zionist right. While they make up around 10 percent of the population within Israel, they now count for a third of those in the West Bank.

Government policies in Jerusalem, which is now acquiring the form of an octopus, expanding east and south, almost exclusively beyond the Green Line, respond to the same thirst for real estate. Currently, about 430,000 Israelis live in the West Bank and 210,000 in government-subsidized projects in East Jerusalem. One could only imagine the cost of the same projects if they were to be located in Israel proper, especially if proximity to the metropolitan centers was to be kept. Billions of dollars in infrastructure subsidies—the sums remain a state secret—were poured in the last two decades into the fantasy of settling Judea and Samaria, far less than into the development townships in Israel's own periphery, whose inhabitants have been for years a captive right-wing electoral vote, shamelessly manipulated by the magic of Likud's nationalist demagoguery.

It is true, as the ardent advocates of the two-state solution argue, that, with all their expansion, the settlements still occupy no more than 1.2 percent of the West Bank. But their jurisdiction and their regional councils extend to about 42 percent, according to the Israeli NGO B'Tselem, a figure disputed by the settlers' council, which claims that their jurisdiction applies to 9.2 percent of the West Bank (Map 7 describes the spread of Israeli settlements in the West Bank).

Percentages can be misleading, however. It is the nature of some settlements as self-contained cities with a stable population in the tens of thousands and with lavish infrastructures, as well as the geographic spread of the smaller settlements, that creates a feature of permanence and irreversibility. The nightmare of negotiating the two-state solution would be even worse if Israel were allowed to implement unilaterally Trump's "Deal of the Century" by annexing the Jordan Valley and building in the E1 area connecting Jerusalem with Maale Adumim, practically cutting in two the West Bank and with it any chance of a Palestinian state with an internally contiguous territory in the future.

The control of Palestinian lands has many more economic benefits for Israel. Think, for example, of the highways crossing the West Bank: Road 90, the north-south highway running along the Jordan River; Road1 (east) from Jerusalem to the Dead Sea; and Road 443, which serves as the much-needed alternative to the constantly jammed highway connecting Tel Aviv to Jerusalem. Imagine the cost of Israeli cars going on long detours west of the Green Line instead of using these roads, or if the Palestinians were allowed to collect tolls on them. Another important example is the Gaza blockade. A *Haaretz* report of June 13, 2009, explained how the decision about which goods would be allowed into the besieged Strip served the needs of Israeli farmers and manufacturers.[6]

That the West Bank is a subjugated colony is also expressed by the Palestinians' lack of access to their airspace, electromagnetic sphere, sea and territorial international borders, as well as by the extra costs of transportation due to the segregation of some West Bank roads. The 1995 Israel-PLO Paris Protocol regulated economic relations between the parties in a way that practically institutionalized overwhelming Palestinian economic dependence on Israel. Israeli companies freely excavate and sell Palestine's natural resources, and the West Bank has become one of Israel's largest captive trade partners. Since the 1990s, Israel has been an almost exclusive destination for more than 90 percent of total Palestinian exports. Israel is also the source of most Palestinian imports, though its share significantly decreased from 75–80 percent in 2000–13 to 65–70 percent in 2014–16. Nevertheless, almost all Palestinian imports from non-Israeli markets still come through Israel, and a large part through Israeli importers. Bilateral trade is largely imbalanced in favor of Israel. Palestinian imports of

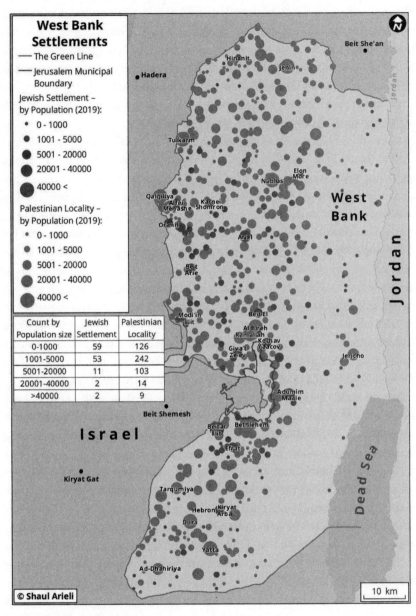

West Bank Settlements

— The Green Line

— Jerusalem Municipal Boundary

Jewish Settlement –
by Population (2019):

- · 0 - 1000
- • 1001 - 5000
- ● 5001 - 20000
- ● 20001 - 40000
- ● 40000 <

Palestinian Locality –
by Population (2019):

- · 0 - 1000
- • 1001 - 5000
- ● 5001 - 20000
- ● 20001 - 40000
- ● 40000 <

Count by Population size	Jewish Settlement	Palestinian Locality
0-1000	59	126
1001-5000	53	242
5001-20000	11	103
20001-40000	2	14
>40000	2	9

© Shaul Arieli

10 km

Map 7 West Bank Settlements, 2019

goods from Israel are still 2.5–3 times higher than Palestinian exports to Israel. Also labor is a potent glue uniting the two economies. By 2016, Palestinian workers' compensation covered about 85 percent of the Palestinian deficit in bilateral trade, reducing it from around $2 billion in 2008–10, and $2.5 billion in 2013, to only $500 million in 2016. Still, with a total of close to $3.5 billion in goods exports a year between 2014 and 2016, the Palestinian market ranks fourth among Israel's top export markets—after the United States, China and Hong Kong, and the United Kingdom—and accounts for 6 percent of total Israeli exports of goods.[7] Additional aspects of Israeli economic colonialism in Palestine are water and land. With Israel's water consumption being almost four times that of the Palestinians, no less than 80 percent of the mountain aquifer in the West Bank is used by Israel and its settlements.

It is not that the occupation is free of material costs for the occupier. Military deployments in the West Bank, rounds of wars and intifadas, and the colossal investments in settlements and infrastructures to serve the occupier represent a heavy financial burden that is difficult to assess because Israel's national budget does not distinguish the territories as separate from Israel. But according to a study conducted in 2014–15, direct and indirect associated defense costs amount to 15 percent of Israeli GDP. This is expected to decline gradually by about half if the conflict is settled. This would mean a 7 percent rise in Israeli GDP should an end of the conflict be reached. Israel's lavish expenditure in the territories and in the periodic wars against Hamas in Gaza should partly explain the stress on the national budget and the subsequent drastic cuts in Israel's welfare policies. Under Netanyahu's rule, Israel consolidated its position as the OECD's most unequal country. A high cost of living, unaffordable housing, and 21 percent of the population below the poverty line have been Netanyahu's record so far.

But the main victim here is the occupied. Since the First Intifada in 1987–93, the Palestinian economy has experienced the loss of around half of its potential growth in GDP under non-conflict conditions. The impact of the conflict is best demonstrated by comparing developments in the West Bank and Gaza. Annual exports from Gaza, which were around $30–40 million in 1996–2006, halted almost entirely in 2008–9. Since 2010, despite a partial relaxation of trade restrictions on Gaza, exports remained insignificant, at an annual level of around $4 million. In the West Bank, meanwhile, an improvement in the security situation enabled an almost fivefold increase in exports, from about $200 million in 2002 (the lowest point of the Second Intifada) to almost $1 billion a year in 2015–16.[8]

Peace would, of course, have economic dividends. Two independent political entities in close economic integration and free of the burden of military conflict with its concomitant closures and blockades could replace the current dependence with a free trade zone highly beneficial to both. Alas, economic considerations are sidelined by the revolutionary mindset of the parties. The economic promise of peace is entirely absent from their political discourse. The threats, the fears, the ideological drive to occupy and expand prevail over the hope and the opportunity for a common future in peace. The Israeli public as a whole lives in a state of denial; it prefers to see the occupation as a lesser evil imposed on it by security needs and by the Palestinian's persistent rejection of Israel's right of existence. This narrative conveniently serves to blur the colonial nature of the occupation.

The Securitization of Peace

In 1961, the then US president Dwight Eisenhower warned of the rise of what he called a "military-industrial complex" that might acquire a "disproportionate power." Eisenhower feared that the "complex," consisting of the military hierarchy and the vast arms industry, might one day take control of the nation's foreign and defense policy. Arguably, the fact that the United States has gone from war to war in the last fifty years can be seen as the vindication of Eisenhower's prophecy.

In Israel's case, the massive penetration of the "security network" into practically every sphere of the nation's life is an unquestionable reality. Abu Ala's complaint to me that we negotiated peace as if we were preparing for the next war was, of course, not baseless. A peace process is always a kind of sublimated warfare; in our case, it tended to be an overly militarized affair, with the security establishment injecting a strong military rationale into Israel's negotiating positions. It all actually started when the military conquered the West Bank in 1967 without any clear directives from the government, which actually never intended that the war be about the acquisition of new territories. After the war, it was the army command that unilaterally extended the boundaries of "liberated" Jerusalem, which the government hesitated about liberating at all, by annexing into it twenty-one neighboring Arab villages.

The Israeli debate over the occupied territories is, then, not just an ideological divide between right and left; it is also overwhelmingly influenced by the all-encompassing "security network" that injects a security rationale into every political move. The securitization of the peace process has had throughout a major role in relegating the potential civilian fruits of peace to a marginal consideration. An Israeli-Palestinian peace could have benefited from political leaders capable of standing up to the security network and establishing the primacy of moral, economic, and political calculations in the quest for peace.[9]

Israel's Dysfunctional Polity

Historically, the Jewish experience in international relations has not been particularly edifying. An independent Jewish state existed for only short periods of the Jews' millennial history, and it twice committed political suicide. The reasons for both were the same: the blunder of ignoring political realities, the drift into Messianic fanaticism, and the defiance of world powers. Ethnocentrism tends to distort a people's relations with the rest of the world. The Israeli nationalistic right today sees "the world" as an almost meta-historical figure with whom the Jews have a dispute pending that cannot be resolved through the traditional tools of international relations. Israel has also conveniently made of the Holocaust a narrative of permanent victimhood and guiltlessness.

Nor is Israel's complex, multifaceted social structure easily conducive to an accommodation with either the Palestinians' or the international community's sensibilities over the conflict. An exciting brand of "Tel Aviv" Israeliness—secular, democratic, high-tech-oriented and peace-seeking—has in recent years been politically overpowered by an uncompromising "Jerusalemite" Israel, much under the radicalizing impact of Israel's occupation practices in Palestinian lands. Embedded in the dire lessons of Jewish history, "Jerusalem" is a magnet for the fears and complexes of a wide rainbow alignment of ethnic minorities yearning for Jewish roots; it is the epitome of a deep-rooted fear of "the Arabs" and an unyielding distrust of the "international community." Jerusalem's ethnocentrism is enhanced by the very nature of the Palestinian conflict as a clash of millennial religious certificates of ownership, not just a banal border dispute. Oslo was made possible when an almost post-Zionist clamor for "normalcy" and peace invaded embattled Israeli society. The "Tel Avivian" depraved drive for laicism, peace, and modernity that had always been vying for supremacy in a constant *Kulturkampf* with traditionalist and peace-skeptic "Jerusalem" got an ephemeral victory in Oslo. But that unpardonable betrayal of Jewish roots and history would not be allowed to last. For the clash between Jerusalem and Tel Aviv was never conducted in a bubble; its outcome always depended on the perception that the Israelis had of their Arab neighbors, particularly the Palestinians. Arafat's rejection of the peace deal that was offered to him in December 2000, and his endorsement of the Intifada not only set on fire the mechanisms of peacemaking, but also dealt an almost mortal blow to "Tel Aviv's" peace camp, and allowed "Jerusalemite" Israel to gain the upper hand in Israel's politico-cultural civil war.

If this were not enough, Israel's peace policy was always determined by her utterly dysfunctional political system being more an obstacle to than a vehicle for assuming historic decisions. One is allowed to wonder whether it is indeed Iran and the Arab world or Israel's own political system that is her major strategic threat. Israel's proportional electoral system would always produce unruly parliaments that are the photocopy of her kaleidoscopic ethnic and religious tapestry. The always inevitable need to form government coalitions grants the smaller parties a veto power on government policies, which then become the hostage of the extremists. In Netanyahu's far-right governments, policies on the Palestinian question were practically defined by a hard-fringe annexationist party, the *Jewish Home*. Ministers in Israeli governments tend to have a leverage over the prime minister that allows them to deviate from his guidelines. It would be perfectly normal for a foreign dignitary visiting Israel to hear from each of the ministers he meets a different "peace plan." Netanyahu's defining political experience happened in 1998. He was then toppled by his right-wing partners for signing with Arafat the Wye River Memorandum. Since then, he would never repeat the "mistake" of negotiating seriously with the Palestinians.

However, Arafat did a better job of mobilizing Israeli peace skeptics than any right-wing leader in Israel's history. Like Cronus, father of the Olympian gods, the Israeli-Palestinian peace process had devoured all its sons and daughters, but unlike Cronus it hasn't vomited them up alive. Hence, Sharon, the benefiter of this logic, refused to follow the pattern of his predecessors for whom peace negotiations had been the prelude to political perdition. The disengagement from Gaza and the dismantling of its settlements was Sharon's way of defying the very logic of the peace process as a bilateral affair and thus avoiding the moment of truth of the final settlement that was bound to lead to the downfall of the prime minister and the meltdown of his coalition. With Sharon, who won back the Palestinian-controlled areas of the West Bank in his 2002 Defensive Shield operation and kept the Chairman under siege in Ramallah until his final days, Arafat finally met his nemesis.

What Is Wrong with No-Peace Anyway?

The conventional wisdom that Israel's international standing is declining irredeemably due to her persistent occupation of Palestinian lands has never been so wrong. The Jewish state now enjoys a global clout unprecedented in its history. The transformation of the Middle East strategic conditions, compounded by the Abraham Accords, Israel's peace agreements with four Arab states, the changing agenda of global politics, and Israel's maneuvering capabilities have diluted the primacy of the Palestinian question. Palestine can always re-emerge from its ashes to trouble the world's conscience, as we saw in the Gaza war of May 2021. But this does not truly change the new global conditions that had allowed Israel's foreign policy, which for years was hostage to one single issue, Palestine, to enjoy the kind of room for maneuver it hardly ever had.

To future-proof itself against mounting popular pressure in the West, Israel has been looking elsewhere for economic and, ultimately, political partners. Her exports to Asia tripled between 2004 and 2014, totaling $16.7 billion, one-fifth of Israel's total exports. Israel now does more trade with the once implacably hostile Asian giants—China, Japan, and India, to which Israel is the second supplier of military technology—than with the United States, with which it has a free trade agreement. The election of the Hindu nationalist Narendra Modi in India, a country with 160 million Muslims, allowed the lifting of the veil off India's growing defense cooperation with Israel. This was highlighted by regular visits of Israel's defense ministers to India, and the historic visits to Israel of both the Indian president, Pranab Mukherjee, and Prime Minister Modi. Nor are Japan and China—the latter is Israel's third largest trading partner—linking the success of peace efforts to their economic ties with the "startup nation" anymore.

Meanwhile, the Eastern Mediterranean is close to becoming Israel's *mare nostrum*, thanks in part to her status as a gas-producing power. Greece's former prime minister, Alexis Tsipras, who while in opposition was fiercely hostile to Israel, ended up becoming a close ally. His visits to Israel for strategic talks became a routine throughout his two terms in office. This marriage of convenience became a tripartite geopolitical bloc, a counterweight to Turkey, at a meeting in Nicosia in January 2015 of Netanyahu, Tsipras, and the president of Cyprus, Nicos Anastasiades. In return for Israeli gas, defense technology, and military intelligence, Greece offered its airspace for the training of Israel's air force. Also, Athens, as the then foreign minister Nikos Kotzias explicitly stated, would not abide by EU sanctions on exports from Israel's occupied territories. Tsipras's current successor, Kyriakos Mitsotakis, is equally committed to Greece's alliance with Israel. No wonder Nabil Shaath, a former Palestinian foreign minister, complained to *Haaretz* on January 27, 2016, of Greece's "betrayal of Palestine." Israel has also made significant inroads into the African continent and Eastern Europe's illiberal axis. Indeed, it is thanks to the stance of that very axis that EU directives on exports from the occupied territories always come out far more attenuated than initially planned by Brussels.

With Russia calling the tune in the Middle East through a nineteenth-century style of power diplomacy, Israel was quick to reach an understanding with Moscow on her freedom of operation against Iranian positions in Syria. Significantly, Israel's neutrality on Russia's annexation of Crimea and its arming of Russian secessionists in Ukraine has set it apart from most Western countries. A similar détente prevails in Israel's relations with her Arab neighbors. Anwar Sadat's Egypt had shown the way. Whenever an Arab state faced a truly existential dilemma or fought for a superior national interest, as Sadat saw this when he went for a separate peace with Israel, Palestine was the first to pay the price. Palestine is now the last of Saudi Arabia's worries; the same applies to the Sunni Gulf dynasties and Egypt, now in intimate security cooperation with Israel against Islamist terrorism and the rising threat of Iran. The loss of their proxy wars in Syria and Yemen, the challenge posed by the rise of a threshold nuclear Iran, the horror of the specter of a Daesh revival, and dismay at what at times looks like US non-committal policies on all these issues combined to make Israel an acceptable, albeit covert partner for the Saudis.

But instead of using this surprising web of alliances and global economic ties to help solve Israel's truly existential problem, her Palestinian conundrum, Israel uses it to vindicate a static strategy on Palestine and shield herself from possible international sanctions for her occupation practices. Israel's international exploits have nurtured her complacency. However busy international opinion might be with Gaza and the periodic wars between Israel and Hamas, to most Israelis the Palestinian "problem" seems to be happening on the dark side of the moon. The wall/fence in the West Bank and Ariel Sharon's disengagement from Gaza have practically done away with the daily friction of the past between Israelis and Palestinians. Absorbed by their booming economy, reassured by America's commitment to never let down Israel, and convinced of their success in defeating Palestinian terrorism, the Israelis have lost the sense of urgency with regard to the Palestinian problem.

They also find satisfaction in the relative prosperity of the West Bank, where order and stability are being secured by well-trained security forces in an intimate cooperation with Israel in fighting terrorism, particularly Hamas's. The Palestinian addiction to international aid makes Israel one of the most convenient foreign occupations in world history; the Israelis control the land and its population without having to bear the burden of direct rule and its financial cost.

But Israel's reluctance to invest in peace did not spring up overnight. It was the Al-Aqsa Intifada in the year 2000 that was the fatal watershed that destroyed Israel's peace constituency and radically shifted popular opinion to the right and far right. Exposed to indiscriminate waves of suicide terrorism, Israelis lost any hope of a negotiated settlement and, in their despair, succumbed to a new self-defeating political religion of unilateralism. The Intifada forced Israelis to turn their backs on the Palestinians, erase them from their consciousness, imprison them behind impenetrable walls while keeping for themselves the essential parts of the land required for their settlements and rising security needs. It still remains to be seen, though, how long the fallout of the latest Gaza war will last in the minds of regional and international stakeholders and how defining the shockwaves it unleashed into the collective psyche of the complacent nation are.

PART IV

DENOUEMENTS

Ominous Unravelings

Without an orderly move to a two-state solution, Israelis and Palestinians would be left with two plausible scenarios. Both—a binational state, and an Israeli unilateral disengagement coupled with the annexation of great parts of the West Bank along contours reminiscent of the 1967 Alon Plan, Ehud Olmert's 2006 Convergence Plan, and Donald Trump's "Deal of the Century"—are ominous, inauspicious plots. The first is already emerging by osmosis; the second would be a desperate attempt to cut short the dystopia represented by the first but, if implemented, would be no less of a calamity.

The Specter of the Single Binational State

The dystopia of a single binational state has always had its intellectual advocates. Some, like the late Tony Judt,[1] are disillusioned former Zionists; others are enlightened Palestinians such as Sari Nusseibeh, a noble fighter for Israeli-Palestinian reconciliation who despaired of the two-state solution.[2] Some, such as the revisionist historian Ilan Pappé, believe in reversing the course of history, undoing the Jewish state, and going back to an imaginary Arcadia, the supposedly harmonious days of Arab-Jewish coexistence in a binational community. This revolutionary romanticism about an archaic golden age is a mirage, a dream shattered by the 1936–39 Arab Revolt and by the 1948 legacy of disinheritance and refugeeism. Since then, lofty visions about coexistence have been further deflated by Arab-Jewish infighting over the same piece of land, a mercilessly effective Israeli occupation, two devastating Intifadas, and wars and blockades in Gaza.

The single binational state is a desperate escape, admittedly gaining sway among desolate masses of Palestinians, to a chimera that is bound to end in lamentation. If it happens, the one-state reality would emerge by osmosis, through the abandonment of responsibility by reckless politicians. Always wavering whether to actually annex Judea and Samaria, Israel's far right coalitions have, nevertheless, consistently created the conditions for such an annexation. It was, indeed, primarily the Palestinians in the occupied territories whom Israel's 2018 Nation State Law pretended to target. For the fear that Israeli Arabs may become a majority and change by democratic means Israel's Jewish character is totally unfounded. Jews can become a minority only by perpetuating their grip on the Palestinian occupied territories. The law paved the way for ensuring that Jewish pre-eminence would be maintained even in a one-state reality with an Arab majority between the sea and the Jordan River. With the two-state solution all but dead, Netanyahu's coalition made its choice between Israel's dual identities, Jewish and democratic, by giving preference to the Jewish identity in Greater Eretz Yisrael. The Nation-State Law is supposed to vaccinate Jewish Israel against the consequences of her drift to a Jewish-Arab binational reality from the sea to the Jordan River, and to secure Jewish pre-eminence in Greater Eretz Yisrael. With Netanyahu, the Republic of Judea and Samaria has defeated the State of Israel.

Prerequisites for a possible annexation of Palestinian areas comprising as much territory with as little population (essentially, Area C, amounting to 60 percent of the West Bank) have been consistently promoted by the more radical members of Netanyahu's right-wing coalitions. Their initiatives included a bill giving the Jerusalem District Court powers of judicial review over the military government in the West Bank, as if the Palestinian territories were a district within Israel. With the same objective in mind, they also advocated imposing Knesset legislation on the disenfranchised Palestinians. Recently, Israel's Supreme Court, to which the government had managed to appoint a number of conservative settler-friendly justices, gave its approval to the confiscation of Palestinian lands to serve the needs of settlers. It can all still be stopped, and even reversed, if a different government coalition is put in place. Otherwise, such provocative steps would one day cease to be seen by the Palestinians just as the normal creeping annexation they have been used to, and become a quantum leap to institutionalized annexation.

It remains a delusion, though, to believe in the viability of an Israeli-Jewish-Muslim-Palestinian state. Here in the Middle East, a multiethnic democracy? This is a recipe for civil war, not the introduction to multiethnic harmony. It would be a forced fusion, "not a marriage, but a rape," as Susie Linfield put it.[3] But even if mutually agreed, it simply will not work because it will not. This can only lead to a situation resembling the old South Africa, with two classes of citizens possessing vastly different political and civil rights. Such a situation would not lend itself to a peaceful South Africa-style solution because Israel, with its superior might, would never concede power to a Palestinian majority. A South African reality without a South African solution is unquestionably a recipe for a state of permanent civil war. An affront to the international community, Jewish supremacy in a binational state would strain beyond reasonable limits her capacity to resist outside pressure. Never the supporter of the two-state solution, Israel's far right is toying these days with the most dangerous of all possible scenarios. An anticipation of what a binational state would look like was offered in the war with Hamas in May 2021. Israeli mixed Jewish-Arab cities that were supposed to be exemplars of coexistence, such as Acre, Ramla, Jaffa, and Lod, erupted in an orgy of violence and vandalism that shocked the nation.

These are days of upheaval when the ominous fragility of the liberal order and the rise of white nationalisms are pulling the West back to its darkest hours. In this age of rampant populism and xenophobia, not even liberal Europe is able to digest multiethnicity. Why on earth would anyone assume that what did not work for Czechs and Slovaks; for Turks and Greeks in Cyprus; for the entire multiethnic universe of the former Yugoslavia that was shattered in an outburst of narcissism of minor differences leading to civil wars, mass slaughter, and ethnic cleansing; and for practically all the Arab countries throughout the Middle East, where minorities are oppressed, gassed, and slaughtered would work in Israel-Palestine? Are our two monumentally divergent national egos, in a state of war for more than a century now, going to coexist peacefully in a region where even Muslims are immersed in an ongoing inter-Muslim war that is tearing apart states and communities, and the only multiethnic democracy—Lebanon—is falling apart? Not exactly a reactionary, Maxime Rodinson acknowledged in 1998 that" bi-national states is not something that works in these modern times."[4]

Significantly, notable figures on the Israeli "civilized" right—among them the former president Ruvi Rivlin and the late defense and foreign minister Moshe Arens, who was also a political mentor of Benjamin Netanyahu—had offered their support for one political space between the Mediterranean and the Jordan River. As always, however, the champions of the idea want the best of all worlds. Theirs is a proposal for an emphatically Jewish state between the sea and the Jordan River where the Palestinians would have citizenship rights, but no national rights whatsoever. Not a bad formula for a state of permanent civil war. My negotiating partner Abu Ala and others on the Palestinian side always maintained that the two-state solution was a historic Palestinian compromise, for they preferred a one-state solution in which Palestinian demography would win for them the definitive battle with Zionism.

Unilateral Disengagement: The Alon Plan Redux

Immediately after the end of the 1967 war, Deputy Prime Minister Yigal Alon presented his plan for the future of the West Bank. In essence, it called for Israel to retain control of the then sparsely populated Jordan Valley and of the eastern slopes of the West Bank hill ridge, which would thus allow her to control the strategic areas of the West Bank as a buffer against possible attacks from the east. Israel would also annex areas in the Jerusalem corridor and the Etzion Bloc. The plan created three populous Palestinian enclaves linked by connected roads, a northern one including Nablus, Jenin, Tulkarm, and Ramallah, a southern enclave around Hebron and Bethlehem, and another around Jericho. The Palestinians' access to Jordan would be facilitated through a corridor under Israel's control (see Map 8).

During the 1948 war, Alon, then a brilliant young general, was prevented by David Ben-Gurion from occupying the West Bank out of concern for the Jewish demographic majority. But now, by retaining the sparsely populated areas of

— Pre-1967 Lines (The "Green Line")
— Municipal boundaries of Jerusalem after 1967
▓ Territories to be annexed to Israel according to Alon Plan

Map 8 "The Alon Plan, 1967"

the West Bank and confining the Palestinians in three enclaves, Alon believed he was securing Israel as the democratic Jewish state promised by the constituent Zionist vision. Eventually, Alon, who first thought the Palestinian enclaves could have a special status as a quasi-independent autonomous entity, proposed a Jordanian-Palestinian state that would include both the enclaves and the Gaza Strip. To Alon, the Jordan Valley with its fertile lands and water resources was not only a strategic asset but also a land for Israeli agricultural settlements. These are today located mostly along two north–south roads, the Alon Road and Route 90. That the valley could also be the breadbasket of the future Palestinian state and the only space where it could absorb its refugees as part of a peace settlement with Israel did not particularly bother Alon in those days of Israeli hubris.

The Alon Plan is, then, not just a historical anecdote, which King Hussein of Jordan turned down as "totally unacceptable" when it was offered to him in 1968 as the basis for a peace agreement between Israel and a Jordanian-Palestinian state. It is also the litmus test of a now rising Israeli national consensus, with Netanyahu's Likud at its main pivot, relentlessly pushing for the annexation of the Jordan Valley and the land reserves of Area C. But for the three blocs of settlements adjacent to the Green Line, which in Alon's days were still in their incipient stage, his map is conceptually the same as that of most of the unilateral annexationist plans toyed with these days, Donald Trump's "Deal of the Century" included.[5] Alon vainly hoped to have this as the basis of a peace agreement with Jordan; his successors ignore Jordan entirely in their drive to confine the Palestinians in three or more dense Bantustans and keep for Israel both the strategic areas of the West Bank and its vital land reserves

Unilateral Disengagement: Ehud Olmert's Version

That the Israeli right toyed at times with a peace process of sorts was not due to the wonders of the two-state solution, but to the need to delineate the geographic limits of Israel's expansion. But with no Palestinian partner willing to accept peace based on Israeli land-grabbing and rising security needs, it was the specter of the loss of Jewish demographic predominance in historical Palestine that gave life to the concept of unilateral disengagement from populated Palestinian areas. The former prime minister Ariel Sharon's Gaza disengagement and the wall he built in the West Bank were his response to the "demographic threat."

Unilateralism has now become a philosophy of life for most Israelis. The vision of the peacemakers from Rabin to Barak and Olmert that peace was the way to achieve security was replaced by a new political philosophy; now security is supposed to bring peace. But Sharon's unilateral pullout from Gaza eventually brought neither. Pursuing his legacy by carrying out a unilateral disengagement in the West Bank was bound to be an especially complex affair. Gaza is a fully fenced, compact strip whose border with Israel was never in doubt. The West Bank, where a maze of settlements and a complex delimitation of areas of responsibility between Israel and the Palestinian Authority overlap each other, would turn unilateral disengagement into a nightmare.

Yet pursuing Sharon's disengagement legacy in the West Bank was exactly what his successor, Ehud Olmert, set out to do immediately upon his election in 2006. After six years of inconclusive chaos that started with the Al-Aqsa Intifada, Olmert came to office with the same sense of desperation as Sharon's with regard to the chances of a negotiated peace. Olmert's Convergence Plan bred the delusion that security could be obtained by retreating in the face of a national movement that had given sufficient proof of its determination to attain its rights by all conceivable means. "Olmert's convergence plan is a recipe for war," warned Ismail Haniyeh, the then Hamas prime minister.[6] The entire purpose of the peace process was the creation of a friendly Palestinian state, but Olmert's disengagement, just like Sharon's from Gaza, was bound to create an enemy state in the West Bank, possibly sustained and financed by Iran, facing Israel's soft belly, that is, its major urban centers in the greater Tel Aviv area. The First Intifada was a crusade of stones; the Second Intifada was marked by suicide terrorism; Olmert's unilateral disengagement would have triggered an Intifada of weapons with a steep trajectory, exactly the same or even worse than the one that Sharon had triggered from Gaza. No wonder the army's reaction to Olmert's plan was that a southern Lebanon-style "security zone" be established along the Palestinian side of the separation wall and a territorial hold be maintained on the Jordan Valley and key sites on the mountain ridges. All this would have amounted to turning the West Bank into a prison for millions of Palestinians, far bigger than the one already existing in Gaza.

Olmert's Convergence Plan (see Map 9) with its promises as well as its monumental flaws is a model upon which the advocates of the idea these days base their own plans. It envisaged the evacuation of seventy thousand settlers as compared with the eight thousand settlers in Gaza. It was like giving away with no quid pro quo part of what had been offered to the Palestinians at Camp David—full sovereignty in the Gaza Strip and in 92 percent of the West Bank—in exchange for peace and stability to an armed, hostile Palestinian state, possibly under Hamas rule. A Hamas state that would have emerged as the product of what would have inevitably been perceived as a capitulation of the "Zionist entity" to the religious fervor of Palestinian resistance would have boosted Islamic groups throughout the Middle East and would have affected the stability of friendly regimes like King Abdullah's Jordan and Mubarak's Egypt. But the Palestinian cause is not only about land. The central ingredients of the Palestinian ethos—Jerusalem, the Temple Mount, and the plight of the refugees—none of

Map 9 Ehud Olmert's Convergence Plan, 2006.

which was addressed by the Convergence Plan, would have continued to fire the spirit of Palestinian resistance. The plan not only promised a unilateral definition of Israel's borders and the beefing-up of arbitrarily outlined settlement blocs, but also contemplated the possibility of connecting Maale Adumim to

Jerusalem, thus creating a huge urban space within the West Bank from the watershed area to the plains of Jericho. Such a megalopolis would have destroyed any chances of territorial contiguity for the Palestinians, for it would have cut off the northern West Bank from the southern part and would have turned the Arab neighborhoods of Jerusalem into isolated islands with no connection to the Palestinian hinterland.

Olmert eventually dropped the idea. But fifteen years after his unilateral delusion and with the idea of a negotiated peace all but dead, Israelis are back in a desperate search for an antidote to the doomsday scenario of a binational state. Unilateral disengagement is a revolt against the specter of the loss of Jewish demographic majority, a priority written into the genetic code of Zionism. It is, indeed, not just the fear of international condemnation that has so far prevented Israel from annexing the occupied territories in the same way as it had annexed the Golan Heights. Zionism was throughout more about demography than about land. Whenever the choice was presented to the movement between more land with an Arab majority and less land with a Jewish majority, it opted for the latter. That was the case with the Zionists' acceptance of the 1937 partition recommendations of the Peel Commission, which, to the Zionists' rejoicing, also called for the transfer of Arabs from the Jewish state, and also with the November 1947 UN partition of Palestine. In the 1948 war, David Ben-Gurion refrained from occupying the West Bank for demographic reasons. The same pattern was reflected in the concept of settlement blocs created by Israeli Labor governments after 1967, and their opposition to what Yitzhak Rabin called "political settlements" deep in the populated West Bank. Ariel Sharon's construction of the wall in the West Bank was tantamount to a philosophical defeat for the Israeli right—its founder, Menachem Begin, had always been adamant that "There should be no border through Eretz Yisrael"—for it meant a recognition that annexation of populated Palestinian areas was out of the question, even for the hawkish Sharon.

In the war in Algeria, Jean-Paul Sartre understood that when peaceful accommodation did not exist, then the hour for a French Algeria was past and pullout was inevitable. But the West Bank is not *outre-mer*; it is a land contiguous with Israel, a unilateral pullout from which would only aggravate the problem. Yet, in spite of the ominous consequences of such a pullout, unilateralism is again resuscitated as a practice of last resort, a desperate move aimed at aborting the decline into a full-fledged binational state that betrays the fundamental purpose of Zionism.

The more enlightened supporters of the idea propose that such a unilateral withdrawal be accompanied with Israel declaring that it is ready to return to negotiations at any time and has no claims of sovereignty on areas east of the security barrier and in the Arab neighborhoods of Jerusalem. It would then advance a plan to evacuate 100,000 settlers who live east of the barrier, 30 percent of whom have already been polled on various occasions as being in support of such a move. Israel could, then, offer sizable parts of Area C, now inhabited by up to 300,000 Palestinians and around 350,000 settlers,[7] to the Palestinians while also evacuating a great number of settlements in that area. In any scenario, however, the hard-line ideological settlers in the heartland of Judea and Samaria would probably remain in their hotbeds of extremism and confrontation. The paradox, however, is that none of these unilateral plans is conceived as the end of the military occupation, for the Israeli armed forces would remain in the areas beyond the security barrier. Unilateral disengagement is about evacuating civilians, not about undoing the IDF's freedom to operate throughout the West Bank.

Donald Trump's "Deal of the Century"

What is it that triggered a president with so many other burning issues on his plate—from North Korea to Syria, from Putin's encroachment on Western spheres of influence, to China's competition with the United States—to venture into an Israeli-Palestinian peace game where the chances of success were always so desperately slim? Certainly, the need to cater to his staunchly pro-Israel evangelical political base called for a peace plan that was markedly biased toward the Jewish state. Also, the prospect of resolving a conflict where all his predecessors failed, more than its strategic utility for America's interest, seemed to have fired the president's imagination. Ridiculed by a liberal elite under whose banner Palestine had been the noblest of causes for the last fifty-four years, Trump wanted to "prove wrong" those who doubted there can ever be an Israeli-Palestinian peace. It was he, the ultimate reactionary, who would give to the liberal elites their most precious gift, a solution to the Israeli-Palestinian conflict.

Arguably, never before had the regional conditions been more favorable for an Arab-Israeli peace. Key Arab actors in the region were now more forthcoming than ever before in offering incentives to Israel on the road to peace in Palestine. Getting the Palestinian problem out of their way would make their strategic alliance with the Jewish state more palatable to the Arab public. These new regional conditions defeated the Israeli left's traditional view of a Palestinian peace being Israel's gateway to the Arab and Muslim world. It turned out to be the other way around: Israel's regional alliances developed without having to pay a price in Palestinian currency.

Be that as it may, Trump's plan had no prospect whatsoever of serving as the premise upon which a bilateral Israeli-Palestinian peace deal could ever emerge. The "Deal of the Century" was a unilateral affair in line with Trump's earlier unilateral recognition of Israel's sovereignty over the Golan Heights and Jerusalem as her capital. The latter too was mostly a tribute to the president's evangelical constituency as well as the result of his compulsive obsession with his predecessors, who, unlike him, presumably lacked the courage to fulfill their electoral pledges to move the US embassy to Jerusalem.

Trump's use of sticks and no carrots with the Palestinians practically turned the entire process into a strictly Israeli-American affair. He offered Jerusalem to the Israelis, cut all aid to the Palestinians, and even declared Israeli settlements not to be illegal. In June 2019, Trump's son-in-law and senior adviser, Jared Kushner, came up with the carrots, which the Palestinians rejected as a clumsy attempt to bribe them into waiving their national aspiration for viable state-hood. Kushner unveiled an ambitious Peace to Prosperity plan to strengthen the Palestinian economy with billions of dollars in investment. Essentially a Marshall Plan for the Middle East, it promised up to $50 billion to boost also the economies of Egypt, Lebanon, and Jordan, all of which are directly affected by the Israeli-Palestinian conflict. The Palestinians remained unimpressed.

The notion that economic incentives can convince the Palestinians to accept Israeli supremacy has a long pedigree. The late British prime minister Winston Churchill, some early Zionists, and even local Arabs argued decades before 1948 that the Zionist enterprise was in the economic interest of the indigenous popu-lation.[8] Shimon Peres suffered from the same illusion that the Palestinians would agree to moderate their national dreams in exchange for economic development. More recently, Netanyahu took up the mantle of "economic peace." There is, of course, nothing wrong with the promise of economic prosperity, but the Israeli-Palestinian clash of national characters cannot be reconciled through economic subsidies; the discordance between the two movements is deeper than what ec-onomic peace could bring.

The Palestinian national movement remains in its revolutionary phase, where economic considerations always come second to national aspirations. The offices of the Palestinian Authority president Mahmoud Abbas and his predecessor, Yasser Arafat, were adorned, when I visited, with images of Jerusalem's Al-Aqsa Mosque and maps of occupied Palestine, not with photos of John Maynard Keynes or Jean Monnet. The Palestinian national movement is driven by the struggle to end the occupation, not by dreams of economic development or of a technological revolution. Accepting an economic deal that is not an annex to a convincing political solution would be tantamount to betraying Palestine for a fistful of dollars. Indeed, in 1923, none other than the founder of the Zionist right, Ze'ev Jabotinsky, denounced as a "childish fantasy" the belief that the Palestinians would "sell out their homeland for a railroad network."[9]

With no input whatsoever on the economic part of the plan, and entirely dis-engaged from talks on the political aspects of Trump's "Deal of the Century," the Palestinians could not be surprised to discover that when the long-awaited political chapter was finally unveiled in the White House at the end of January 2020, it turned out to have gifted Israel most, if not all, of its demands. No wonder the audience of American and Israeli officials at the ceremony—it looked more as a meeting of Likud's central committee—could barely contain their delight. As shown in Map 10, the state the Palestinians were offered was a crippled territorial entity dotted with Israeli settlements and surrounded on all sides by Israeli sovereign territory.

Nor did the plan meet any of the core Palestinian narrative issues, such as Jerusalem and refugees. Not even one refugee would be allowed to return to Israel, and the Palestinian capital would be located in one of the outer Palestinian neighborhoods of a city that is defined by the plan as Israel's "undivided" capital. Forfeiting any pretense of fairness, the plan truly read as if it was Israeli government talking points. Israeli security, not Palestinian self-determination, stood at the center of the plan.

Key clauses of the plan were:

- Recognition of the vast majority of Israeli settlements in the West Bank as part of the sovereign state of Israel. This also included "enclaves" that are not contiguous with Israel but would have access to Israel and be under Israeli protection.
- The Jordan Valley, the intended breadbasket of a future Palestinian state, and the northern shores of the Dead Sea would be a sovereign part of Israel.
- The Palestinian state would be established on 70 percent of the West Bank and the Gaza Strip. It would be compensated for the loss of 30 percent of the land with the equivalent of 14 percent within Israeli territory, mostly desert, which would thus bring the total size of the Palestinian state to 84 percent of the West Bank in addition to the entire Gaza Strip. Gaza and the West Bank would be linked by high-speed rail. Given that no Israeli settlement would be dismantled, the Palestinian state turns out to be a series of cantons linked by bridges and tunnels but entirely surrounded by sovereign Israeli territory. Israel was also to retain overarching "security control" over the entire area west of the Jordan River.
- The plan raised the possibility that, as part of the scheme of territorial swaps, the so-called triangle, an Israeli corridor inhabited by Israeli Palestinian Arabs bordering with the West Bank, might be included in the future Palestinian state, which would mean stripping 300,000 Arab Israelis of Israeli citizenship.
- The Palestinian state would be demilitarized. And the "complete dismantling of Hamas" in Gaza was a precondition for Palestinian statehood.

The Trump team, all consisting of right-wing American Jews closely linked to the Israeli governing right, produced a plan that was "negotiated" with only the

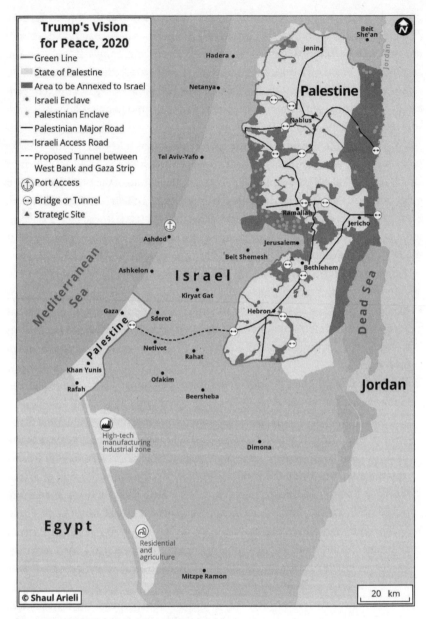

Map 10 Trump's Vision for Peace, 2020

Israeli side and therefore departed from all previous concepts of peacemaking.
It practically institutionalized the imperatives of Israeli security and the philosophy underlying its settlement policy. It also read like a political platform aimed
at boosting Netanyahu's electoral chances and distracting public attention from
both Trump's and Netanyahu's legal woes.

More than a peace plan aimed at addressing the Palestinians' national yearnings, it is a plan aimed, as its drafters put it in patronizing terms, at "improving their lives." Two-thirds of the 181-page peace document is about the economic potential of Palestine. It endorses the entire Israeli national, religious, and security narrative—"Israel's valid historical claims," Judea and Samaria as the Jews' biblical homeland, the withdrawal from a territory taken in a war of self-defense being "unprecedented"—and none of the Palestinians'. It even endorses Israel's far-right ethnocratic ambitions by offering to strip Israeli Arabs of their citizenship. Israel would also control all access (by sea, air, and border crossings) to the Palestinian state. To gain the right for this sham state, the Palestinians would still have to disarm Hamas and prove they are a democratic community governed by the rule of law. And it is not only that Israel would not make any concessions on the right of return, but that she would also have the last word on how many would be allowed to return to the Palestinian state, lest this pose a threat to her security. As was the case with the British 1939 White Paper that limited Jewish immigration to Palestine, the return of refugees would depend on the economic capacity of the Palestinian state. What is also truly shocking is that Israel and the United States, not the Palestinians or any international body, would have the final word on whether the Palestinians had met the conditions for statehood. This is a self-appointed Israeli-American mandate on Palestine with utter disregard for international law and rules of conduct in the transition from war to peace.

Such a plan could be produced only against the background of a radically transformed Middle East where Palestine is the last of the regional actors' worries. The ambassadors of Bahrain, the United Arab Emirates, and Oman were present at the White House ceremony publicly showing their endorsement. But also those absent from the event, such as Jordan, Egypt, Saudi Arabia and other Gulf states, did not sound the alarm at such a blatantly biased peace project. In fact, they all—obliquely, one should say—supported it. Saudi Arabia, in particular, had been an intrinsic part of the lead-up process; its Crown Prince Mohammed bin Salman was fully complicit in the elaboration of the plan. Palestine has been dramatically demoted from being the unifying battle cry of an otherwise fragmented Arab world into the status of a nuisance, a financial and political burden for the Saudis and other Gulf States, an obstacle in the way of a new policy of rapprochement with the Jewish state. Saudi Arabia and the Gulf states are now, for the first time ever, relaxing travel bans on citizens of Israel, a country that is no longer viewed as a foe. Particularly surprising was the almost muted reaction in Jordan and Lebanon, both most likely to be affected by the plan. Jordan was bound to protest, but judging by its ambiguous attitude to Palestinian statehood, one must wonder whether it would not prefer having Israel, with which it had traditionally colluded in reining in Palestinian aspirations, rather than the Palestinians, as its neighbor. Hezbollah's reaction was right on target. Trump's "deal of shame," it said, would not have happened without the "complicity and betrayal" of several Arab states.

What now? In practice, nothing. Not one Palestinian would be found to negotiate on the basis of such terms. This is an utterly unimplementable plan. But catastrophe lurks behind the corner. The plan was born as a unilateral project and can only be implemented unilaterally if, say, Joe Biden were to be succeeded in 2024 by a Trump-like president.

Exit Oslo, Enter Madrid

The Oslo Accords proved to be a failed circumvention of the now forgotten parameters of the 1991 Madrid Peace Conference, where the Palestinian cause was represented by a Jordanian-Palestinian delegation, in principle in order to address Israel's opposition to a strictly Palestinian delegation under PLO control, but still alluding to a Jordanian-Palestinian solution as well. Oslo has long run its course. Is a return to Madrid just a mirage? Certainly no more than the undeliverable two-state solution.

Either of the ominous scenarios presented in Chapter 33 are likely to draw Jordan, out of sheer survival instinct, deeper into the affairs of the West Bank, as Egypt had been drawn against her will back into the affairs of Gaza. Both countries were the sovereign in these parts of the Palestinian homeland until Israel occupied them in 1967, and both were happy to let Israel be entangled in the unrewarding task of dealing with Palestine's ever unsatisfiable national yearnings. But with Gaza turning into Egypt's border with Iran, as Egypt's Chief of Intelligence Omar Suleiman put it to me in a meeting at his office in early March 2008, Egypt was forced to be drawn, perhaps irreversibly, into the affairs of Gaza. A similar reality was always in play with regard to Jordan and the West Bank. Palestine's and Jordan's destinies are intertwined. A major crisis in the West Bank will always be an inexorable domestic concern for Jordan. Recovering her presence in the West Bank can become, at highly threatening junctures, a vital necessity for the Hashemite kingdom.

The "peace industry" of the Israeli left has never suffered from a lack of ideas. Now, after all has failed and the specter of the one-state reality or a violent Israeli partial disengagement becomes ever closer, an architect of Oslo who despaired of his own creature, Yossi Beilin, has come up with the idea of an Israeli-Palestinian Confederation. In this "two states, one fatherland" concept, Jews and Arabs would move freely within their common space, no Israeli settlement in the Palestinian state would be dismantled, and Israel would accept Palestinian refugees in numbers similar to the Jewish population of the settlements, that is, more than half a million Palestinian refugees from Syria and Lebanon.

A mishmash of concepts that introduces the binational state through the backdoor, the Israeli-Palestinian Confederation would for all practical purposes be one state with a Palestinian demographic majority. It would not spare the parties the daily clash between two divergent nationalisms, one seeing itself part of the larger Arab and Muslim world and the other looking at the West as its natural point of reference. Moreover, what kind of a confederation is this between a pluralistic democracy, however imperfect, and an authoritarian system, which is what Palestine might turn out to be, in line with the general trend throughout the entire Arab world? How does one create common institutions uniting such politically disparate cultures and systems? Would the hundreds of thousands of Israeli settlers in Palestine be willing to live under the jurisdiction of a Palestinian state? Would Israelis and Palestinians accept having rotating presidencies, which is what confederations are supposed to have? Significantly, unlike a federation, a confederation is a political invention that exists nowhere in the world—for all practical purposes, Switzerland is a federation, not a confederation—for it means a union of two or more fully sovereign states.

The economic disparities between the two components of the confederation and the restless creativity of the Israeli socioeconomic system would still leave the Israelis as the dominant master race exploiting cheap Palestinian labor. In 2019, Israel's per-capita income was above $45,000 and rising, while that of the West Bank stood at $3,000. The consumption per capita in Israel is 32,000 shekels; in the West Bank it is 4,000. Israel has practically no unemployment (less than 4 percent before the pandemic); in the West Bank it is 30 percent. The average daily salary in Israel is 470 shekels; in the West Bank, 110. An OECD member, Israel ranks within the top twenty nations in the world in the latest report of the UN's Human Development Index. Colossal disparities exist also in the quality of infrastructures, both physical and scientific. Israel has all the harbors, railroads, power plants, desalination plants, nuclear reactors, highways, industrial complexes, international trade centers, top-class universities and research institutions, and high-tech belts on a par with Silicon Valley. Israel dedicates about 5 percent of its GDP, more than any other OECD country, to research and development. She has the second largest number of startup companies in the world after the United States. High-tech giants, such as Intel, Microsoft, and Apple, built their first overseas research and development facilities in Israel, and other high-tech multi-national corporations, such as IBM, Google, HP, Cisco Systems, Facebook, and Motorola, have also opened research and development centers in Israel.

An Israeli-Palestinian confederation would be a socially and culturally explosive merger between a prosperous Western society and millions of destitute Palestinians. Israeli cities would be filled with Palestinian ghettos of exploited cheap day laborers, and the friction between a master race of Israelis and the discriminated-against Palestinians would not be different than that which existed under South Africa's apartheid system. In fact, even after the end of apartheid, the black population in South Africa continues to be exploited and marginalized in an economy completely dominated by the white minority. One should not expect that the Palestinians would fare better under the economic domination of the nation that presumed to be "a light unto the nations." One has only to look at the despicable way the Israelis treat immigrants from Africa, and sometimes their own African Jews, the black Ethiopian communities. Israel would not behave with the Palestinians in the same way as West Germany met, after the fall of the Berlin Wall, her lost East German fellow citizens. And even there, thirty years after reunification, a widening gulf in practically all socioeconomic indicators is apparent as Eastern and Western social and political tribes are drifting apart in lingering mutual incomprehension.[1]

* * *

A Jordanian-Palestinian confederation, or federation, has a more compelling historical and sociopolitical logic. This would be a stable state, homogeneous in terms of religion, Arab history, and socioeconomic structures. The idea of a Jordanian-Palestinian state, indeed, has a long pedigree. It was actually in 1947 the position of Emil Sandström, the Swedish chairman of the United Nation's Special Committee on Palestine (UNSCOP) who was assigned to explore the feasibility of the partition of Palestine. Sandström, who saw no realistic possibility of accommodating two viable states west of the Jordan River, thought, against the view of the majority in the committee, that the partition of Palestine should have been between a Jewish and a Jordanian-Palestinian state.[2]

Years later, though morally committed to a "homeland" for the Palestinians, President Jimmy Carter (1977–81) toyed with the Jordanian option. In his conversations with the then prime minister Yitzhak Rabin, who insisted that there should not be a third state between Jordan and Israel, but only one Palestinian-Jordanian state consisting of "two entities, but only in one state," Carter suggested a possible model of two states within a federation, where Jordan would control defense and foreign policy and the West Bank state would be demilitarized. Countering the Israeli and American-Jewish outcry against his "homeland" idea, Carter later stated that he had never called for an independent Palestinian state, and if there was to be a Palestinian entity established in the West Bank, "It ought to be associated with Jordan." He reiterated the concept to Prime Minister Menachem Begin in 1977.[3]

Candidly, Carter's own legal counsel, Robert Lipshutz, accused of double talk those Arab leaders who called for Palestinian statehood. "They all recognize that it is in their worst interest to see that happen . . . The best outcome of all that is to end up in a federation of some type with Jordan."[4] Despite Anwar Sadat's rhetorical support for the Palestinians, his peace talks with Menachem Begin revealed a great deal of Egyptian antipathy toward the PLO and Palestinian nationalism, the same antipathy that I myself found in Morocco's King Hassan II when I met him in the summer of 1993. "Some of the PLO men are Soviet agents," Begin remarked. "All of them," Sadat replied. In concluding their talks, Begin reiterated his opposition "to a Palestinian state of Arafat and [Fatah leader] Kaddoumi." Sadat agreed: "As you know I have always been in favor of a link with Jordan—a federal or a confederal."[5]

During Ronald Reagan's presidency, instead of reviving a full-scale Israeli-Palestinian peace initiative, US officials again explored the Jordanian option of a moderate Palestinian infrastructure under the aegis of an Israeli-Jordanian arrangement.[6] Actually, when Reagan was still president-elect, Henry Kissinger, who was no longer in office, took the liberty of lobbying among Arab leaders for the Jordanian option. He also was prophetically of the view that the PLO was bound to radicalize the peace by raising issues "the Israelis can't handle." Kissinger wanted the United States to encourage a Jordanian-Palestinian federation, a view espoused at the time also by Richard Allen, Reagan's future national security adviser.[7] The resilience of the idea in Washington so many years after Jordan had given up in 1988 its right on the occupied West Bank was again manifested in Donald Trump's explicit call for it. As King Abdullah II confided to a team from the United States Middle East Project in 2018, Trump had suggested to him that Jordan take back the West Bank and create a Jordanian-Palestinian confederation. Abdullah's rejection of the idea did not dissuade Trump from offering a role to the Hashemite kingdom in his peace plan. "By virtue of territorial proximity, cultural affinity and family ties," Trump's "Deal of the Century" expected Jordan to play a "distinctive role in assisting the Palestinians on . . . institution building and municipal services." This sounded, admittedly, more like an attempt to harness Jordan to the task of laundering Israel's overarching domination west of the river, a key stipulation of Trump's peace plan.

When Israelis spoke in the past of the "Jordanian option," it was, as stipulated by the Alon Plan, in order to conveniently annex the strategically important parts of the West Bank, while ceding the densely inhabited areas to the Hashemite kingdom. The Israeli right has its own version of the Jordanian option, essentially annexing the whole of the West Bank and driving its population over the Jordan River, since "Jordan is anyway already a Palestinian state." They have always seen the Hashemite kingdom as an artificial British colonial project doomed to disappear. Its demise is now considered by Israel's far right vital to the grand project of annexing the West Bank without falling into the trap of a binational state. They hang their hopes on US withdrawal from Iraq, which is bound to strengthen Iran's grip on that country and allow her to extend her clout into Jordan's borders in a way that would further destabilize the Hashemite kingdom. This, in its turn, would facilitate the Israeli right's annexation schemes by turning Jordan into the

Palestinian homeland. The end of the Hashemite monarchy is then a joint project of Iran, the Israeli right, and America's messianic evangelicals.

It is true that Jordan was always seen as a fragile entity, a "political anomaly and a geographical nonsense," as Professor Avi Shlaim put it. Winston Churchill boasted that he created it with a stroke of his pen in 1921. A desert kingdom suffering from an endemic water deficit and an economy that is largely dependent on foreign aid, Jordan is also surrounded by belligerent neighbors such as Iraq and Syria. Yet, since Jordan's rise out of Mandatory Palestine, its destiny has been intimately linked to the Israeli-Palestinian conflict. Jordan successfully integrated most of the Palestinian refugees of the 1948 *Nakba*, and is the only Arab country that granted them full citizenship. Today, they and their descendants are the most dynamic element in the kingdom's economy.

Jordan has also outlasted all the predictions about its "inevitable" dissolution. Ruling Jordan has been for both King Hussein and the current king, Abdullah II, a permanent exercise in political jugglery at home—co-opting the leaders of protest movements, playing up divisions between Islamists and secularists, and Palestinians and East Bankers, and weathering the permanent tensions between rich and poor—and strategic cunning in dealing with external forces. Jordan has yet to find ways, however, to recover the role she lost to Egypt as the main mediator in the Israeli-Palestinian conflict. Israel's peace with the Gulf States without this being linked to a solution of the Palestinian problem was another setback to the Hashemite kingdom. But Jordan has one vital asset in Palestine. Her 1994 peace agreement with Israel codified her custodianship of the Muslim holy shrines in Jerusalem, including the Al-Aqsa Mosque. Israel is obligated to give due regard to Jordan's primary role in the exercise of her custodianship.

A Palestinian-Jordanian federate or confederate state has, then, a compelling historical logic and a political sense. It would satisfy the Palestinian yearning for statehood and would enhance Jordan's regional standing through the creation of a robust Jordanian-Palestinian entity, whose viability should be boosted by financial assistance and development schemes of great magnitude that the international community under US leadership must put in place. Such an updated "Jordanian option" also entails the abandoning by the Israeli far right of their dream of Jordan as the "alternative homeland" of the Palestinians to which they could be transferred. Jordan's former foreign minister, Marwan Muasher, rightly recently called upon the international community to help forestall any such plan that Israel might harbor.[8] But through a Jordan-Palestine peace with Israel, King Abdullah II would make true the dream of his great-grandfather, Abdullah I (whose kingdom included the West Bank as well), who was assassinated by a Palestinian in 1951 at the Al-Aqsa Mosque in Jerusalem for trying to make precisely such a peace with Israel.

How, then, would such a paradigm shift affect the parties? And why would Israel contemplate offering Jordan the kind of territorial concessions in the West Bank she resisted offering to the Palestinians? Why is it that when Israel negotiated peace with Arab states, she always accepted a return to the 1967 borders—Rabin made such a pledge to Syria's Hafez al-Assad without even meeting him, and Egypt got its land back to the last grain of Sinai's sand—but when it comes to the Palestinians she has always been adamant in rejecting the antebellum status quo?

Israel's Palestinian interlocutor is an unpredictable movement, not a state with a "Westphalian" behavior. Israel's peace treaty with Egypt was respected by the Egyptian state throughout all the turmoil of Egyptian politics—from President Sadat's assassination to the rise of the Muslim Brotherhood—while in the Golan Heights not one shot has been fired since the 1974 agreement on the separation of Israel's and Syria's military forces. States tend to have considerations of regional stability and are normally deterred by their enemy's military capabilities. National movements waging asymmetric wars are by definition revolutionary entities undisturbed by considerations of the balance of power. The Palestinians are today a movement institutionally invertebrate, devoid of a tradition of state-building, and split between pan-Islamist Hamas and ineffective secular nationalists still clinging to utterly unrealizable expectations.

With Jordan back in the equation, Israel would finally have a reliable, "Westphalian" interlocutor in an orderly state with a tradition of, and a vested interest in, compliance. Israel's security establishment has always had a high regard for Jordan's security forces; it would certainly prefer them as part of a neighboring security regime. With Jordan as an integral part of the solution, Israel could no longer use the convenient pretext of Palestinian institutional weakness to perpetuate the occupation of the West Bank, or, as Trump's plan has it, to encircle a crippled, fragmented Palestinian state under an overarching Israeli domination.

It is the widespread sense of despair at a deceitful peace process that should account for the considerable levels of support for the Jordanian-Palestinian confederation among Palestinians. Polls conducted by the Palestinian Center for Policy and Survey Research on June 13–15, 2013, showed that 55 percent of West Bank Palestinians supported the idea, a 10 percent increase since 2008. On May 13, 2016, a research institute affiliated with An-Najah National University in Nablus published the results of a survey indicating that 42 percent of Palestinians supported the establishment of a Jordanian-Palestinian confederation and 39 percent opposed it.[9] The Palestinians who welcome the idea of a confederation with Jordan are those who see the end of occupation as a more compelling necessity than separate statehood. President Abbas himself had expressed interest in the idea in a meeting with a group of Israelis on September 2, 2018.

Admittedly, the Jordanian option is no easy matter for the Palestinians. Traditionally, Jordan colluded with the Jewish state in reining in Palestinian nationalism. While the United Nations was debating the partition of Palestine into a Jewish and a Palestinian state in November 1947, an understanding was being reached between the Zionists and King Abdullah I of Jordan to partition Palestine between them. Also, Jordan's Black September (1970) ruthless war against the PLO, which resulted in the death of thousands of Palestinians, remains a sad landmark in the history of Palestinian nationalism. Jordan's opposition to the creation of a Palestinian state persisted even beyond King Hussein's 1988 decision to waive Jordan's claim to the West Bank, a decision he might not have taken if it were not for the pressure of the Arab League.

Jordan's Palestinian vocation is an innate reality built into the very origins of the Jordanian state. In the collective memory of Palestinian West Bankers, Jordan, where between 60 to 70 percent of the population is of Palestinian origin, represents a common past, a benign hinterland, the lost promise of freedom of movement, an outlet into the Arab world and the opportunities it offered. Even today, Amman, not Tel Aviv, is the business capital for West Bank Palestinians. Governments in Amman always had, as they still do, Palestinian representatives. Jordan was never seen in the West Bank as an alien power or a foreign oppressor; the Jordanian Arab Legion was seen as a protector, not an occupying force. Abu Ala, my Palestinian interlocutor, used to lament that the Hashemite monarchy had "distanced itself from the Palestinian question," since, he insisted, "a solution between Israel and Palestine is bound to have a Jordanian context." Traditionally, Palestinian nationalism was a Gaza affair, and Fatah was fundamentally a Gazan creature founded in 1959 by Yasser Arafat at Cairo University with a strong component of Palestinian refugees from Gaza. The West Bank was home to more pan-Arab movements, such as the Movement of Arab Nationalists founded in the late 1940s by George Habash at the American University of Beirut, and it never developed a legacy of separate Palestinian state-building.[10]

But history has of course, moved on. Palestinian nationalism in the West Bank was inflamed and galvanized through the resistance to Zionism and the Israeli occupation, and the new generations of Palestinians no longer share the memories of a remote past under Jordanian rule. But, as the polls suggest, the unfulfilled yearning for an end to the Israeli occupation edges Palestinians to a sober weighing of options where the Jordanian option can potentially win adherents. The international credibility of a Palestinian state would be boosted through a confederative arrangement with Jordan, probably one of the most orderly states in the Arab world. Also, the key issue of refugee resettlement would be better facilitated in a broader Jordanian-Palestinian economic structure.

Already home to more than 2,000,000 Palestinian refugees, 400,000 of whom are still living in camps, Jordan should expect a massive international effort, in which Israel has to participate out of a moral and political obligation, to finance schemes of resettlement and rehabilitation.

King Hussein, in line with most Arab leaders, never favored a fully independent Palestinian state. They all feared it could be radicalized and fall into the hands of a "Qadhafi-like leader," as Jimmy Carter had put it. To Hussein, such a scenario was an imminent existential threat to Jordan, given that a Palestinian state could not but inherit the revolutionary traits of the Palestinian national movement. Palestine, he feared, would develop irredentist aspirations toward Jordan and irremediably destabilize the kingdom. This was what pushed him as early as 1972 to propose turning the two sides of the Jordan River into a "Joint Arab Kingdom," and in 1977 to advance the idea of a federation with the West Bank. The PLO, he said then, was the creation of Arab summits, not the choice of the Palestinian people.[11] Hussein's plans represented a challenge to the nationalists in the kingdom who viewed the creation of a separate Palestinian state as the best way to demarcate clear lines between Jordan's identity and Palestinian nationalism. But Hussein persisted nevertheless, and in 1985 he again promoted his confederation idea. At that point, Arafat also saw the confederation as a realistic strategy for him to get control of the West Bank. On February 11, a joint Jordanian-Palestinian communiqué was issued whereby "Palestinians will exercise their inalienable right of self-determination . . . within the context of . . . a confederated Arab States of Jordan and Palestine," for which the two parties called for an international conference where they would negotiate peace with Israel through a "joint Jordanian-Palestinian delegation."[12]

However, on February 19, 1986, the king was forced to end the Jordan-PLO initiative. As it turned out, Arafat refused to endorse UN Resolutions 242 and 338 as the basis upon which peace would be negotiated with Israel. Hussein lamented the PLO's departure from "the shared destiny of Jordan and Palestine." The confederation, he said, was "a matter of shared history, experience, culture, economy and social structure . . . a confluence of interest." The Palestinians were thus missing an opportunity to link their political salvation to Jordan, "a sovereign state which enjoys credible international standing," as the king put it. He rejected as utterly unconvincing Arafat's pretext that for him to accept Resolution 242 he needed American acceptance of the Palestinian right of self-determination within the context of the Jordanian-Palestinian confederation. That was a matter, Hussein explained, that did not concern the Americans; it was "a matter for Jordanians and Palestinians . . . as long as we are committed" to the February 1985 accord. Hussein made it clear, however, that notwithstanding the failure of this phase of the process, he still believed in the "equality of rights and obligations in facing our joint destiny."[13]

But Jordan was now on a collision course with the PLO. In retaliation, the king closed down the PLO office in Amman, and in his drive to sideline the PLO, he intensified his attempt to have a foothold in the West Bank through an economic development plan which he conceived, with American backing, together with his Israeli interlocutors at the time, Prime Minister Shimon Peres and Defense Minister Yitzhak Rabin. Economic development was to the king a way to stem the radicalization of the West Bank, which he always saw as an existential threat to Jordan. But the attempt to circumvent the PLO could not succeed. On July 31, 1988, King Hussein was forced by the pan-Arab consensus to declare Jordan's disengagement from the West Bank. Admittedly, the international and regional impact of the Palestinian uprising—the First Intifada was then in full swing—was perceived as a Palestinian affirmation of national identity which the king could not be seen as standing against. "Jordan is not Palestine," he now said, and the "independent Palestinian state should be created in the occupied Palestinian state after its liberation."[14]

But the king did not succumb to the pan-Arab consensus before he had made a last-ditch attempt to reach an agreement with Israel's then foreign minister, Shimon Peres, to solve the Palestinian question within a Jordanian context. Although it essentially dealt with the procedures of an international conference where the Palestinian cause would be represented by a Jordanian-non-PLO Palestinian delegation, the April 1987 London Agreement was a desperate attempt to rescue the "Jordanian option" and derail what both Israel and Jordan saw as a threat, the Palestinian drive to an independent state. But Israel's hardline prime minister Yitzhak Shamir disavowed his foreign minister and buried the entire London package.

Did the 1993 Oslo Accords establishing a roadmap for Palestinian statehood settle the debate in Jordan in favor of an independent Palestinian state in the West Bank? If anything, Hussein's fears only increased. The moment he knew of the Oslo Accords he ordered the closure of the bridges linking the West and the East Banks for fear of a mass exodus of Palestinians that would end up subverting the kingdom. The May 1994 Israeli-PLO economic agreement was another setback for the king, who now saw the emergence of an Israeli-Palestinian economic space that would undermine Jordan's economic ties with the West Bank and produce, as a result, unemployment and political instability in the kingdom. Not in vain did he persist in his efforts to always have a foothold in the West Bank, particularly in East Jerusalem.

It is intriguing, indeed, why King Hussein became the only Arab leader to publicly endorse Benjamin Netanyahu in Israel's 1996 elections and rejoice in the defeat of Shimon Peres. One reason was his total lack of trust in Peres. More important was the king's fear that, with the architect of Oslo in power, the road might be paved to a Palestinian state, whereas Netanyahu could be the undertaker of Oslo, which he had promised to be throughout the campaign. That in 1995 Netanyahu shared with an incredulous Jordanian ambassador in Israel, Marwan Muasher, his hope that the two countries could collaborate in preventing the creation of a Palestinian state was because he sensed that this was not too outlandish an assumption to share with the king. As the late Eitan Haber, Yitzhak Rabin's chief of Cabinet and confidant, related to me, on the eve of the signing of the peace agreement between Israel and Jordan in October 1994, King Hussein still mentioned to Rabin, certainly with a degree of levity, the return of the West Bank to Jordan's sovereignty as the best way to prevent the creation of a Palestinian state neither of them truly wanted.

Today, the question is whether the bride, Jordan, is interested anymore in the dowry. She is not, but with a nuance. The Jordanian establishment has lost none of the fears and concerns of King Hussein with regard to the potential threat represented by a radical, disorderly Palestinian state. True, King Abdullah II professed more than once to be "fed up" with talks of a Jordanian-Palestinian confederation. He defined this as "a conspiracy against both Palestine and Jordan." Yet he always left a door open to the possibility that "once a Palestinian state is created" in negotiations with Israel, "Palestinians and Jordanians will decide the nature of relations between them." It is safe to assume, however, that the mistrust and fear of a revolutionary Palestinian state was not just the particular obsession of his father. It struck me when, during a visit I made to the king in Amman ahead of the Camp David summit, he advised me to shift back to the Syrian track and relegate the Palestinian process to a secondary priority. Did he truly trust that the Palestinians could create an orderly state that would not put at risk the stability of his kingdom? As the then Secretary of State Condoleezza Rice told me in a meeting in Washington in March 2008, King Abdullah had agreed to consider, as part of the Annapolis process, having an international force stationed on the Jordanian side of the border, as if it were Jordan not Israel, that needed security guarantees against the threats emanating from a disorderly Palestinian state.

This sequence—a Palestinian state first and confederation later—represents a consensus among the supporters of the confederation idea in Jordan. When, in December 2012, rumors spread of President Abbas's support and lobbying for the confederation, even the Jordanian Muslim Brotherhood, which back in 1988 had opposed King Hussein's decision to waive Jordan's rights on the West Bank as an unacceptable deviation from the principle of Arab and Islamic unity, insisted that the Jordanian option could be addressed "only after the liberation of Palestine."

But national security options are generally weighed against an environment of threats and opportunities. Jordan would consider the Jordanian option only as a last resort to safeguard its national security, not as a way to solve an Israeli predicament or respond to a Palestinian necessity. Although Jordan no longer refers to the West Bank as a lost territory that should be recovered, it is from the West Bank that a major Israeli-Palestinian crisis can produce streams of Palestinian refugees who can put in jeopardy the delicate demographic balance in the kingdom and undermine its independent identity. But what if the two-state solution continues to elude us? The alternative fantasy of Israel's growing far right, the one-state project, binational but under Jewish primacy—a potential, unilateral implementation of Trump's plan *does* make possible precisely such an ominous fantasy—is bound to usher in a state of permanent civil war between Arab and Jew, the effects of which are bound to spill over into Jordan.

Notwithstanding Jordan's official position, the Jordanian option dies hard even in Amman. King Hussein's 1988 decision to waive Jordan's claim on the West Bank was never ratified in Parliament, and is still seen by many as unconstitutional. Also, eminent Jordanians, among them a former royal adviser, Adnan Abu-Odeh, and two former prime ministers, Abdel Salaam Majali and Taher al-Masri, had been on public record for their blunt support of the confederation. Majali even arrived in Israel to lobby for the idea.[15]

Significantly, the trigger for Majali's Jordanian-Palestinian confederation plan of 2007 was his fear that Ehud Olmert's convergence plan would lead to massive migration or forced transfer of desperate Palestinians into Jordan. Jordan can never be unaware of the threat of a Hamas takeover of the West Bank in the aftermath of such an Israeli disengagement. That Abbas and his PLO continue to govern in Ramallah is today principally due to their cooperation with Israel's security services in persecuting Hamas activists and local leadership. With Israel redeploying, Hamas could recover in the West Bank just as it did in Gaza in the wake of Israel's withdrawal. This in its turn could embolden the Islamic Action Front, the Jordanian extension of the Muslim Brotherhood, to a degree not acceptable to the Jordanian establishment.

If it is to have any positive effect on the possibility of an Israeli-Palestinian settlement, the Jordanian-Palestinian confederation and all the guarantees that go with it should be part of a tripartite peace deal, not an item to be negotiated after a Palestinian state has been created, something that, left to their own devices, Israelis and Palestinians are inherently incapable of producing. Jordan's involvement in negotiations on the future of the West Bank is crucial only if it is bold, robust, and free of complexes.

This was exactly what Abdel Salaam Majali proposed. As an old chief negotiator with Israel, he knew how remote the chance of an Israeli-Palestinian bilateral peace was. He, therefore, explained that a Jordanian-Palestinian state was the mechanism through which the two-state solution might materialize, for only Jordan had the credibility to give the necessary security assurances to Israel. He assumed that Jordan would be in a far better position than the Palestinians to get from Israel a deal based on its return to the 1967 lines with agreed border modifications and land swaps. Majali's plan was an updating of King Hussein's federation plan of March 1972 and the 1985 agreement between Arafat's PLO and Jordan to seek Palestinian self-determination within a Jordanian-Palestinian confederation. Majali also introduced into his plan elements of the Lebanese consociational constitution. Both the legislative and the executive authorities would be based on equal representation for the two states, with a Palestinian and a Jordanian rotating in the positions of speaker and prime minister. The king would be the head of state not in his capacity as Jordan's king, but as a descendent of the Hashemite dynasty and, as such, also of the Prophet, and the Palestinians living in Jordan would have the option of choosing between Palestinian or Jordanian nationality. A serious sticking point is what would become of Gaza. Would it be part of the confederation once it finally merges with the West Bank under a united leadership? Would it stay as an Islamic independent quasi-state? Or would it absorbed as an Egyptian protectorate? In the grand peace designs of King Abdullah I, Gaza was to be part of the Hashemite Kingdom.

Majali's plan was far from being universally applauded in Jordan. But it dies hard. On a visit to the West Bank on May 22, 2016, Majali reiterated his conviction that the confederation was the best option for both Jordanians and Palestinians. This triggered the dispatch of a delegation of 350 Palestinian notables to plead with King Abdullah to reactivate the confederation plan. Their call was reinforced by an An-Najah National University poll in the West Bank suggesting a slight majority (42.9 percent to 39.3 percent) for the supporters of the idea among Palestinians.[16] President Abbas's expiring leadership and the Diadochi war that would probably follow his departure would possibly boost the popular call for a Jordan connection.

Most probably, Majali's plan was a trial balloon that could not have been launched without King Abdallah's acquiescence. It shows that when the context calls for it—now, the death of the two state solution, and then, in 2007, it was the civil war in Gaza, the fear of a spillover of the fight between Hamas and Fatah to the East Bank, and Prime Minister Olmert's convergence plan that threatened to trigger a stream of Palestinian refugees from the West Bank into Transjordan—decision-makers in Jordan, with the king at their head, might be willing to challenge Jordanian nationalists and other opponents of the Jordanian-Palestinian option. An Israeli unilateral implementation of Trump's plan would be an even more ominous scenario than Olmert's convergence plan. Both Israel's unilateralism and her osmotic decline into a one-state reality are extreme scenarios, each of which could lead Jordan, out of a genuine sense of self-defense, to be drawn back into the Palestinian question. With the demise of the classic two-state paradigm, an agreement within a Jordanian-Palestinian-Israeli triangle might still be the Palestinians' last remaining hope of building a viable state. The Jordanian option would give Israel the security guarantees it needs, but would not save her the territorial price of peace.

Jordan's understandable reluctance might be attenuated by its renewed capacity to control adverse processes in Palestine that threaten her stability. Such a confederation would also allow Jordan to acquire geostrategic critical mass in an ever more dangerous region. The Jordanian option would also represent a paradigm shift that the international community should join the Arab world in supporting. Historians and prophets have never lived in peace with each other, and there is, of course, no certainty that the Jordanian solution would come to pass. But it is worth earnestly exploring, if only because, if all we ever do is all we ever did, then all we will ever get is all we ever got, and possibly worse.

PART V

DEFYING THE LOGIC
OF CONFLICT RESOLUTION

Palestine: A Comparative Perspective

God, it's hard. It's nothing like I have ever dealt with—all the negotiations with the Irish, all the stuff I have done with the Palestinians before this and with the Israelis, the Balkans at Dayton.
Bill Clinton, *The New York Daily News*, July, 17, 2000 [in the middle of the Camp David summit]

"Happy families are all alike; every unhappy family is unhappy in its own way." Tolstoy's opening words in *Anna Karenina* are applicable to conflict-ridden societies unhappy in their own way. This does not mean that similarities cannot be found or analogies made. Like a number of other multidimensional conflicts around the world, Palestine transcends facile analogies and has been singularly resistant to a peaceful denouement. A comparative perspective that looks at other conflicts and the way they were or failed to be resolved may help illustrate why the promise of peace in Palestine has remained so tragically unfulfilled. This should not exempt us from the responsibility we bear for our failures, but it would perhaps make our shortcomings more comprehensible.

War as a Prelude to Peace

Winston Churchill's assertion that "nothing in history was ever settled except by wars" is a sad truth borne out by the history of international conflicts. Conflicts become ripe for diplomatic solution only when the parties get trapped in unbearably painful military deadlocks. Without such a deadlock, the 1973 Yom Kippur War could hardly have ushered in an Israeli-Egyptian peace. It was the first Gulf War and the first Palestinian Intifada that created the conditions for the 1991 Madrid Peace Conference and the subsequent Oslo Accords. History teaches us that without such mutually damaging deadlocks, neither UN resolutions nor premature peace initiatives can cut short the war dynamic. As my friend Joaquín Villalobos, a former guerrilla commander in El Salvador's civil war, instructed me, the conflict became ripe for a solution once the failure of the

Farabundo Martí National Liberation Front's (FMLN) 1989 offensive showed the insurgents that they could not trigger a popular uprising, and the army that it could not protect the right-wing establishment anymore. In a different theater of conflict, it was the precarious military stalemate created by the June 1988 Techipa-Calueque battles that led to the resolution of the Cuba-Angola-South Africa conflict. Diplomacy has hardly ever succeeded in solving a conflict before war, or the threat thereof, has forced the parties to the negotiating table. It was NATO's robust military intervention that created the conditions for the end of genocide and ethnic cleansing in the former Yugoslavia. Martti Ahtisaari's success in resolving the Kosovo conflict would not have materialized before Serbia was militarily humbled.

This is also the case in struggles for self-determination. States were normally born amid dramas of blood and self-sacrifice. The peaceful split of Norway and Sweden and the amicable divorce of the Czech and Slovak republics have never been the norm, which is not an irrelevant message these days to Catalonia in its extravagant drive for an amicable split from Spain. The Palestinian president Mahmoud Abbas's strategy of getting a Palestinian state through the goodwill of the international community is flawed. Equally flawed was the hope of the Irish nationalists in 1919 of getting statehood on a silver platter from the Versailles peace conference. They would have it two years later, but only after making life unbearable for the British occupier. Lloyd George's envoy to the Irish negotiations, Sir Alfred Cope, ended up advising his boss,

> We are willing to acknowledge that we are defeated. There is nothing else for us to do but draft . . . four hundred thousand men and exterminate the whole population of the country, and we are not willing to do that. . . . We are willing to withdraw our whole establishment from the lowest policeman to the highest judge.[1]

Algeria's bitter struggle for independence is another case in point; 300,000 Algerians died in one of the most savage wars of the postcolonial era. Rooted in the merciless behavior of France's imperial army, the war conducted by the 450,000 French troops sent to quell the resistance of the Algerian National Liberation Front (FLN) was of such cruelty and scope as the Palestinian occupied territories have never experienced. This might partly explain why the war's outcome, just as the US defeat in Vietnam, was eventually decided by the collapse of the imperial power's home front. "It is not their violence, but ours, turned back," noted philosopher Jean-Paul Sartre.[2] The abhorrence of what their army was doing in their name was overwhelming; in a referendum, 65 percent of the French supported independence for Algeria. France's Fourth Republic simply disintegrated under the strains of the war. The man who was placed in power by the army, General Charles de Gaulle, was eventually forced to negotiate with the FLN and, in the Évian peace settlement of March 1962, grant independence to Algeria. The agreement stipulated that a million French settlers who had conducted a scorched earth campaign in a desperate attempt to prevent the inevitable could stay in Algeria. But, being no longer the master race in a colonized country, most of them returned to France. More recently, East Timor and parts of the former Yugoslavia also achieved independence because they exhausted their occupiers or their internal rivals. And so did South Sudan, a new, now failing state that emerged out of a twenty-two year civil war that left behind more than two million dead.

Alas, blood and sacrifice are not always sufficient. Ask the Kurds, the Chechens, the Tibetans, or the Palestinians. The Israeli-Palestinian conflict does not respond to history's lesson that diplomacy produces results only when backed by overwhelming power. The logic of statesmen and leaders facing insurgencies or bloody wars—de Gaulle in Algeria, Kissinger in Vietnam, Mandela and de Klerk in South Africa, Anwar Sadat in the Yom Kippur War with Israel, Gerry Adams and Ian Paisley in Northern Ireland, Juan Manuel Santos in Colombia—who ended up recognizing the limits of what power can achieve failed to work in Palestine. Nor has Israel's oppression of the Palestinians shaped public perception of the conflict in the way it did in France and the United States during the Algerian and Vietnam Wars respectively, and even in Russia during the first phase of the Chechnya war. In all these cases the occupying armies were defeated by strong antiwar sentiment back home.[3] In Israel, the opposite is true: the war on Palestinian "terror" boosts popular support for what the army is doing in the nation's name.

Arguably, however, the real meaning of the transformation of the battlefield from interstate wars to the asymmetric conflicts of today lies in that the Clausewitzian convention of military action facilitating a political solution is hardly applicable anymore. The idea of war as a major conclusive diplomatic event has simply become obsolete. The era of glorious wars is over, and "victory" no longer brings peace, simply because there will always be another war after the war. The war in Kosovo lasted for two months only to usher in a six-year asymmetric conflict. And America's three-week "shock and awe" campaign in Iraq ended in "mission accomplished" with the toppling of Saddam Hussein, but opened the gates of hell for the forces of occupation for more than a decade. The return of the Taliban in Afghanistan many years after their regime was dismantled is now an uncontested reality. As in Vietnam, the world's superpower broke into the run in Afghanistan with helicopters shuttling American diplomats from their embassy. Nor could the Israelis with their overwhelming technological capabilities claim victory over Hezbollah in the 2006 Lebanon war, and against Hamas in Gaza in four consecutive wars. Fifteen years after the merciless pounding of Hezbollah positions, the organization is today even stronger than it was before the war. With more rockets and missiles falling on the north of Israel in thirty-three days than the sum of all German V1s and V2s hitting Britain in World War II, the Israelis had to reckon with an entirely new phenomenon, an asymmetric entity with a nation-state firepower.

Civil wars seem to have their own logic. They tend to evoke the most intense passions, which make peace offers into fragile equilibria that are almost impossible to enforce. That was the case of the Laotian civil war (1962–75) and that in Cyprus (1974), where the settlement only became the avenue to a new conflict. Almost invariably, therefore, civil wars end with the predominance of one of the parties, as was the case in the two most notable civil wars in modern history, the American (1861–65) and the Spanish (1936–39). Such was also the case in the civil wars in Greece (1946–49), China (1927–49), and Russia (1917–22), and the Malayan Emergency (1948–60). More recently, Syria's civil war has shown that victory is possible only when the superior power is willing to break all the rules of warfare, show no mercy for the defeated, and defy the sensibilities of the international community. Many years of mediation and endless peace proposals in Sri Lanka's conflict with the Tamil Tigers failed to end the war. "Peace" came about with the total and unconditional defeat of the Tamils. What sometimes separates victory from stalemate is the question of whether the superior power is a democracy respectful of the humanitarian rules of war or a dictatorship blind and deaf to humanitarian concerns and international opprobrium. Colombia, a democratic state with a vocation for an improved international status, discarded the Sri Lanka way, and turned the military deadlock into an avenue to peace. But President Putin in Russia and President Mahinda Rajapaska in Sri Lanka oppressed the Chechens and the Tamils respectively with utter indifference to international opinion.

The Israeli-Palestinian conflict started in 1947 as a civil war that the Israelis won resoundingly, but then became a clash between two separate national entities that belies the logic of war and peace being connected vessels. This is so because either the mutual deadlock suffered by the parties is not unbearable enough or, what is more probable, the parties prefer to pay the price of conflict rather than compromise their irreconcilable national dreams. And though it is a democracy for which the threat of international opprobrium is a major strategic concern, Israel could only go as far as she could in her peace offers, but certainly not beyond, in order to meet the Palestinians' unrealistic expectations. For, this is no normal sort of conflict; it is not just a collision over territory, or a banal border dispute; it is a clash of rights and memory. Jewish millennial certificates of ownership clash with the Palestinian longing for the abandoned fig tree and terrace farming. The yearning for the same landscapes, the mutually exclusive claims on religious sites and symbols, ánd the ethos of dispossession made the parties' national narratives practically irreconcilable. A mirror image of each other, Israelis and Palestinians compete for the monopoly on victimhood, "exile," "holocaust," and "return."

Even without possessing such a military arsenal as Hezbollah does in Lebanon or Hamas in Gaza, Arafat's PLO did not arrive in Camp David as a defeated nation willing to compromise its core national demands for the sake of peace with the occupier. Nor have fifty-four years of military occupation and the unceasing punishment of the Palestinian population in two Intifadas, as well as a fifteen-year-long inhumane siege of, and a number of wars against, Gaza, changed an iota of what the Palestinians see as their minimum requirements for peace with Israel. In Israel-Palestine, war was a defining event only in so far as it led to negotiations; it could never force on the parties a peace settlement that compromised their core narratives and national security interests.

Northern Ireland and Colombia

Inevitably, there are always notable similarities between conflict situations whatever their origin and evolution might be. In the cases of Northern Ireland and Palestine, they range from the parties' competing narratives of victimhood to the role of external enablers. Irish-Americans and the Republic of Ireland supported the IRA and Sinn Fein, the Israel lobby in the US and American administrations lined up with Israel, while Arab states backed, and even went to war for the sake of, Palestine. At some point, both conflicts even had the same US mediator, Senator George Mitchell for the Clinton administration in Northern Ireland and later for Barack Obama in Palestine.

But Palestine has serially defeated each and every mediator. How revealing it is that George Mitchell succeded in Northern Ireland and failed in Palestine. He who affirmed in an address to the United States Instititute of Peace in May 2010 that "there is no such a thing as a conflict that can't be ended . . . I saw it happen in Northern Ireland . . . I believe deeply that with committed, persevering, and patient diplomacy, it can happen in the Middle East"[4] eventually lost patience with the tantalizing difficulties of the Israel-Palestinian situation and simply gave up his mission.

In 2016, after fifty years of armed conflict that left behind more than a quarter of a million dead, almost double the number of casualties in the Israeli-Palestinian century-old conflict, and seven million displaced persons, Colombia signed a historic peace agreement with the FARC guerrilla group, the last hangover of the Cold War in the Western hemisphere. But, unlike the case of Palestine, Colombia's conflict had one key "advantage": it was a sociopolitical insurgency

free of any religious, ethnic, or territorial contentions. Conversely, the characteristics of the Northern Ireland conflict—an ethnosectarian divide between two
competing communities, Republican Catholics and Protestant Unionists—are
presumably closer to those prevailing in Israel-Palestine. But only presumably,
for the notable differences are indeed of a defining nature. Israel-Palestine is a
bitter dispute between warring nations, not an intercommunity schism where,
as in Northerm Ireland, power-sharing could attenuate the conflict, and in
Colombia's case make the guerrillas' political integration the end of conflict.

Israel-Palestine is a hybrid conflict that has in it the traits of a resilient civil
war—the fight over the same fatherland by people inhabiting the same area—
that always called for the unconditional exclusion, even destruction, of the other,
and a national conflict over borders and self-determination. For the Palestinians,
Israel is both an occupying power and a homeland. Their war with Zionism is
a uniquely powerful clash marked by the yearnings of the dispossessed nation
for a lost land and for the holy shrines of Islam. For the Israelis, the conflict is
about the return to their ancestral, biblical cradle, as well as about the Zionist
constituent ethos of settling the land and defining the state's political borders
along the lines of its outer settlements. "We are a generation that settles the land,
and without the steel helmet and the canon's maw, we will not be able to plant a
tree and build a home," was how then Chief of Staff General Moshe Dayan put
it in a defining elegy for a murdered soldier in 1956. The parties' drive to alter
the demographic balance—Israel through Jewish immigration and the expansion of settlements and the Palestinians through the threat of the refugees' right
of return—is another vital component of the conflict driving Israelis to create
segregagtion walls, and fueling the Palestinians' hope of a victory through what
Arafat himself defined as "the biological weapon . . . the womb of the Palestinian
mother."[5]

Peace in Colombia and Northern Ireland was essentially a trade-off between
disarmament and political participation, between demobilization and power-
sharing. In both cases, the neighboring states played a vital role in smoothing
the way to the peace settlement. Peace in Northern Ireland was immensely
facilitated by the full collaboration of the Irish Republic, which in its December
1993 joint Downing Street Declaration with the British government agreed to
abandon an endgame based on a united Ireland. Similarly, peace in Colombia
was made possible thanks also to the radical change of attitude of Venezuela,
Ecuador, and Cuba, all old allies of the guerrilla group, which actively pushed
the FARC insurgency to the negotiating table.

Such a regional envelope of proactive and unbiased support, which had also
existed in the Central American Esquipulas Peace Accords of the mid-1980s,
in the form of the "friendly states" ("países amigos") headed by Costa Rica's
President Óscar Arias, for which he was later awarded the Nobel Peace Prize,

never existed in the case of Palestine. The Arab states were there only as the advocates of the Palestinian cause, which was understandable but not particularly helpful in the negotiating process.

The peace process in both Northern Ireland and Colombia also benefited from a uniquely engaged civil society. True, Israel has known throughout the years mass demonstrations in support of a historic compromise in Palestine; millions of dollars from foreign donors helped finance projects of "people to people"; and Israeli NGOs like B'Tselem, Peace Now, Breaking the Silence, and many others such as joint Israeli-Palestinian associations of bereaved families or Women in Black, which protests the treatment of Palestinians at army checkpoints, still do admirable work in alerting Israeli society to the sins of occupation. But they never had a truly transformative impact on the peace process. Oslo was not a bottom-up process. Like the 1993 Arusha Peace Accords for Rwanda, Oslo was an elite affair negotiated in a secluded Norwegian castle that left not only the public at large but even the state's bureaucracy and the army's hierarchy without a perceived stake in the process.[6]

Conversely, throughout the Northern Ireland process, many thousands of NGOs were involved in creating contact between the warring communities. By conferring the 1976 Nobel Peace Prize on Betty Williams and Mairead Corrigan, co-founders of Community of Peace People, a civil society organization dedicated to promoting a peaceful resolution to the Troubles, the Nobel Committee acknowledged how vital the work of NGOs was in carrying out pedagogical work within the communities to help them overcome their inflexible perception of the other. NGOs practically acted as indigenous mediators working to take the prerogative for political discussion from the sole ownership of the politicians. Initiative 92 was a major cross-community program that gathered over a long period of time the views of local communities on the future of Northern Ireland. The resulting Opsahl Report was a compilation of hundreds of peace proposals emanating from society, which eventually helped generate the final agreement.

Like synagogues in Israel and mosques in Palestine, churches in Northern Ireland resisted endorsing cross-community projects. But, unlike the synagogues and the mosques, where the other is feared and demonized, churches in Northern Ireland eventually succumbed to social pressure and started to host cross-community projects. Initiatives such as Joint Bible Study Groups, joint services following acts of violence, including inviting clergy of the other denomination to preach, became significant in moderating the cross-community discourse in a country with one of the highest levels of church attendance in Western Europe.

Not unlike Israel's occupation practices in Palestine, the police and the military in Northern Ireland used harsh tactics of control and domination. In both cases, checkpoints, house searches, abusive language, blackmail of individuals to turn them into police spies, beatings, and arbitrary arrests were all daily practices. The diference was, however, that the challenge of NGOs in Northern Ireland bore fruit, and civil society groups such as the Londonderry Peace and Reconciliation NGO succeded in moderating the behavior of the security forces, which started to improve their recruitment processes and develop social skills in dealing with intercommunity tensions. No such impact was produced on Israel's practices in occupied Palestine. The overwhelming popular backing for the IDF's fight against "Palestinian terrorism" is an iron-clad domestic foundation for Israel's occupation practices. The Supreme Court, not civil society, is the only possible brake on the IDF's behavior in Palestinian lands.

Walls in both Northern Ireland and Palestine are tragic monuments to the fear of the other. Israeli NGOs that persistently protested against the inhumane encirclement of Palestinian communities behind the separation wall and tried to develop cross-wall social and economic projects could never have the effect that NGOs in Belfast and other cities in Northern Ireland did in turning areas of war and blockade into peace spaces. They also incorporated in such endeavors ex-prisoners returning to their communities. Though never lacking in NGOs and in important sectors of society intimately attuned to the plight of the Palestinians, Israeli society at large never embraced these effective ways of reaching out to the other; it saw the separation wall as a legitimate, vitally necessary means to keep terrorists at bay, and looked at the Palestinian prisoners as bestial murderers. NGOs in Northern Ireland ran projects to counter the ghettoizing factor of the so-called "peace walls" that separated communities. One such initiative was the "Interface Project" that metaphorically built doors into the walls throughout Belfast by helping break the emotional and physical walls that separated warring communities. By creating the necessary conditions for a dialogue between Protestant paramilitaries and Catholic communities, NGO's in Northern Ireland became key agents of peacemaking. Without their invaluable contribution it would have been impossible to conceive the 1998 Good Friday Agreement.[7]

Central to the Colombian peace process were the victims. The United Nations and the National University in Bogotá followed the official negotiations with a gathering of a thousand people from victims organizations to make proposals to the negotiators in Havana. The latter eventually got from these gatherings a whole twelve volumes of comments and suggestions, which gave them a sense of the way the victims saw the entire process. The negotiators also opened a "virtual postbox" through which other victims could send their own proposals. Dozens of victims were also invited to Havana to offer their own testimonies of the atrocities they suffered at the hands of FARC. The guerrilla leaders at the negotiating table confronted their victims for the first time. As one negotiator later told me, several members of FARC were seen crying in the corridors. The entire mechanism of transitional justice agreed in Havana was actually elaborated with input from the victims. This was how a concept—the

"Comprehensive System of Truth, Justice, Reparation, and Non-Repetition"—was agreed upon to meet the rights of the victims. This required putting in place a whole range of institutions: the Special Jurisdiction for Peace, the Commission for the Clarification of Truth, Coexistence, and Non-Repetition, and the Special Unit for Disappeared Persons.

It is one thing to end an armed conflict, quite another to build peace on the ground. Citizen participation was also encouraged in Colombia during the phase of the implementation of the peace accords. The entire three-hundred-page peace settlement is full of measures on how to mobilize citizens around the implementation of every point in the agreement, from rural development to the justice mechanism, from political participation to the admission into the community of reintegrated guerrillas. Measures passed through the filter of citizen deliberations allowed peace to respond to the genuine needs of the population and thus acquire a broad-based popular legitimacy. Participatory models of peacemaking were tried successfully in other conflicts too, from South Africa to Guatemala, from Mali to the Philippines. In Mali, indigenous traditions of community decision-making were harnessed to create spaces for social involvement in deliberations leading to localized peace agreements. In the Guatemalan peace process, a Civil Society Assembly operated in parallel to the official negotiations mandating diverse sectorial groupings to develop detailed proposals that were incorporated into the final agreement. To heal the wounds of apartheid, South Africa also developed mechanisms for engaging civil society at national, regional, and local levels.

That civil society's mobilization in Israel did not have the same transformative impact on the chances of peace has to do with the radically different nature of the conflict as a bitter national, even existential dispute as opposed to an insurgency or an intercommunity cleavage. Colombia's was a conflict between a legitimate government and an insurgency that started as an ideologically driven Marxist rebellion and ended up as a criminal project funded by the drug industry. And while Catholics in Northern Ireland aspired to form part of the Republic of Ireland and Protestans upheld the union with Britain, the Republic eventually ruled out the unification of the island, thus framing the conflict in strictly intercommunity terms.

Parties in conflict have always clung to distinctive political vocabularies and inflammatory symbols as a way to assert their identity and define the nature of their peace objectives. In Northern Ireland, the Republicans referred to the Republic of Ireland as "the twenty-six counties," and to the entire Island as "the thirty-two counties," or just "Ireland" or "Eire," all of them terms that called for a solution that excluded partition. For the Unionists, "Northern Ireland" and the "Republic of Ireland" were the only valid definitions of the nature of the conflict and of its solution through partition. This divisive embrace of the contrarian semantics of conflict was fought through the "In Search of a Settlement" public questionnaires that helped formulate a common language where most of the participants accepted the validity of terms such as "North" and "South," or the "Council of the Isles" instead of the "Council of the British Isles."

That the parties to the Israeli-Palestinian process cling to totally conflicting vocabularies only deepens the irreconcilability of their expectations. The "Arabs of Eretz Yisrael" was how the late prime minister Menachem Begin preferred to call the Palestinians, definite progress compared with Golda Meir's assertion, "There is no such thing as Palestinians." What for the Palestinians are the "occupied territories," represents for the Israelis "the administered (or liberated) territories"; the terrorists for the Israelis are the freedom fighters of the Palestinians; the Israeli obsessive quest for total security is for the Palestinians a euphemism for occupation; what the West Bank is for the Palestinians, Judea and Samaria are for the Israelis; the Palestinian right of return clashes with the Israeli law of return of the Jews to their ancestral homeland; the Israelis' Jerusalem is the Palestinian Al-Quds; and the Jewish holy of holies, the Temple Mount, is the Palestinian/Muslim Haram al-Sharif.

The Colombian Law of Land Restitution and Victims does rhyme with the call of the Palestinians for restitution and, indeed, for the need to address the roots of the conflict as the only acceptable way to peace. But a crucial difference is that the dispossessed Colombian peasants were recovering lands in their own country, and the millions of displaced persons were returning to their villages in their own Colombia. In Palestine, restitution is about a return in time and space to the Palestinians' homeland, now an entirely different state, sometimes literally to the fig and olive tree left behind in a war their leaders had started in defiance of the November 1947 UN Partition Plan and lost. The Palestinians refuse to see a return to the Palestinian state, and even to areas *within* Israel they were supposed to receive as part of the land swaps stipulated by all peace plans, as the realization of the right of return. Settling in those areas would deny the refugees, they said, the right to chose where exactly in Israel they would like to live. The right of return would be, then, applied à la carte, and each refugee would make his own choice. There is, indeed, no historical precedent for a national movement struggling for a state of its own just in order to ingather its exiles in a neighboring state.

Multidimensional Conflicts

India-Pakistan, Pakistan-Bangladesh, north and south Cyprus, South Africa-Namibia, Sudan and South Sudan, Morocco and Western Sahara, Kosovo, Bosnia,

Ethiopia-Eritrea, and Israel-Palestine are all conflicts that transcend a struggle for a disputed territory; they are complex knots of intractable contentions about historic homelands and mutually exclusive national or religious narratives. They all suffered ethnic cleansing, occupation, displacements, even the creation of settlements and, inevitably, resistance to occupation by every conceivable means from diplomacy to terror and guerrilla warfare. Some of these conflicts, like the Israeli-Palestinian conundrum, still resist peaceful solutions, and when a solution is found, it always looks ephemeral.

The phenomenon of major demographic changes and massive migrations produced by war and the redelimitation of borders has been common to most of these conflicts. The standard solution, or the reality imposed by war, has been divorce, the bisection of the land along religious and ethnic lines. This was how Muslim Pakistan emerged out of mostly Hindu India in 1947. Bangladesh received its independence from Pakistan in 1971 after a war of liberation against a mainland 2,200 kilometers away that oppressed and misgoverned the province. Eritrea seceded from Ethiopia to become an independent state in 1993 after a long and bloody civil war. Similarly, it took a savage civil war for the separation of mostly Christian South Sudan into independent statehood in 2011 from the Arab-Muslim north. In Israel-Palestine, this vital paradigm of partition was rejected by the Palestinians in 1947 and, after 1967, persistently eluded by Jewish dreamers of a biblical homeland, and by Palestinian maximalists.

In the Morocco-Western Sahara conflict that started with the withdrawal of Spain from the province in 1975 and its immediate occupation by Morocco, the latter followed the pattern of Israeli governments with regard to Palestine. They staunchly resisted Sahrawi independence, settled the land, and blocked the return of Sahrawi refugees. A similar fait accompli resisting all peace initiatives is the Turkish occupation in 1974 of northern Cyprus, where at least half of the population now consists of settlers from mainland Turkey. Also, South Africans in Namibia occupied the land by settling it.

But the Israeli-Palestinian case is, nonetheless, unique in how central ethnic and religious claims are in driving Israel's expansion of its settlements. Also, in none of the cases mentioned above have the occupied and the occupier claims over each other's land. Morocco has a claim on the Sahara, but the Sahrawis have no claim on Morocco, nor did Namibia have any claim on South Africa, the Bangladeshis on West Pakistan, or the Turks on Greek Cyprus. Sudan and South Sudan have still unresolved claims on border areas and so do Pakistanis and Indians on one particular border zone, Kashmir, an ever explosive conflict. But in neither case is the mutual longing for the land of the other such a central ethos as in the case of Israel-Palestine. Upon the collapse of the Camp David summit, Israeli author and peace activist Amos Oz defined the right of return as "an Arab euphemism for the liquidation of Israel."[8] But equally unacceptable is Israel's land-grabbing of what remained for a possible Palestinian state, whose creation Oz supported fervently.

Historically, the Palestinian dream of uprooting the Zionists, whose state was born in the sin of the Palestinian *Nakba* and, after 1967, expanded into the little that remained for the Palestinians, the biblical, God-promised lands of Judea and Samaria, is a pattern of conflict that has no parallel. In no other case have the borders of a state been so clearly defined by the extension of its settlements. That was the case before 1967, and it has been the case throughout the peace process as well in which the Israelis' insistence on annexing their settlement blocs in the Palestinian occupied lands was such an obstacle to an agreement.

Last but not least, in all of the other cases, security has not been so predominant a consideration as it is in the Israel-Palestine case. Palestine is seen by the Israelis as part of an immense Arab hinterland of mortal enemies, for it served either as the trigger or as the mobilizing pretext of most of the Arab-Israeli wars. And when Israel finally pulled out of occupied lands, be it in southern Lebanon or in Gaza, the vacuum was filled by Hezbollah and Hamas respectively and, with massive Iranian support, they became launching pads for an incessant war on Israel. It is truly difficult to exaggerate the impact that this sequence of withdrawals followed by wars had on Israel's resistance to taking security risks in future peace negotiations.

The Colonial Paradigm

Empires in modern times have been incubators of nations and generators of free states. But unlike Algeria and so many other nations liberated from the yoke of a colonial power—more recently, East Timor, a country occupied by Indonesia from 1975 to 1999, achieved independence after years of struggle and brutal repression—Palestine is not a classic case of colonial occupation. It would, of course, be absurd to deny the colonial practices of Israel's occupation of the West Bank—Albert Memmi's brilliant concept of the "self denying colonizer" (*le colonisateur qui se refuse*) comes to mind—her exploitation of its human and natural resources, and the way she turned the Palestinian population into the hewers of wood and drawers of water of the Israeli economy. Nor can it be denied that, just like the French settlers in Algeria, the Israeli settlers in the West Bank do have a country to return to. The Palestinians have, then, sufficient reasons to project globally the image of a nation occupying the moral high ground in its struggle against a merciless colonial power.

Yet it would be wrong to frame the Israeli-Palestinian conflict in strict terms of a clash between a reactionary colonial power and a colonized, socially progressive people as many in the Western left tend to see it.[9] The Palestinians brought untold tragedies upon themselves by their paradigmatic blindness to the true nature of the force of will driving the "Zionist entity." Analogies with Algeria and Vietnam are shallow sloganeering. None other than Noam Chomsky, the critic-in-chief of Israel's immoral conduct, warned against these facile analogies between the Palestine conflict and the anticolonial struggles in Algeria and Vietnam.[10] Since the early days of Zionism, the Palestinians have displayed a blind refusal to acknowledge the authenticity of the Jews' drive to reclaim their spiritual and political roots. The Palestinians did not have to accept that; but, by overlooking and ignoring how compelling the driving force of the Jewish national movement was, they framed their struggle in the wrong terms, as if it were a simple colonial enterprise. In their negation of free choice and moral responsibility, and by casting all blame on the dark forces of Zionism and Western imperialism for the tragedies that had befallen them, the Palestinians trapped their cause in a paradigmatic blind alley.

For Zionism was not an extension of Europe's nineteenth-century grab for colonies and raw materials. Unlike the European colonialists who behaved as the beachhead and the promoters of the strategic interests of the mother country, the Zionists cut off their links with their countries of origin and inaugurated for themselves a new beginning, a radical break with Jewish history. Decimated by the Jewish catastrophes in Eastern Europe, the Jews who came to build a national home in the midst of the vast Arab Middle East were the emissaries of no foreign power; they were idealistic pioneers, genuine in their aspiration not to exploit the local population. They saw their ideal in creating a new Jewish society based on self-help and manual labor. And before the clash with the Arabs drifted into open war, they did not evict the Palestinian peasants, but bought poor land for their settlements from their legal owners and improved it. Unlike the European invaders during the imperialist drive of the late nineteenth century, the Zionists were driven by an ideology of national revival based on human improvement and social utopia. A new culture and an old-new language were to be two fundamental pillars of this new beginning. Zionism was a social and cultural revolution, a movement that, in its beginning, believed innocently that it would not even require the use of force in order to assert itself. When the early Zionists spoke of "conquest," they referred to "conquering" the wilderness and the desert. They wanted to redeem the Jewish people by "conquering" work, toiling on the land they had "acquired legally rather than by theft or military conquest," and by excluding the exploitation of the Arab workforce, as none other than Maxime Rodinson—probably the most notable anti-Zionist in France—acknowledged. Rodinson, nevertheless, defined Israel in a 1967 article as a "colonial reality," but years later, in 1998, without retracting from his definition, he still thought that Israel was a special case, "not a state like all the others." Hannah Arendt, whose attitude to the Zionist project was throughout ambivalent, was unequivocal in her rejection of the colonial comparison. What the Zionists created, she wrote in 1948, had no precedent; "it could not possibly fit into the political scheme of imperialism because it was neither a master nor a subject nation." To Arthur Koestler, another disappointed Zionist, the Zionists were no colonialists, but, yes, "the executors of the amoral working of history."[11] Nor was Israel a gift Western imperialism gave to the Jews in compensation for the Holocaust. A case unique in its kind, Israel was already a political entity with all the features of statehood—an army subject to political authority, a democratic polity with its parties and elected parliament, a system of trade unions, a vibrant economy, a welfare state system, and advanced, utopian social experiments—when the news about the Shoah started to have its international impact.

Since the early 1960s, that is, before Israel had occupied the West Bank, Arafat's PLO framed its struggle against the "Zionist entity" through the colonial paradigm in line with the wars of national popular liberation of the Vietnamese and the Algerians. Israel's colonial nature, certainly in the eyes of Hamas, now the most vital force in Palestinian nationalism, also applies to Israel proper and to her rule over the "1948 Palestinians," as the sizable Palestinian minority in Israel is normally defined. But if the colonial paradigm were truly applicable to the Jewish state, Israel should have long ago left the occupied territories or, as the PLO expected, collapsed altogether rotten and disintegrated as the "invented" and "artificial" entity that it supposedly was. Even today, Hamas's war on Israel continues to be inspired by the conviction that, if Israel is not defeated, since it is "weaker than a spiderweb," as Hezbollah's Hassan Nasrallah likes to put it, it would collapse sooner or later as the Crusaders' kingdom did in the twelfth century. No colonial power in history, however mighty, has resisted such a long struggle of national liberation, now half a century old in the Palestinian terri- tories and seventy-four years in Israel proper. A genuine colonial occupation is never so existentially vital for the colonial power that it should be willing to per- sist in it against a continuous national uprising, the ever-increasing opprobrium of the international community and, in Israel's case, the hostility of the entire Arab world, which, moreover, fought one war after another against the "Zionist crusader state," supposedly for the sake of Palestine.

Even assuming the validity of the colonial paradigm, a major difference exists between an overseas colony, which has invariably been the case of Western impe- rialism in faraway lands, and an occupied land that is territorially contiguous with the home territory, as is Israel's case with the West Bank and Gaza. It is this ter- ritorial contiguity that has bedeviled Israeli negotiators, for they have imagined it paved with threats such as political instability in the adjacent Palestinian state, the probability that a radical Islamist group would rise to power, Palestinian irre- dentism and revisionism, faltering state-building in Palestine, and the possibility that the new state would forge alliances with Israel's enemies in the region's outer circle. These days, Gaza offers an example of a liberated land which Hamas, with the robust assistance of Iran, turned into a launching pad of missiles onto Israeli territory.

It is doubtful whether Israel's critics in Western governments would have conducted peace negotiations under similar conditions in a more flexible way than we did in both the Camp David and the Annapolis process. Historically, the dismantling of Western colonial rule has been the "end of conflict" as far as the colonial power was concerned. But the newly independent states, as we saw throughout Asia and Africa, still had a long and uncertain way of state- and institution-building ahead of them, their economies frequently faltered, many of them collapsed into civil wars compounded by genocides of entire tribes, and the lofty dreams of workable democracies and the rule of law ended up frequently in monumental disappointments. But the failing statehood of their former colonies did not truly affect the security and well-being of the former colonial powers. It does not require a high degree of imagination to figure out what would have been Britain's fears of withdrawing from, say, Uganda or Kenya, France from Algeria, or Belgium from the Congo if these colonies were territorially contiguous with the colonial powers' home countries. My Palestinian interlocutor, Abu Ala, was right when he observed, "Instead of making peace, you seem to be getting ready for the next war." He referred to the many security arrangements that we wanted to put in place. It would not be a wild guess to assume that Britain, France, and Belgium would have done the same, and possibly more, in the cases mentioned above. The "end of conflict" in clear-cut processes of the decolonization of overseas lands is a straightforward affair, for the failures of the former colony no longer truly affect the security of the former colonial power. Such a promise could never be taken for granted in the case of a contiguous territory, even if it is, like the West Bank, defined as a colony.

End of Conflict?

Israel's pursuance of an "end of conflict" with the Palestinians was a delusive aspiration. Any agreement, inevitably imperfect, would have provided the Palestinians, and Israeli-Jewish radicals, with manifold pretexts for harboring revisionist sentiments. In Arafat's enigmatic mind there was always room for conciliatory rhetoric when addressing Western audiences and a jihadist vocabulary at home. Ending the conflict was a liberal Western notion of peace which Arafat found unsuited to the awesome magnitude of the contention over narratives that separated him from a Jewish state born in sin. It is highly probable that both Palestinian and Jewish-Israeli fanatics would have seen compromises over sacred assets in the same way as France saw Germany's annexation of Alsace-Lorraine in 1870 as an inevitably necessary evil to be revisited in the future. Moreover, any solution to the conflict that Israel would agree to would require the Palestinians to com-promise the driving motif of their cause, the refugees ethos. The Palestinian state would then be delivered amid a consequential crisis of legitimacy in the eyes of the Palestinians themselves.

In the case of internal conflicts—for example, Northern Ireland, Colombia, South Africa—and in that of a contiguous occupied territory, the case of the West Bank, faltering state-building is the main, albeit not the only, threat to the prospects of an orderly post-conflict phase. Unlike peace agreements between orderly states that focus essentially on the delimitation of borders—Israel-Egypt and Israel-Jordan, for example—the end of internal conflicts and that of an oc-cupation of territorially contiguous territory entails complex and prolonged state-building assignments. Alas, state-building has never been central to the Palestinian national ethos. Torn between the irreconcilable strategies of the Islamist Hamas in Gaza and the supposedly secular nationalism of the PLO with its corrupt and incompetent Palestinian Authority, the Palestinian territories risk becoming a politically invertebrate state whose unfulfilled national dreams would betray Israel's illusion of an end to the conflict.

Another threat has to do with the resilience of divergent narratives. The clash of narratives is, indeed, an obstacle that is always more difficult to crack than tangible differences. This is precisely the reason why in Colombia and Northern Ireland, and in many other peace processes, narratives were relegated to bilateral commissions to be dealt with *after* the peace agreement had been signed and the tangible is-sues of power-sharing, the evacuation of territories, disarmament, and so forth had been resolved. In the case of Palestine, the narrative stands at the center of the process to be addressed and resolved here and now. The Israelis wanted an end of conflict that is essentially based on the resolution of the problems created by the 1967 war. The Palestinians would not settle for anything that did not address 1948, that is, the core of the Palestinian national narrative, here and now.

But such is the resilience of the narrative divide that it tends to persist be-yond the formalities of the peace agreement. Many years after the Good Friday Agreement, tensions over flags, identities, politics, and unreconcilable narratives still persist in Northern Ireland. The New Irish Republican Army created by dis-sident Republicans is dreaming of a return to the good old days of the Troubles. They have on their side the fact that the fruits of peace have not reached the Catholic community. There are still regions in the province where two-thirds of the children in Catholic communities are born into poverty.[12] Since the Good Friday Agreement, to this day, all attempts to reinstate power-sharing have failed, owing to ongoing disagreements between the Protestant Democratic Unionist

Party (DUP) and the Catholic Sinn Fein. And when reinstated, power-sharing governments frequently faltered, and Westminster had to reimpose direct rule. From 2017 to 2020, Northern Ireland was the region holding the world record for the longest period without a sitting government. The potency of the old feuds between the Catholics who want to be part of the Republic of Ireland and the Protestant Unionists was again demonstrated in violent clashes following Britain's exit from the European Union.

Post-conflict Colombia is also mired in major dysfunctionalities. One is the fact that a peace settlement signed with the Santos government had to be implemented by a revisionist government consisting of the fiercest opponents of the agreement. The Israeli parallel was the signing of the Oslo Accords by Rabin and their destruction by his revisionist successor, Benjamin Netanyahu. In Colombia, President Iván Duque has yet to decide whether to throw water or gasoline on the peace agreement. According to a watchdog group, the International Commission on Human Rights Verification, the government has so far complied with only 18.5 percent of the reforms and laws stipulated by the peace accords.[13]

The second is the challenge of the formidable structural deficiencies presented by a vast, ungoverned geography where the state's absence is always filled by insurgent or simply criminal groups. An all-out war is still going on between FARC fronts that resisted demobilization, paramilitary groups, the ELN (the Army of National Liberation), a still fully mobilized Marxist militia that resisted President Santos's offer of a separate peace deal, and criminal bands (BACRIM) vying for FARC's abandoned illicit economy. Also coca, the raw material for cocaine on which FARC based its entire illicit economy, continues to be a major problem. In 2017, a year after the signing of peace, coca grew on 146,000 hectares, three times the area it covered in 2012. Most of the fighting for these and other illicit assets takes place in about a quarter of the country's municipalities. Just 5 percent of that area is now under state control.[14]

The peace Colombians dream of will not happen unless the historically titanic mission of reconstructing the country's abandoned rural periphery is accomplished. But economic vested interests and their friends among the mainstream politicians have done their best to block structural reform. Big agro-industrial companies, unhappy with the justice done by the peace agreement to the evicted peasants, stand to profit from much of this renewed violence. Small landowners are intimidated into selling at bargain prices to these magnates the stolen lands they had recovered as part of the Law of Victims and Land Restitution, which Former President Santos had the vision to start implementing while the conflict with FARC was still ongoing. Santos's reform was made for the sake of the small, disinherited peasants; his political adversaries have been more interested in the big landowners.[15] The evacuation of the Colombian Amazon by FARC has also paved the way for the opening of these hitherto inaccessible territories to big companies bent on destroying huge areas of virgin forest, thus degrading an ecosystem so vital for the balance of the global climate. According to the World Resources Institute, Colombia has lost almost half a million hectares of forest cover in 2017, a jump of 46 percent over 2016.[16]

South Africa is another example where the end of conflict betrays expectations. The end of apartheid and the birth of democracy in South Africa were two of the most dramatically significant events of our times. But almost thirty years later, Nelson Mandela's vision of forgiveness and reconciliation is still far from living up to his ideals of justice and equality for black people. Black-led governments preside over an economy that is white-dominated and frequently ranks among the most unequal in the world. Clearly, the white population has reaped greater economic benefits from the end of apartheid than the black population. Since the end of apartheid, the proportion of white people with skilled jobs has risen from 42 to 61 percent, while the proportion of black people during the same period has gone up only from 12 to 18 percent.[17] In his Nelson Mandela lecture in October 2015, Thomas Piketty claimed that black empowerment did not alter the country's course so that it is even more unequal than it was under apartheid. The statistics that he presented showed that 60–65 percent of South Africa's wealth is concentrated in the hands of just 10 percent of the population (compared to 50–55 percent in Brazil, and 40–45 percent in the United States), a group that is predominantly white. Within the top 1–5 percent, it will be up to 80 percent.[18] Strikingly, as Panashe Chigumadzi, the founder and editor of *Vanguard Magazine*, put it, South Africa continues to be anti-black so many years after apartheid.[19] Nor has the segregative urban architecture of apartheid in South Africa's biggest cities changed.[20]

Nelson Mandela's fatherland is also betraying the pan-African spirit upon which it had built its struggle against apartheid. South Africa has now become home to heinous xenophobia and hate speech against black immigrants for whom South Africa was supposed to be a land of promise. Just like any other populist autocrats in Europe and America, leaders of Mandela's African National Congress who failed to transform the lives of their people have now resorted to the diversion of anger and frustration at African foreigners. Free of the pretentious rhetoric of the South African National Congress, Uganda and Ethiopia, among other countries in Africa, have been far more generously open to hosting hundreds of thousands of African refugees.[21]

Refugees

People have been forced to leave their countries since the very notion of a country was created.[22] Wars, famines, failing states, and genocides moved millions of people across seas and continents. The twentieth century is replete with cases of mass displacement of communities in the storm of war. The birth of India and Pakistan in 1947 produced 14 million refugees and the massacre of more than half a million people. Hundreds of thousands of Chinese arrived in Hong Kong after the 1949 Communist takeover of China. The Korean War in the early 1950s pushed 1.3 million refugees from North to South Korea. The Vietnam War moved a million refugees from the north to the south. The suppression of Chechnya's bid for independence in the 1990s turned 600,000 Chechens into refugees; millions of Afghans were displaced in the 1980s by civil war and Russia's intervention; the civil war in Rwanda in the 1990s produced 4 million refugees, that of Bosnia more than 800,000, Liberia's almost 2 million, and in Central America's civil wars in the 1980s about a million Salvadoreans and Guatemalans were made refugees. Lately, 4.8 million Venezuelans fled the chaos of the Bolivarian revolution to neighboring countries, 1.6 million of whom were generously admitted by Colombia. In total, 70 million people throughout the world were defined in 2020 by the UNHCR as displaced and refugees.

Normally, the separation of warring ethnic groups through a forced exchange of populations for the sake of the ethnic homogeneity of states was seen necessary for peace and stability. After World War I, 1.2 million Greeks were sent back home from Turkey and 600,000 Turks living in Greece went back to their homeland. A similar exchange of populations took place between Greece and Bulgaria, 50,000 Greeks for about 100,000 Bulgarians. In the wake of World War II, about 12 million Germans were expelled or fled back to Germany from the Baltic States and Eastern Europe. Asia was particularly given to massive exchanges of populations. The 14 million refugees produced by the dramatic birth of India and Pakistan were split with Hindu and Sikhs going to India and Muslims to Pakistan. The end of Bangladesh's war of independence from Pakistan in 1972 brought back home 10 million Bangladeshis who had fled to India during the war. The common denominator in all these cases was the principle of refugees returning to the country in which they represented the majority ethnic group, never the minority. There is, seemingly, not even one precedent of a minority return.[23]

By all accounts, the Palestinian refugee problem has been treated by the international community as a singular case. The December 1948 UN General Assembly Resolution 194 opened the door to the return of Palestinian refugees. It stipulated that "refugees wishing to return to their homes and live at peace with their neighbours should be permitted to do so at the earliest practicable date." For Israel, the good news was that the resolution linked return to a peace settlement. But the Arab states wanted the resolution, which being a General Assembly resolution was anyway not binding, to be implemented through automatic repatriation and outside any peace settlement with Israel. The ethos of return was cultivated, even if unwittingly, also by the United Nations Relief and Works Agency for Palestine Refugees in the Near East (UNRWA), which was created in December 1949. It singled out Palestinian refugees as the only ones who would have their own separate UN agency to deal with their problem. All the other many millions of refugees were to be dealt with by the UN High Commissioner for Refugees (UNHCR). UNRWA's generous definition of refugees as "persons whose normal place of residence was Palestine during the period 1 June 1946 to 15 May 1948," meant that with only two years of residence, a condition that affected some of those who were attracted to emigrate from neighboring Arab countries to work in the relatively prosperous Mandatory Palestine, a person could come under the protective umbrella of UNRWA. In 1954, UNRWA decided to include in the category of Palestine refugees all the descendants of refugees forever. This is how the current number of almost 6 million refugees was reached. And so the hundreds of thousands of Palestinians who might have restored their lives, made careers, and become respectable property owners in Arab countries or elsewhere would still be defined as refugees.

In the past, Israel did not rule out a sizable return of refugees and displaced persons so long as it was done in the framework of a peace agreement. During the Arab-Israeli UN-sponsored peace talks in Lausanne in the spring of 1949, Israel proposed incorporating the Gaza Strip and its entire 300,000 Palestinian population into Israel. Prime Minister David Ben-Gurion was even willing to compensate Egypt with land within Israel. Egypt turned down the offer. The Arab side in Lausanne also rejected an Israeli offer to admit 100,000 Palestinian refugees. But by her annexation of East Jerusalem in 1967, Israel had unwittingly absorbed about 300,000 Palestinians and integrated them into her social security system. On the basis of reports from Israel's Population and Immigration Authority, Professor Menachem Hofnung of Jerusalem's Hebrew University concluded that since 1967, hundreds of thousands of West Bank and Gaza Palestinians had settled in Israel. While the Arabs' fertility rate is close to that of Jewish society, their relative rate in Israel's population has grown from 11 percent in the late 1950s to 21 percent in 2018,[24] in spite of the fact that 2.4 million Jews immigrated to Israel during that period. The Israeli Ministry of Interior does not keep records or a database of persons, or categories of persons, who were naturalized under family reunification schemes. Yet, Danny Rubinstein, a respected expert in Palestinian affairs, wrote that he could reach ministry of the interior data showing that from 1994 to 2012, 130,000 Palestinians arrived in Israel through family reunification schemes and got full citizenship. Demographer Arnon Soffer, a serious scholar but admittedly known as an alarmist, calculated that since 1967 to 2020 about 250,000 Palestinians from the occupied territories were naturalized in Israel with full citizenship. It is, he argued, "an implementation of the right of return through the back door."[25]

Even if these figures are overblown—in 2003, during the Al Aqsa Intifada, a Citizenship Entry Law was enacted banning family unification schemes—there should be no doubt about the high number of Palestinians that "returned" to Israel before and also after the 2003 ban. Even without annexing the occupied territories, Israel is already practically a binational state, a reality that her Nation-State Law aims to arrest.

Undeniably, UNRWA was necessary as a tool of much needed relief for refugees. But under the pressure of the Arab states which wanted to keep alive the ethos of return and the refugees as a tool of war against the Jewish state, it never truly focused on a mandate of rehabilitation. UNRWA became, through its education projects, an important incubator of Palestinian nationalism. The rise in the 1970s of the Soviet-backed bloc of non-aligned, mostly third-world states shifted the balance in UN institutions in a way that gave a tailwind to UNRWA's philosophy. A UN section was now created to promote "the inalienable rights of the Palestinians," an item that was to be automatically added every year to the General Assembly's agenda, and a long series of resolutions were passed supporting Palestinian "return."

The singularity of the Palestinians' plight, born when Palestine was bisected by the sword in 1948 and 700,000 people either fled or were evicted by the victors, lies in that the dream of return to the fig tree, the abandoned village, and home is not always just a metaphor; it is frequently meant literally. An Israeli settler society has disinherited an indigenous people, and, as courageously observed in 1955 by Israel's then Chief of Staff, General Moshe Dayan, the refugees "have been sitting in the refugee camps in Gaza, and before their eyes we have been transforming the lands and the villages where they and their fathers dwelt into our estate."[26] This, the unachievable dream of return, is only one among other concerns that made all Israeli peace proposals so desperately non-attractive to the Palestinian leadership.

It has been a conventional norm to define people who were forced to leave their homes, but remained in their homeland—the case of the bulk of the Palestinian refugees who remained in Mandatory Palestine, that is, in Gaza and the West Bank—as displaced persons, not refugees. In the case of the Turkish invasion of Cyprus in 1974, the thousands of Greeks who were either evicted or fled to the Greek part of the island were not recognized as refugees by the UNHCR. The same criterion was also applied to the Serbs who fled Kosovo in the late 1990s. Also, return in post-conflict situations was always addressed as a return of the refugee to his "homeland," never to his "home." Hence, in his peace parameters, Bill Clinton was loyal to the accepted standards of international law and the UN Declaration of Human Rights, according to which a refugee is entitled to return to his country, not necessarily to his home. He, therefore, spoke of a return to "historical Palestine," as he put it, not to the home left behind. But in the PLO's ideal, the right of return is a personal matter for each refugee, and nobody can give it up in his name. When in 2012, President Abbas said that he had given up his right to return to his hometown Safed, he also made it clear, "I wasn't giving up the right of return; I was just speaking personally." "No one," he said, "can give up the right of return in the name of the Palestinians."[27] In an article he wrote five years later, Abbas spoke of "7 million refugees," saying that each of them is "free to choose" about his own right of return, thus implicitly affirming that the PLO has no right to speak on behalf of these refugees or to agree with Israel in their name about "the finality of claims and end of conflict."[28] Moreover, Clinton's stipulation that the refugees return to the "State of Palestine," or to "historical Palestine," was rejected by the PLO because the whole issue was a strictly Palestinian sovereign matter that did not belong to a bilateral peace settlement. The creation of a Palestinian state as such, they said, was by no means the solution of the refugee problem.

This should help explain why the Palestinians found it so difficult to digest the concept of "two states for two peoples." When I was invited to Doha by *Al Jazeera* in 2011 to debate the Palestine Papers, a leaked archive of memos pertaining to the peace process, I realized how deep the Palestinians' conviction was that the right of self-determination for the two peoples, Israelis and Palestinians, posed a risk to the right of return. For it could mean that the exercise of self-determination resolves the problem of return. Additionally, accepting Israel as a Jewish state was tantamount to giving up on the right of return. In internal Palestinian position papers, complaints were made about Palestinian "red lines" on the refugee file being "unclear," which obviously made Israelis imagine, or fear, the worst. Dr. Einat Wilf and Adi Schwarzman mention, indeed, some extravagant Palestinian expectations as to the number of refugees Israel could and should admit. They found that a study commissioned by the PLO, in 2008—"Israel's Capacity to Absorb Palestinian Refugees"—claimed that Israel was capable of absorbing between 600,000 and 2 million refugees without compromising its Jewish majority. Another document suggested that the PLO ask for a return of a million refugees. But, Palestinian position papers prepared ahead or during negotiations were definitely much more moderate. In such a paper of April 28, 2007, during the Annapolis process, they suggested 100,000 returnees spread over ten years. I can't recall such a number being mentioned during the Barak government-led negotiations. What was then explicitly mentioned by Arafat himself were "my dear refugees in Lebanon," whose number stood around 300,000. During the Annapolis negotiations, the Palestinians would affirm that "a just solution (to the plight of the refugees) in line with Resolution 194, was a compromise position." They would also ask Israel to compensate the refugees for both their refugeehood and for loss of property, and they called for compensation also for the Arab states that had hosted the refugees for long decades.

This was not an unjust requirement, and it was addressed throughout the entire process. What the Palestinians could not accept was Israel's refusal to make its compensation through the refugees' "Absentee Property" in Israel. Inherent in the debate about the Absentee Property are the moral and historical origins of the conflict. The financial problem is resolvable, but Israel could be more generous with regard to the moral dimension of the conflict. Ideally, a Truth and Reconciliation Commission to deal with the origins of the *Nakba* and, as Israel would certainly insist, also the political responsibilities that brought it about, could serve as a moral panacea. In such conflicts, truth telling offers a moral compensation that can be as important as the plight over property. Short of such a commission, leaders willing to shift the traditional discourse from denial to empathy could make a difference.

Peace and Justice

The Nuremberg trials provide an ideal model for post-conflict justice. But in cases where no side has been defeated, a trade-off between reconciliation and accountability is inescapable. The fundamentalist notion of the International Criminal Court (ICC) that in the transition from war to peace the "rule of law" replaces politics is utterly unrealistic. Transitional justice is not a strictly legal affair; it is fundamentally a political deal. A fundamentalist obsession with justice would always derail peace enterprises.

The Colombian way in transitional justice was a brilliant exercise in what Archbishop Desmond Tutu defined as restorative justice. Justice was not applied as a vindictive tool, and the victims were given moral and material compensation, but not full and unqualified justice. The peace agreement also established a special subcommission to examine the origins of the conflict and the plight of victims affected by it. Israelis and Palestinians preceded the Colombian experiment in the attempt to reconcile conflicting narratives, but failed. In our own last-ditch attempt to save the peace process, in January 2001, at Taba, the then Israeli minister of justice Yossi Beilin and the Palestinian minister Nabil Shaath made substantive progress in drafting precisely such a reconciliation of opposed narratives.

They also got down to a practical discussion of the number of refugees who could return to Israel. But the point of equilibrium between symbolic Israeli gestures and Palestinian expectations of sizable numbers of returnees could never be reached. In Palestine, the understandable quest for justice has constantly defeated the yearning for peace. "Return" might be a morally compelling requirement, but it cannot and will not happen. Hence, the model of transitional justice in an Israeli-Palestinian peace would have to follow the patterns of transitional justice established in Colombia and South Africa, where confessing the truth mattered more than the punishment. The case par excellence of such a reconciliation based on truth-telling is, of course, the South African Truth and Reconciliation Commission, in which an end to the denial of past crimes created the conditions for a new chapter in the relations between the two communities. Amnesty was granted in many cases as a plausible way to achieve peace and bring democracy, but truth denial would always haunt the affected nations. Spain's transition to democracy in the late 1970s was based on amnesty and forgiveness for the crimes committed during the Francisco Franco dictatorship. But, the painful past could not be silenced, and in 2018, forty years after the dictator's death, the government announced the establishment of a Truth Commission.

But a conflict between two righteous victims vying for the monopoly of victimhood, the Israeli-Palestinian dispute suffered throughout from a total lack of magnanimity and forgiveness. Israel is particularly fond of the awkwardly false symmetry she makes between the Palestinian refugee crisis and the forced emigration of 600,000 Jews from Arab countries following the creation of the State of Israel, as if it were "an unplanned exchange of populations." In fact, envoys from the Mossad and the Jewish Agency worked underground in Arab countries and Iran to encourage Jews to go to Israel. More importantly, for many Jews in Arab states, the very possibility of emigrating to Israel was the culmination of millennial aspirations. It represented the consummation of a dream to take part in Israel's resurgence as a nation. No matter how painful the memory of their eviction or how humiliating their second-class status in Israel, these new Israelis never sought to return to their lands of origin. By contrast, the yearning for return became the Palestinians' defining national ethos, which it certainly was not for Jews evicted from Arab lands.

Peace is frequently not about justice but about stability, which calls not only for the Palestinians to attune their discourse to what is realizable, but also for Israel to settle its own contradictions and address the refugee problem in a way that would secure the legitimacy and durability of a future peace agreement. It is precisely because justice for the Palestinians cannot be based on an automatic concept of return that not only material but also genuine moral compensation is called for. Instead of suppressing the memory of the Palestinian refugees, Israel needs to recognize that the Jewish state came into being much on the basis of the massive uprooting, dispossession, and disinheritance of Palestinian communities. Israel failed to develop the necessary self-confidence in its solidity as a nation in order to integrate into the curriculum of its schools the tragedy of the Palestinian *Nakba*. The solution of conflicts of this nature requires that historical memory be recovered and that the narratives of both parties be given a proper hearing. This, I am afraid, is not today on the agenda of any of the main political or even social forces in Israel.

Negotiations, Trust, and Would-be Mediators

The Israeli-Palestinian peace process is a monument to the utter inadequacy of Henry Kissinger's negotiating technique of "constructive ambiguity." Constructive ambiguity facilitated an agreement in Oslo at the price of creating irreconcilable misconceptions with regard to the final settlement at Camp David and beyond. Ambiguous, full of lacunae, essentially built on the delusion that trust could be built between the occupied and the occupier, the Oslo Accords contained the seeds of their own destruction. Trust between peacemakers is highly desirable, of course. But its significance may be overrated. Peace processes are not about making love; they are about making peace. Ask Gerry Adams and Ian Paisley in Norther Ireland, or Charles de Gaulle and Ahmed Ben Bella in Algeria. A genuine peace process also requires respect for the adversary. Israel made peace with Egypt without this having been preceded by long years of trust-building. Menachem Begin was forced to give back the entire Sinai peninsula because he respected Anwar Sadat and Egypt's power. For similar reasons, Rabin was ready to give back the whole of the Golan Heights in exchange for peace, while Syria's President Hafez al-Assad was not even ready to meet him. Such generosity was always missing in the case of Palestine.

Third-party involvement can frequently be vital in the shift from war to a diplomatic phase; but it often requires that the mediator transform into a manipulator and arm-twister. America's only successful attempts at peacemaking in the Middle East involved coercive diplomacy, a masterly combination of power, manipulation, and pressure. Henry Kissinger, a proficient practitioner of coercive diplomacy, utterly rejected the definition of conflict resolution as the naive attainment of a non-coercive solution that is derived from the parties themselves. America's blunder in the Korean War, he said, stemmed from its perception of power and diplomacy as distinct and separate phases of foreign policy. It acted as if the process of negotiation operated on its own inherent logic, independent of the military balance. Treating force and diplomacy as distinct phenomena, as Bill Clinton, George W. Bush, and Barak Obama did in their failed attempts to broker an Israeli-Palestinian peace, caused American power to lack purpose and its negotiators to lack clout.

The credibility of third-party guarantors also lies in their capacity to respect their commitments to the parties in conflict. A defining moment in Israel's loss of trust in the international community's mediating role happened in 1967. The then UN Secretary General U Thant and world powers paved the way for war by ignoring the guarantees they had given after the 1956 Sinai War for Israel's freedom of navigation in the strategic Straits of Tiran. Menachem Begin later ridiculed the pretentions of international peace brokers. "I have no problem with guarantees," he said, "but what I need are guarantees to guarantee the guarantees." Or take the case of Ukraine. In the 1994 Budapest Protocol, she agreed to waive her nuclear capabilities in exchange for international guarantees of her territorial integrity. Crimea might possibly have still been hers, and Vladimir Putin might already have ceased his harassment of eastern Ukraine if Kiev had kept her nuclear arsenal.

Apologia for Political Betrayal

War and foreign enemies unite nations; it is the search for peace that divides them. Leaders in the transition from war to peace have almost invariably been prophets without honor who had to betray the national consensus in their search for peace. This could also be said of President Santos in Colombia. Pursuing the war against FARC, instead of engaging in a divisive and uncertain peace process that ended with his approval rates at their lowest ebb ever, would have certainly been a more politically rewarding strategy. Peace came together with his political decline. The leader in quest of peace will too often have a split nation and a divided polity threatening to derail his entire peace enterprise.

Egypt's Anwar Sadat was another such "traitor." For a major problem in the Arab-Israeli conflict, as in many other intricate conflicts throughout history, has always been the incapacity of leaders to conduct a peace policy that is not supported by the paralyzing national consensus. Leaders, more frequently than not, act as the hostages of the sociopolitical environment that produces them instead of shaping it. Anwar Sadat gained a privileged place in history the moment he fled from the comfortable prison of the pseudo-solidarity and hollow rhetoric of Arab summits. A visionary much ahead of his time, Sadat was eventually to be isolated by the rest of the Arab world. His assassination in 1981 by an Islamist fundamentalist reflected how far away he had gone from the Egyptian people's consensus over the satanized image they had of the Jewish state. It would have been, in the short term, more politically rewarding for Sadat if he had stayed within the warmth of the inter-Arab consensus.

Throughout our Camp David peace enterprise we, the Israelis, never put party before country. Unlike Arafat and Netanyahu, Rabin, Barak, and Olmert were willing to divide the nation and make peace at the cost of their political survival. Netanyahu's long premiership rested on his obsession with never departing from the grip of his political power base, even if it meant being the willing accomplice of a messianic settler community. With him, the lust for power prevailed over the search for peace. Alas, the power of his message to the nation was perhaps short-sighted, but also politically compelling: Did his predecessors' political suicide for the sake of peace bring Israel any closer to reaching peace with the Palestinians? So why not leave things as they are?

Most peacemakers were forced to betray their political base. "In politics, it is necessary either to betray one's country or the electorate. I prefer to betray the electorate," explained Charles de Gaulle, a philosophy he certainly applied in his peace in Algeria. King Abdullah I of Jordan, Anwar Sadat, and Yitzhak Rabin paid with their lives for such a "betrayal." Nor could have Ariel Sharon performed the single most important move against Israel's settlements obsession—the dismantling of the entire Israeli presence in Gaza—without betraying his electorate, and indeed his own political biography. This is all about turning Machiavelli on his head. The author of *The Prince* praised leaders who did not keep their word to respect peace agreements. Making peace while risking one's grip on power was to Machiavelli an exercise in unpardonable political naivete. When it comes to Palestine, the Israeli right, in power through most of the fifty-four years that followed the 1967 war, would blindly second Machiavelli's proposal.

Epilogue

In more than half a century of Israeli occupation of Palestinian lands, Israelis and Palestinians have tried it all. The record is disheartening: two Intifadas, the second of which was an all-out war of suicide terrorism and crippling collective punishment; four wars in Gaza with thousands of civilian deaths; desperate Palestinian oscillation between international diplomacy and resistance; a global boycott, divestment, and sanctions campaign against the Jewish state; an ever tighter Israeli control of the occupied nation; and a host of peace initiatives, two of which by forward-looking Israeli governments—Ehud Barak's and Ehud Olmert's—were defeated by a combination of domestic opposition and Palestinian rejection. Almost every American president since 1967 has tried his luck at breaking the code of this desperately intractable dispute. They all failed. The dwindling Israeli peace camp, shattered and demoralized by its irremediable defeats, still agonizingly resists accepting that the buds of the two-state solution have irretrievably atrophied and that the old consensus of peacemaking has been terminally swept away by history.

Ours was a signal failure to shape Palestinian statehood; the right, which gained momentum after our defeat, stymied it altogether. The peace tribe has been defeated and the emotional power of peace negotiations is no longer sufficient to gather it, let alone extend its reach. The emotional vacuum we have created with our condescending, presumably superior peace culture was filled by a new dominant tribe that has drawn strength from the disappointments of the peace process. Its political triumph has become a foregone conclusion in every election since 2001, and its discourse of annexation has become open and free of complexes. The Jordan Valley and large parts of Area C, where most of the Israeli settlements are located were, after all, promised by Trump's promiscuous so-called peace plan. But sovereignty is not a right that a "sovereign" can apply selectively in a territory that, according to Netanyahu's far-right allies, "belongs" to them by providential promise. It has to be applied to the entire land and their inhabitants without any discrimination on ethnic or religious grounds. Sovereignty means responsibility for the security and well-being of all who live in the land, and it also requires conferring on them citizenship rights such as freedom of movement, social benefits, and the right to vote for the Knesset. But the Israeli right wants the best of all worlds. It wants to "apply sovereignty" on an ethnic and national basis in order to eschew giving political rights to the Palestinians, who would thus remain stateless or, at best, politically undefined individuals. "Only with stateless people," Hannah Arendt reminded us, "one could do as one pleased"; but then she had the Jews in mind. Netanyahu's governments have displayed no sense of urgency for getting back to peace negotiations; nor was there any domestic constituency or international pressure to coerce them. A 2020 poll found that 72 percent and 81 percent of Palestinians and Israeli Jews respectively did not believe in the feasibility of a two-state solution.[1]

Indeed, why would myopic governments plunge again into the pains of a peace process when Israel had never had it so good? The 2002 Arab Peace Initiative, to which Israel reacted with cavalier disdain, fed the illusion that Israel had won its war with Palestinian and Arab nationalism. By the time the coronavirus pandemic threw the entire world economy into sharp decline, Israel was thriving, its economy was booming, and the start-up nation was a technological superpower courted by neighbors and faraway admirers, particularly among the giant Asian economies. Also, relations with the United States had never been better, with Trump practically offering a blank check to Israel in the occupied territories. Busy with its existential dilemmas, Europe—"a power vacuum between two major powers," as Arthur Koestler defined it many years ago—let the United States and her own East European illiberal democracies shield Israel against EU initiatives. Closer to home, the eastern Mediterranean has become Israel's *mare nostrum* thanks to the massive gas fields she has developed in her maritime Exclusive Economic Zones. To galvanize the nation against real and imaginary enemies, Benjamin Netanyahu has framed BDS, the Palestinian-led Boycott, Divestment, Sanctions movement, as a global octopus about to strangle the Jewish state. But the truth is that BDS has had a pathetically marginal effect on Israel's expanding global clout.

If anything, the coronavirus pandemic and the consequent turning of the major world actors to their own existential troubles only bolstered Israel's license to relegate Palestine. Israel has been the first to control the pandemic and recover her economic vigor. Even when tethered by the burden of the Palestinian problem, which re-emerged from its temporary lethargy following the last Gaza war, Israel would still continue to be, as she had never been before in her history, free to develop her global economic and political networks. Notwithstanding the many flaws of her democracy, Israel can still boast of representing the vindication of the nation-state in a region where states are melting down and economies getting stuck in a cycle of civil wars and deepening poverty. With a per-capita income in line with the OECD average, and thanks to the turbocharged growth of her innovation-based economy and high-tech military industry, Israel has made herself an indispensable partner for countries in the region and far beyond. Overwhelmed by their own troubles with terror, Iran, and the mounting rage of the younger generations at the disappointments of the Arab Spring, Arab regimes got weary of the annoying distraction of Palestine.

Israel's static strategy on Palestine also gets a powerful tailwind from the evident decline in the vigor and sense of purpose of the Palestinian national movement. Conveniently for the occupier, the split and disoriented Palestinians, whose poor leadership is crippled by a serious deficit of democratic legitimacy, offer no sense of being a reliable interlocutor for peace negotiations. The conflict between the Fatah-controlled West Bank and Hamas in Gaza has thrown Palestine into a state of war with itself. That these are also the twilight days of the ailing Mahmoud Abbas's rule, with all the uncertainties that this entails, does not make the Palestinians' situation any more promising.[2]

But Israel's international dilemma is not confined only to the corridors of power in world capitals; the case of Israel, more than that of any other country in the planet, is frequently decided in the international tribunal of public opinion. The fallout of the last Gaza war with its waves of anti-Israel and anti-Jewish demonstrations may perhaps dissipate, but only temporarily. A BBC world survey conducted following Israel's November 2012 war with Gaza found that Israel ranked as the fourth most hated country in the world, after North Korea, Pakistan, and Iran.[3] It is true that in recent years Israel's ranking improved as a result of the decline in the global resonance of the Palestinian problem, but the effects of Israel's occupation of Palestinian lands and her wars in Gaza are still the conventional reason for her rejection. Israel's quest for security in a hostile Middle East is understood by the international community. That she was not subjected to irresistible international pressure to relinquish her territorial gains either in 1948 or in the immediate aftermath of the 1967 war was due to the perception of her victory being the result of a legitimate war of self-defense. But when the war of salvation and survival turned into a war of conquest, occupation, and settlement, world opinion recoiled and Israel went on the defensive. She has remained there ever since.

Israel must reckon with the fact that Palestine represents a uniquely resonating story. Seven million refugees and close to 500,000 dead in the Syrian carnage mean far less to the Western conscience than Palestinians killed in Gaza. The Syrian hecatomb, the hundreds of thousands of casualties of the Iraq war, the obliteration of Grozny by the Russian army, and hundreds of civilians killed in NATO's aerial bombings in Kosovo and Afghanistan have never unleashed such worldwide hatred as in Israel's case. For years, stories about Israel focused almost exclusively on the Palestinian conflict. Joyce Karam, the Washington bureau chief of the pan-Arab *Al-Hayat*, believes that the reason is that "Muslim killing Muslim seems more acceptable than Israel killing Arabs."[4]

Israel's siege of Gaza is wrongheaded morally and politically unwise. But Gaza is also for all practical purposes an enemy state terrorizing its own civilian population and the Israeli villages outside its borders. And not only do Gaza's humanitarian conditions not begin to approach other infamous humanitarian crises of recent decades, but the entire Arab-Israeli conflict has produced in more than a century (from 1882 to this very day) fewer than a third the number of casualties in Syria's civil war,[5] not to mention catastrophes in the Democratic Republic of Congo, Sudan, Iraq, and Afghanistan. Gunnar Heinsohn, who compiled statistics ranking conflicts since 1950 for *Front Page Magazine Online*, ranked the Arab-Israeli conflict as forty-ninth in terms of fatalities.[6]

It is a despicable flaw of the UN system that the application of the lofty principles of universal justice should be conditioned by the global balance of power and that the world's most notorious abusers should be allowed to posture as the guardians of human rights in UN agencies. The United Nations Human Rights Council, where more resolutions condemning human rights abuses have been passed against Israel than against the rest of the world combined, is a unique case of political and moral obscenity. The same council would not dare put Russia in the dock for razing Grozny, Chechnya's capital, to the ground, or China for brutally oppressing the people of Tibet and the Muslim Uighur minority. Nor have the United States or Britain ever been called to order by the council for the massive casualties they have inflicted on the civilian population in Iraq and Afghanistan. Forever anonymous will also remain the many thousands of Yemenis, 25 percent of them children,[7] who were killed in a war involving celebrated champions of human rights, such as Iran and Saudi Arabia, a war that spawned the world's worst humanitarian crisis in decades. The same is true of the five hundred confirmed civilian deaths and six thousand wounded in NATO's massive bombing campaign in the Balkans in the 1990s, a case that was never investigated by the International Criminal Tribunal for the former Yugoslavia.

Anti-Semitism, ironized Isaiah Berlin, is "hating Jews more than is absolutely necessary." By the same token, much of the anti-Israel diatribe is sometimes a magnified cocktail of undeniable truths mixed with dubious assertions, sincere sympathy for the Palestinians' plight, old anti-Semitic atavisms, and sheer ignorance. Israel's critics too frequently defeat their case by their grotesque coupling of legitimate solidarity with Palestine with an anti-Jewish invective that degenerates into a supposedly politically correct form of anti-Semitism. The vilification of Israel and her singling out for opprobrium in such noxious terms as are never used against other states has long gone beyond legitimate criticism, for it has turned into an international Bacchanalia of character assassination.

Israel's actions are often described by her critics in obscenely disproportionate terms. A British newspaper editorialized in 2002 that Israeli actions in
Jenin—a fierce urban battle in which twenty-three Israeli soldiers and fifty-two
Palestinians, some of whom excelled at blowing up buses and kindergartens,
died—were "every bit as repellent" as the terrorist attacks of September 11 that
left behind the staggering death toll of three thousand innocent civilians. Others
prefer Holocaust metaphors. Obscenities like the late writer José Saramago's
comparing Jenin to Auschwitz are not rare.[8] A cruel urban battle, with a moderate number of casualties—compare this to Grozny, to the casbah of Algiers,
or to Najaf and Fallujah—has been likened to a death factory where thirty thousand Jews were murdered daily. "The Holocaust," Thomas Keneally wrote in
Schindler's Ark, "is a Gentile problem, not a Jewish one." In a seemingly paradox-
ical insight, the psychiatrist Zvi Rex quipped that Europe will probably never
forgive the Jews for Auschwitz. The late Israeli author and peace activist Amos
Oz used to say that one day the Jewish state would probably make peace with
Islam, but its conflict with the Christian West has all the traits of eternity.

The far left's Jewish problem in the West is the real intractable issue here, and,
as Princeton's political theorist Michael Walzer rightly observed, anti-Zionism
has joined anti-Semitism to become what August Bebel brilliantly defined as
the "socialism of fools." The now fashionable ivory tower nonsense about a one-
state solution to the Israeli-Palestinian dispute still draws its rationale from the
old topic that religion is not a proper basis for statehood, as if the European
states were not historically born as Christian republics and as if the Arab states
surrounding Israel are a monument to religious diversity. Israel has much soul-
searching to do, but so do her critics. Had not Zionism been put in the dock by
its detractors years before the 1967 occupation? And was it not that thirty years
after the Holocaust, when there were hardly any settlements in the territories
and the Palestine Liberation Organization had not yet endorsed the two-state
solution, an infamous UN resolution equating Zionism with racism was passed?

The truths about the occupation are sad enough, but an unholy alliance of pro-
gressive Western activists, Islamist groups, and, sometimes, white supremacists
as well has harnessed an entire industry of fake news to their onslaught on
Zionism and the Jews. Supporters of tyrannical fundamentalist Islamists like
Hamas and Hezbollah are among those who pushed Jews out of Jeremy Corbin's
British Labour Party. To my own dismay, I had the chance of witnessing that al-
liance in action when I joined an antiwar demonstration in London's Trafalgar
Square during the early days of the 2003 Iraq War. The rally, it turned out, could
hardly be distinguished from an anti-Israel demonstration. In both Europe and
America, such demonstrations did not exactly offer a congenial company to
Jews, who, like me, might have opposed the war and Ariel Sharon's policies but
could not feel at ease in places where the Israeli flag was being burned. That in

Hamas's and Hezbollah's social order of religious obscurantism and the debasement of women there would be no room for this progressive left's core principles is immaterial to the Corbyns, the Noam Chomskys, and many other possessors of what George Orwell defined as the "shallow self-righteousness of the leftwing intelligentsia."

On the left of America's Democratic Party these days, anti-Jewish and anti-Israel diatribes are serially produced by passionate, possibly even well-intentioned, albeit ill-informed public figures, some of whom flirt openly with reactionary bigots of the Louis Farrakhan kind. Branding American Jews as traitors, Congress as controlled by Jewish money, and Israel as America's top enemy are appallingly popular notions in such circles. Some members of the progressive "squad" in Congress have been particularly outspoken in this regard.

Not all of Israel's critics are the usual suspects, though. Changes in the perception of Israel are occurring also in traditionally friendly constituencies, such as Democratic white American liberals, many of whom are Jewish. This has to do with the racial lens becoming central to the way American *bien-pensants* frame the Palestinian conflict as one between a white colonial power trampling the rights of a colonized third-world nation.

Benjamin Netanyahu's alliance with America's fundamentalist evangelicals, hard-line Republicans, and other Trumpian constituencies, combined with Israel's drift to ultranationalist policies under his rule bear much, but not all, of the blame for this state of affairs. An American public, admittedly particularly among Democratic voters, that increasingly sees the Palestine-Israel conflict in human rights terms is now more ready to challenge the pro-Israel consensus in the face of Israel's occupation practices in Palestinian lands. There are also divisions along generational lines: more than twice as many Americans under 30 than older Americans felt Israel's wars in Gaza were unjustified.[9]

When all is said and done, Israel should not use the malignant flaws of her critics as a cover for her wrongheaded policies. It is improper to conveniently dismiss each and every attack against her reproachable policies as anti-Semitism. The memory of the Holocaust, too frequently used and abused by Israel's own leaders, should not be allowed to launder Israel's repressive practices in Palestinian lands. Nor should she be consoled by the macabre arithmetic of blood. This is a changing world where Israel is the last developed Western nation oppressing a non-Western people. Most of the conflicts known these days—Colombia, Somalia, Democratic Republic of Congo, Sudan, Iraq, and Afghanistan—are fundamentally internal conflicts, not stories of occupation. Israel does not have the luxury of dismissing legitimate criticism. Her democracy is a strategic asset that is being compromised by her illiberal governments. Russia gets punished by biting sanctions not only for refusing to relinquish an occupied land, Crimea, but also for being a revisionist, destabilizing autocracy. Israel has so far been immune to such punishment because she is a democracy and, yes, also because the Western guilt complex for centuries of persecutions of Jews still prevails over the malignant sentiments of Israel's indiscriminate critics in a way that shields, for now, the Jewish state from crippling sanctions.

* * *

Does Israel today have a national strategy that would address her Palestinian predicament? The answer would normally be that she aspires to be a "Jewish democratic state" with a Jewish majority. But how does one achieve this? With the two-state solution all but dead—"It is embarrassing to even talk about it seriously in polite or impolite company," observed a brilliant Palestinian friend—what would Israel do to prevent its slide into a one-state reality with an Arab majority in a latent state of civil war? Israel has yet to answer US President Lyndon Johnson's question in 1968 to the then Israeli prime minister, Levi Eshkol: "What kind of Israel do you want, Mr. Prime Minister?" Israel has never truly had a grand design for Palestinian lands. Everything always seemed to happen by osmosis and under domestic political pressures. Governments tended to push land-grabbing only to the limits that the international community could live with, that is, until Donald Trump came on the scene and, together with Netanyahu, reshaped the nature of the conflict and the foundations upon which it should be resolved.

Behind the cynical political manipulator there lies Netanyahu the ideologue. He has survived so many years in power precisely because the two pillars of his strategy—an unrelenting war against Iran's hegemonic ambitions and the drive to defeat and obliterate the Palestinian national movement—are shared by the overwhelming majority of Israelis and their political parties. Netanyahu is the embodiment of the Israelis' fear of and contempt for the Palestinians, and, like them, he never truly believed that the Palestinians would ever accept any Israeli peace plan or ever recognize the legitimacy of a Jewish state. Trump's peace plan fully coincided with Netanyahu's vision that for the Palestinians to get a crippled state they needed to be stripped of their entire national ethos and abandon the armed struggle.

Donald Trump and Benjamin Netanyahu worked on the assumption that the Palestinian national project had been defeated, and, through Trump's "Deal of the Century," they believed they had irreversibly revolutionized the paradigm for an Israeli-Palestinian peace. Trump also managed to make it reasonably acceptable to the Arab world and the international community. Iron-clad principles such as the 1967 borders, the illegality of Israeli settlements, the partition of Jerusalem, the Jordan Valley as part of the Palestinian state, and the inviolability of the right of return suddenly lost their sacrosanct status. Both Trump and Netanyahu managed to reach out to those Arab countries willing to relegate the

Palestinian problem in their quest for security cooperation with the Jewish state. It is revealing how sanguine the Arab reaction was to Trump's recognition of Jerusalem as Israel's capital; suffice to recall how staunchly Arab leaders backed Arafat when he serially rejected each and every compromise on Jerusalem we had made at Camp David and after.

The mute, even supportive reaction to Trump's plan from Europe, the heartland of the principles traditionally underlying the Palestinian cause, spoke volumes. Boris Johnson's government in the United Kingdom welcomed the peace plan as "a serious proposal" and "a positive step forward." Most significantly, the "unilaterally imposed humiliating terms" of the deal, a Russian publication commented, were a blessing to Russia, because "it provides a precedent for major powers dictating terms to weaker ones," and vindicates Russia's occupation of Crimea, which the *Moscow Times* defined as "Russia's West Bank." "Limited sovereignty," it said, was exactly what Moscow wanted to give to the former Soviet republics.[10]

In 2020, the then presidential candidate Elizabeth Warren rightly defined the Trump plan as "a rubber stamp for annexation [that] offers no chance for a real Palestinian state." President Joe Biden is of the same view today. The Biden administration is also right to resume humanitarian and economic assistance for the Palestinians and to reopen a decent diplomatic dialogue with the Palestinian Authority. The problem lies with the final objective. Secretary of State Antony Blinken indicated that assistance would be offered as part of the long-term objective of moving the parties back to the old peace process leading to a two-state solution. He does not see "near-term prospects for moving forward on that," but he would like to make sure that neither party takes steps that could compromise such a solution. This is all commendable. Investing in Palestinian society and institutions, and shifting policies to a rights-centered approach for the disenfranchised Palestinians, as proposed by some Middle East experts,[11] is a noble proposition but it would not in itself lead to a two-state solution. The old peace diplomacy is dead, and Biden himself realized it when he became the first president in more than thirty years not to appoint a Middle East peace envoy. It could be resuscitated if the Biden administration was willing to create a real cost for Israel's annexationist policies, and to invest the necessary political capital in order to harness Congress and major global powers in a grand multilateral effort to reaffirm "international law as a source of authority" in the Israel-Palestine situation. Nor is there any guarantee that reviving the old two-state diplomacy would be more effective now that the political environment in Israel, Palestine, and, no less importantly, the region has changed so radically since the better days of the old diplomacy.

Trump has gone, but for the Israelis he has managed to change the contours of the debate on Palestine. Israel's drive to implement the Trump plan's annexation provisos has been cut short by his departure, but it remains a project waiting for the right conditions in both Washington and Jerusalem. Self-defeated by their own rejectionist attitude with regard to all former peace plans and now betrayed by an Arab world weary with Palestine, and an indifferent international community, the Palestinians are politically disoriented. Abbas's rule in the West Bank depends to a large degree on the Israeli security services, and Hamas in Gaza is engaged in an intermittent war with Israel. Abbas's decision in April 2021 to suspend the legislative elections—the first in fifteen years—in the Palestinian territories was mainly due to his fear of a Hamas victory.

Donald Trump was, of course, wrong to assume that he had "solved" the Palestinian problem. History is about change and movement, and Palestine's agony can still be a galvanizing Arab cause and a renewed international concern. Nor should Israel be so complacent in assuming that her Arab alliances are more than a circumstantial and ephemeral affair. Saudi Arabia, for example, is reaching out these days to Israel's nemesis Iran. Israel's Arab alliances are the result of a changing geostrategic setup, and they might not last beyond a change in the regional strategic equation or a not improbable domestic upheaval affecting the Arab regimes. So long as the Jewish state does not have internationally recognized borders, it will continue to be perceived by the Arabs as possessing an irresistible propensity to expand. The incumbent Arab regimes have exhausted their already limited stores of legitimacy, and they are too weak to persist in ignoring their domestic constituencies, particularly if the political landscape is transformed, and simply hand over Palestine on a silver platter to Israel's fundamentalist right. The Arab states and Israel's new friends in Asia do not share with Israel the same outlook on the world to a degree that is essential for a true strategic alliance, and they certainly cannot replace her vital links with the West.

Resolving the Palestinian problem continues to be the vehicle through which Israel could legitimize and boost her now-covert alliances in the Arab world, enhance the chance of a regional system of security being ever created, and allow herself to consolidate her international standing. Without internationally recognized borders Israel will never be able to acquire a binding link with, perhaps even membership in, NATO, and an even closer association with the European Union. Peace in Palestine has additional strategic benefits that Israeli policymakers fail to appreciate. The approach of Israel's mortal enemies—the Iran-Hezbollah-Hamas axis—is to publicly support the two-state solution while actually doing everything in their power to derail it. A Palestinian peace that would legitimize the existence of the Jewish state in the region is the strategic nightmare of the region's "axis of resistance."

By disguising an agrarian appetite under the mantle of a security argument Israeli governments have distorted military thinking and turned the IDF into an army of occupation with a police mentality, away from their natural task of preparing for war against external enemies. The deficient performance and sapped morale of Israel's ground forces in the Gaza and Lebanon wars were a direct consequence of this. If Trump's plan is unilaterally implemented, Former High Military Commanders, an organization opposed to the plan, warned that Israel would have to deploy in the West Bank between three and five divisions and recruit 300,000 reservists in order to control a maze of 169 isolated Palestinian "islands" that together create a border 1,800 km long with annexed Israeli lands. The economic tag price would also be astronomical.[12]

Nations in history hardly ever get assassinated; they commit suicide, and the occupation is cruising into Israel's self-destruction. The real existential threat facing Israel is not nuclear Iran; rather, it is to be found in the morally corrosive effects of the oppressive occupation of the Palestinian people. Fifty-four years of occupation have taken their toll. Israel's grip on the Palestinian territories is key to understanding the reasons for the illiberal zeitgeist that has overtaken Israel's public life. The unlawful practices of occupation were bound to spill over into the country's recognized boundaries and further enhance its ethnocentrist impulses. Israel's unapologetically annexationist governments spearheaded the attack on Israel democracy's last frontier, the Supreme Court and the free press. We saw "disloyal" artists being stripped of government subsidies, and peace-seeking NGOs being scrutinized as foreign agents while right-wing groups got lavish aid from the government, Jewish foreign donors, and casino magnates. Some time ago, a novel on a love affair between a Palestinian and a Jewish girl was banned from the school curriculum. And a bill aimed at Israeli Arabs' representatives in Parliament has been passed that would allow the dismissal of MPs for "disloyalty" to the state. In its reckless flirtation with illiberal democracy, Benjamin Netanyahu's far-right coalition produced in 2018 the Nation-State Law, which stands in stark contradiction with both Israel's 1948 Declaration of Independence and the 1992 Constitutional Law: Human Dignity and Liberty, both of which recognize the full and unconditional individual rights of all, Jews and Arabs, in the "Jewish and Democratic" State.

Significantly, the Nation-State Law was enacted when the Israeli Arabs' integration was progressing apace. The 2017 Israel Democracy Institute Index of Arab-Israeli relations found that 70 percent speak fluent Hebrew, 77 percent are not interested in separation, and 80 percent support the two-state solution. Professor Amal Jamal of Tel Aviv University studied the consistent rise of an Arab middle class, and an empowered Arab civil society eager to share in the revolution of opportunities that Israeli governments are finally facilitating.[13] There is still a long way to go. But despite the violent feuds between Jews and Arabs in Israel's so-called mixed cities during the last war with Gaza, the process of Arab "Israelization" seems irreversible. In the last seven years, the number of Arab students in Israel's universities increased by 80 percent, 50 percent in computing sciences, and 60 percent in postgraduate and doctoral programs. In 2019, a third of the new students matriculated in the Technion–Israel Institute of Technology, ranked as the best university in the country, were Arabs. In the last decade, the number of Arabs employed in high-tech went up by 1,800 percent, with women representing 25 percent of this increase. In total, 10 percent of the start-up nation's employees and 15 percent of Israel's physicians are Arabs. This is partly the result of the narrowing of the budgeting gap per pupil between the Jewish and Arab sector from 27 percent in 2013 to 12 percent in 2018.[14]

It is, then, a travesty of reality to tag Israel, as some of her critics do with malicious frivolity, as an apartheid state. There is still a long way to go for full equality for Israel's sizable Arab minority, but the trend of greater Arab emancipation described here is promising. It was an Arab judge who sent to jail Israel's former president Moshe Katsav, and the government that now rules Israel relies on the support of an Arab Islamist party that managed to get for its constituency a long overdue package of social and economic improvements. Not exactly a South African state of affairs. The term apartheid cannot be applied to the Palestinian occupied territories either. Occupation practices, however oppressive, should not be confused with apartheid. Every Western occupation in Asia and Africa resorted to similar practices. Full military and civilian control of the local population is occupation, not apartheid. Also, the separation wall in the occupied territories was built for political and security reasons, essentially to stop the waves of suicide terrorism of 2001–2, not as a device of racial segregation. The Palestinians are in a fully justified struggle for national and political self-determination, and for an end to Israel's repressive and reproachable military occupation, not for the end of racial segregation.

My view in this book has indeed been that the threat of apartheid does exit. It lies not in the occupation as such, however heinous and oppressive, but in the lurking danger of the annexation of the occupied territories and the decline into a binational state under Jewish supremacy. This is where I see the danger of the Nation-State Law. It was supposed to vaccinate Jewish Israel against the consequences of her drift into a Jewish-Arab binational reality from the sea to the Jordan River. Nor do I underestimate the law's inherent bleak consequences inside Israel proper. Like Trump and the mushrooming number of illiberal and xenophobic populist leaders throughout Europe, Netanyahu and his right-wing coalitions accumulated political capital by appealing to tribal instincts and by pitting groups against each other. His rule by incitement and ultranationalistic, anti-Arab rhetoric compounded by the death of the peace process destroyed past optimism among Israelis that their country could be both Jewish and democratic. This has now become, according to polling by the Israeli Democracy Institute, a minority position.[15] Even so, the Nation-State Law clashes with the changing socioeconomic reality of the Arab minority. I have not lost hope in its obliteration at some point in the foreseeable future.

* * *

Zionism was born as a rupture with Jewish past, but to the ideological right, the State of Israel is the messianic culmination of Jewish history, and Judea and Samaria are a spiritual empire, a surrogate religion, not a political project. They would dismiss their "defeatist" detractors with the claim that the entire Zionist enterprise was an unrealistic dream that miraculously came true. Faith and ideology tend to blind people from seeing reality as it is, for there was nothing miraculous about Zionism's exploits. Zionism materialized because the historical conditions and the political circumstances favored it, and because Zionist diplomacy wisely navigated through the waters of international diplomacy. The 1967 victory is not a license for Israel to set to herself utterly unmoral and unrealistic objectives, such as the eternal occupation of a disenfranchised people. Not every fantasy is a vision. The ethos of Israel's far right lies in its insistence on blurring this distinction. The right's fantasies belie the fundamental teaching of international relations that political positions are always susceptible to change. Nor is it true that nothing can distract the Arab world from its hostility. They will never accept the *moral foundations* of Zionism, but, as Israel's peace with Egypt and Jordan and the 2002 Arab Peace Initiative indicate, they would consider accepting the *political legitimacy* of a Jewish state. The peace process is not supposed to deliver paradise, but its qualified promise requires superseding fatalism.

Nor is succumbing to the delusionary comfort of the status quo an option. Of all people, it was Ariel Sharon who taught the settlers, the Lords of the Land for so many years, that their hubris was out of tune with Israel's longing for normalcy. In the 2005 Gaza disengagement, it looked as if the notion finally percolated through to Israelis that this Jewish republic of settlers on the golden sands of Gaza and the hilltops of Judea and Samaria, at times in lawless defiance of the state and more frequently in complicity with it, had become an unbearable moral and political burden. Once considered a patriotic vanguard, the settlers were then an entanglement that needed to be untied if Israel were to maintain its Jewish and democratic character. In the summer of 2005, it looked as though Israel was a society mature enough to face the formidable challenge of defining its final borders without cataclysmic upheaval. The precedent was established and, for the first time since 1967, the State of Israel challenged Eretz Yisrael and survived.

After long decades of rule by the right, Israel vitally needs a political change that would craft a new narrative and help reshape the zeitgeist. A high-tech, Westernized society living in an explosive revolutionary region, Israel cannot withstand a state of perpetual war indefinitely. To set the course for a generous policy on Palestine, the Israelis' tendency to minimize internal frictions through a self-defeating, hollow consensus would need to be superseded. Even Rabin's assassination is no longer being commemorated as the divisive ideological debate over war and peace that it was, as if the man died in his bed of a heart attack. And, as if there were no hard choices to be made, the overwhelming majority of Israelis voted in four consecutive elections in the last two years for a paralyzing dead-lock between the right and an ideologically amorphous center and left of center. Recently, Tel Aviv University disgracefully closed down its Tami Steinmetz Center for Peace Research "for lack of public interest in the subject." The deep divide of the Rabin years, Camp David, and Annapolis need to be recovered for Israel to be able to face the difficult choices of her existential dilemmas. This requires confronting head-on the annexationist right's Hobbesian view of the Palestinian problem as an equation of naked power. Jewish statehood is a gen-uine reality, a historic necessity. But is it truly written in the stars, as the Israeli messianic right, always glutted with the divine certainty and exhilaration of vic-tory, believes, that the Palestinians would always be history's losers and we its winners? Are the Palestinians doomed to submit to our encroachments forever and be what Giuseppe Mazzini defined as "the bastards of humanity" who have neither country of their own nor rights nor admission as brothers in the fellow-ship of peoples?[16]

"To be defeated and not submit is victory," Poland's national hero Józef Piłsudski told his countrymen. "To be victorious and rest on one's laurels is de-feat." While victorious Israel rests on its laurels, the Palestinians' defeat does not mean they have lost the will to pursue their objectives. Defeats in history were frequently a wellspring of political and intellectual recovery, as our own Jewish history shows, while the hubris of the victor was often the avenue to a reck-oning, particularly if the fruits of his victory are widely seen, as is the case with Israel's colonization of Palestinian lands, as illegitimate and illegal profiteering. In his angry prophecy "The Homeland Is in Danger" of March 1980, when no more than seventeen thousand settlers lived in the occupied territories, the re-nowned historian of the French Revolution and its offspring, political messia-nism, Jacob Talmon warned of the bitter fruits of victory, namely, Israel's return to the patterns of thought and action characteristic of an isolated, exilic religious sect with the mentality of a master race. The 1967 victory was to Talmon a curse in disguise, the moral and political defeat of the victor,[17] exactly the way that Heinrich Mann referred to Germany's 1870 victory over France: *Vae Victoribus* ("Woe to the victors!").[18]

But for such a course of history to be kind to the defeated, the Palestinians must undergo a deep and long overdue process of national renewal and polit-ical soul-searching. Their serial rejection of reasonable peace plans in recent years was a typical Pavlovian reaction that exposed the built-in flaw in the Palestinian movement, a despairing incapacity to turn historical conjunctures into opportunities. Anger is not a strategy. In its indignation at US policies and the indifference of other international powers the Palestinian leadership fre-quently fell into the realm of the imaginary.

President Abbas asserted at the Islamic Summit in Istanbul on December 13, 2017, that "from now on" he would not accept "any role" for the United States in the peace process, and even called the world to reconsider its recognition of Israel.[19] Abbas presumably is also still waiting for the United Kingdom to apologize for the 1917 Balfour Declaration. The same Abbas was heard in a Fatah Central Committee meeting on April 29, 2021, vulgarly cursing the whole world including China, Russia, the United States (which had just renewed financial and political assistance to the Palestinian Authority), and most importantly, all the Arabs. He only spared Israel.[20]

The international community has a crucial role in facilitating Palestinian renewal. Western indulgence of Palestinian comportment, be it in war or in moments where difficult decisions on peace needed to be addressed, has been highly detrimental to the Palestinian cause. The international pampering of the national Palestinian movement is unparalleled in modern history and, no less importantly, was in vital crossroads of the conflict an obstacle to a settlement. Rarely—if ever—is history familiar with a similar case of a disparity between the high degree of international support enjoyed by a national movement and the poor results thereof. International support was frequently interpreted by the Palestinian leadership as an implicit encouragement to persist in its almost built-in incapacity to take decisions, and find instead satisfaction in Israel's decline into the position of a state put in the dock of the court of international opinion.

International indulgence is, of course, only one of the many reasons why an orderly peace process is not in the offing anymore. With a new superpower emerging in the region, Russia, with neither the capacity nor the vocation of the peacemaker, *Pax Americana* is not about to be replaced by *Pax Russiana*. Hence, the Israel-Palestine situation might have to wait for a major geostrategic shift in the region that could come in a variety of ways and forms, such as a violent, abrupt Israeli disengagement from the West Bank or, conversely, a unilateral implementation of Trump's annexation promises, a mega-terror event, a major conflagration, or a new and much more determined explosion of an Arab and Palestinian Spring that would sweep away regimes and borders. Each of these scenarios carries the potential to reshape the attitudes of the parties to the conflict. The result would not necessarily be either of the scenarios described in this book, but could also create the conditions for either of them. After all, whatever progress toward peace ever occurred in the Israeli-Arab conflict came about only after such major strategic shake-ups. If politicians and statesmen continue to fail, as they have done so far, the floor would have to be left to the impersonal forces of history, to Clio, its goddess, and to her wild cards and unexpected turns. The iron law of unintended consequences can humble an arrogant and complacent nation once it is forced to face such a cataclysm. With Israel compulsively rejecting diplomacy as a way of addressing security challenges, the cataclysm of a total war with Iran is not too farfetched a specter.

Another possible cataclysmic scenario that could force Israelis and Palestinians back into the search for a diplomatic solution is the question of Jerusalem, currently the most visible vortex of instability in the Israeli-Palestinian situation. Israeli poet Yehuda Amichai wrote of Jerusalem after 1967: "You look in vain for the barbed wires / You know well that such / things don't really disappear." In this house divided against itself, a divided Jewish-Muslim Belfast, two national collectives live under a different set of laws, and different rights and entitlements. The void created by the vanishing Palestinian Authority's presence in East Jerusalem has been filled by a mostly secular young Palestinian generation that turned the Haram Al-Sharif into the ultimate icon of their resistance to Israeli occupation. It is through the narrative of religious violence, so omnipresent around them (significantly, the terror by knife by young Jerusalemite Palestinians is an ISIS symbol), that they fulfill their mission as rebels against the docility of their fathers and the incompetence of the Palestinian leadership.

By using Al-Aqsa as the defining symbol of the Palestinian cause, the young generation of rebels in Jerusalem and beyond brings the conflict with Israel to the level of an apocalyptic confrontation that can inflame the entire region. This is so precisely because a similarly dangerous Jewish messianism has been building up in recent years around the Temple Mount, the home of Judaism's destroyed sacred temples. Strict Halachic rulings have always prohibited Jews from ascending to the Mount lest they profane this most sanctified of Jewish shrines before it is redeemed by the coming of the Messiah. But, now, a political theology claiming Jewish sovereignty over the Mount in order to rebuild the temple has been gaining ground not only among religious fanatics—more than a dozen messianic foundations work to retrieve the Temple Mount for Jewish cult—but also within Israel's ruling party, Likud, whose soft wing has been decimated. This is all an open invitation to millions of Muslims throughout the world to what could be the mother of all jihads.[21]

Hamas and Islamic Jihad in Gaza are driven precisely by such a political faith. In their May 2021 war on Israel they gained a strategic victory by connecting all the dots needed to gain primacy in the Palestinian national movement. They positioned themselves as the protectors of Jerusalem and Al-Aqsa and as the spearhead of Islam's struggle against the Israeli-Jewish occupier. The Gaza war also shook the prevailing consensus among Israelis that Palestinian nationalism had been defeated and thus that a political solution to the conflict was no longer necessary. But, notwithstanding the strategic setback that Israel's recent Abraham Peace Accords with four Arab states meant to the Palestinians, their national cause can always re-emerge with a vengeance. The Gaza war also taught the complacent Israelis that the era of glorious wars and uncontested victories is over.[22] And if Hamas's ultimate objective to take over the PLO and control the West Bank as well materializes, Israel would face a neighbor that would require a truly Damascene conversion to abandon its utter rejection of a Jewish state on Palestine's sacred Waqf land in order to be a negotiating partner. If proof were still needed, Hamas's battle for Jerusalem reaffirmed the definition of the conflict in irreconcilable religious terms.

We bear, then, a heavy responsibility to persist in conceiving bold and generous solutions. History teaches that interim arrangements, such as the political limbo the Palestinians are in, cannot last. The autonomies of the Habsburg Empire eventually ushered in sovereign states, and France's abortive attempts to force Tunisia and Algeria to settle for an autonomy ended in their full independence. Nor do we have precedents that democratic societies ever terminally subdued national movements. The great Palestinian saga needs to end in a piece of real estate out of a far larger historical Palestine. Alas, the classical two-state solution we fought for is a structural impossibility. My conviction is that only by introducing Jordan—which not only has a particular link to the question of Palestine but also holds the status of the Muslim guardian of the Haram al-Sharif—into the equation, could the idea of Palestinian statehood be salvaged from the debris of so many failing attempts to reach peace.

Israel's Arab neighbors have come a long way from the philosophy of utter rejection and denial toward accepting the legitimacy of a Jewish state within internationally recognized boundaries. The era of procrastination must be ended. It would be an unpardonable blunder if we were to persist in our refusal to draw lessons from our past mistakes and succumb instead to the strategy of doomsday of the forces in our midst, particularly the Jewish zealots in Judea and Samaria, of the kind which had twice in our millennial history brought about the destruction of Jewish sovereignty.

NOTES

A Note on Vocabulary

1. See Tarifi's declarations (and mine) in "Israel: Jerusalem: Safe Passage Agreement Signed," October 5, 1999, *AP Archive*. http://www.aparchive.com/metadata/youtube/03d8dc1a77b 68bcc9f79f689a1cfec68.

Introduction

1. See https://www.brookings.edu/wp-content/uploads/2016/06/israel_palestine_key_fin dings_telhami_FINAL.pdf, accessed August 3, 2021.
2. Robert Fisk, *The Great War for Civilization: The Conquest of the Middle East* (London: Fourth Estate, 2005), 540.
3. See Seth Anziska, *Preventing Palestine. A Political History from Camp David to Oslo* (Princeton, NJ: Princeton University Press, 2018).
4. Quoted in Adnan Abu Odeh, "Religious Inclusion. Political Inclusion: Jerusalem as an Undivided Capital," *Catholic University Law Review* 45, no. 3 (1996), https://scholarship.law. edu/lawreview/vol45/iss3/4/, accessed August 3, 2021.
5. Aaron David Miller, *The Much Too Promised Land: America's Elusive Search For Arab-Israeli Peace* (New York: Bantam Dell, 2008), 173.
6. Albert Camus, *Algerian Chronicles*, ed. Alice Kaplan, trans. Arthur Goldhammer (Cambridge, MA: Belknap Press of Harvard University Press, 2013), 28
7. Noam Chomsky, *American Power and the New Mandarins* (New York: Pantheon Books, The New Press, 1969).
8. James C. Thomson, "How Could Vietnam Happen? An Autopsy," *The Atlantic* (April 1968), https://www.theatlantic.com/magazine/archive/1968/04/how-could-vietnam-happen-an-autopsy/306462/.
9. Shaul Arieli, *All Israel' Borders: A Century of Struggle for Independence, Identity, Settlement and Territory* [in Hebrew] (Tel Aviv: Yedioth Ahronoth, 2018), 176.
10. For the full quote from Rabin's speech, see Shaul Arieli, *12 Myth About the Israeli-Palestinian-Conflict* (in Hebrew) (Tel Aviv: Yedioth Ahronoth, 2021), 351.
11. Idith Zertal, *Israel's Holocaust and the Politics of Nationhood,* Cambridge University Press, 2005.
12. 1 Samuel 14:32.
13. The full English text of Amr's letter to Arafat can be found at http://imra.org.il/story.php?id= 13508.
14. Gilead Sher, *Just Beyond Reach: The Israeli-Palestinian Peace Negotiations 1999–2001* [in Hebrew] (Tel Aviv: Yedioth Ahronoth, 2001), 408.
15. Elsa Walsh, "The Prince," *The New Yorker*, March 24, 2003, https://www.newyorker.com/magazine/2003/03/24/the-prince-3, accessed August 8, 2021.

16. Shlomo Ben-Ami, "The Only Way Out: A Solution in The Middle East Must be International, Led by the United States with the Participation of Europe, Russia and Key Arab States," *Newsweek*, August 20, 2001; Shlomo Ben-Ami, "A New Paradigm for an Israeli-Palestinian Peace" *The Financial Times*, October 31, 2001.

Chapter 1

1. Ahmed Qurie ("Abu Ala"), *Beyond Oslo: The Struggle for Palestine; inside the Middle East Peace Process; from Rabin's Death to Camp David* (London: I. B. Tauris, 2008), 110–14.

Chapter 2

1. Danny Yatom, *The Confidant: From Sayeret Matkal to the Mossad.* [in Hebrew] (Tel Aviv: Yedioth Ahronoth, 2018), 355–56.
2. Shaul Arieli, *12 Israeli Myths*, 350.
3. Qurie ("Abu Ala"), *Beyond Oslo*, 115, 118.
4. Qurie ("Abu Ala"), *Beyond Oslo*, 258.

Chapter 3

1. Henry Siegman, "Israel: A Historic Statement," *The New York Review of Books*, February 8, 2001, https://www.nybooks.com/articles/2001/02/08/israel-historic-statement/, accessed August 3, 2021.

Chapter 4

1. National Security Council, *Initial Positions for the Negotiations* (in Hebrew), December 22, 1999.

Chapter 5

1. Qurie ("Abu Ala"), *Beyond Oslo*, 147.
2. See above, p. 38.
3. Dennis Ross, *The Missing Peace: The Inside Story of the Fight for Middle East Peace* (New York: Farrar, Straus, and Giroux, 2005), 634–40 .

Chapter 6

1. Qurie ("Abu Ala"), *Beyond Oslo*, 148–55.
2. Martin Indyk, *Innocent Abroad: An Intimate Account of American Diplomacy in the Middle East* (New York: Simon and Schuster, 2009), 300–302.
3. Ehud Barak, *My Country, My Life: Fighting for Israel, Searching for Peace* (New York: St. Martin's Press, 2018), 352–53.
4. Qurie ("Abu Ala"), *Beyond Oslo*, 163–70.

Chapter 7

1. "Abu Mazen: If We Were to Meet Again in Camp David We Would Take the Same Positions," *Al Ayyam*, July 29, 2001, https://www.memri.org/sd/SP25001.html.
2. See p. above, pp. 45–46.

Chapter 8

1. Qurie ("Abu Ala"), *Beyond Oslo*, 174.
2. Danny Yatom, *The Confidant*, 379.
3. Danny Yatom, *The Confidant*, 374.

4. See Chapter 5, pp. 45–46.
5. Miller, *The Much Too Promised Land*, 298.

Chapter 9

1. See Arieli, *12 Myths*, 360
2. Qurie ("Abu Ala"), *Beyond Oslo*, 210.
3. Qurie ("Abu Ala"), *Beyond Oslo*, 227.

Chapter 10

1. Yatom, *The Confidant*, 382–83.
2. Ahmed Qurie ("Abu Ala"), *The Peace Negotiations in Stockholm, Camp David and Taba* [in Arabic] (Beirut: Palestine College, 2006), 262; Qurie ("Abu Ala"), *Beyond Oslo*, 201–2.
3. The text in Qurie ("Abu Ala"), *Beyond Oslo*, 202–3.

Chapter 11

1. Free of political catchwords and nationalistic demagoguery, Nir Hasson's *Urshalim: Israelis and Palestinians in Jerusalem 1967–2017* [in Hebrew] (Tel Aviv: Yedioth Ahronoth, 2017) offers a fascinating and most elaborate portrait of the real, socio-culturally divided Jerusalem as it evolved after 1967.

Chapter 12

1. Barak, *My Country, My Life*, 372–74.
2. Clinton's mention of Arafat's pledge to allow such high percentages of Israeli annexation casts doubt on the Palestinians' claim that Arafat withdrew his offer immediately after making it. See above, pp. 73–74.
3. Barak, *My Country, My Life*, 374–375.
4. Barak, *My Country, My Life*, 378.

Chapter 13

1. See above, p. 74.
2. See Chapter 22, pp. 153–54.
3. Yatom, *The Confidant*, 416–17.
4. Yatom, *The Confidant*, 419.
5. Akram Haniyah, "The Camp David Papers," *Journal of Palestine Studies* 30, no. 2 (Winter 2001), 32.
6. Indyk, *Innocent Abroad*, 335–36.

Chapter 14

1. Excerpts from Saeb Erakat's archive are in Yossi Beilin's archive. The excerpts are quoted by Beilin's biographer, in Avi Shilon, *The Left-Wing's Sorrow* [in Hebrew] (Tel Aviv: Kinneret Zmora-Bitan Dvir, 2017), 367–69.
2. Marwan Kanafani, *Sanawat al-Amal* (Cairo: Dar al-Shorouk, 2007), 419, quoted in Daniel Kurtzer et al., *The Peace Puzzle: America's Quest for Arab-Israeli Peace, 1989–2011* (Ithaca, NY: Cornell University Press, 2013), 137.
3. See Chapter 13, p. 95.
4. Indyk, *Innocent Abroad*, 336.
5. Barak, *My Country, My Life*, 380.
6. Yatom, *The Confidant*, 421.
7. Yatom, *The Confidant*, 423.

Chapter 15

1. "Abu Mazen, "If We Were to Meet Again in Camp David We Would Take the Same Positions," *Al Ayyam,* July 28, 29, 2001, http://www.memri.org.il/cgi-webaxy/sal/sal.pl?lang=he&ID= 875141_memri&act=show&dbid=articles&dataid=391.
2. Qurie ("Abu Ala"), *Beyond Oslo,* 247–48.
3. Ross, *The Missing Peace,* 715.
4. Haniyah, "The Camp David Papers," *Journal of Palestine Studies* 30, no 2, Winter 2001, 17–18.
5. See above, Chapter 12.

Chapter 16

1. Miller, *The Much Too Promised Land,* 306.

Chapter 18

1. *Al-Hayat al-Jadida,* "Towards the Declaration of an Independent Palestinian State," July 2, 2000, http://www.memri.org.il/cgi-webaxy/sal/sal.pl?lang=he&ID=875141_memri&act= show&dbid=articles&dataid=196, accessed August 7, 2021.
2. *Al Ayam,* "The Background to the Outbreak of Violence in the Occupied Territories and Its Objectives," July 24, 2000, http://www.memri.org.il/cgi-webaxy/sal/sal.pl?lang=he&ID= 875141_memri&act=show&dbid=articles&dataid=229, accessed August 7, 2021.
3. See above, Chapter 6, pp. 48–50.
4. https://www.ynet.co.il/articles/0,7340,L-22146,00.html, accessed August 7, 2021.
5. The editor of the Hebron-based *Akhbar el Halil*—the same weekly in which Barghouti warned of a military confrontation—Khalid Amayreh, claimed he was constantly harassed and threatened by Arafat's intelligence services: https://ifex.org/journalist-threatened-by-pale stinian-intelligence-services-in-hebron/, accessed August 7, 2021.
6. See the evolution of Palestinian opinion with regard to the peace process and Palestinian institutions in Jacob Shamir and Khalil Shikaki; *Palestinian and Israeli Public Opinion: The Political Imperative in the Second Intifada* (Bloomington, IN: Indiana University Press, 2010), esp. 61.
7. For a thorough account of the Intifada, see Amos Harel and Avi Isacharoff, *The Seventh War: How Did We Win and Why Did We Lose in Our War against the Palestinians?* [in Hebrew] (Tel Aviv: Yedioth Ahronoth, 2004).
8. Ahmed Qurie, ("Abu Ala"), *Peace Negotiations in Palestine: From the Second Intifada to the Roadmap* (London: I. B. Tauris, 2015), 12.
9. On the Sharm El-Sheikh conference, see Chapter 20, pp. 140–142.
10. See Chapter 20, pp. 143–144.
11. Qurie ("Abu Ala"), *Peace Negotiations in Palestine,* 16–17.
12. Qurie ("Abu Ala"), *Peace Negotiations in Palestine,* 21.
13. Qurie ("Abu Ala"), *Peace Negotiations in Palestine,* 26.
14. Yezid Sayigh, "Arafat and the Anatomy of a Revolt," *Survival* 43, no. 3, Autumn 2001, 47–60.
15. See a discussion of the anticolonial paradigm on pp. 310–313.
16. Qurie ("Abu Ala"), *Peace Negotiations in Palestine,* 32.
17. Qurie ("Abu Ala"), *Peace Negotiations in Palestine,* 31.
18. Qurie ("Abu Ala"), *Peace Negotiations in Palestine,* 32; Khalil Shikaki, "Palestinians Divided," *Foreign Affairs 81,* no. 1 (2002): 89, https://www.foreignaffairs.com/articles/palestinian-au- thority/2002-01-01/palestinians-divided, accessed August 7, 2021.
19. Susie Linfield, *The Lion's Den: Zionism and the Left from Hanah Arendt to Noam Chomsky* (New Haven, CT: Yale University Press, 2019), 199.
20. Qurie ("Abu Ala"), *Peace Negotiations,* 20.

Chapter 19

1. Henry Kissinger, *Does America Need a Foreign Policy? Toward a Diplomacy for the 21st Century* (New York: Simon and Schuster, 2001), 185.

2. Mario Andrea Rigoni, *Elogio dell'America* (Rome: Fondazione Liberal, 2003).
3. See Chapter 27, pp. 204–206.

Chapter 21

1. Ross, *The Missing Peace*, 746–47.
2. Raphael Cohen-Almagor, "History of Track Two Peace Negotiations: Interview with Hussein Agha," *Israel Studies* 26, no.1 (2003): 47–72.
3. Ross, *The Missing Peace*, 748.

Chapter 22

1. Indyk, *Innocent Abroad*, 346–47.
2. Yatom, *The Confidant*, 407.
3. On my peace offers see Indyk. *Innocent Abroad*, 364–66.
4. Indyk. *Innocent Abroad*, 335.
5. Indyk, *Innocent Abroad*, 366.
6. Quoted in Indyk, *Innocent Abroad*, 364.
7. For the full text, see https://www.usip.org/sites/default/files/Peace%20Puzzle/10_Clinton%20Parameters.pdf.
8. For the Carter State Department's peace plan, see Anziska, *Preventing Palestine*, 29–31.

Chapter 23

1. Bill Clinton, *My Life* (London: Hutchinson, 2004), 936–46 defined our reservations as still being inside the parameters and the Palestinians' outside.
2. Yasser Arafat, "The Palestinian Vision of Peace," *New York Times*, February 3, 2002, https://www.nytimes.com/2002/02/03/opinion/the-palestinian-vision-of-peace.html, accessed August 8, 2021.
3. "NSU Memo Regarding President Clinton's Proposals," January 2, 2001, http:/transparency.aljazeera.net/en/projects/thepalestinepapers/20121821232131550.html, accessed August 8, 2021.
4. "The 44 Reasons Why Fatah Movement Rejects the Proposals made by US President Clinton" in Fatah Movement Central Publication, *Our Opinion*, January 1–7, 2001. Discussed in David Makovsky, "Time Running Out on Clinton Proposals," *Washington Institute for Near East Policy*, January 11, 2001, https://www.washingtoninstitute.org/policy-analysis/view/time-running-out-on-clinton-proposals, accessed August 8, 2021, 3.
5. Elsa Walsh, "The Prince," *The New Yorker*, March 24, 2003, https://www.newyorker.com/magazine/2003/03/24/the-prince-3, accessed August 8, 2021.
6. Ross, *The Missing Peace*, 757.

Chapter 24

1. The full document is in Qurie ("Abu Ala"), *Beyond Oslo*, 285–93.
2. Khalil Shikaki, "There is No Returning to the Pre-Intifada Period", *Palestine-Israel Journal* 7, no. 4 (2000). https://pij.org/app.php/articles/250/there-is-no-returning-to-the-preintifada-period. See a more elaborate account in Khalil Shikaki, "Palestinians Divided," *Foreign Affairs* 81, no. 1 (2002): 89–105. https://www.foreignaffairs.com/articles/palestinian-authority/2002-01-01/palestinians-divided.

Chapter 25

1. Qurie ("Abu Ala"), *Beyond Oslo*, 308
2. Gilead Sher, *Just beyond Reach*, 408.

3. Reported in Elsa Walsh, "The Prince," *The New Yorker*, March 24, 2003.
4. Qurie ("Abu Ala"), *Peace Negotiations in Palestine*, 7.
5. Qurie ("Abu Ala"), *Beyond Oslo*, 310–11. "Taba Negotiations: The Moratinos Non-Paper," www.mideastweb.org/moratinos.htm
6. "Clinton Addresses Open Letters to Israelis, Palestinians," https://edition.cnn.com/2001/WORLD/meast/01/19/mideast.03/.
7. The truth is that these were all standard pronouncements by both Amr Moussa and El-Baz with regard to Israel in the Middle East. In 2001, Moussa's anti-Israel tirades got him pop-icon status. Egyptian pop singer Shaaban Abdel Rahim released then a song with the line, "I hate Israel and I love Amr Moussa." See, "The Throwback," *The New Republic*, April 30, 2011 on "The anti-Israel demagogue," https://newrepublic.com/article/87607/moussa-biography-egypt-arab-league-mubarak. On Moussa's pronouncements, see https://www.ynet.co.il/articles/0,7340,L-396488,00.html, accessed August 9, 2021, and https://www.ynet.co.il/articles/0,7340,L-418269,00.html, accessed August 9, 2021.
8. http://www.ahewar.org/debat/show.art.asp?aid=162860&r=0, accessed August 9, 2021.
9. Quoted by Tracy Wilkinson, "Once Applauded as a Hero, Clinton Bows Out Amid Palestinian Catcalls", *Los Angeles Times*, January 19, 2001, https://www.latimes.com/archives/la-xpm-2001-jan-19-mn-14350-story.html.

Chapter 26

1. https://www.pcpsr.org/en/node/461, accessed August 9, 2021.
2. https://www.democracynow.org/2006/2/14/fmr_israeli_foreign_minister_if_i, accessed August 9, 2021.
3. Akram Haniyah, "The Camp David Papers," p. 14.
4. https://www.pcpsr.org/en/node/461, accessed August 9, 2021.
5. Linfield, *The Lion's Den*, 295, 296.
6. Haim Ramon, *Against the Wind* [in Hebrew] (Tel Aviv: Yedioth Ahronoth, 2020), 585.
7. Abu Mazen, "If We Were to Meet Again in Camp David We Would Take the Same Positions."
8. Henry Kissinger, *Does America Need a Foreign Policy?*, 175.

Chapter 27

1. Ewen MacAskill, "Arafat Approves Taba Plan Too Late," *The Guardian*, June 22, 2002, https://www.theguardian.com/world/2002/jun/22/israel.
2. Alan Philps, "Desperate Arafat Grasps Clinton Peace Plan," *The Telegraph*, June 22, 2002, https://www.telegraph.co.uk/news/worldnews/middleeast/israel/1398064/Desperate-Arafat-grasps-Clinton-peace-plan.html, accessed August 11, 2021.
3. Ari Shavit, "Dov Weissglas Interview: The Big Freeze," *Haaretz*, 8 October 2004.
4. Ari Shavit (ed.), *Partition: Disengagement and Beyond* [in Hebrew] (Jerusalem: Keter Publishing, 2005). My own contribution is in 66–71.
5. Ramon, *Against the Wind*, 403–6.
6. "Prime Minister's Ariel Sharon Address to the Knesset Prior to the Vote on the Disengagement Plan (October 25, 2004)," https://www.knesset.gov.il/docs/eng/sharonspeech04.htm. For Sharon's political battles over his disengagement plan see, Nir Hefez and Gadi Bloom, *The Shepherd: The Life Story of Ariel Sharon* [in Hebrew] (Tel Aviv: Yedioth Ahronoth, 2005), 724–73.
7. See a discussion of Olmert's Convergence plan in Chapter 33, pp. 273–277.
8. Omer Zanany, *The Annapolis Process (2007–2008): Negotiation and Its Discontents* (Jerusalem: The Tami Steinmetz Center for Peace Research and Molad—The Center for the Renewal of Israeli Democracy, 2015) is a thorough, exhaustive study of Annapolis.
9. Udi Dekel and Lia Moran-Gilad, *The Annapolis Process: A Missed Opportunity for a Two-State Solution?* The Institute for National and Security Studies (INSS), Tel Aviv University, May, 2021, https://www.inss.org.il/publication/annapolis/, accessed August 10, 2021, 30, 119.

10. Condoleezza Rice, *No Higher Honor: A Memoir of My Years in Washington* (New York: Crown, 2011), 723.
11. Omer Zanany, *The Annapolis Process*, 30–31.
12. Udi Dekel and Moran-Gilad, *The Annapolis Process*, 5, 7.
13. The entire plan is in Ehud Olmert, *In Person* [in Hebrew] (Tel Aviv: Yedioth Ahronoth, 2018), 838–40.
14. Udi Dekel and Moran-Gilad, *The Annapolis Process*, 48, refers to the case of Annapolis.
15. Quoted in Dekel and Moran-Gilad, *The Annapolis Process*, 93.
16. Dekel and Moran-Gilad, *The Annapolis Process*, 52–57, offers a detailed description of the discussions on security.
17. Omer Zanany, *The Annapolis Process*, 101.
18. Condoleezza Rice, *No Higher Honor*, 652.
19. Tom Najem, Michael Molloy, Michael Bell, and John Bell (eds.), *Governance and Security in Jerusalem: The Jerusalem Old City Initiative,* UCLA Center for Middle East Development (London and New York: Routledge), 2017.
20. Dekel and Moran-Gilad, *The Annapolis Process*, 74.
21. Dekel and Moran-Gilad, *The Annapolis Process*, 60–70.
22. Olmert, *In Person*, 829.
23. Dekel and Moran-Gilad, *The Annapolis Process*, 66.
24. Dekel and Moran-Gilad, *The Annapolis Process*, 4, 120.
25. Olmert, *In Person*, 814.
26. Condolezza Rice, *No Higher Honor*, 724.
27. For Olmert's meeting with the Secretary of State, see Olmert's account, *In Person*, of his meeting with the Secretary, 830–33.
28. Condolezza Rice, *No Higher Honor*, 652.
29. Olmert, *In Person*, 842–43; See also Olmert in an interview to *Australian*, November 11, 2009.
30. Olmert, *In Person*, 844.
31. Dekel and Moran-Gilad, *The Annapolis Process*, 89.
32. Avi Issacharoff, "Olmert: 'I Am Still Waiting for Abbas to Call,'" *The Tower Magazine*, May 24, 2013, is a most elaborate account of the Olmert-Abbas talks.
33. Jackson Diehl, "Abbas Waiting Game on Peace with Israel,", *The Washington Post*, May 29, 2009, https://www.washingtonpost.com/wp-dyn/content/article/2009/05/28/AR20 09052803614.html.
34. Dekel and Moran-Gilad, *The Annapolis Process*, 5.
35. "Erakat: Israel Agreed to Give Up all the Land, There is no Reason to Hurry,", ad Dustour, Amman, June 25, 2009, http://www.memri.org.il/cgi-webaxy/item?2060&findWords= %D7%A2%D7%A8%D7%99%D7%A7%D7%90%D7%AA%20%D7%90%D7%95%D7 %9C%D7%9E%D7%A8%D7%98.
36. Olmert, *In Person*, 835.

Chapter 28

1. Ramon, *Against the Wind*, 585.
2. The text of Abbas's letter is in Haim Ramon, *Against the Wind*, 605–8, https://www.timesofisr ael.com/text-of-abbas-letter-to-netanyahu.
3. An intelligent insider account is Michael Herzog, "Inside the Black Box of Israeli-Palestinian Talks," *The American Interest*, February 27, 2017. Nahum Barnea published in a series of articles versions of the text leaked to him, presumably by Minister Tzipi Livni: Nahum Barnea, "The Concessions' Document," "Netanyahu's Concessions," "Almost Peace," *Yediot Ahronoth*, March 4, 6, and 8, 2015, file:///C:/Users/Shlomo/AppData/Local/Temp/%D7%A2%D7%A8%D7%944-1.pdf file:// /C:/Users/Shlomo/AppData/Local/Temp/%D7%A2%D7%A8%D7%942.pdf file:///C:/ Users/Shlomo/AppData/Local/Temp/%D7%A2%D7%A8%D7%94%203.pdf
See also https://www.haaretz.com/israel-news/.premium.MAGAZINE-exclusive-obamas-plans-for-mideast-peace-revealed-1.5481322, accessed August 11, 2021.
4. Mark Lander, "Mideast Peace Effort Pauses to Let Failure Sink In," *The New York Times*, May 15, 2014.

5. On the paradoxes of Abbas's persona, see Grant Rumley and Amir Tibon, *The Last Palestinian: The Rise and Reign of Mahmoud Abbas* (New York: Prometheus Books, 2017).
6. See Mark Landler and Jonathan Weisman, "Obama Fights a Push to Add Iran Sanctions," *New York Times*, January 13, 2014, https://www.nytimes.com/2014/01/14/world/middlee ast/obama-fights-a-push-to-add-iran-sanctions.html, accessed August 11, 2021.

Chapter 29

1. See Shaul Arieli, *All Israel's Borders: A Century of Struggle for Independence, Identity, Settlement and Territory* [in Hebrew] (Tel Aviv: Yedioth Ahronoth, 2018), 324–25. See a Palestinian perspective in Mohammad Shtayyeh, *Israeli Settlements and the Erosion of the Two-State Solution* (Cairo: Dar Al-Shorouk, 2015). The now PA prime minister concludes that unless stopped, Israeli settlements expansion would kill the two-state solution.
2. http://www.geneva-accord.org/, accessed August 12, 2021.
3. See Chapter 22, pp. 153–155.
4. http://www.pcpsr.org/en/node/245, accessed August 12, 2021.
5. The Lebanese *Daily Star*, December 3, 2003.
6. *Haaretz*, June 23, 2002.
7. See, Shaul Arieli, "Have the Settlements Made the Two-State Solution Impossible"; Jan de Jong, "Settlements II: Technical Aspects. Response to Shaul Arieli: 'It's Quality not Quantity'," in *Moment of Truth: Tackling Israel-Palestine's Toughest Questions*, ed. Jamie Stern-Weiner (London and New York: OR Books, 2018), 83–116.
8. See my own comments about the limited sense of the issue of technical feasibility in "Saving the Parties from Themselves," in *Moment of Truth*, ed. Stern-Weiner, 69–71.
9. See Chapter 34, p. 283.
10. Robert Malley and Agha Hussein, "Camp David: The Tragedy of Errors," *New York Review of Books*, August 9, 2001, https://www.nybooks.com/articles/2001/08/09/camp-david-the-tragedy-of-errors/, accessed August 12, 2021.
11. For an examination of Fatah's website's reservations with regard to the parameters, see Makovsky, "Time Running Out on Clinton Proposals," https://www.washingtoninstitute.org/policy-analysis/view/time-running-out-on-clinton-proposals.
12. See https://www.pcpsr.org/en/node/731, accessed August 12, 2021. See also, Dahlia Scheindlin, "The Shrinking Two-State Constituency," in Jamie Stern (ed.), *Moment of Truth*, 73–81.
13. See David Pollock, "Younger Palestinians More Moderate on Tactical Issues, But Not on Long-Term Peace with Israel," *Washington Institute for Near East Policy*, September 6, 2019, https://www.washingtoninstitute.org/policy-analysis/view/younger-palestinians-more-moderate-on-tactical-issues-but-not-on-long-term, accessed August 12, 2021.
14. CBC/Radio-Canada, "Young Palestinians See No End to the Israeli Occupation," October 13, 2019, https://www.youtube.com/watch?v=fVuAYE5W0zI, accessed August 12, 2021.
15. Miriam Berger, *Newsweek*, July 11, 2018, "Middle East Peace? Can Young Palestinians' Rejection of the PA Lead to a Binational State with Israel?," *Newsweek*, July 11, 2018, https://www.newsweek.com/2018/07/20/palestinians-israel-abbas-gaza-west-bank-peace-pa-pale stinian-authority-hamas-1016978.html, accessed August 11, 2021.
16. See Felicia Schwartz and Dov Lieber, "Israeli Millennials, Tilting Right, Helped Elect Netanyahu," *Wall Street Journal*, April 11, 2019, https://www.wsj.com/articles/israeli-mill ennials-tilting-right-helped-elect-netanyahu-11555002403, accessed August 11, 2021.

Chapter 30

1. See David Shearer, "The Humanitarian Crisis in the Occupied Palestinian Territory: An Overview," *Humanitarian Practice Network*, November 2004, https://odihpn.org/magazine/the-humanitarian-crisis-in-the-occupied-palestinian-territory-an-overview/, accessed August 12, 2021.
2. Anziska, *Preventing Palestine*, 83–85.

3. See http://www.israelnationalnews.com/News/News.aspx/125809, accessed August 12, 2021.

4. Amira Hass, "The Cult of the Angel of Peace Has Gone out of Control," *Haaretz*, December 20, 2019.

5. Ghazi Hamad, "Now I Understand How and Why the Palestinians Lost Palestine," *The Times of Israel*, January 2, 2015, http://www.timesofisrael.com/writers/ghazi-hamad, accessed August 12, 2021; see also http://www.timesofisrael.com/now-i-understand-how-and-why-the-pales tinians-lost-palestine/#comments, accessed August 12, 2021.

6. A tweet from Israel's channel 13, https://twitter.com/newsisrael13/status/113037121842 5765888?s-03, quoted in Ramon, *Against the Wind*, 417.

7. https://www.haaretz.co.il/opinions/premium-1.9850009, accessed August 12, 2021.

8. See an extended discussion of the Palestinian refugee issue from a Fateh perspective http://www.mideastweb.org/fatah_refugee_statement.htm, accessed August 12,2021. See also http:/mideastweb.org/fatah_program_2009.htm, accessed August 12, 2021.

Chapter 31

1. Anziska, *Preventing Palestine*, 96.

2. See Chapter 34, p. 290.

3. http://www.brookings.edu/~/media/research/files/reports/2015/12/04-american-pub lic-opinion-israel-middle-east-telhami/2015-poll-key-findings-final.pdf, accessed August 13, 2021.

4. George W. Ball, "The Middle East: How to Save Israel in Spite of Herself?" *Foreign Affairs*, April, 1977, https://www.foreignaffairs.com/articles/israel/1977-04-01/middle-east-how-save-israel-spite-herself, accessed August 13, 2021.

5. https://www.haaretz.com/1.4875383, accessed August 13, 2021.

6. Brian Whitaker, "Pragmatist Whose Two-State Solution Cuts No Ice with Israel," *The Guardian*, August 22, 2003, https://www.theguardian.com/world/2003/aug/22/israel1, accessed August 13, 2021.

7. Shlomo Ben-Ami, "Labourite Sees Momentum towards an International Solution," *The Forward*, April 2, 2002 (based on a paper I submitted to the Labor Party: see Shlomo Ben-Ami, "Internationalizing the Solution: Multilateralism and International Legitimacy," *Palestine-Israel Journal* 13, no. 4 [2007], https://pij.org/articles/969/internationalizing-the-solution-multilat eralism-and-international-legitimacy, accessed August 13, 2021); Shlomo Ben-Ami, "Bush's Mideast Opportunity," *New York Times*, April, 5, 2002, https://www.nytimes.com/2002/04/ 05/opinion/bush-s-mideast-opportunity.html, accessed August 13, 2021; Shlomo Ben-Ami, "Un mandato internacional para Palestina," *El País*, June 11, 2002, https://elpais.com/diario/ 2002/06/11/internacional/1023746418_850215.html?outputType=amp, accessed August 13, 2021.

8. See https://www.un.org/press/en/2019/sc13895.doc.htm, accessed August 13, 2021.

9. George Orwell, "Catastrophic Gradualism," *Politics*, September 1946, 268–69, http://www. unz.com/print/politics-1946sep/, accessed August 13, 2021.

Chapter 32

1. Michael Sfard, *The Wall and the Gate: Israel, Palestine, and the Legal Battle for Human Rights* (New York: Metropolitan Books, Henry Holt, 2018), 379.

2. Meron Benvenisti, "West Bank Data Project: A Survey of Israel's Policies" *Foreign Affairs*, Summer 1984. https://www.foreignaffairs.com/reviews/capsule-review/1984-06-01/west-bank-data-project-survey-israels-policies, accessed August 13, 2021.

3. Hugh Naylor, "Two-State Solution Loses Its Champion," *The National*, April 13, 2012, https:// www.thenational.ae/world/mena/two-state-solution-loses-its-champion-1.380369, accessed August 13, 2021.

4. For a far more up-to-date analysis than Benvenisti's, see Yael Berda, *Living Emergency: Israel's Permit Regime in the Occupied West Bank* (Stanford, CA: Stanford University Press, 2017).

5. http://www.israelnationalnews.com/News/News.aspx/269748, accessed August 13, 2021.

6. www.haaretz.co.il/misc/1.1559271, accessed August 13, 2021. See also https://972mag. com/who-profits-from-keeping-gaza-on-the-brink-of-humanitarian-catastrophe/133549/, accessed August 13, 2021.

7. https://institute.global/insight/middle-east/israeli-palestinian-trade-depth-analysis, accessed August 13, 2021.

8. https://institute.global/insight/middle-east/israeli-palestinian-trade-depth-analysis, accessed August 13, 2021.

9. Uri Ben-Eliezer, *War Rather than Peace: One Hundred Years of Nationalism and Militarism in Israel* [in Hebrew] (Tel Aviv: Modan Publishers, 2019), highlights Israel's compulsive tendency to address political challenges by military means.

Chapter 33

1. Toni Judt, "Israel: The Alternative," *The New York Review of Books*, October 23, 2003.

2. Naylor. "Two-State Solution Loses Its Champion."

3. Linfield, *The Lion's Den*, 211.

4. Régine Dhoquois-Cohen, "Israël, fait colonial? 30 ans après." https://iremmo.org/wp-cont ent/uploads/2016/02/2605.rodinson.pdf, accessed August 14, 2021.

5. See below, pp. 279–281.

6. Ismail Haniyeh, "A Just Peace or No Peace," *The Guardian*, March 31, 2006. https://www.theg uardian.com/commentisfree/2006/mar/31/Israel, accessed August 14, 2021.

7. Amira Hass, "UN Report: 300,000 Palestinians Live in Area C of West Bank," *Haaretz*, March 5, 2014, https://www.haaretz.com/.premium-un-300k-palestinians-live-in-area-c-1.5329286, accessed August 14, 2021. The B'tselem assessment is 180,000–300,000 Palestinians and a settler population of at least 325,500 living in 125 settlements and approximately 100 outposts; see https://www.btselem.org/topic/area_c, accessed August 14, 2021.

8. Winston S. Churchill (ed.), *Never Give In! The Best of Winston Churchill's Speeches* (London: Pimlico, 2004), 80; Nathan Weinstock, "The Impact of Zionist Colonization on Palestinian Arab Society before 1948," *Journal of Palestine Studies* 2, no. 2 (Winter, 1973): 49–63.

9. Ze'ev Jabotinsky, "The Iron Wall (We and the Arabs)," *Jewish Herald*, November 26, 1937, http://www.marxists.de/middleast/ironwall/ironwall.htm, accessed August 14, 2021.

Chapter 34

1. See https://www.ft.com/content/a22d04b2-c4b0-11e9-a8e9-296ca66511c9, accessed August 14, 2021.

2. Elad Ben-Dror, *The Road to 29 November: The UNSCOP Story and the Origins of the UN Involvement in the Arab-Israeli Conflict* [in Hebrew] (Jerusalem: Yad Ben-Zvi, 2019), 197–204.

3. Anziska, *Preventing Palestine*, 39, 44, 58.

4. Anziska, *Preventing Palestine*, 120–21.

5. Anziska, *Preventing Palestine*, 107–8.

6. Anziska, *Preventing Palestine*, 243.

7. https://www.jta.org/1980/12/31/archive/kissinger-discusses-jordanian-option-in-meet ing-with-sadat, accessed August 14, 2021.

8. https://www.ynet.co.il/articles/0,7340,L-5661767,00.html, accessed August 14, 2021.

9. https://www.memri.org/reports/idea-jordanian-palestinian-confederation-resurfaces-only-be-rejected-both-sides, accessed August 14, 2021.

10. Rashid Sammy, "The Emergence and Evolution of Palestinian Nationalism," *International Journal of Multicultural and Multireligious Understanding* 2, no. 2 (2015), 1–7.

11. Anziska, *Preventing Palestine*, 46.

12. Walter Laqueur and Barry Rubin, eds., *The Israel-Arab Reader: A Documentary History of the Middle East Conflict* (New York: Penguin Books, 2001), 298–99.

13. Laqueur and Rubin, *The Israel-Arab Reader*, 299–313.

14. Laqueur and Rubin, *The Israel-Arab Reader*, 338–41.

15. See Reuven Pedazur, "The Jordanian Option: The Plan that Refuses to Die," *Haaretz*, July 25, 2007. https://www.haaretz.com/1.4954947. See also comments on Majali's plan in Ian Bremmer, "A Difficult Plan Whose Time Has Come," *The New York Times*, June 6, 2007, https://www.nytimes.com/2007/06/15/opinion/15iht-edbremmer.1.6153154.html, accessed August 14, 2021.

16. On Majali's meeting with the West Bank notables, see a comment by Hillel Frisch, "The Future Lies in the Past: The Jordanian Option", *Carnegie Endowment for International Peace*, September 9, 2017, https://carnegieendowment.org/2017/09/08/future-lies-in-past-jordanian-option-pub-73040, accessed August 14, 2021

Chapter 35

1. Quoted in Ronan Fanning, *Éamon de Valera: A Will to Power* (Cambridge, MA: Harvard University Press, 2016), 98.

2. Ian Birchall, "Sartre and Terror," in *Sartre Today: A Centenary Celebration*, ed. Adrian Van den Hoven and Andrew Leak (New York: Berghahn Books, 2005), 257.

3. For Chechenia, see Arkady Ostrovsky, *The Invention of Russia: The Journey from Gorbachev's Freedom to Putin's War* (London: Atlantic Books, 2018), 183–89.

4. https://www.youtube.com/watch?v=VvkpH7Q37qE, accessed August 14, 2021.

5. https://www.goodreads.com/quotes/383672-arafat-had-said-that-the-womb-of-the-pale stinian-woman, accessed August 14, 2021.

6. Thania Pfaffenholz, Darren Kew, and Anthony Wanis-St. John, "Civil Society and Peace Negotiations: Why, Whether, and How They Could Be Involved," Paper Presented at the 47th Annual Convention of the International Studies Association, San Diego, March, 2006 (https://www.hdcentre.org/wp-content/uploads/2016/07/CivilSocietyandPeaceNegot iations-WhyWhetherandhowtheycouldbeinvolved-June-2006.pdf), found strong evidence that peace negotiations characterized by high civil society involvement have been more conducive to sustained peace, while most negotiations with low civil society involvement resulted in the resumption of warfare.

7. Mari Fitzduff, "Breaking Down the Walls: Northern Ireland Lessons," *Palestine-Israel Journal* 12, no. 4 (2005) offers an instructive survey of NGO'scontribution to peace in Northern Ireland.

8. Amos Oz, "The Specter of Saladin," *New York Times*, July 28, 2000, https://www.nytimes.com/2000/07/28/opinion/the-specter-of-saladin.html, accessed August 15, 2021.

9. See Rashid Khalidi's emphasis on the colonial nature of the conflict in *The Hundred Year's War on Palestine: A History of Settler Colonialism and Resistance* (London: Profile Books, 2020).

10. Susie Linfield, *The Lion's Den*, 267.

11. See Rodinson's "Israël, fait colonial?" in Jean-Paul Sartre, dir., *Les Temps Modernes*, (no. 22, 1967), 17–88. Also, his interview in 1998 in Régine Dhoquois-Cohen, "Israël, fait colonial? 30 ans après," https://iremmo.org/wp-content/uploads/2016/02/2605.rodinson.pdf. See also Linfield, *The Lion's Den*, 24–25, 103, 119.

12. Sinead O'Shea, "A Frail Peace in Northern Ireland Still," *The New York Times*, April 27–28, 2019). Sinead O'Shea, "Northern Ireland Unfinished Peace", the New York Times, April 25, 2019 https://www.nytimes.com/2019/04/25/opinion/lyra-mckee-northern-ireland.html

13. https://www.elespectador.com/noticias/paz/solo-se-ha-cumplido-el-185-del-acuerdo-de-paz-c.

14. https://www.crisisgroup.org/latin-america-caribbean/andes/colombia/67-risky-business-duque-governments-approach-peace-colombia, accessed August 14, 2021.

15. See an International Crisis Group report on the gap between Santos's investment in rural reform and that of his successors: "Crucial Reforms Languish as Colombia Seeks to Consolidate Peace", July 19, 2019. https://www.crisisgroup.org/latin-america-caribbean/andes/colombia/crucial-reforms-languish-colombia-seeks-consolidate-peace

16. https://www.wri.org/news/2018/07/release-colombia-becomes-first-country-latin-america-commit-deforestation-free, accessed August 14, 2021.

17. Ajay Singh, "South Africa Is Not Working," *Freedom Magazine* 47, no. 6, (https://www.fre edommag.org/magazine/201507-infrastructure/world/south-africa-is-not-working.html, accessed August 14, 2021.

18. https://www.nelsonmandela.org/news/entry/transcript-of-nelsonmandela-annual-lecture-2015.

19. Panashe Chigumadzi, "Why Is South Africa Still So Anti-Black, So Many Years after Apartheid?" *The Guardian*, March 10, 2017,https://www.theguardian.com/commentisfree/2017/mar/10/south-africa-anti-black-violence-afrophobic, accessed August 14, 2021.

20. Justice Malala, "Why are South African Cities Still So Segregated 25 Years after Apartheid?" *The Guardian*, October 21, 2019, https://www.theguardian.com/cities/2019/oct/21/why-are-south-african-cities-still-segregated-after-apartheid, accessed August 14, 2021.

21. David Pilling, "Xenophobia Sours the Legacy of Pan-Africanism", *The Financial Times*, September 25, 2019.

22. I am indebted for having greatly benefitted from Adi Schwartzman and Einat Wilf's *The War of Return* [in Hebrew] (Tel Aviv: Kinneret Zmora-Bitan, Dvir, 2018) in the preparation of this section on refugees. Other sources pertaining to the Palestinian philosophy on refugees came from my own exposure to the Palestine Papers when I was invited to discuss them in Doha by *Al Jazeera* in 2011.

23. Howard Adelman and Elazar Barkan, *No Return, No Refuge: Rites and Rights in Minority Repatriation* (New York: Columbia University Press, 2011), pp. ix–xx, quoted by Adi Schwartz and Einat Wilf, *The War of Return*, pp. 58–59.

24. Tzvi Joffre, "Palestinian Migrants Flood into Israel: Report," *Jerusalem Post*, February 13, 2019, https://www.jpost.com/israel-news/palestinian-migrants-flood-into-israel-report-580605, accessed August 14, 2021; https://www.haaretz.co.il/misc/article-print-page-prem ium-1.9004591, accessed August 14, 2021. https://www.jewishvirtuallibrary.org/total-immigration-to-israel-by-year, accessed August 14, 2021.

25. Danny Rubinstein, "Israeli Citizenship is Worth 130 Shekel", *Calcalist (Yedioth Ahronoth)*, November 26, 2012. Soffer's assessment is in Nadav Shragai, "Why the Temporary Provision That Prevents Terror Needs to Be maintained?", *Israel Hayom*, June 24, 2021, https://www.israelhayom.co.il/magazine/hashavua/article/2544116, accessed August 14, 2021.

26. "Moshe Dayan: Eulogy for Ro'i Rotberg," https://tikvahfund.org/collegiate-forum/moshe-dayan-eulogy-for-roi-rothberg/

27. *The Times of Israel*, November 4, 2012, quoted by in Schwartz and Wilf, *The War of Return*, p. 189.

28. Mahmoud Abbas, "Lord Balfour's Burden," *The Cairo Review of Global Affairs*, November 2, 2017.

Epilogue

1. https://www.pcpsr.org/en/node/731, accessed August 14, 2021. See also Perry Cammack, Nathan Brown, and Marwan Muasher, *Revitalizing Palestinian Nationalism: Options versus Realities* (Washington DC: Carnegie Endowment for International Peace, 2017), 9–24.

2. See Hussein Agha and Ahmad Samih Khalidi, "The End of This Road: The Decline of the Palestinian National Movement," *The New Yorker*, August 6, 2017, https://www.newyorker.com/news/news-desk/the-end-of-this-road-the-decline-of-the-palestinian-national-movem ent, accessed August 14, 2021.

3. https://www.bbc.com/news/world-europe-22624104, accessed August 14, 2021.

4. Quoted in Jeffrey Goldberg, "Obsessing about Gaza, Ignoring Syria (and Most Everything Else): Trying to Understand Why Syrian Deaths No Longer Seem to Matter," *The Atlantic*, 23 July, 2014.

5. https://www.jewishvirtuallibrary.org/total-casualties-arab-israeli-conflict, accessed August 14, 2021.

6. Gunnar Heinsohn and Daniel Pipes, "Arab-Israeli Fatalities Rank 49th," *Likoed*, October 8, 2007, https://likoed.nl/2007/10/arab-israeli-fatalities-rank-49th-likoed-nederland/, accessed August 14, 2021.

7. https://www.aljazeera.com/news/2021/3/23/children-25-of-civilian-casualties-in-yemen-relief-agency, accessed August 14, 2021.

8. Richard Bernstein, "The World: An Ugly Rumor or an Ugly Truth," *New York Times*, August 4, 2002, https://www.nytimes.com/2002/08/04/weekinreview/the-world-an-ugly-rumor-or-an-ugly-truth.html, accessed August 14, 2021.

9. Shibley Telhami, "Americans Are Increasingly Critical of Israel," *Foreign Policy*, December 11, 2018, https://foreignpolicy.com/2018/12/11/americans-are-increasingly-critical-of-Israel/ , accessed August 14, 2021; Ben White, "News Agencies Still Whitewashing Israeli Forces' Lethal Violence," *Middle East Monitor*, February 1, 2017, https://www.middleeastmonitor.com/news/, accessed August 14, 2021.

10. Vladimir Frolov, "Goodbye Palestine! Why Trump's 'Peace Deal' Is Good for Moscow," *Moscow Times*, January 31, 2020, https://www.themoscowtimes.com/2020/01/31/good bye-palestine-why-trumps-peace-deal-is-good-for-moscow-a69121, accessed August 14, 2021.

11. Zaha Hassan, Daniel Levy, and Hallaamal Keir, and Marwan Muasher, "Breaking the Israel-Palestine Status Quo," *Carnegie Endowment for International Peace*, April 19, 2021, https://carnegieendowment.org/2021/04/19/breaking-israel-palestine-status-quo-pub-84167, accessed August 14, 2021.

12. https://www.cis.org.il. See also an unusually elaborate advert in *Haaretz*, April 24, 2020 by Commanders for Israel's Security.

13. Haggai Matar, "Civil Society Groups Join Forces to Protect Freedom of Speech," +972 *Magazine*, May 13, 2017, https://972mag.com/civil-society-groups-join-forces-to-protect-freedom-of-speech/127286/, accessed August 14, 2021.

14. https://www.haaretz.co.il/magazine/.premium-MAGAZINE-1.8018656, accessed August 14, 2021.

15. https://en.idi.org.il/publications/20280, accessed August 14, 2021.

16. Giuseppe Mazzini, *The Duties of Man Addressed to Workingmen* (New York: Funk & Wagnalls, 1898), ch. 5.

17. J. L. Talmon, "'The Homeland Is in Danger.' An Open Letter to Menahem Begin," *Dissent* (1980), https://www.dissentmagazine.org/article/the-homeland-is-in-danger-an-open-let ter-to-menahem-begin, accessed August 10, 2021.

18. For an interesting examination of the elusive meaning of victory throughout history, see Wolfgang Schivelbusch, *The Culture of Defeat: On National Trauma, Mourning and Recovery* (London: Granta Books, 2001).

19. http://english.wafa.ps/page.aspx?id=15EtyQa95597878332a15EtyQ, accessed August 14, 2021.

20. Edy Cohen, "Palestinian President Curses Half the Planet," *Israel Today*, April 27, 2021, https://www.israeltoday.co.il/read/palestinian-president-curses-half-the-planet/, accessed August 14, 2021.

21. See a Palestinian perception of the religious-political conflict over the Haram al-Sharif in Nazmi Jubeh, "Jerusalem's Haram al-Sharif: Crucible of Conflict and Control," *Institute for Palestine Studies* 45, no. 2, (2016): 23–37. For how the efforts of Temple Mount Jewish activists to alter the status quo with the connivance of Netanyahu's governments got additional encouragement from Donald Trump's Abraham Accords, see Daniel Seidemann, "The Status Quo on Temple Mount/ Haram Al Sherif: Dodging A Bullet (For Now)," in *Terrestrial Jerusalem*, October 12, 2020, https://t-j.org.il/0202/10/12/the-status-quo-on-the-temple-mount-haram-al-sharif-dodging-a-bullet-for-now/, accessed August 14, 2021.

22. See Shlomo Ben-Ami, "The End of Israel's Illusion," *Project Syndicate*, May 13, 2021, https://www.project-syndicate.org/commentary/palestinian-resistance-shatters-israeli-consensus-by-shlomo-ben-ami-2021-05, accessed August 14, 2021.

BIBLIOGRAPHY

1. Israel-Palestine Process

Abbas, Mahmoud. "Lord Balfour's Burden." *The Cairo Review of Global Affairs*, November 2, 2017.

"Abu Mazen (Mahmoud Abbas): If We Were to Meet Again in Camp David We Would Take the Same Positions," *Al Ayyam*, July 28, 29, 2001, http://www.memri.org.il/cgi-webaxy/sal/sal. pl?lang=he&ID=875141_memri&act=show&dbid=articles&dataid=391, accessed August 3, 2021.

Abu Odeh, Adnan. "Religious Inclusion, Political Inclusion: Jerusalem as an Undivided Capital." *Catholic University Law Review* 45, no. 3 (1996): 687–694, https://scholarship.law.edu/lawreview/vol45/iss3/4/, accessed August 3, 2021.

Aburish, Saïd. *Arafat: From Defender to Dictator*. London: Bloomsbury, 1998.

Agha, Hussein, and Samih Ahmad Khalidi. "The End of This Road: The Decline of the Palestinian National Movement." *The New Yorker*, August 6, 2017, https://www.newyorker.com/news/news-desk/the-end-of-this-road-the-decline-of-the-palestinian-national-movement, accessed August 14, 2021.

Agha, Hussein, and Robert Malley. "Camp David: An Exchange." *New York Review of Books*, September 20, 2001.

Agha, Hussein, and Robert Malley. "Camp David: The Tragedy of Errors." *The New York Review of Books*, August 9, 2001.

Albright, Madeleine. *Madam Secretary*. New York: Miramax Books, 2003.

Alpher, Yossi. *And the Wolf Shall Dwell with the Wolf: The Settlers and the Palestinians*. [in Hebrew]. Tel Aviv: Hakibbut Hameuhad Publishing House, 2001.

Anziska, Seth. *Preventing Palestine: A Political History from Camp David to Oslo*. Princeton, NJ: Princeton University Press, 2018.

Arafat, Yasser. "The Palestinian Vision of Peace." *New York Times*, February 3, 2002, https://www.nytimes.com/2002/02/03/opinion/the-palestinian-vision-of-peace.html, accessed August 8, 2021.

Arieli, Shaul. *A Border between Us and You: The Israeli-Palestinian Conflict and Ways to Solve It*. [in Hebrew]. Tel Aviv: Yedioth Ahronoth, 2013.

Arieli, Shaul. *All Israel's Borders: A Century of Struggle for Independence, Identity, Settlement and Territory*. [in Hebrew]. Tel Aviv: Yedioth Ahronoth, 2018.

Arieli, Shaul. *The Truman Institute Atlas of the Jewish-Arab Conflict*. Hebrew University of Jerusalem, 2020.

Arieli, Shaul, "Have the Settlements Made the Two-State Solution Impossible?" in *Moment of Truth: Tackling Israel-Palestine's Toughest Questions*. Edited by Jamie Stern-Weiner. London and New York: OR Books, 2018, 101-106-111-114

Arieli, Shaul. *12 Myths about the Israeli-Palestinian Conflict*. [in Hebrew]. Tel Aviv: Yedioth Ahronot, 2021.

Avesar, Josef. "The Israel-Palestinian Confederation Proposal", *Palestine-Israel Journal* 14, no. 2 (2007), https://pij/org/articles/1073/the-israelpalestinian-confederation-proposal.

Avishai, Bernard. "Confederation: The One Possible Israel-Palestine Solution." *The New York Review of Books*, February 2, 2018.

Ball, George W. "The Middle East: How to Save Israel in Spite of Herself?" *Foreign Affairs*, April, 1977, https://www.foreignaffairs.com/articles/israel/1977-04-01/middle-east-how-save-israel-spite-herself, accessed August 13, 2021.

Barak, Ehud. *My Country, My Life: Fighting for Israel, Searching for Peace.* New York: St. Martin Press, 2018.

Barnea, Nahum "The Concessions' Document", "Netanyahu's Concessions", "Almost Peace", Yedioth Ahronoth, March 4, 6, and 8, 2015 file:///C:/Users/Shlomo/AppData/Local/Temp/%D7%A2%D7%A8%D7%944-1.pdf   file:///C:/Users/Shlomo/AppData/Local/Temp/%D7%A2%D7%A8%D7%942.pdf   file:///C:/Users/Shlomo/AppData/Local/Temp/%D7%A2%D7%A8%D7%94%203.pdf

Beilin, Yossi. *Manual for a Wounded Dove.* [in Hebrew]. Tel Aviv: Yedioth Ahronoth, 2001.

Ben-Ami, Shlomo. "End of a Journey." (Interview with Ari Shavit). *Haaretz*, September 14, 2001.

Ben-Ami, Shlomo. "A New Paradigm for an Israeli-Palestinian Peace." *Financial Times*, October 31, 2001.

Ben-Ami, Shlomo. "The Only Way Out: A Solution in The Middle East Must Be International, Led by the United States with the Participation of Europe, Russia and Key Arab States." *Newsweek*, August 20, 2001.

Ben-Ami, Shlomo. "Bush's Mideast Opportunity." *New York Times*, April 5, 2002, https://www.nytimes.com/2002/04/05/opinion/bush-s-mideast-opportunity.html, accessed August 13, 2021.

Ben-Ami, Shlomo. "Un mandato internacional para Palestina." *El País*, June 11, 2002, https://elpais.com/diario/2002/06/11/internacional/1023746418_850215.html?outputType=amp, accessed August 13, 2021.

Ben-Ami, Shlomo. "So Close and Yet So Far: Lessons from the Israeli-Palestinian Peace Process." *Israel Studies* 10, no. 2 (2005): 72–90.

Ben-Ami, Shlomo. "Internationalizing the Solution: Multilateralism and International Legitimacy." *Palestine-Israel Journal* 13, no. 4 (2007): 9–14, https://pij.org/articles/969/internationalizing-the-solution-multilateralism-and-international-legitimacy, accessed August 13, 2021.

Ben-Ami, Shlomo. "Saving the Parties from Themselves.'" In *Moment of Truth: Tackling Israel-Palestine's Toughest Questions.* Edited by Jamie Stern-Weiner, 69–71. London and New York: OR Books, 2018.

Ben-Ami, Shlomo. "The End of Israel's Illusion." *Project Syndicate*, May 13, 2021, https://www.project-syndicate.org/commentary/palestinian-resistance-shatters-israeli-consensus-by-shlomo-ben-ami-2021-05, accessed August 14, 2021.

Ben-Dror, Elad. *The Road to 29 November: The UNSCOP Story and the Origins of the UN Involvement in the Arab-Israeli Conflict.* [in Hebrew]. Jerusalem: Yad Ben-Zvi, 2019.

Ben-Eliezer, Uri. *War Rather Than Peace: One Hundred Years of Nationalism and Militarism in Israel.* [in Hebrew]. Tel Aviv: Modan Publishers, 2019.

Benvenisti, Meron. *West Bank Data Project: A Survey of Israel's Policies.* Washington, DC: AEI Press, 1984.

Berda, Yael. *Living Emergency: Israel's Permit Regime in the Occupied West Bank.* Stanford, CA: Stanford University Press, 2017.

Berger, Miriam. "Middle East Peace? Can Young Palestinians' Rejection of the PA Lead to a Binational State with Israel?." *Newsweek*, July 11, 2018, https://www.newsweek.com/2018/07/20/palestinians-israel-abbas-gaza-west-bank-peace-pa-palestinian-authority-hamas-1016978.html, accessed August 11, 2021.

Bergman, Ronen. *Authority Given: Where Did We Go Wrong? This Is How the Palestinian Authority Became a Serial Producer of Corruption and Terror.* [in Hebrew]. Tel Aviv: Yedioth Ahronoth, 2002.

Bernstein, Richard. "The World: An Ugly Rumor or an Ugly Truth." *New York Times*, August 4, 2002, https://www.nytimes.com/2002/08/04/weekinreview/the-world-an-ugly-rumor-or-an-ugly-truth.html, accessed August 14, 2021.

Bremmer, Ian. "A Difficult Plan Whose Time Has Come," *The New York Times*, June 6, 2007, https://www.nytimes.com/2007/06/15/opinion/15iht-edbremmer.1.6153154.html, accessed August 14, 2021.

Cammack, Perry, Nathan Brown, and Muasher Marwan. *Revitalizing Palestinian Nationalism: Options versus Realities*. Washington, DC: Carnegie Endowment for International Peace, 2017.

CBC/Radio-Canada. "Young Palestinians See No End to the Israeli Occupation." October 13, 2019, https://www.youtube.com/watch?v=fVuAYE5W0zI, accessed August 12, 2021.

Churchill, Winston S., ed. *Never Give In! The Best of Winston Churchill's Speeches*. London: Pimlico, 2004.

Clinton, Bill. *My Life*. London: Hutchinson, 2004.

Cohen, Edy. "Palestinian President Curses Half the Planet." *Israel Today*, April 27, 2021, https://www.israeltoday.co.il/read/palestinian-president-curses-half-the-planet/, accessed August 12, 2021.

Cohen-Almagor, Raphael. "History of Track Two Peace Negotiations: Interview with Hussein Agha." *Israel Studies* 26, no. 1 (2003): 47–72.

Dekel, Udi, and Lia Moran-Gilad. *The Annapolis Process: A Missed Opportunity for a Two-State Solution?* Institute for National and Security Studies (INSS), Tel Aviv University, May, 2021, https://www.inss.org.il/publication/annapolis/, accessed August 10, 2021.

Edelist, Ran. *Ehud Barak: Fighting the Demons*. [in Hebrew]. Tel Aviv: Zmora-Bitan Publishers, 2003.

Enderlin, Charles. *Le Rêve brisé: Histoire de l'échec du processus de paix au Proche-Orient, 1995–2004*. Paris: Fayard, 2002.

"Erakat: Israel Agreed to Give Up All the Land, There Is No Reason to Hurry", Interview in ad Dustour, Amman, June 25, 2009, http://www.memri.org.il/cgi-webaxy/item?2060&findWords=%D7%A2%D7%A8%D7%99%D7%A7%D7%90%D7%AA%20%D7%90%D7%95%D7%9C%D7%9E%D7%A8%D7%98

Fisk, Robert. *The Great War for Civilization: The Conquest of the Middle East*. London: Fourth Estate, 2005.

Frisch, Hillel. "The Future Lies in the Past: The Jordanian Option," *Carnegie Endowment for International Peace*, September 9, 2017, https://carnegieendowment.org/2017/09/08/future-lies-in-past-jordanian-option-pub-73040.

Frolov, Vladimir. "Goodbye Palestine! Why Trump's 'Peace Deal' Is Good for Moscow." *Moscow Times*, January 31, 2020, https://www.themoscowtimes.com/2020/01/31/goodbye-palestine-why-trumps-peace-deal-is-good-for-moscow-a69121, accessed August 14, 2021.

Goldberg, Jeffrey. "Obsessing about Gaza, Ignoring Syria (and Most Everything Else): Trying to Understand Why Syrian Deaths No Longer Seem to Matter." *The Atlantic*, July 23, 2014.

Jabotinsky, Ze'ev. "The Iron Wall (We and the Arabs)." *Jewish Herald*, November 26, 1937, http://www.marxists.de/middleast/ironwall/ironwall.htm

Hamad, Ghazi. "Now I Understand How and Why the Palestinians Lost Palestine." *The Times of Israel*, January 2, 2015.

Haniyah, Akram. "The Camp David Papers." *Journal of Palestine Studies* 30, no. 2: (2001): 75–97.

Haniyeh, Ismail. "A Just Peace or no Peace." *The Guardian*, March 31, 2006 https://www.theguardian.com/commentisfree/2006/mar/31/Israel

Harel, Amos, and Avi Isacharoff. *The Seventh War: How Did We Win and Why Did We Lose in Our War against the Palestinians?* [in Hebrew]. Tel Aviv: Yedioth Ahronoth, 2004.

Hass, Amira. "UN Report: 300,000 Palestinians Live in Area C of West Bank." *Haaretz*, March 5, 2014, https://www.haaretz.com/.premium-un-300k-palestinians-live-in-area-c-1.5329286, accessed August 14, 2021.

Hass, Amira. "Mahmoud Abbas' Cult of Personality Has Gone Out of Control." *Haaretz*, December 22, 2019. https://www.haaretz.com/middle-east-news/palestinians/.premium-mahmoud-abbas-cult-of-personality-is-out-of-control-and-sparking-protest-1.829.

Hassan, Zaha, Daniel Levy, and Hallaamal Keir, and Marwan Muasher. "Breaking the Israel-Palestine Status Quo." *Carnegie Endowment for International Peace*, April 19, 2021, https://carnegieendowment.org/2021/04/19/breaking-israel-palestine-status-quo-pub-84167, accessed August 14, 2021.

Hasson, Nir. *Urshalim: Israelis and Palestinians in Jerusalem 1967–2017.* [in Hebrew]. Tel Aviv: Yedioth Ahronoth, 2017.

Hefez, Nir, and Gadi Bloom. *The Shepherd: The Life Story of Ariel Sharon.* [in Hebrew]. Tel Aviv: Yedioth Ahronoth, 2005.

Heinsohn, Gunnar, and Daniel Pipes. "Arab-Israeli Fatalities Rank 49th." *Likoed* October 8, 2007, https://likoed.nl/2007/10/arab-israeli-fatalities-rank-49th-likoed-nederland/, accessed August 14, 2021.

Helmick, Raymond G., S. J. *Negotiating Outside the Law: Why Camp David Failed.* London and Ann Arbor, MI: Pluto Press, 2004.

Herzog, Michael. "Inside the Black Box of Israeli-Palestinian Talks." *The American Interest*, February 27, 2017.

Hirsh, Michael. "Clinton to Arafat: Its All Your Fault." *Newsweek*, June 27, 2001. https://www.newsweek.com/clinton-arafat-its-all-your-fault-153779

Hirschfeld, Yair. *Oslo: The Formula for Peace.* [in Hebrew]. Tel Aviv: Am Oved Publishers, 2000.

Indyk, Martin. *Innocent Abroad: An Intimate Account of American Diplomacy in the Middle East.* New York: Simon and Schuster, 2009.

Israeli, Raphael. "From Oslo to Bethlehem: Arafat's Islamic Message." *Journal of Church and State* 43, no. 3 (2001): 423–445.

Issacharoff, Avi. "Olmert: 'I Am Still Waiting for Abbas to Call,'" *The Tower Magazine*, May 23, 2013. http://www.thetower.org/exclusive-olmert-i-am-still-waiting-for-abbas-to-call-will-abbas-ever-say-yes/.

Jabotinsky, Ze'ev. "The Iron Wall (We and the Arabs)." *Jewish Herald*, November 26, 1937, http://www.marxists.de/middleast/ironwall/ironwall.htm, accessed August 14, 2021.

Joffre, Tzvi. "Palestinian Migrants Flood into Israel: Report." *Jerusalem Post*, February 13, 2019, https://www.jpost.com/israel-news/palestinian-migrants-flood-into-israel-report-580605, accessed August 14, 2021.

Jong, Jan de. "Settlements II: Technical Aspects. Response to Shaul Arieli: 'It's Quality not Quantity.'" In *Moment of Truth: Tackling Israel-Palestine's Toughest Questions.* Edited by Jamie Stern-Weiner, 53–114. London and New York: OR Books, 2018.

Jubeh, Nazmi. "Jerusalem's Haram al-Sharif: Crucible of Conflict and Control." *Institute for Palestine Studies* 45, no. 2 (2016): 23–37.

Judt, Toni. "Israel: The Alternative." *The New York Review of Books*, October 23, 2003 https://www.nybooks.com/articles/2003/10/23/israel-the-alternative/.

Kanafani, Marwan. *Sanawat al-Amal.* Cairo: Dar al-Shorouk, 2007.

Kerry, John. *Every Day Extra.* New York: Simon and Schuster, 2018.

Khalidi, Rashid. *The Iron Cage: The Story of the Palestinian Struggle for Statehood.* Boston, MA: Beacon Press, 2006.

Kissinger, Henry. *Does America Need a Foreign Policy? Toward a Diplomacy for the 21st Century.* New York: Simon and Schuster, 2001.

Klein, Menachem. *Shattering a Taboo: The Contacts towards a Permanent Status Agreement in Jerusalem, 1994–2001.* [in Hebrew]. Jerusalem: Jerusalem Institute for Israel Research, 2001.

Klein, Menachem. *A Possible Peace between Israel and Palestine: An Insider's Account of the Geneva Initiative,* New York: Columbia University Press, 2007.

Kristol, Irving. "Conflicts That Can't be Resolved." *Wall Street Journal,* September 5, 1997.

Kurtzer, Daniel, Scott Lasensky, William Quandt, Steven Spiegel, and Shibley Telhami. *The Peace Puzzle: America's Quest for Arab-Israeli Peace, 1989–2001.* Ithaca, NY: Cornell University Press, 2013.

Landler, Mark. "Mideast Peace Effort Pauses to Let Failure Sink In. *New York Times*, May 15, 2014 https://www.nytimes.com/2014/05/16/world/mideast-peace-effort-pauses-to-let-failure-sink-in.html.

Landler, Mark, and Jonathan Weisman. "Obama Fights a Push to Add Iran Sanctions." *New York Times*, January 13, 2014, https://www.nytimes.com/2014/01/14/world/middleeast/obama-fights-a-push-to-add-iran-sanctions.html, accessed August 11, 2021.

Laqueur, Walter, and Barry Rubin, eds. *The Israel-Arab Reader: A Documentary History of the Middle East Conflict.* New York: Penguin Books, 2001.

Lavie, Ephraim, Yael Ronen, and Henry Fishman, eds. *The Oslo Peace Process: A Twenty-Five Years' Perspective.* [in Hebrew]. Tammi Steinmetz Center for Peace Research, Tel Aviv University. Jerusalem: Carmel Publishers, 2019.

Linfield, Susie. *The Lion's Den: Zionism and the Left from Hanah Arendt to Noam Chomsky.* New Haven, CT: Yale University Press, 2019.

Lutwak, Edward. "Give War a Chance." *Foreign Affairs* 78, no 4: https://www.foreignaffairs.com/articles/1999-07-01/give-war-chance.

MacAskill, Ewen. "Arafat Approves Taba Plan Too Late." *The Guardian*, June 22, 2002, https://www.theguardian.com/world/2002/jun/22/israel.

Makovsky, David. "Time Running Out on Clinton Proposals." *Washington Institute for Near East Policy*, January 11, 2001, https://www.washingtoninstitute.org/policy-analysis/view/time-running-out-on-clinton-proposals, accessed August 8, 2021.

Masalha, Nur. *Politics of Denial: Israel and the Palestinian Refugee Problem.* London and Sterling, VA: Pluto Press, 2003.

Matar, Haggai. "Civil Society Groups Join Forces to Protect Freedom of Speech." +972 *Magazine*, May 13, 2017, https://972mag.com/civil-society-groups-join-forces-to-protect-freedom-of-speech/127286/, accessed August 14, 2021.

Miller, Aaron David. *The Much Too Promised Land: America's Elusive Search for Arab-Israeli Peace.* New York: Bantam Dell, 2008.

Mishal, Shaul, and Nadav Morag. "Political Expectations and Cultural Perceptions in the Arab-Israeli Peace Negotiations." *Political Psychology* 23, no. 2, 2002: 325–353.

Mitchell, George, and Alon Sahar. *A Path to Peace: A Brief History of Israeli-Palestinian Negotiations and a Way Forward in the Middle East.* New York: Simon and Schuster, 2016.

Morris, Benny. "Camp David and After: An Exchange (1. An Interview with Ehud Barak)." *New York Review of Books*, June 13, 2002, https://www.nybooks.com/articles/2002/06/13/camp-david-and-after-an-exchange-1-an-interview-wi/, accessed August 10, 2021.

Najem, Tom, Michael Molloy, Michael Bell, and John Bell, eds. *Governance and Security in Jerusalem: The Jerusalem Old City Initiative.* UCLA Center for Middle East Development. London and New York: Routledge, 2017.

National Security Council, *Initial Positions for the Negotiations.* [in Hebrew], December 22, 1999.

Naylor, Hugh. "Two-State Solution Loses Its Champion," *The National*, April 13, 2012, https://www.thenational.ae/world/mena/two-state-solution-loses-its-champion-1.380369, accessed August 13, 2021.

Olmert, Ehud. *In Person.* [in Hebrew]. Tel Aviv: Yedioth Ahronoth, 2018.

O'Malley, Padraig. *The Two-State Delusion: Israel-Palestine; a Tale of Two Narratives.* New York: Viking, 2015.

Orwell, George. "Catastrophic Gradualism," *Politics*, September 1946, 268–269, http://www.unz.com/print/politics-1946sep/, accessed August 13, 2021.

Orwell, George. *Seeing Things as They Are: Selected Journalism and Other Writings.* London: Harvill Secker, 2014.

Oz, Amos. "The Specter of Saladin." *New York Times*, July 28, 2000, https://www.nytimes.com/2000/07/28/opinion/the-specter-of-saladin.html, accessed August 15, 2021.

(The) *Palestine Papers.* "Refugee Committee – Talking Points for December 14 2008." https://www.jewishvirtuallibrary.org/jsource/arabs/PalPaper121408a.pdf

(The) *Palestine Papers*, "Principles of Permanent status agreement between Israel and Palestine." April 28, 2007, https://www.jewishvirtuallibrary.org/jsource/arabs/PalPaper042807.pdf

(The) *Palestine Papers*. "NSU Draft Language on Core Issues." November 18, 2007, https://www.jewishvirtuallibrary.org/jsource/arabs/PalPaper111807d.pdf

(The) *Palestine Papers*. "FAPS Based on Arab Peace Initiative." January 1, 2002, https://www.jewishvirtuallibrary.org/jsource/arabs/PalPaper010102.pdf

Pedazur, Reuven. "The Jordanian Option. The Plan that Refuses to Die." *Haaretz*, July 25, 2007. https://www.haaretz.com/1.4954947.

Philps, Alan. "Desperate Arafat Grasps Clinton Peace Plan." *The Telegraph*, June 22, 2002, https://www.telegraph.co.uk/news/worldnews/middleeast/israel/1398064/Desperate-Arafat-grasps-Clinton-peace-plan.html, accessed August 11, 2021.

Pollock, David. "Younger Palestinians More Moderate on Tactical Issues, But Not on Long-Term Peace with Israel." *Washington Institute for Near East Policy*, September 6, 2019, https://www.washingtoninstitute.org/policy-analysis/younger-palestinians-more-moderate-tactical-issues-not-long-term-peace-israel, accessed August 12, 2021.

Pressman, Jeremy. "Visions in Collision: What happened in Camp David and Taba?" *International Security* 28, no. 2 (2003): 5–43.

Pundak, Ron. "From Oslo to Taba: What Went Wrong?" *Survival* 43, no. 3 (2001): 31–45.

Qurie, Ahmed ("Abu Ala"). *Beyond Oslo: The Struggle for Palestine; inside the Middle East Peace Process; from Rabin's Death to Camp David*. London: I. B. Tauris, 2008.

Qurie, Ahmed ("Abu Ala"). *Peace Negotiations in Palestine: From the Second Intifada to the Roadmap*. London: I. B. Tauris, 2015.

Rabinovich, Itamar. *Waging Peace: Israel and the Arabs, 1948-2003*. Princeton, NJ: Princeton University Press, 2004.

Rabinovich, Itamar. "Palestine Portrayed." In *Jewish Review of Books*, Fall 2010. https://jewishreviewofbooks.com/articles/192/palestine-portrayed/.

Ramon, Haim. *Against the Wind*. [in Hebrew]. Tel Aviv: Yedioth Ahronoth, 2020.

Rice, Condoleezza. *No Higher Honor: A Memoir of My Years in Washington*. New York: Crown, 2011.

Rigoni, Mario Andrea. *Elogio dell'America*, Rome: Fondazione Liberal, 2003.

Ross, Dennis. "Camp David: An Exchange: Dennis Ross and Gidi Grinstein, Reply by Hussein Agha and Robert Malley," *The New York Review of Books*, September 20, 2001. https://www.nybooks.com/articles/2001/09/20/camp-david-an-exchange/

Ross, Dennis. *The Missing Peace: The Inside Story of the Fight for Middle East Peace*. New York: Farrar, Straus, and Giroux, 2005.

Ross, Dennis, and David Makovsky. *Myths, Illusions and Peace: Finding a New Direction for America in the Middle East*. New York: Viking, 2009.

Rubin, Barry, and Judith Rubin. *Yasir Arafat: A Political Biography*. New York: Oxford University Press, 2003.

Rubinstein, Danny, Robert Malley, Hussein Agha, Ehud Barak, and Benny Morris. *Rashomon Camp David*. [in Hebrew]. Tel Aviv: Yedioth Ahronoth, 2003.

Rubinstein, Danny. "Israeli Citizenship Is Worth 130 Shekel." *Calcalist (Yedioth Ahronoth)*, November 26, 2012.

Rumley, Grant, and Amir Tibon. *The Last Palestinian: The Rise and Reign of Mahmoud Abbas*. New York: Prometheus Books, 2017.

Safieh, Afif. *The Peace Process: From Breakthrough to Breakdown*. London: Saqi Books, 2011.

Said, Edward. *The End of the Peace Process: Oslo and After*. London: Granta Books, 2002.

Sammy, Rashid. "The Emergence and Evolution of Palestinian Nationalism." *International Journal of Multicultural and Multireligious Understanding* 2, no. 2 (2015): 1–7.

Savir, Uri. *The Process: 1100 Days that Changed the Middle East*. New York: Knopf Doubleday, 2010.

Sayigh, Yezid. "Arafat and the Anatomy of a Revolt." *Survival* 43, no. 3 (2001): 47–60.

Scheindlin, Dahlia. "The Shrinking Two-State Constituency." In *Moment of Truth: Tackling Israel-Palestine's Toughest Questions*. Edited by Jamie Stern-Weiner, 73–81. London and New York: OR Books, 2018.

Schivelbusch, Wolfgang. *The Culture of Defeat: On National Trauma, Mourning and Recovery.* London: Granta Books, 2001.

Schwartz, Adi, and Einat Wilf. *The War of Return.* [in Hebrew]. Tel Aviv: Kinneret Zmora-Bitan Dvir, 2018.

Schwartz, Felicia, and Dov Lieber. "Israeli Millennials Tilting Right, Helped Elect Netanyahu." *Wall Street Journal*, April 11, 2019, https://www.wsj.com/articles/israeli-millennials-tilting-right-helped-elect-netanyahu-11555002403, accessed August 11, 2021.

Seidemann, Daniel. "The Status Quo on Temple Mount/ Haram Al Sherif: Dodging A Bullet (For Now)." in *Terrestrial Jerusalem*, October 12, 2020, https://t-j.org.il/0202/10/12/the-status-quo-on-the-temple-mount-haram-al-sharif-dodging-a-bullet-for-now/.

Shikaki, Khalil. "There Is No Returning to the Pre-Intifada Period." *Palestine-Israel Journal* 7, no. 4, 2000, https://pij.org/app.php/articles/250/there-is-no-returning-to-the-preintifada-period.

Shikaki, Khalil. "Palestinians Divided," *Foreign Affairs* 81, no. 1, 2002, https://www.foreignaffairs.com/articles/palestinian-authority/2002-01-01/palestinians-divided.

Shragai, Nadav. "Why the Temporary Provision That Prevents Terror Needs to Be maintained. *Israel Hayom.* June 24, 2021, https://www.israelhayom.co.il/magazine/hashavua/article/2544116.

Serry, Robert. *The Endless Quest for Israeli-Palestinian Peace: A Reflection from No Man's Land.* London: Palgrave Macmillan, 2017.

Sfard, Michael. *The Wall and the Gate: Israel, Palestine, and the Legal Battle for Human Rights.* New York: Metropolitan Books, Henry Holt, 2018.

Shamir, Jacob, and Khalil Shikaki. *Palestinian and Israeli Public Opinion: The Political Imperative in the Second Intifada.* Bloomington, IN: Indiana University Press, 2010.

Shavit, Ari. "Dov Weissglas Interview: The Big Freeze." *Haaretz*, 8 October 2004. https://www.haaretz.com/1.4710587

Shavit, Ari. *Partition: Disengagement and Beyond.* [in Hebrew]. Jerusalem: Keter Publishing, 2005.

Shearer, David. "The Humanitarian Crisis in the Occupied Palestinian Territory: An Overview." *Humanitarian Practice Network*, November, 2004, https://odihpn.org/magazine/the-human itarian-crisis-in-the-occupied-palestinian-territory-an-overview/, accessed August 12, 2021.

Sher, Gilead. *Just beyond Reach: The Israeli-Palestinian Peace Negotiations 1999–2001.* [in Hebrew]. Tel Aviv: Yedioth Ahronoth, 2001.

Shilon, Avi, *The Left-Wing's Sorrow.* [in Hebrew]. Tel Aviv: Kinneret Zmora-Bitan Dvir, 2017.

Shlaim, Avi. "The Rise and Fall of the Oslo Peace Process." In *The International Relations of the Middle East.* Edited by Louise Fawcett, 241–261. Oxford: Oxford University Press, 2005.

Shlaim, Avi, *The Iron Wall. Israel and the Arab World*, Penguin Books, London, 2014

Shtayyeh, Mohammad. *Israeli Settlements and the Erosion of the Two-States Solution.* Cairo: Dar Al-Shorouk, 2015.

Siegman, Henry. "Israel: A Historic Statement." *The New York Review of Books*, February 8, 2001, https://www.nybooks.com/articles/2001/02/08/israel-historic-statement/, accessed August 3, 2021.

Sontag, Deborah. "Quest for Mideast Peace: How and Why It Failed?" *New York Times*, July 26, 2001. https://www.nytimes.com/2001/07/26/world/and-yet-so-far-a-special-report-quest-for-mideast-peace-how-and-why-it-failed.html.

Stern-Weiner, Jamie, ed. *Moment of Truth: Tackling Israel-Palestine's Toughest Questions.* London and New York: OR Books, 2018.

Swisher, Clayton. *The Truth about Camp David. The Untold Story about the Collapse of the Middle East Peace Process.* New York: Nation Books, 2004.

Talmon, J. L. "'The Homeland Is in Danger.' An Open Letter to Menahem Begin." *Dissent* (1980), https://www.dissentmagazine.org/article/the-homeland-is-in-danger-an-open-letter-to-menahem-begin, accessed August 10, 2021.

Telhami, Shibley. "Americans Are Increasingly Critical of Israel." *Foreign Policy*, December 11, 2018, https://foreignpolicy.com/2018/12/11/americans-are-increasingly-critical-of-Isr ael/, accessed August 14, 2021.

Thomson, James C. "How Could Vietnam Happen? An Autopsy." *The Atlantic*, April 1968. https://www.theatlantic.com/magazine/archive/1968/04/how-could-vietnam-happen-an-autopsy/306462/.

Walsh, Elsa. "The Prince." *The New Yorker*, March 24, 2003, https://www.newyorker.com/magaz ine/2003/03/24/the-prince-3, accessed August 8, 2021.

Wasserstein, Bernard. *Divided Jerusalem: The Struggle for the Holy City*. New Haven, CT, and London: Yale University Press, 2002.

Weinstock, Nathan. "The Impact of Zionist Colonization on Palestinian Arab Society before 1948." *Journal of Palestine Studies* 2, no. 2 (1973): 49–63.

Whitaker, Brian. "Pragmatist Whose Two-State Solution Cuts No Ice with Israel." *The Guardian*, August 22, 2003, https://www.theguardian.com/world/2003/aug/22/israel1, accessed August 13, 2021.

White, Ben. "News Agencies Still Whitewashing Israeli Forces' Lethal Violence." *Middle East Monitor*, February 1, 2017, https://www.middleeastmonitor.com/news/, accessed August 14, 2021.

Wilkinson, Tracy. "Once Applauded as a Hero, Clinton Bows Out Amid Palestinian Catcalls." *Los Angeles Times*, January 19, 2001, https://www.latimes.com/archives/la-xpm-2001-jan-19-mn-14350-story.html.

Yatom, Danny. *The Confidant: From Sayeret Matkal to the Mossad*. [in Hebrew]. Tel Aviv: Yedioth Ahronoth, 2009.

Zanany, Omer. *The Annapolis Process (2007–2008): Negotiation and Its Discontents*. Jerusalem: Tami Steinmetz Center for Peace Research and Molad—Center for the Renewal of Israeli Democracy, 2015.

Zertal, Idith. *Israel's Holocaust and the Politics of Nationhood*. Cambridge: Cambridge University Press, 2005.

Zertal, Idith, and Akiva Eldar. *The Lords of the Land: The War over Israeli Settlements in the Occupied Territories, 1967–2007*. New York: Nation Books, 2007.

2. Comparative Perspectives

Adelman, Howard and Elazar Barkan. *No Return, No Refuge: Rites and Rights in Minority Repatriation*. New York: Columbia University Press, 2011.

Arias Sánchez, Oscar. *Bringing Peace to Central America*. New York: Chelsea House Publishers, 2007.

Arnson, Cynthia, ed. *Comparative Peace Processes in Latin America*, Stanford, CA: Woodrow Wilson Center Press and Stanford University Press, 1999.

Bensouda, Fatou. "International Justice and Diplomacy." *New York Times*, March 19, 2013.

Birchall, Ian. "Sartre and Terror." In *Sartre Today: A Centenary Celebration*. Edited by Adrian Van den Hoven and Andrew Leak, 251–264. New York: Berghahn Books, 2005.

Camus, Albert. *Algerian Chronicles*, ed. Alice Kaplan, trans. Arthur Goldhammer. Cambridge, MA: Belknap Press of Harvard University Press, 2013.

Chigumadzi, Panashe. "Why Is South Africa Still So Anti-Black, So Many Years after Apartheid?" *The Guardian*, March 10, 2017, https://www.theguardian.com/commentisfree/2017/mar/ 10/south-africa-anti-black-violence-afrophobic, accessed August 14, 2021.

Cobban, Helena. "Uganda: When International Justice and Internal Peace Are at Odds." *Christian Science Monitor*, August 24, 2006.

Czarnetzky, John M. "The International Criminal Court: An Obstacle to Peace?" *First Things*, May 15, https://www.firstthings.com/web-exclusives/2007/05/the-international-criminal-court-an-obstacle-to-peace, accessed August 10, 2021.

Dhoquois-Cohen, Régine. "Israël, fait colonial? 30 ans après." https://iremmo.org/wp-content/ uploads/2016/02/2605.rodinson.pdf, accessed August 10, 2021.

Doudaki, Vaia, and Nico Carpentier. *Cyprus and Its Conflicts: Representations, Materialities and Cultures*. New York: Berghahn Books, 2017.

Fanning, Ronan. *Éamon de Valera: A Will to Power*. Cambridge, MA: Harvard University Press, 2016.

Fitzduff, Mari. "Breaking Down the Walls: Northern Ireland Lessons." *Palestine-Israel Journal* 12, no. 4 (2005), https://pij.org/articles/405/breaking-down-the-walls-northern-ireland-lessons.

Fitzduff, Mari. "Breaking Down the Walls: Lessons from Northern Ireland; the Irish Case and the Effectiveness of Community Involvement in Peace-Making." *Palestine-Israel Journal* 22, no. 1 (2017).

Freeman, Marc. *Necessary Evil: Amnesties and the Search for Justice*. Cambridge: Cambridge University Press, 2011.

Gidron, Benjamin, Stanley Katz, and Yehezkel Hasenfeld. *Mobilizing for Peace: Conflict Resolution in Northern Ireland, Israel-Palestine, and South Africa*, Oxford: Oxford University Press, 2002.

Horne, Alistair. *A Savage War for Peace: Algeria 1954–1962*. New York: The Viking Press, 1978.

International Crisis Group Report. "Crucial Reforms Languish as Colombia Seeks to Consolidate Peace." July 19, 2019, https://www.crisisgroup.org/latin-america-caribbean/andes/colombia/crucial-reforms-languish-colombia-seeks-consolidate-peace.

Irwin, Colin. *20 Peace Lessons from Northern Ireland to Israel and Palestine*. Scotts Valley, CA: CreateSpace, 2012.

Keynes, Maynard John. *The Economic Consequences of the Peace*. New York: Dover Publications, 2004.

Khalidi, Rashid. *The Hundred Years' War on Palestine: A History of Settler Colonial Conquest and Resistance*. London: Profile Books, 2020.

Malala, Justice. "Why Are South African Cities Still So Segregated 25 Years after Apartheid?" *The Guardian*, October 21, 2019, https://www.theguardian.com/cities/2019/oct/21/why-are-south-african-cities-still-segregated-after-apartheid, accessed August 14, 2021.

Mazzini, Giuseppe. *The Duties of Man Addressed to Workingmen*. New York: Funk & Wagnalls, 1898.

Memmi, Albert. *Portrait du colonisé précédé du Portrait du colonisateur*. Paris: Gallimard, 1985.

O'Shea, Sinead. "Northern Ireland Unfinished Peace." *New York Times*, April 25, 2019, https://www.nytimes.com/2019/04/25/opinion/lyra-mckee-northern-ireland.html, accessed August 10, 2021.

Ostrovsky, Arkady. *The Invention of Russia: The Journey from Gorbachev's Freedom to Putin's War*. London: Atlantic Books, 2018.

Paul, T. V., ed. *The India-Pakistan Conflict: An Enduring Rivalry*. Cambridge: Cambridge University Press, 2005.

Pfaffenholz, Thania, Kew, Daren, Wanis-St.John. Anthony, Wanis-St.John, A./Kew. "The Missing Link? Civil Society, Peace Negotiations: Contributions to Sustained Peace." *Paper Presented at the 47th Annual Convention of the International Studies Association, San Diego*, March 23, 2006, https://www.american.edu/sis/faculty/upload/wanis-civil-society-and-peace-negotiations.pdf.

Pilling, David. "Xenophobia Sours the Legacy of Pan-Africanism." *Financial Times*, September 25, 2019.

Powell, Jonathan. *Great Hatred, Little Room: Making Peace in Northern Ireland*. New York: Vintage Books, 2009.

Powell, Jonathan. *Talking to Terrorists: How to End Armed Conflicts*. New York: Vintage Books, 2015.

Rodinson, Maxime. "Israël, fait colonial?" In Jean-Paul Sartre (dir.), *Les Temps Modernes* no. 22 (1967), 17–88.

Santos Calderón, Juan Manuel. *La batalla por la paz*. Barcelona: Editorial Planeta, 2019.

Singh, Ajay. "South Africa Is Not Working." *Freedom Magazine* 47, no. 6, https://www.freedommag.org/magazine/201507-infrastructure/world/south-africa-is-not-working.html, accessed August 14, 2021.

Zunes, Stephen, and Jacob Mundy. *Western Sahara: War, Nationalism, and Conflict Irresolution*. Syracuse Studies on Peace and Conflict Resolution. Syracuse, NY: Syracuse University Press, 2010.

INDEX